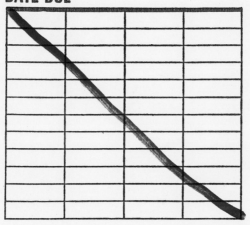

CONFRONTING INJUSTICE
The Edmond Cahn Reader

CONFRONTING

The Edmond Cahn Reader

Edited by LENORE L. CAHN

INJUSTICE

Foreword by Hugo L. Black

*General Introduction and Prefatory Chapter Notes
by Norman Redlich*

Essay Index Reprint Series

BOOKS FOR LIBRARIES PRESS
FREEPORT, NEW YORK

Library of Congress Cataloging in Publication Data

Cahn, Edmond Nathaniel, 1906-1964.
  Confronting injustice.

  (Essay index reprint series)
  Reprint of the 1966 ed.
  Includes bibliographical references.
  1. Civil rights--United States--Addresses, essays,
lectures. 2. Law--United States--Addresses, essays,
lectures. I. Cahn, Lenore L., ed. II. Title.
[KF4749.A2C3 1972]   342'.73'085   72-8525
ISBN 0-8369-7308-9

Many of the selections in this book have previously appeared in print. We are grateful for permission to include the following copyrighted material:
"The Consumers of Injustice" from *Social Research*, vol. 26, 1959. Reprinted by permission of *Social Research*.
"Law in the Consumer Perspective" from the *University of Pennsylvania Law Review*, vol. 112, 1962. Reprinted by permission of the *University of Pennsylvania Law Review*.
"John Marshall — Our 'Greatest Dissenter' " from the *New York Times Magazine*, August 21, 1955; "Hamiltonians and Jeffersonians" (originally published as a review of *The Right of the People* by William O. Douglas) from the *New York Times Book Review*, January 19, 1958; "Brief for the Supreme Court" from the *New York Times Magazine*, October 7, 1956; "Justice Frankfurter's 'Dominating Humility' " (originally published as a review of *Of Law and Men — Papers and Addresses of Felix Frankfurter*, edited by Philip Elman) from the *New York Times Book Review*, May 27, 1956. © 1955, 1956, 1958 by The New York Times Company. Reprinted by permission of The New York Times Company.
"Madison and the Pursuit of Happiness," 1952; "The Inherent Radicalism of the Legal Profession," 1952; "Fact-Skepticism and Fundamental Law," 1958; all from the

New York University Law Review. Reprinted by permission of the School of Law of New York University.

"Supreme Court and Supreme Law: An American Contribution" (originally entitled "An American Contribution") from *Supreme Court and Supreme Law* by Edmond Cahn, published by the Indiana University Press. Copyright 1954 by the Law Center Foundation of New York University. Reprinted by permission of the Law Center Foundation of New York University.

"The Firstness of the First Amendment" from the *Yale Law Journal*, vol. 65, p. 464. Copyright 1956 by the Yale Law Journal Company. "Jerome Frank's Fact-Skepticism and Our Future" from the *Yale Law Journal*, vol. 66, p. 824. Copyright 1957 by the Yale Law Journal Company. Both reprinted by permission of the Yale Law Journal Company and Fred B. Rotham & Co.

"The Parchment Barriers" from *The American Scholar*, vol. 32, no. 1, 1962–1963. Copyright © 1962 by Lenore L. Cahn.

"Correspondence with David Ben-Gurion: A Debate" (originally entitled "Defamation Control vs. Press Freedom: A Current Chapter in Israel") from the *Journal of Public Law*, 1964. Reprinted by permission of the *Journal of Public Law.*

"Freedom of the Press: The Libertarian Standard" and "Freedom of the Press: Responsibility for Defamation" were lectures delivered in Israel, December 1962. © Edmond Cahn 1962.

"How to Destroy the Churches" from *Harper's Magazine,* November 1961. Copyright 1961, by Harper's Magazine, Inc.

"The 'Establishment of Religion' Puzzle," 1961; "On Government and Prayer," 1962; "Skepticism in American Jurisprudence," 1952; "'Courts on Trial': An Analysis" (originally published as a review of *Courts on Trial* by Jerome Frank, adapted from a review in the *Yale Law Journal,* 1950), 1950; "Fact-Skepticism: An Unexpected Chapter," 1963; "A Dangerous Myth in the School Segregation Cases," 1954; "The Lawyer, the Social Psychologist, and the Truth," 1955; "The Lawyer as Scientist and Scoundrel," 1960; all from the *Annual Survey of American Law.* Reprinted by permission of the School of Law of New York University and the Law Center Foundation of New York University.

"A Lawyer Looks at Religion" from *Theology Today,* April 1958. Reprinted by permission of *Theology Today.*

"The Binding of Isaac: A Case Study" (originally entitled "The Juristic Approach to Moral Problems: A Case Study") from the *Yearbook of the Central Conference of American Rabbis,* vol. 70, 1960. Reprinted by permission of the Central Conference of American Rabbis.

"Some Reflections on the Aims of Legal Education" from the *Journal of Legal Education,* vol. 11, no. 1. Copyright 1958 by the Association of American Law Schools. Reprinted by permission of the Association of American Law Schools.

"Ethical Problems of Tax Practitioners" from the *Tax Law Review,* vol. 8, 1952. Reprinted by permission of the School of Law of New York University and the Law Center Foundation of New York University.

"Eavesdropping on Justice" from *The Nation,* January 5, 1957. Reprinted by permission of *The Nation.*

"Reflections on Hanging: Preface for Americans" from *Reflections on Hanging* by Arthur Koestler. Copyright © 1957, by Arthur Koestler. Reprinted by permission of The Macmillan Company.

"Drug Experiments and the Public Conscience" from *Drugs in Our Society* edited by Paul Talalay, 1964. Reprinted by permission of The Johns Hopkins Press.

"The Democratic Resolution" from *The Predicament of Democratic Man* by Edmond Cahn. Copyright © 1961, by Edmond Cahn. Reprinted by permission of The Macmillan Company.

Note: all sources are cited in full on pages 408–428.

For what gives justice its special savor of nobility? Only the divine wrath that arises in us, girds us, and drives us to action whenever an instance of injustice affronts our sight.

— EDMOND CAHN

Foreword

IT is both a pleasure and an honor to write this brief foreword for *Confronting Injustice: The Edmond Cahn Reader*, a book containing some of Edmond's articles and speeches compiled by Lenore, his wife, who loved and helped him during his all too brief life.

Edmond was a cherished personal friend with whom I spent many but not nearly enough happy hours discussing problems of life, society, our Constitution and government. His vital interest in and information about current affairs, together with his vast knowledge of history and the cultures of the past, made him a fascinating conversationalist with whom hours passed as minutes. For me Edmond's charming conversational style carries over into his speeches, articles and books, and this in itself is more than enough to call for their printing here. But I think there are far stronger reasons for this and future reprints of Edmond's works. Few books ever outlive their own generations. Most are written for temporary entertainment or to appeal to some transient interests, emotions or prejudices. Edmond Cahn, however, did not write about fleeting problems that are here today and gone tomorrow but about the ideal of equal justice for all people which is neither transient nor unimportant. A major purpose of his books, and indeed of his life, was to promote, through analysis and discussion, governmental processes that would achieve justice. I find in his writings the same kind of inspiring arguments for equal justice for all people that is found in those enduring books which contain the maxims and precepts of the great religions and philosophies of the world. The achievement of justice is a problem which, in the final analysis, depends on what kind of government and laws control society. Edmond Cahn did not believe that equal justice could be achieved if the basic rights of the people were left dependent upon a mysterious, unwritten, fluctuating "natural law." He believed, as I do, in a government of definite and precise laws enacted under the authority of a written Constitution which clearly marks the boundaries of governmental power. He believed in a system of government where judges interpret laws and are not left free to make decisions according to their own personal notions of what is just and reasonable at the moment. While he thought of our Constitution as the best in the world and of our judicial system as a model institution for the administration of justice, he wanted judges administering the law to keep themselves securely tied to the text of the Constitution. On this subject he quaintly said, "A judge untethered by a text is a dangerous instrument." He went on to say:

> When the American Revolution was over and the people set up free governments, they swiftly composed Bills of Rights, federal and state, to convert so-called "natural" rights (and some other rights like trial by jury) into explicit and enforceable positive guarantees. They put their trust not in natural law but in positive constitutions, positive guarantees and a government that would stand responsible to the people.

I am distinctly honored to have my name linked with this book and the views so clearly and eloquently expressed in the writings of Edmond Cahn, a great legal philosopher.

Hugo L. Black
Associate Justice,
Supreme Court of the
United States

May 2, 1966

Acknowledgments

My husband and I had often talked about assembling his most important articles and speeches into a book. This, he always said, was something he would do in his old age when he no longer had any new ideas. He did not assemble this book, but he was able to transmit the core of his beliefs to those who helped me. I could not have attempted or completed this collection without the assistance of the many who expressed their devotion to him, through the help they gave me.

I wish to thank all who have made possible *The Edmond Cahn Reader:*

My daughter Mary for her unceasing aid, perceptive guidance and affectionate companionship throughout every phase of this book; Edward Wise for his invaluable assistance in assembling and summarizing all of my husband's articles, helping to plan, organize, select material and prepare the final manuscript for publication; Norman Redlich, close friend and student of my husband, for his insightful Introduction and Prefatory Notes, for his wise counseling in the selection and organization of materials and for his careful scrutiny of the entire manuscript; Evelyn Redlich for her sympathetic and constant encouragement; my son Edgar for his confidence in me and his ready assistance; Ephraim London and Robert McKay for their acute evaluation of material; Virginia and Albert Rosenberg for their infinite and varied help; my son-in-law Herman Schwartz for his discerning suggestions and remarkable tolerance; Lisa McGaw for her meticulous and skillful checking of proofs.

I wish to express my particular thanks to Justice Hugo L. Black for his continuing friendship and his penetrating Foreword. I also wish to thank A. L. Hart, Jr., of Little, Brown and Company for his complete understanding of what his friend Edmond Cahn would have wanted for this book.

LENORE CAHN

Introduction

Edmond Cahn: "His Spirit Worketh in Me"

EDMOND CAHN brought to the study of law the cosmic insights of a philosopher, and he approached philosophy through the practical workings of the law. This explains in large part why his public career as a legal philosopher did not commence until his fortieth year, when he published what was to become the first chapter of *The Sense of Injustice*. Until then he practiced law, wrote in the more traditional fields of taxation and estates and acquired the learning of philosophy.

When he died on August 9, 1964, at the age of fifty-eight, his days as a practicing lawyer were far behind him. As a teacher and writer he had successfully blended the disciplines of law and philosophy. In the short span of eighteen years, Edmond Cahn had emerged as one of the handful of outstanding judicial philosophers ever produced in this country.

During this period he wrote three books and over one hundred scholarly articles and reviews for professional and popular journals. This book contains a selection of these articles and reviews and the beginning of a fourth book. It has been prepared to make available in one volume the most important of his shorter works which, together with his three books, constitute Edmond Cahn's legacy to democratic thought.

Edmond Cahn wrote in order to reach people. Legal or philosophic abstractions did not interest him. He sought to move minds and hearts and to stir men to action. A memorial issue of the *New York University Law Review*, published a few months after his death, was eloquent testimony to his success. It evoked not merely an appreciation of his intellectual attainments, but a deeply moving emotional reaction among judges, scholars and friends.

"I have missed him," wrote Supreme Court Justice Hugo L. Black, "and shall keep on missing him — his letters through which I came to know him better as a thinking, loving, aspiring and inspiring human being; his conversations, which I venture to say lifted us both above the commonplace things and to a greater appreciation of our country and its Constitution, with its promise of freedom for the mind and spirit of man to seek new light — always freedom to think and speak and write and believe."

He was described by another leading jurist, Stanley Fuld of the New York Court of Appeals, as an "aristocrat of democracy," by his dean as "the only irreplaceable man on our faculty," and by a fellow teacher as "the most remarkable teacher I have ever known." Professor Joseph F. Fletcher of the Harvard Divinity School may have best expressed the common sentiment when he wrote, ". . . but most of all he was a scholar and a democratic man. . . . His spirit worketh in me."

Edmond Cahn's spirit does, indeed, work in those who shared his belief that the law should aspire to express society's highest moral values. Pronouncements of morality and justice, if divorced from law, are at best sermons of exhortation and at worst pretentious hypocrisies. And a legal system which is oblivious to moral concerns and individual dignity cannot serve the needs of a self-governing democratic society.

Edmond Cahn looked continuously to the practical operation of the law as the testing ground for democracy's success or failure. Few would question, in abstract terms, the moral superiority of representative government over its totalitarian rivals. But to the individual citizen government is not an abstraction. An urban dweller who is unfairly taxed because of the votes of a malapportioned state legislature, or a young man who is drafted because he participates in an antiwar protest, or an injured plaintiff who must settle a negligence claim for less than its value because he cannot afford a trial delayed for years by crowded court calendars — to these individuals the law has become the method of frustrating rather than fulfilling the high moral purposes of democratic government.

Nor does it suffice to compare our virtues with the shortcomings of a totalitarian society. An indigent and uneducated suspect who confesses to a crime he did not commit, after being questioned for days by the police without counsel, draws little solace from the fact that in other countries the writ of habeas corpus is not available to correct the wrong. In his case it might not be available either and, even if it were, one can hardly heap praise on a legal system because of its ability to correct injustices which should never have occurred.

A legal philosophy gleaned from the perspective of the person upon whom the law acts, which was the essence of Edmond Cahn's "consumer perspective," provides little opportunity for smugness. Comparisons with other countries assume less importance, as do sweeping and self-serving generalizations about historical trends. One hundred years from now, for example, the twelve-year period following the

Supreme Court's decision in *Brown v. Board of Education,* which held that racially segregated public schools were unconstitutional, will be described accurately as years in which giant strides were taken toward achieving racial equality. But at the end of those twelve years hundreds of thousands of children who were not yet born when the *Brown* case was decided still face their remaining years burdened by the handicap of an inferior education resulting from state-imposed racial segregation. Whatever may have been the justification for the Supreme Court's decision to postpone immediate desegregation and to proceed instead "with all deliberate speed" (and the reasons were persuasive at the time), we must never ignore the consequences of that postponement on a generation of Negro children.

Edmond Cahn's philosophy, however, does not direct us toward a morbid concentration on society's shortcomings. If the principal test of a democratic legal order is that of the just decision here and now, each day offers opportunities and optimism for those imbued with the democratic ideal. By eschewing abstract generalizations, Edmond Cahn led us away from pronouncements about inevitable trends which serve only to dampen the enthusiasm of the human spirit. In the forum of the live case or controversy man is free to fulfill his role in democratic society.

A single citizen's voice raised in protest, a single case of an official misdeed corrected, a single life saved, one hand extended in help — these acts will forever change the lives of the individuals who were involved. From the doing of such deeds, moreover, the principles of justice emerge. It was, for example, the concern of individual citizens, first ignored and then heard, which led to the United States Supreme Court's decision in 1964 guaranteeing to all Americans that their right to vote could not be diluted through malapportionment.

Viewing the law in these terms, Edmond Cahn created a philosophy which will have increasing meaning to lawyers, judges, and government officials. These, and the individuals upon whom the law acts, are all "consumers of law." In the final analysis they will determine the quality of the product. They do so by the nature of their decisions — in the courtroom, the legislatures, the ballot boxes and in the offices of government. Edmond Cahn's role was to provide a philosophy for democratic man which could enable him, through the everyday processes of law and government, to produce a more humane and just social order.

As one reads these chapters, it is apparent how well Edmond Cahn did his work. A legal philosophy for democratic man must make its judgments in terms of the individual upon whom the law acts, and, while concerned with the interests of all the people, must constantly strive to achieve justice in a particular case. These pages abound, therefore, with specific examples drawn from actual decisions in the law.

A democratic philosophy cannot be based on mere utilitarian considerations but must recognize the role of moral values in the law. These chapters reflect the constant interplay between law and morals which was the theme of Edmond Cahn's book *The Moral Decision.*

A democratic society must constantly question in order to seek the truth. Thus, fact-skepticism was an essential ingredient of Edmond Cahn's approach to legal problems. Democracy must be imaginative and bold in social and economic areas, where experimentation is the essence of progress. But it must hold fast, with no exceptions, to the basic political and personal liberties which alone set democracy apart from other forms of government.

Most important, if the individual in a democracy is to utilize his full intelligence to achieve a more just society here and now — and not in some distant Golden Age — he must do so in a legal order which provides complete intellectual and political freedom. Any restriction on these freedoms prevents the individual from fulfilling his proper role and prevents the state from asserting in good conscience that its decisions rest on a firm moral base.

In the two years which have elapsed since Edmond Cahn's death, new issues have moved to the forefront of the American legal scene. Edmond Cahn would be the first to agree that his value as a philosopher of justice must be appraised not in terms of how well he dealt with the issues confronting him while he lived, but rather by whether he provided the insights which can enable those who shared his values to cope with the challenges and opportunities of a democratic society in a continuous state of flux.

Advances in electronic technology, for example, have placed the controversy over government eavesdropping in a wholly new legal framework. In 1928, the United States Supreme Court, by a five to four majority, ruled that wiretapping did not violate the Fourth Amendment's prohibition against unreasonable searches and seizures because that Amendment had reference to the search and seizure of "things." A telephone message was not a material thing, according to Chief Justice Taft. Moreover, a wiretap did not involve a trespass by the police of the person's premises.

Congress responded in 1934 by making the interception and divulgence of telephone conversations a federal crime, and the Supreme Court supported this ban by ruling, in a series of cases, that wiretap evidence was inadmissible in federal court even if obtained by state law enforcement officials. State wiretapping could still be used in state trials, but to an increasing extent state law enforcement officials have been reluctant to base prosecutions on testimony obtained in violation of a federal law.

Other types of electronic eavesdropping have, until recently, been circumscribed by relying on the portion of the original *Olmstead* opinion which emphasized the absence of a police trespass of the premises. Thus, driving a "spike" microphone into the common wall between two houses was held to be an unreasonable search and seizure because of the protrusion of the microphone into the home. Recently, however, congressional testimony has brought forward evidence of eavesdropping techniques which do not violate the federal statute and which can be employed without any physical invasion of the premises. Conversations in a room can be picked up through a telephone wire even though the telephone remains on the hook. Quiet conversations in a public restaurant, on a street corner, or in the privacy of one's car are no longer safe from electronic eavesdropping.

Traditionally, the appeal for the protection of the individual's privacy against encroaching surveillance by the government is personalized only by reference to the individual whose privacy is invaded. It is understandably difficult to develop empathy for the gamblers, tax evaders and other alleged criminals who generally protest against the use of "bugged" conversations.

Since the old legal doctrines, based on whether there was a trespass, or whether a conversation is a "thing," appear inadequate to deal with modern problems of government surveillance, judges and lawyers must develop new criteria. A valuable point of reference would be Edmond Cahn's last book, *The Predicament of Democratic Man,* in which he sought to define the citizen's responsibility for the wrongdoing of his government. It would then be apparent that in deciding whether government may validly transcribe a conversation between two individuals, neither of whom has reason to suspect that he is engaging in a public conversation, we can no longer think of the person who is doing the "bugging" as a faceless and nameless institution called "government."

The judge must place himself not merely in the role of the person whose privacy is invaded, but, of perhaps greater significance, in the role of the person who is doing the eavesdropping. The proper posture of democratic man is surely not that of a snooper crouching over a recording device listening to the intimate and private conversations of two individuals. When we recognize fully the moral degradation created by our own involvement in these practices, our courts will exclude this type of evidence once and for all.

Another growing danger to personal liberties in the current legal scene results from augmented federal and state welfare programs. In some respects these programs pose a greater threat to personal liberties than the cold war pressures of the 1950's, when it was argued that the dangers of internal subversion justified such things as loyalty oaths and the dismissals of public employees on the basis of hearsay evidence and without such elemental protections as the right of confrontation or cross-examination. Those who sought to defend the rights of the individual during this period could argue forcefully that the government's entire premise was false — that the danger to American security was external and that the internal menace was the product of hysteria and political opportunism.

Today, however, the various government programs which are infringing on individual rights do serve a valid public purpose, and if they are significantly curtailed, large numbers of citizens would suffer privation. For example, those who saw a threat to the separation of church and state in the federal aid-to-education bill, enacted in 1965, threatened by their opposition a program which was desperately needed and which they would have wholeheartedly endorsed if it were stripped of its provisions benefiting religious institutions. Similarly, when local governments use churches and church-supported institutions to wage the war against poverty, civil libertarians are forced to defend First Amendment freedoms by attacking programs whose objectives they applaud.

Here again, Edmond Cahn's insight provides us with the courage and the philosophic support for continuing the fight for a principle which James Madison regarded as the most important in the Bill of Rights, the separation of church and state. By observing what happens to churches themselves when they become the recipients of a government handout, Edmond Cahn dramatizes in these pages the importance to religious freedom of strong and independent religious institutions.

His writings also help us to appraise individual guilt for the erosion which has taken place of this uniquely American concept. An official of an organization which supports the separation of church and state, but which accepts a program of indirect assistance to religious schools because the national need for education is great and the compromise with the First Amendment is only minor — such an official, if he remains silent, bears a heavier responsibility than his counterpart in a group that openly supports aid to church-supported schools. Persons with particular expert knowledge of church-state relationships — historians, constitutional lawyers, law professors — have a greater opportunity for effective action than their less trained neighbors. Accordingly, the responsibility for doing nothing is greater. And those who bear the greatest responsibility of all would be the leaders of the minority religious groups, such as the orthodox Jewish schools, who, while recognizing that government aid to religion may destroy the religious freedom which Americans have enjoyed under our Constitution, nevertheless line up to receive the money like docile turkeys in the fall.

Finally, we have seen in recent years the degrading conditions which governments often impose on those who are the recipients of welfare benefits. This has even included the requirement that our elderly citizens submit to the equivalent of a loyalty oath in order to obtain medical benefits under federal law. We have also seen unconscionable invasions of privacy by local governments in order to determine whether a wife has, in fact, been deserted by her husband or whether she is merely claiming desertion in order to obtain welfare benefits. Only by a callous application of what Edmond Cahn would call the "imperial or official perspective" can one conclude that the government, as a condition of paying welfare benefits to its poorer citizens, may invade privacy through methods which would be regarded as outrageous if applied to more affluent citizens.

Perhaps a note of fact-skepticism might be useful here. On what basis does government conclude that welfare recipients have lower moral standards than our wealthier citizens who have no need of welfare programs, or our government officials who dispense the benefits? If we are to believe statistics concerning broken marriages, gambling, adultery, tax evasion and the use of narcotics, it is apparent that no economic group in our society has a monopoly on moral virtue. The twin tools of fact-skepticism and the consumer perspective will help expose the moral bankruptcy of a policy which assumes otherwise.

Although written over a period of two decades, the following pages vibrate with a sense of immediate concern for the problems of today. As long as this nation continues to live under a representative government, Edmond Cahn's voice will span the years and help with the work of the hour. That is why "his spirit worketh in me."

NORMAN REDLICH

New York, 1966

Contents

1

THE CONSUMER PERSPECTIVE

*E*DMOND CAHN compressed into one phrase—the consumer perspective — a concept which was pivotal to his entire approach to law and to life. Since he chose words with the precision of a diamond cutter, it is significant that he described his most important idea not as a "theory" or "philosophy" but as a "perspective." He shunned conceptualized theories of law. Instead he asked us to view the law as it acts on the individual, and from that perspective he provided the insights and the philosophic thought that illumine these pages.

Most political and legal philosophers view the law from the vantage point of the state, as do most judges and other public officials. From this "imperial" perspective the "common good" or, in modern parlance, the "consensus" looms large in the foreground, while at the far end of the telescope appears a mass of completely fungible units called "the people." But in reading Edmond Cahn's books and articles we are compelled to turn the telescope around and view the legal landscape with the individual dominating the scene.

From the consumer perspective the visceral reaction to a specific case of injustice becomes a more potent force in human affairs than the pursuit of an ill-defined concept of justice. The search for moral values in the law leads, under this approach, to a study of actual court cases in which moral questions are decided, for this is where the ultimate product of our legal system is consumed. And in an age when democratic governments have demonstrated the capacity for both great good and monstrous evil, the morally sensitive citizen cannot ignore his involvement in the actions of his government. These were the themes of Edmond Cahn's three books.

Whether exploring questions of free speech, criminal justice, racial segregation, or state-imposed prayers in public schools, he always infused new life into old legal questions and could stir men not merely to think but to act. How much more immediate and compelling is the call to action when the concern is not a remote and often unobtainable goal, but rather the prevention of a single case of wrongdoing here and now. "Only in the consumer perspective," he wrote, "can a passing skirmish count as much as a long campaign and the rescue of a single life as much as either."

This chapter contains Edmond Cahn's formulation of the consumer perspective, but the reader will share this perspective through all that follows.

N.R.

The Consumers of Injustice

THERE was an incident in 1781 that symbolized the beginning of a new age for government and law. The Revolutionary War had been going on since 1775, and the final battle was fought at Yorktown on the coast of Virginia during the month of October 1781. The British army, sent to subdue the colonists, found itself hopelessly wedged between a formidable French fleet on one side and the American forces under General Washington on the other. The British commander decided that capitulation was inevitable, and General Washington granted him generous and honorable terms. The last great body of imperial troops paraded on the Yorktown plain in surrender to a threadbare and despised collection of amateur soldiers, who had resolved to pursue their national destiny under a free, republican government. As the brilliant ranks of redcoated soldiers filed across the plateau, the British bandmaster signaled to his band and they began playing a popular English tune of the time. It was to this tune that the defeated army marched stiffly away from the scene of battle. Though no one knows even now whether the bandmaster selected the tune purposely or by chance, the name of the tune furnished an inspired commentary. It was "The World Turned Upside Down."

Ever since that time philosophers have been attempting either to ignore or to build upon the historic fact which the British band acknowledged so candidly. Some have perceived quite clearly, others have refused to perceive, that the world of political and legal relations had been turned upside down and the old systems and perspectives would never be adequate again. Henceforth, though a philosopher looking at the legal world would see all the established and familiar elements which his predecessors had been describing since ancient times, everything could look different to him, for he could see all the concepts and phenomena of the institution in a radically new perspective. Everything had turned 180 degrees. What had once looked trivial now became important, and what had previously dominated the stage shifted now to the deep background.

The new factor is the power and responsibility of the citizen entitled to a free vote in a representative democracy. As the right to vote has expanded, group by group and class by class, it has revolutionized the functions of law in the democratic countries. In one form or another the scene at Yorktown has been reenacted again and again in other lands and on other shores all over the world, and we may safely predict there will be other Yorktown surrenders until there is no further occasion for them. In the emancipated countries (including, of course, Britain itself, which was emancipated by Yorktown only slightly less than America), the right to vote spread slowly and tediously as parliaments gradually eroded the old barriers of religion, property, race, and sex. Though the process is incomplete, we know that every impulse and current in human affairs operates to favor it. More and more, men realize that there is no hope of genuine enfranchisement unless they have the franchise.

What then is this new perspective that is based on the vantage point of the voting citizen, and how does it differ from the old, pre-democratic perspective? The new perspective is the perspective of the democratic citizen in the role of consumer of the law. The old perspective, developed while observing an empire, a kingdom, a landed aristocracy, or an oligarchy, was essentially a ruler's or at best an official's perspective; what democratic legal theory has been trying to attain since 1781 is a consumer's perspective.

How does a person become a consumer of the law? The most obvious way consists in being safeguarded and regulated from day to day by official rules or becoming involved directly with the legal mechanism — for example, being charged with a crime or engaging in a lawsuit. A second way, which representative government makes available to its citizens, is to influence the shape and form of law, as by voting, by advocating reforms, by asserting group interests. Then there is the third way, which is perhaps the most characteristically democratic. It is the way of assuming and shouldering responsibility for those acts that our representatives do in our name and by force of our authority, the evil acts as well as the good, the oppressive and unjust and the foolish, too.

This is the way that is new. The philosophy that does not reckon with it is talking a pre-democratic language and addressing us in terms that are fit for powdered wigs and knee breeches. To cope with the problems of our democratic era we need to reassess all the familiar, accepted doctrines. We need to ascertain how suitable they are for the specific, homely experiences of individual human beings. This alone is the genuinely democratic perspective. And when we do adopt it and do concern ourselves with the individual human being as consumer of the law, what will we think about the traditional notions of law and justice? How adequate are they for the new age of representative government? . . .

The old perspectives and traditions are tenacious, and I suppose that none of us has thrown them off entirely. Perhaps there are some who fear to turn the juristic world upside down and adopt the new democratic perspective because they confuse the consumer's point of view with obsolete economic individualism. Perhaps they believe, or pretend to believe, that concern with individual human beings is some sort of casuistic cloak for a gospel of unregulated private enterprise. Of course, they are entirely mistaken. The consumer perspective – or "anthropocentric" view of law (as I have called it) – is not welded to any specific tenure system or mode of social organization. It is determined by our changing needs, claims, and aspirations as human beings and citizens living under a representative government. For us, many of the old ways of thought no longer suffice, and we insist, in Horace Kallen's words, "The ultimate consumer is the basic social reality. He is the *natural* terminus of any chain of change in human life. He is the end for whose sake things are not merely used but used up. He is the topmost turn of any economy, the seat of value, the individual in whom the processes of life, whatever their course, begin and end and find their meaning."

The ugliest sign of our thralldom to the old outlook is that it tends to desensitize men of fine intellect and good will. Somehow they learn not to notice what happens to [individuals], and even to suppress, though they cannot entirely forget, their own inevitable involvement. As it was customary for an emperor, king, or despot to think of the people in large quantitative terms, as raw material for programs or convenient fodder for cannon, a view of law conceived in the old imperial perspective will almost inevitably adopt the same wholesale approach. Fancying himself a ruler of the destinies of men, or perhaps a species of pagan god, the old-style philosopher assumed a post of lofty remoteness where he could look down on the scurryings of the populace as one might watch a swarm of interesting but not very important insects. If curiosity happened to draw him closer to the scene, they might appear somewhat larger to his eye and then, instead of assimilating them to a beehive or an anthill, he might call them "the herd."

This is what mere quantity or numerical mass or preoccupation with arithmetic can do to blunt the moral sensibilities of intelligent men. Perplexed by the marvelous variety of human personalities and transactions, the modern professional theorist gropes for some reassuring formula or other, consisting if possible of arithmetical measurements and statistics. The rage to quantify that we witness today goes back to ancient times, as we know from the example of King Solomon, who smugly recorded that he possessed a total of 700 wives and 300 concubines. Solomon's maxim of procedure is extremely popular today in sociology, opinion research, and communication theory. It is, "If you cannot understand them, you can at least contrive to count them."

If they are properly organized and interpreted, statistical studies have genuine utility, and modern society cannot operate without them. For one thing, they may serve to condense and recapitulate the experience of the past, which they preserve for the benefit of the present and future, and thus they may constitute a major factor in the transmission of a cultural heritage. How, indeed, could anyone learn to exercise the faculty of judgment unless he could take into account the averages established by previous social experience and use them to build his expectations of his neighbors' behavior?

Yet how far can we trust a mere average? To a reflective observer, an average may indicate much or nothing. Standing by itself, it does not reveal any sufficient reason for our approving or disapproving. The "average man" who emerges from scientific statistical studies should not be confused with the "reasonable man" whom the law uses as a conceptual model of behavior that it will approve or disapprove. Neither of them is a very attractive fellow. The "reasonable man" concocted by legal theory never violates the law or gets into trouble with government officials. How can he? He is too careful, too prompt, too foresighted, too prudent, too obedient — in point of fact, just too dull. I have never met a completely "reasonable man," and I doubt that one exists. Nor have I ever met the "average man" of scientific statistics: that quaint person who owns 2.6 suits of clothes, marries 1.2 times, and is blessed with 2.8 children. The world either does not know or does not heed what the lawyers and statisticians have prescribed for it, and continues to behave in ways that startle and shock them.

Consequently, averages can furnish only the beginning of understanding. The register and range of the items, their scope and peculiarities of distribution — these speak much more revealingly to a sensitive mind, which never allows collectives or averages to dull its interest in concrete particulars. The man who stops at averages and feels no concern with particulars is rather like one who refuses to read novels, short stories, poems, essays, dramas, and epics, yet keeps on demanding "literature."

Once we examine law and government from the consumer perspective, we are less likely to be beguiled by averages. If one-half of the statutes passed at a legislative session are too lavish and extravagant with the people's money, and the other half too scant and niggardly, it is not probable that an intelligent electorate will be satisfied just because the averages come out well. If a foreign office is too aggressive and bellicose in certain affairs, can it gain public confidence by being too backward and diffident in others? And if an innocent man . . . is wrongfully convicted of a crime, who will have the impudence to solace him by pointing out how many guilty men escape altogether from punishment? In the anthropocentric view, the quality of government and law is to be tested and approved or found wanting, case by case. While the particular case may involve a whole nation, a class or group within the nation, or a single individual, it is by what they do here — in this case — that the legislators, executives, or judges must vindicate themselves. . . .

Somehow the old imperial perspective still continues to sway men's thinking. . . . Whenever popular protests are raised against police lawlessness or whenever the Supreme Court endeavors to require lawful methods of the police, some very conscientious lawyers will protest that efficiency in punishing crime is the more important consideration and that the "third degree" and like horrors are not used frequently — or, at least, are not exposed frequently. Here is a typical rationalization in a recent book: "The dangers of encouraging police lawlessness are not to be minimized; but surely there is a good deal of hyperbole, if not nonsense, in the current judicial apprehension. It leaves out of account the question of the scale of police lawlessness. The danger to civil liberties is not great so long as the misconduct of the police is no more than occasional."

I shall not tarry with this passage, the fallacies of which seem apparent as soon as one considers that the so-called "occasional" case . . . may readily become one's own. Let me rather present a less obvious instance of the error, taken from the pen of no less a figure than Benjamin N. Cardozo. Justice Cardozo may rightly be regarded as a paragon of moral insight on the American bench. If, therefore, the fallacy of averaging types of judges or philosophies or litigants or their cases, one against the other, could influence a mind like Cardozo's, surely no one else has the right to feel immune from it. I believe it did infect these passages, which I quote from his most celebrated work, *The Nature of the Judicial Process:*

The eccentricities of judges balance one another. One judge looks at problems from the point of view of history, another from that of philosophy, another from that of social utility, one is a formalist, another a latitudinarian, one is timorous of change, another dissatisfied with the present; out of the attrition of diverse minds there is beaten something which has a constancy and uniformity and average value greater than its component elements. . . .

Ever in the making, as law develops through the centuries, is this new faith which silently and steadily effaces our mistakes and eccentricities. I sometimes think that we worry ourselves overmuch about the enduring consequences of our errors. They may work a little confusion for a time. In the end, they will be modified or corrected or their teachings ignored. The future takes care of such things.

Lawyers have a way of hailing these fine paragraphs and drawing comfort from the assurance that "the eccentricities . . . balance one another" and "the future takes care of such things." But if we are candid with ourselves we must recognize that the comfort is sorely insufficient. Revere Cardozo as we may, we cannot help retorting that averages in the administration of justice do not avail the person who is wronged grievously in his own, particular case. The appeal to time and patience may assist in evolving better concepts and techniques for future use of the profession, but it cannot excuse or exonerate our sending an innocent man to the penitentiary here and now. Enlightenment tomorrow or elsewhere will not serve, for his destiny rests in our hands today, and our sense of injustice (for that is what I call it) forbids us to be patient at his cost.

Why do I propose we speak of the "sense of injustice" rather than the "sense of justice"? There are various reasons, each of them related in one way or another to our taking a consumer's or anthropocentric perspective. When we adopt this perspective we investigate the meaning of a concept by observing the occasions when it becomes relevant to the common, earthy experiences of individual human beings. When then does the concept of "justice" achieve this relevance? In the existential sense, when is a citizen in a democratic society disposed to invoke the name of justice?

I believe he invokes it when, personally or vicariously, he experiences the impact of an act of injustice. It is not his custom to meditate in his study and search for self-evident juristic propositions or tidy utopian diagrams about abstract justice. If justice were only an ideal mode or state or condition, our response as human beings would be merely contemplative, and — as we all know — contemplation bakes no loaves. But the response with which men meet a real or imagined instance of injustice is entirely different; it is alive with warmth and movement that courses through the entire human organism. How often when we are faced with a social problem and cannot determine which of many alternative solutions would be just, we find ourselves certain and unanimous that one particular solution would be utterly unjust!

If it is preferable to speak of the "sense of injustice," what shall we mean when we find occasion to use the term "justice"? We cannot be satisfied to employ it in the traditional ideal or static sense because, in that sense, justice — like goodness — is a hopelessly ambiguous concept. Since the time of Immanuel Kant philosophers have reiterated that justice is a term too ambiguous and multivalent to convey a definable meaning in human relations and social arrangements. The most they are disposed to grant is that justice may be regarded as a quality of the human will or, in other words, a type of good motive or volition.

This is indeed a sad demotion for a concept as sublime and inspiring as justice. To treat justice as a mere quality of the will and nothing more is to trivialize it and impoverish ourselves unnecessarily. In the context of our consumer's or anthropocentric view, which focuses on the "sense of injustice," the word "justice" can bear a much more estimable meaning. For us, justice will mean neither a static diagram on the one hand nor a mere quality of will on the other; it will mean the active process of remedying or preventing what would arouse the "sense of injustice." It will be taken not as a condition or a quality but as a species of human activity.

In conducting this activity or process, while there is no single, orthodox formula to prescribe for universal application, we generally obtain the worthiest results when we use the methods of pragmatism as James, Dewey, Peirce, and Kallen have outlined them. But with a certain difference or refinement, for the pragmatism that serves us best in practicing justice is a *graded* pragmatism. I call it "graded" because it classifies and grades the beliefs that we happen to possess at any given moment. It insists that our beliefs, judgments, prehensions, meanings, and warranted assertions are not created equal and cannot be rendered equal in terms of either verification or verifiability. Weak verification and weak verifiability are not equal to strong verification and strong verifiability. Therefore beliefs must be ranked and graded according to the conceived cost that may follow from proceeding to act on them. What is clearly a warranted assertion for a low price in prospective human consequences may not be warranted at all if the prospective price is raised.

A graded pragmatism is concerned with two main centers of cost: cost to the human subject of the conceived action, and cost to the human object. The subject inquires what will be the initial cost, what the prospective upkeep and maintenance that the idea offered to him may require him to assume, and his belief will be graded according to the highest cost-level he feels willing and able to maintain. For example, people may believe quite sincerely in the idea of education at one cost-level and not believe in it at another. Some may believe sincerely in secular public education, but not at the cost of sending their own children to certain public schools in New York City. Judges may believe sincerely in the idea of speedy justice at the cost-level of opening court at ten o'clock, but not at the cost-level of nine o'clock.

Then there is the factor of conceived cost to the human object of the action. Here all our experience in the law endorses the wisdom of using a graded pragmatism. If a charge against a man amounts to mere gossip or hearsay we refuse to predicate any sort of liability on it. We do not impose liability for money damages unless our belief is based on a preponderance of credible evidence; we do not impose civil liability for the commission of fraud unless our belief is verified further and is based on clear and convincing proof; and we do not impose a prison sentence for crime unless our belief is entirely firm and is based on proof beyond a reasonable doubt. Thus by consciously and critically grading our beliefs according to their prospective costs and human concussions, we enlist the teachings of pragmatism in the service of the sense of injustice.

When do men experience the "sense of injustice"? Typically, when officials violate or threaten to violate their demands for equality, for recognition of desert, for respect of human dignity, for conscientious adjudication, for the confinement of government to its proper functions, and for the fulfillment of the common expectations of the society. These are the circumstances that arouse the sense of injustice and summon it into operation. For example, whenever officials misuse their power, or oppress the innocent and unoffending, they provoke our sense of injustice.

When we see or hear or read about this sort of conduct we feel that sympathetic reaction of outrage, resentment, and anger and those affections of the viscera and adrenal secretions that prepare human beings to resist attack, for our physiology has equipped us to regard an act of injustice to another as a personal aggression against ourselves. Empathy or imaginative interchange projects us into the place of the one who is wronged, not merely to pity or compassionate him but to resist and defend. The sense of injustice transmutes the wrong into an act of assault, and prepares our psychic organs for measures of self-defense.

This is the way justice can acquire a public meaning. Through mutual communication and discussion the men who live in a particular ethos may perceive the same threat and experience the same bodily reactions. The fact that they are roused individually and jointly gives us sufficient warrant to speak of "justice" without utter relativism or subjectivism or solipsism. Anyone who desires empirical proof can observe and verify this interchangeability for himself. It is real and demonstrable. It is also indispensable to the preservation of society. If man did not have the capacity to recognize oppression of another as a species of attack on himself he would be unprepared — in the glandular sense — for survival as a political being. In short, the human animal as we know him is equipped and predisposed to fight injustice.

This predisposition, like other natural capacities, being designed to end in action, is finite and limited. Each of us is bound by the perspective predicament to his own brief time and narrow place, and though the sense of injustice gives him a lengthening tether to enable him to wander some distance away from self and its immediate setting, he does remain tethered. Since he lives a finite existence in a finite world, his survival does not require that the sense of injustice encompass infinitude; nor need he wait for assurance that what it admonishes him to do would be universally right and valid, for when he faces any particular crisis of his own he does not feel compelled to legislate for the universe. If we were to ask him whether the voice of his sense of injustice is right in all times and all places he would reply — quite reasonably — that the injustices he needs to subdue arise invariably in particular times and particular places. Injustice does not threaten him *semper et ubique* but here and now. He can safely assume that he will never be called to combat it in all times and all places.

Nevertheless, the tether that holds us is a rather elastic one. If the circumstances of the specific case permit us to engage in imaginative interchange we can respond to an injustice despite great disparities of time, place, culture, law, and ethical tradition. For example, the trial and condemnation of Socrates will stir men's sense of injustice as long as they can conceive the danger of corrupt judges and mob passions.

Here, then, is the sense of injustice at work within men and the law. Is it nothing more than a reasonless compound of glandular secretions and angry emotions, a mere syndrome of outraged feelings, a "sense," as it were, that is completely without sense? Clearly not. While the sense of injustice uses empathy, projection, and emotion, it simultaneously summons perception, reasoning, intelligence, and judgment — all the capacities that make for understanding and the application of sense. In the experience of the sense of injustice, thinking and feeling suffuse each other reciprocally, reason and empathy blend together indissociably, and the rational directs the emotional while the emotional impels the rational. The combined process enables men to develop and communities to advance. Without reason the sense of injustice could not serve the purposes of social utility, which only observation, analysis, and science can discern, while without empathy it would lose its warm sensibility and cogent drive. Compounded indissolubly of both reason and impulsion, it is an active, spontaneous source of law. It makes a practical, working difference in courts, legislatures, and administrative tribunals.

In this compound the democratic citizen and the democratic state find their best, eventual hope of cohesion and survival. The public experience of the sense of injustice can work the greatest of social transformations, because it incites men to join one another and participate — first in recognizing a jeopardy, then in resisting it, and finally in exulting side by side whenever they have practiced justice successfully. All of these are public acts of solidarity, which weld a people together and fill them with a patriotism of irresistible power. There is no established interest, no sinister influence, no outworn institution or superstition that can stand against it. If, by way of metaphor, we imagine the ancient stronghold of Jericho as a citadel of injustice, then no wonder its walls collapsed — not, however, as some have thought, when the priests blew their trumpets but, as the Scripture makes clear, when the people shouted in unison with a great and mighty voice. In less dramatic circumstances the public sense of injustice is equally solidary. Though like any other human capacity it is finite and fallible, it can create its own cumulative rewards by addressing the weak, the insecure, and the deviant ones of the community with a promise of mutual support and confidence.

In public life or private, the sense of injustice offers us no categorical warranty; how amid the ways of this world should we ever come to expect one? What it does offer should supply hope and certainty enough for the responsible citizens of a free land. It promises men that, if they only will, they can close ranks in mutual defense, collaborate with their neighbors in the enterprises of justice, and from day to day become increasingly secure. It promises that persuasion and free assent can triumph over brute force and build the foundations of a happier commonwealth.

From the Horace M. Kallen Lecture for 1959 at the New School for Social Research, published in Social Research, *1959.*

Law in the Consumer Perspective

THE TASK FOR LEGAL PHILOSOPHY

ALMOST two centuries ago the German scientific philosopher Georg Christoph Lichtenberg said, "For a long time now I have thought that philosophy will one day devour itself." If Lichtenberg had a chance to observe the low morale of our contemporary faculties of philosophy, he would probably claim that his prediction had come true. In ancient Greece, when philosophy began its career, it proudly called itself "the love of wisdom," but today it seems that if there ever was a love affair between wisdom and the professors of philosophy, each of them has gradually lost interest in the other. A typical statement by a prominent Oxford moral philosopher, R. M. Hare, reads: "To get people to think morally it is not sufficient to tell them how to do it; it is necessary also to induce in them the wish to do it. And this is not the province of the philosopher. It is more likely that enlightened politicians, journalists, radio commentators, preachers, novelists, and all those who have an influence on public opinion will gradually effect a change for the better—given that events do not overtake them." A highly regarded American scientific philosopher, Hans Reichenbach, says: "Whoever wants to study ethics, therefore, should not go to the philosopher; he should go where moral issues are fought out." With few exceptions, the professors of philosophy have despaired of trying to influence the political and moral decisions of their fellow citizens.

It would be a gloomy day for mankind if this failure of nerve were to infect legal philosophy and jurisprudence. Our world offers innumerable invitations, challenges and opportunities to juristic theorists. Never in previous history have so many social and individual problems been put under the sway of law. Law has absorbed substantial slices of relations and transactions that used to belong to homes, churches, voluntary associations, and other disciplinary organs of social environment. Law has assumed burdens that our ancestors left to corporate religion, private benevolence, group ethics, the play of market and economic forces, and the unpredictable shifts of weather and climate. It has recently begun to bear certain responsibilities that the men of the past called "political" and consigned to the tender mercies of state legislatures. Never has law had so much to do; never has it stood in greater need of philosophic guidance and enlightenment. Jeremy Bentham spoke to our time when he declared, "If it be of importance and of use to us to know the principles of the element we breathe, surely it is not of much less importance nor of much less use to comprehend the principles, and endeavour at the improvement of those *laws,* by which alone we breathe it in security."

No one can charge that the theorists of law have defaulted in their strictly critical function. There has been no deficiency of what we may call the "prudence" in jurisprudence. Our modern realists and skeptics have excelled in analyzing legal standards, exposing latent fallacies, testing the relevant insights of the social sciences, and generally disclosing the role of personal psychological factors that affect the processes of judgment and decision. The only significant deficit on the skeptical side of modern jurisprudence has been a deficit of fact-skepticism.

It is not the critical or aporetic function that has lagged. In point of fact, legal philosophers have been working so devotedly at systematic doubt that most of them have come to think of it as their whole task. The consequences are not altogether wholesome. As reflective thought that remains too long barred from release in action may lead to mere carping and abulia, a jurisprudence that is exclusively critical may conclude, as Lichtenberg warned, by "devouring itself." He had another remark that is pertinent to our era: "To be frequently alone, and meditate about oneself, and create a world from within oneself, may well afford us great pleasure; but in this way we come imperceptibly to evolve a philosophy according to which suicide is right and permissible. It is a good thing, then, to grapple oneself to the world again by means of a girl or friend, so as not to fall off altogether." What legal philosophy needs is constantly to grapple itself to the world.

As I see it, the single most important fallacy of twentieth-century thought is that we have homogenized our relativism. Spurred by semantics and anthropology, philosophy has taught that all propositions and judgments are relative, and legal philosophy has echoed the teaching. Depending on the point of view, every statement and its contrary are fungibly true, fungibly false. Yet, oddly enough, the philosophers who so assure us have failed to apply their dialectical and critical talents to their own relativism. Relativism alone stands undifferentiated, untested, unassorted, and unclassified. Since values are merely relative without discrimination or distinction among them, Adolf Hitler may be regarded as relatively bad or good in the same sense that Albert Schweitzer is relatively good or bad and Charles Darwin is relatively superior or inferior to an anthropoid ape. In the spirit of homogenized relativism, a professor of philosophy may insist that all standards and judgments are equally flexible and equally unreliable, that a female ape, for example, may likely prefer her mate to Mr. Darwin. Yes, well she may; but is her case really ours? Granting her the privilege of choosing according to simian standards, may we not reply that in the present state of human affairs we have not only a right but also a most urgent duty to rank Mr. Darwin higher?

It is time for relativism, too, to acquire a measure of self-consciousness and functional sophistication.[1] If, as we are assured, everything depends on and varies with the point of view, then the point of view, the angle of vision, the chosen perspective necessarily becomes the most decisive factor in the formation of responsible judgment. If everything depends on the point of view, we are under a pressing need to select the best, wisest, and most enlightened among available points of view. If everything depends on the point of view, one of the prime tasks of legal philosophy is to examine diverse points of view, contrast their respective implications for a free society, and indicate the point of view that intelligent judges may esteem and just judges may adopt.

THE IMPERIAL OR OFFICIAL PERSPECTIVE AND
SOME OF ITS RHETORIC

All the modern legal systems have inherited a single characteristic way of viewing the problems of society. We may call it "the imperial or official perspective" because it has been largely determined by the dominant interests of rulers, governors, and other officials.[2] A similar perspective can be found throughout the history of legal philosophy and jurisprudence. At least from the death of Aristotle down to recent times the classic philosophers of government and law developed their theories while observing the ways of empires, kingdoms, aristocracies, and republican oligarchies. This circumstance left distinct marks on their thinking.

Whenever a concrete question arises for decision in a given society, most of the inhabitants will be seen to accept more or less the same list of factors as relevant to resolving it, and if some disagree with others in their answer, it is mainly because they appraise the respective factors in different proportions of size and materiality. Almost everything in the process of deliberation depends on where they take their stand while they appraise them, on what we correctly call their "point of view." Of course, extreme passion and prejudice may blind some people to the very existence of relevant factors; by like token, a magistrate who is a small man may not be able to see over the mace of authority that lies on the bench before him. But, by and large, the principal differences among valuations will be attributable not so much to myopia as to differences of habitual perspective. In the law, the habitual perspective has been imperial or official.

During the third century B.C., the Emperor Asoka of India, a monarch of extraordinary enlightenment, expressed the imperial or official perspective in the following attractive terms:

> Just as a man feels confident when he has entrusted his child to a skilled nurse, thinking, "This skilled nurse will take good care of my child," so I have appointed the provincial governors for the welfare and happiness of my provincial people.
>
> In order that they may perform their duties fearlessly, confidently, and cheerfully, they have been given discretion in the distribution of honors and the infliction of punishments.
>
> Impartiality is desirable in legal procedures and in punishments. I have therefore decreed that henceforth prisoners who have been convicted and sentenced to death shall be granted a respite of three days. [During this period their] relatives may appeal to the officials for the prisoners' lives; or, if no one makes an appeal, the prisoners may prepare for the other world by distributing gifts or by fasting.

As Asoka illustrates, the imperial or official perspective does not necessarily convey a cruel or oppressive purpose. What it constitutes is a sort of "internal colonialism" whose motive may be kindly and benevolent. To take a modern example, when our representatives in Congress directed the Postmaster General of the United States to censor mail from abroad and make sure that Communist propaganda sent to American citizens was labeled as such, they employed the old imperial or official perspective. In this perspective, one assesses the factors of freedom and security from the point of view of the official processors of government.[3]

It would be misleading to assume that the official or imperial perspective operates within the sphere of public law only. While easier to notice in constitutional law and criminal procedure, it leaves unmistakable traces throughout the legal system and controls the value judgments of the majority of lawyers in every country. The official perspective is not confined to despotic and tyrannical regimes. Implementing as it does the inveterate "we — they" attitude of the professional processors toward the lay consumers, it remains characteristic of bench and bar even in the Western democracies.

The official perspective has a typical rhetoric which, when expertly manipulated, can seem very persuasive. Like effective rhetoric in other domains of social activity, it employs phrases and maxims that would sound quite reasonable if they were restricted to their proper uses. As the proper uses keep depositing money in the bank of our experience, we may easily become confused and extend credit when we meet the same phrases in improper or dishonest references.

Some of the familiar phrases are: the public interest in getting things finally settled; the duty to abide by established principles and precedents; the necessity of showing respect for expert judgment and administrative convenience; the dominant need for certainty in the law; the obligation to preserve the law's predictability so that men will know how to order their affairs; the danger of opening the floodgates of litigation; the danger of opening the gates of penitentiaries; the danger of inviting collusion, fraud, and perjury; the deference due to other organs of government; the absurdity of heeding mere speculations; the necessity of leaving certain wrongs, however grievous they may be, to the province of morals; the paramount need to maintain strict procedural regularity; and (by way of solace to a man on his way to the electric chair) the undeniable right to petition for executive clemency.

Whoever wishes further examples may turn to Bentham's *Handbook of Political Fallacies* and convert the respective political locutions that he finds there into legal counterparts. Surveying obstructionism in all its guises, Bentham affixed a label to almost every conceivable species of rhetorical hypocrisy. Our day has produced only a single item to add to his list; it would be called the "Fallacy of Self-assumed Superiority" and would declare, in effect, "I, the judge, am personally ready for a better, more humane rule of law in this case, but my duty requires me to decide according to the people's standard, and of course the people are not."

It would be redundant to multiply examples of the imperial or official perspective.[4] Not long ago, when I asked some of my colleagues what they considered its most heinous use in the reports of the United States Supreme Court, they offered a variety of nominations and finally chose the decision in *Daniels v. Allen*.[5] The case involved two North Carolina Negro youths, seventeen years old, who were under sentence of death. The Supreme Court of North Carolina and the United States Supreme Court refused to consider their very substantial constitutional claim (based on systematic exclusion of Negroes from the jury lists) because their lawyer had served a notice of appeal one day late, and the North Carolina court, although possessed of full discretionary power under state law to accept a tardy notice, had curtly refused.

During the 1920's and 1930's the United States Supreme Court was occasionally unfaithful to the official perspective and began to move away from it. In those days there was no sign that the Court consciously intended to disavow the old point of view; it intended only to employ it with stricter system and decency. The game of litigation was expected to remain the same old game, the sporting theory of justice was still to prevail, but the officials were to be held more closely to established rules. Mr. Justice Holmes epitomized the official perspective at its most ambitious when, dissenting in the *Olmstead* case, he protested against the government's engaging in "dirty business."

We can see the start of the movement (which no one suspected of launching a transition) if we look at the ordeal of Tom Mooney.[6] Mooney was convicted of murder for participating in the San Francisco bombing of 1916. After his time to apply for a new trial had expired under California law, it was discovered that the district attorney had received information before the trial, which he did not disclose, showing that the two principal eyewitnesses for the prosecution were offering wholly false testimony. In 1918, despite this specific evidence of fraud and perjury directly involving the prosecutor, the Supreme Court of California decided unanimously that Mooney had no remedy. It adopted in its opinion the following statements of the lower court:

> The defendant in such case is without remedy. In this state it is the settled law that a judgment cannot be set aside because it is predicated upon perjured testimony, or because material evidence is concealed or suppressed. The fraud which is practiced in such cases upon both the court and him against whom the judgment is pronounced is not such fraud as is extrinsic to the record; and it is only in cases of extrinsic fraud that such relief may be had. . . .
>
> Nor can it be said that the duty of a district attorney differs in the trial of criminal actions from that of counsel in civil actions. Each has an equal duty imposed upon him by the oath he has taken and by the law of the land to present to the court and to the jury only competent and legitimate evidence from which may be determined the truth of the issues involved. If that obligation be violated, and perjured testimony produced, or material evidence suppressed by either, as we have seen, in so far as the judgment is concerned, the injured party is without remedy.

It is embarrassing to add that the Supreme Court of the United States denied Mooney's petition for certiorari.

By 1934 the law was ready for a transitional step. Mooney, after more than sixteen years of imprisonment, turned to the Supreme Court's original jurisdiction and moved for leave to file a petition for habeas corpus. At last the Court put its foot down on the issue of official honesty. Though it denied the petition without prejudice, ingeniously distinguishing the 1918 determination and remitting Mooney to the use of state habeas corpus, it declared categorically that if he could prove the fraud he asserted, his conviction must be nullified. Due process, it said, is a requirement that cannot be deemed to be satisfied by mere notice and hearing if a State has contrived a conviction through the pretense of a trial which in truth is but used as a means of depriving a defendant of liberty through a deliberate deception of court and jury by the presentation of testimony known to be perjured. Such a contrivance by a State to procure the conviction and imprisonment of a defendant is as inconsistent with the rudimentary demands of justice as is the obtaining of a like result by intimidation.

Thereupon, weary of fraud, delay, and injustice, the governor of California declared his belief in Mooney's innocence and gave him an unconditional pardon. No one returned sixteen years of life to Tom Mooney. Few even considered the question whether the official prosecutor and the legal system that had denied a remedy ought to admit their guilt and petition for a pardon. The whole episode demonstrated that although on some occasions "hard cases make bad law" on others bad law makes hard cases. Significantly enough, the former is a familiar saying among lawyers, and the latter is not.

Following the *Mooney* decision, the United States Supreme Court and various high state courts developed and elaborated its doctrine with commendable firmness. During the quarter century after Mooney's release, though it cannot be said that prosecutors' behavior improved, the courts at least endeavored to elevate their standards of due process and fair trial. The more revolting instances of official misbehavior came to be generally regarded as indecent, undutiful, and "dirty business." We shall see that this phase, impressive as it seemed, was only a transition.

EMERGENCE OF THE CONSUMER PERSPECTIVE

The democratic revolution that began in the seventeenth century and is still under way in the twentieth is gradually providing the law with a new and different perspective. The old point of view — the imperial or official — was that of the processors; the new point of view which we may call the consumer perspective, is that of the consumers of law and government. A free and open society calls on its official processors to perform their functions according to the perspective of consumers.

How does a person become a consumer of government and law? The obvious and traditional way consists in living amid conditions of reasonable public order and being safeguarded and regulated from day to day as one goes about the chores of his life and fills his place in society; in this sense, one consumes law whenever one talks or writes, walks or sits, buys or sells, rents or rides, pays or receives. In addition, there is a more dramatic way to consume the law. One may engage in a lawsuit, or be charged with a crime.

Under democratic government, a citizen also consumes law in a more extensive fashion.[7] He influences the shape of policy and legislation, casts his vote, supports his political party, urges reforms, asserts the interests of a special group or of the whole community.

Finally, there is a third way to consume government and law. It consists in examining, judging, and assuming responsibility for what our officials do in our name and by our authority, the unjust and evil acts as well as the beneficent and good.

Suppose we consider a case like Tom Mooney's in the consumer perspective and ask whether the doctrine reached in the 1930's was adequate. Is it enough to hold that a conviction is unconstitutional and subject to collateral attack when the prosecutor with guilty motive introduces evidence that he knows to be false, suppresses evidence that would exonerate the accused or, if you will, stands silent in the courtroom when he hears prosecution witnesses testifying falsely?

Granted that from the imperial or official point of view, the prosecutor's guilty purpose may make a decisive difference, how much difference can it make in the consumer perspective? As far as the public is concerned its interest is in having trials conducted fairly and in minimizing, though it cannot eliminate, the risk of convicting innocent persons. As far as the accused is concerned, he suffers from the giving of false testimony or the suppressing of favorable evidence just as much, whether the prosecutor's motive be good or bad, well intentioned or vicious. The harm to him is the same either way. True, a prosecutor with good intentions may cast a lesser onus of disgrace on the community and its law-enforcement apparatus; yet what consolation can that be to an innocent defendant who is left to remain in the penitentiary? The best of official motives cannot make prison walls acceptable to an innocent man. Thus in the consumer perspective the *Mooney* doctrine fell short.

The next evolutionary phase began in 1956 when the New York Court of Appeals upheld an attack on a conviction when the prosecutor had remained silent in court though he knew that the state's principal witness was giving false answers to questions that bore directly on his credibility.[8] Judge Stanley H. Fuld's opinion for the unanimous court adopted a consumer view of the prosecutor's motive: "That the district attorney's silence was not the result of guile or a desire to prejudice matters little, for *its impact was the same,* preventing, as it did, a trial that could in any real sense be termed fair."

Five years later in *Brady v. State,* the Court of Appeals of Maryland unanimously embraced the new doctrine and when the case reached the United States Supreme Court, the Court's opinion by Justice William O. Douglas consolidated the advance.[9] Under the Fourteenth Amendment it is now unconstitutional for a prosecutor in any state to withhold "evidence on demand of an accused which, if made available, would tend to exculpate him or reduce the penalty" annexed to the offense. Affirming the Maryland court, Mr. Justice Douglas stated: "We now hold that the suppression by the prosecution of evidence favorable to an accused upon request violates due process where the evidence is material either to guilt or to punishment, *irrespective of the good faith or bad faith of the prosecution.*"

It will be noticed that the Supreme Court's statement still requires (a) a demand or request for the pertinent item, and (b) some knowledge or information on the prosecutor's part by which the item can be connected with him. In all likelihood, the Court will soon begin to erode the former requirement and dispense with demand, particularly where the defense has no cause to suspect that the item of evidence exists. Surely Judge Edgerton was right when he remarked a number of years ago: "The case emphasizes the necessity of disclosure by the prosecution of evidence that may reasonably be considered admissible and useful to the defense. When there is substantial room for doubt, the prosecution is not to decide for the court what is admissible or for the defense what is useful."[10]

To complete the evolution and provide a doctrine that comports fully with the consumer perspective, it will also be necessary to eliminate the requirement that the prosecutor or police know about the item at the time of trial. If the prosecutor's motive is deemed irrelevant as it now is, the same ought to be true of his knowledge or information. If a conviction rests on perjury, what difference does it make to the public or the defendant that the prosecutor and police have no cause to suspect the testimony when they offer it at the trial? It may even be that a prosecutor who credits the veracity of his false witnesses can work more harm than one who distrusts them. At any rate, the right to collateral attack on a conviction obtained by perjury should not be made to depend on the prosecutor's subjective state of information. The conviction is equally unjust however much or little the prosecutor may have known when he obtained it. Once its injustice comes to light there is no warrant in the consumer perspective for permitting it to stand.

Of course, this does not imply that a convict who has had a completely fair trial is entitled to submit the same conflicting evidence to another jury. It does mean that if at any time he offers concrete, newly discovered evidence to establish that he was convicted through perjury, his right to a new trial should not be denied simply because he cannot implicate the prosecutor.[11] In the consumer perspective, convictions and penitentiary terms should not rest on clearly demonstrable perjury under any circumstance.

Nor for that matter should they rest, as experience demonstrates they sometimes do, on the mistaken identification of sincere and respectable eyewitnesses whose powers of observation have been confused by anger, excitement, or panic fear.[12] Suppose a convict at any time offers newly discovered evidence that is not merely cumulative and not substantially contradicted by contrary evidence; suppose the newly discovered evidence is sufficient in quality and probative effect to convince a judge that the man was wrongly convicted: surely on these conditions the court ought to set aside the conviction without finding it necessary to label either the prosecutor or his witnesses as scapegoats. It should be enough to find that the trial process, which we all acknowledge to be imperfect, has manifestly miscarried and condemned an innocent man. Our courts, which have come a long way during the past generation, ought to be ready to take the remaining steps.

WHAT THE CONSUMER PERSPECTIVE IS NOT

So much for a particular illustration of the consumer perspective. What is it in general? Perhaps, to minimize misunderstanding, we should begin by saying rather flatly what it is not.

For one thing, it is not an attempt to repudiate the values that the traditional perspective has emphasized (or overemphasized) — governmental efficiency, public order, respect for authority, and national security. Far from banishing the traditional values, the consumer perspective puts them in their proper rank and proportion as instruments of the people's welfare.

For another thing, when we regard the general citizenry as consumers of law and government, we are not assigning them a merely passive role. We do not mean they are like a flock of Strasbourg geese that have grain pushed down their throats in order to hasten their conversion into pâté de foie gras. On the contrary, the people are consumers in much the same sense that a farmer is one, who grows his wheat and sends it to the miller to be ground into flour, which he takes away and consumes, the lesser part of it directly in the form of home-baked bread and the greater part indirectly by sale or exchange for other merchandise which in turn he uses or consumes. It would be a strange miller who believed that farmers, because they were consumers, were merely passive. Such millers, of course, there may be; there may also be tailors who fancy that men have arms in order that they may make sleeves, and legs in order that they may fit trousers. But no one who has ever had a baby in the house can long believe that the role of a consumer — even of a sleeping consumer — is truly passive. In a free society, no influence is more cogent and active than the citizen-consumers' needs, demands, and complaints.

This does not mean that we are furnishing officials with excuses for abdicating their lawful authority. The judge who uses the consumer perspective still has to decide individual cases as they come before him; he still has a solemn duty to sift the evidence, deliberate over the issues, and reach his own conscientious determination.[13] So too, the President, senator, congressman, or commissioner who uses it is still obliged to think for himself; he cannot delegate his thinking to public opinion polls. The perspective is not an escape from official responsibilities, nor a signal for installing so-called "people's courts" in the free nations.

Nor is it an attempt to take sides between the individual and the social group, or between material and economic interests, on the one hand, and intellectual, cultural, and ideal interests, on the other. It does involve shifting the focus of law and government from processors to consumers; but among the various consumers and their diverse interests, it offers no simplistic formula, no *a priori* preference, no lazy hierarchy of values. Some consumers need bread; others need Shakespeare; others need their rightful place in the national society — what they all need is processors of law who will consider the people's needs more significant than administrative convenience.

Finally, to avoid one more conceivable misunderstanding, let us add that in a criminal case the accused is obviously not the only pertinent consumer of law. The community is likewise a consumer, and so, too, are the persons whom the crime has injured directly. It would travesty our theme to take it as suggesting that we look at criminal trials exclusively from the point of view of the accused. We have proposed nothing so fatuous.

WHAT THE CONSUMER PERSPECTIVE IS

So much for what the consumer perspective is not. Turning now to its positive attributes, one sees what is new about them in the following operations.

Quoad the Targets and Occasions of Law's Impacts. In the consumer perspective, the significance of any principle, rule, or concept, however exalted, is investigated by observing the specific human targets of its impacts and the occasions when it becomes material to concrete experiences of the members of the community. It was this method that disclosed that the sense of injustice — rather than a purported sense of justice — exerted vital influence within the operations of law.[14]

Current trends in the court reports provide a variety of encouraging positive illustrations. For example, anyone who has been watching the field of products liability must see how the concern with consumer impacts has steadily eroded conventional concepts of warranty and the requirement of privity. Justice Roger J. Traynor, writing for the Supreme Court of California, recently broke through the barrier of warranty and declared, "A manufacturer is strictly liable in tort when an article he places on the market, knowing that it is to be used without inspection for defects, proves to have a defect that causes injury to a human being."[15] Not only a purchaser, mind you, not only a privy or relative or connection of a purchaser, but a "human being" pure and simple. Recognizing that "the injured persons . . . are powerless to protect themselves," the California court brushed past warranties with all their technical refinements, and boldly imposed liability on the manufacturer. If legal philosophers would examine concepts like freedom, truth, security, welfare, and sovereignty with a comparable sensibility to human impacts, they might bring a bright new light to the law.

Quoad the Concretization of Men. In law as elsewhere, conceptual statement tends to make even a gray notion seem black along its edges. This happens because whenever our concept says "A is this," it seems silently to imply that "A is not that," and it may make the implication all the more dangerously because it does it mutely. By avoiding an explicit statement that "A is not that," it escapes open qualifications and disagreements. To say, for example, "This juvenile delinquent is a lawbreaker" seems to imply (by means of the truth itself) that this is the aspect of his total personality we ought to attend to; it seems silently to ask us not to notice what else he may be.

Since we certainly cannot dispense with abstractions and concepts in the ordering of human affairs, our only working approach to the whole personality of a human being is to employ a consumer perspective. Though the law classifies its consumers as facets or fragments of men, it touches them as whole men. It puts the whole man in jail, hangs the whole man, takes away money, status, and property that affect the life of the whole man. When it imposes guilts, they pervade the whole man. It protects the physical and psychic safety of the whole man, and the property on which he may depend. The law guarantees social values, ideals, and freedoms that make life meaningful for the whole man.

There is no denying that the whole man, whoever he may be, is fearfully and wonderfully complex. In the consumer perspective we put aside the convenient marks and statistical dots that stand for human beings and see our congeners in their diverse mixtures of rationality and irrationality, altruism and selfishness, decency and viciousness, magnanimity, cupidity, and repulsive pettiness. Peacocks for vanity, goats for lubricity, and monkeys for conformity they may be — yet strangely endowed with nobility, valor, devotion, and passionate intelligence.

Permeating these singular beings is the unpredictable and highly various chemistry of sex. According to the consumer perspective, sex may make a difference not only in the person judged but also in the person judging; the Supreme Court has taken the proposition seriously enough to overturn a criminal conviction because women had been intentionally eliminated from the jury panel.[16] Thus the perspective not only directs our attention to concrete data of human behavior which the old official perspective ignored, it employs the data more functionally, flexibly, and equitably.

Quoad the Relative Proportions and Weights of Items. Judgment in the consumer perspective tends to reverse the respective proportions and weights attributed to the traditional concerns of law. Though responsive to the interests of internal efficiency and convenience, it accords larger significance to the felt needs of the general citizenry.

Quoad the Concern with Particular Cases. It is traditional for jurists of the official perspective to justify the legal system in terms of averages, wholesale statistics, and overall performances. In point of fact, they are prone to disparage an interest in the outcomes of particular cases as unscientific, unphilosophic, and unlawyerlike. The system, they submit, would not be a system if it were not impersonal and indifferent; it works well enough for them if it meets its purpose in the long run.

Seen in the consumer perspective, these defenses seem dubious. If an innocent man is sent to prison or the electric chair, there is something not quite adequate about assuring him (or his widow) that miscarriages do not happen very often; the man may have a stubborn feeling that he is entitled to justice in his particular case. So too, for that matter, may the litigant in a civil action with a good claim or a good defense. In the consumer perspective, there is something repulsive about the complacent grin with which we are assured that not many judges have been caught taking bribes, that the third degree is not so common as it used to be, and that not many prosecutors suppress evidence favorable to the defense or, if they do, it is seldom proved.

If a layman goes to a surgeon who bungles his operation and he loses an arm or a leg, it is not likely that he will recommend the surgeon to his friends just because other patients have had more satisfactory results. Why should laymen use a different standard when they judge the legal system? How can one expect to solace them by promising that some day the law will awake to needs like theirs?[17] Unless a litigant happens to be an Olympian philosopher or a legal historian, he probably desires justice here and now. He can understand that the law is imperfect like any other human contrivance, that juries may err, and that judges — even the best of them — are restricted by the law and are neither omnipotent nor omniscient. What he cannot understand is inertia and smug indifference.

ARE JUDGES CONSUMERS OF THE LAW?

Legal philosophy in its long career has found a score of ways to ask whether judges are themselves consumers of the law. Does a judge assume any personal responsibility of an ethical nature when he enforces an immoral private law (i.e., a contract) or an inhumane public law (i.e., a statute)? If he does, has he a *legal* right to refuse enforcement?

Without attempting to examine these perennially vexing issues in all their ramifications, we can surely say that the long histories of civil law and common law alike confirm the status of the judge as a consumer of law. Both systems have recognized his legal right to deny enforcement under certain circumstances. At times his authority for refusing may be explicit, at others implied or assumed; at times it may be expansible, at others fixed and rigid. But that judges may be authentic consumers of law seems beyond doubt in our tradition. They have not been mere menials of the political branches.

The systems provide various techniques to enable a judge to defend his integrity. In the first place, he is authorized and expected to construe the provisions of contracts and statutes so as to avoid socially obnoxious, oppressive, immoral, or inhumane results. In the second place, he is expected, under the aegis of public policy, to refuse enforcement of contracts that serve illegal, immoral, or antisocial purposes. In the third place, by disavowing the notion of parliamentary supremacy, the American system rescues him even from acts of legislation if they transgress the specified limits and prohibitions of the written constitution. In our time, the judicial review of constitutionality has come to prevail in more than thirty nations, perhaps because the humiliating spectacle afforded recently by Nazi Germany and Fascist Italy, and presently by the Republic of South Africa, showed what degradation might befall judges without it. The tragic experiences of these countries imply that a free society owes a written bill of rights not only to its general citizenry but also to its decent and honorable judges. When law affects basic human values, judges cannot dispense it to others without partaking of it themselves.

The proposition that judges too may be consumers of the law has immediate practical applications. Suppose, for example, we consider the subject of "entrapment" and its consequences in criminal jurisprudence. For almost forty years the United States Supreme Court has fumbled with entrapment doctrine, and for about thirty years — ever since *Sorrells v. United States* — the respective justices have attached themselves to two different theories of its import.[18]

In general, entrapment takes place "when the criminal design originates with the officials of the Government, and they implant in the mind of an innocent person the disposition to commit the alleged offense and induce its commission in order that they may prosecute." According to the Supreme Court majority, a trial judge must assume that Congress in enacting a criminal statute did not intend it to apply to instances of entrapment, must construe the statute accordingly, and on receiving evidence that government officials may have instigated the crime, must submit the defense of entrapment to the jury. Though this approach to the problem has irrefutable merit, it suffers from two defects: (a) it concedes the power of Congress to eliminate the defense of entrapment by express enactment; and (b) it leaves the judge unprotected if he feels convinced that entrapment took place, but the jury, for whatever reason, feels otherwise.[19]

According to the minority, the doctrine should not rest on imputed legislative intent or statutory construction. It should rest on public policy and the preservation of the court's integrity. Consequently, the minority contend:

> It is the province of the court and of the court alone to protect itself and the government from such prostitution of the criminal law. . . . Proof of entrapment, at any stage of the case, requires the court to stop the prosecution, direct that the indictment be quashed, and the defendant set at liberty. If in doubt as to the facts it may submit the issue of entrapment to a jury for advice. But whatever may be the finding upon such submission the power and the duty to act remain with the court and not with the jury.

Although this approach likewise has merit, it too shows defects: (a) relying as it does on a general notion of judge-made policy, it leaves the court vulnerable to a statute that might expressly eliminate the issue of entrapment; and (b) though it safeguards the judge's position, it leaves the issue of entrapment entirely to his judgment and allows no other protection for the defendant, the jurymen, or the general community.

I suggest that each of these views is inadequate. The majority have neglected the interest of the judge as a consumer of law while the minority have concentrated on his interest to the exclusion of everyone else's. The majority have evinced respect for the motives of the legislature and the minority for the honor of the judiciary as though these were irreconcilable alternatives and the law must make a choice between them. But would it be unreasonable to assume that neither judges nor legislators approved the vicious practice called entrapment? If so, what has so long been treated as a problem of either/or is not one at all, it is a problem of both/and.

In order to satisfy all the pertinent consumer interests, we need a procedure that would combine the minority with the majority solution. In short, whenever the evidence of entrapment is sufficient to convince the trial judge, he should stop the prosecution and quash the indictment, and whenever it is substantial but insufficient to convince him, he should submit the defense of entrapment to the jury. In either situation, there should be no need for proof of entrapment beyond a reasonable doubt; a preponderance of credible evidence should suffice.

Finally, in the improbable event that a legislature should expressly forbid the judge or jury to consider entrapment, the statute should be held unconstitutional. If an act of Congress, its invalidity would stem from violating the separation of powers (Article III) as well as denying due process of law (Fifth Amendment) and inflicting cruel and unusual punishment (Eighth Amendment). If a state statute, its invalidity would rest on corresponding provisions of the state constitution together with the due process clause of the Fourteenth Amendment. By means such as these, judges could preserve their own high status as consumers of law.

STRIFE

It would be pleasant to infer that the positive advances we have been noting betoken a dependable trend in the law, that democratic and humane standards must sooner or later supersede the old imperial ways of viewing and deciding, and that once the judges become conversant with the consumer perspective their attachment to it will be not only complete but irrevocable. It would be pleasant to engage in reveries like these, pleasant but altogether groundless. For us who are witnessing the course of the twentieth century (the century that rediscovered genocide), there is no excuse for a bland and shallow optimism.

There are, of course, a number of gains and reforms under way on the legal scene which, though they cannot guarantee future developments, do furnish occasions for hope. The libertarian judges of our era are displaying an admirable and increasing capacity for psychological projection, social insight, and creative intelligence. Empathy is at work as never before in the judicial process.

On the other hand, we have grimly to admit that the counterforces — the impulsions that resist the consumer perspective — can never suffer a final defeat in human society as we know it. Even if subdued locally and temporarily, which seems unlikely, they would be sure to rise again and renew the contest. The first great counterforce is man's insatiable lust for power, inviting temptations and corruptions that an honorable official may dismiss from his psyche today only to succumb to their poison tomorrow. No one can retain official authority and immunize himself totally from them.

The second counterforce — equally irrepressible — is man's inveterate propensity to distinguish "we" from "they," to wall off "we" from "they," and eventually to promote "we" and subordinate "they." Who has ever met a human being exempt from the predisposition? In all probability none exists. It is part of the way our species is wont to behave and misbehave, part of what we mean by the loyalty we admire and the bigotry we detest. It is the incorrigible jack that will not stay down but keeps popping up in our human box.

Though all we can be sure of is contention and strife, we have abundant incentives to continue striving. Our legal order already displays extensive shifts away from the old, harsh official perspective. Every move toward a consumer perspective demonstrates how much intelligence and resolution are able to achieve for the law. And even if the trend should change one day for the worse and all our hopes prove to be dupes, no one could cancel what we should have gained in some individual case on behalf of some individual human being, no one could strip us of some concrete good that we should have redeemed then and there, some particular act of equality that we should have performed, some specific exercise of freedom that we should have made whole. Only in the consumer perspective can a passing skirmish count as much as a long campaign and the rescue of a single life as much as either.

From the University of Pennsylvania
Law Review, *1963*.

2

THE BILL OF RIGHTS
AND THE JUDGES

*W*E generally think of the Bill of Rights as a set of guarantees enacted by the Founding Fathers for the protection of the people. It is somewhat startling, therefore, to read Edmond Cahn's statement that ". . . every democratic nation owes its judges a bill of rights."

Why the judges? Because without a formal text judges would be left with the impossible task of substituting their own personal judgments for those of the legislature or the executive. On occasion they would exceed their rightful role, but their most common pose would be that of deference to other arms of the government. It would be a courageous judge, indeed, who would uphold, during the Vietnam war, a Communist's refusal to register as a party member if the Constitution used such phrases as "unfair" or "unreasonable" or "contrary to natural principles of justice." But armed with a specific constitutional prohibition against compulsory self-incrimination the Supreme Court unanimously invalidated such a provision in the fall of 1965 and the waves of protest from the public were surprisingly mild.

Civil libertarians do not generally rank John Marshall — our greatest Chief Justice — as among their heroes, but Edmond Cahn wrote with great feeling of Marshall's contribution to American freedom. That contribution consisted of a willingness to use the text of the Constitution — whether the supremacy clause, the commerce clause, or the privilege against self-incrimination — to decide specific cases. John Marshall, in other words, established at the outset of our national experience that the Constitution was law and that a judge in the lowliest state or federal tribunal could rely on the words of the Constitution in deciding that a statute was invalid, or that a prisoner was unlawfully detained, or that a government official had prescribed rules which were forbidden by the Constitution.

But John Marshall's concept of the Constitution has been seriously undermined in recent years by those who would uphold statutes abridging freedom of speech if, after applying a "balancing" test, the interests of the government are found to outweigh the rights of the individual. Edmond Cahn described as "ink-eradicators" those who urged this watered-down version of our national charter. If John Marshall could read these pages, his greatest regret would be that someone other than John Marshall coined so apt a phrase. He would recognize, however, that in Edmond Cahn he had found a kindred constitutional spirit.

N. R.

John Marshall — Our "Greatest Dissenter"

NEXT Wednesday a ceremony will be held on Philadelphia's new Independence Mall commemorating the two hundredth anniversary of the birth of John Marshall. The event is one of a number this year in which patriotic Americans of various political faiths are honoring the great jurist. Born on September 24, 1755, in what is now Fauquier County, Virginia, Marshall served as Chief Justice of the United States from 1801 until his death in 1835.

There may be many conflicting opinions as to who was the nation's greatest President, or senator, or congressman. But there is complete agreement that John Marshall stands without rival as our greatest Chief Justice. In a recent address which inaugurated the bicentennial ceremonies, Chief Justice Earl Warren said: "Stone by stone, he built the foundation of our constitutional structure, and he constructed it sufficiently strong to support everything we have since built upon it."

There were three basic principles in Marshall's constitutional philosophy. He believed that the United States Constitution, as drafted in 1787, provided for a federal government with powers strong enough to solve the problems of a developing nation and flexible enough to succeed and endure permanently. He also believed that every governmental action — whether federal or state — which conflicted with the Constitution was null and void. Finally, he believed that when a legal case or controversy arose presenting a constitutional issue, it was the specific function of the Supreme Court to interpret the Constitution and pronounce a judgment of validity or invalidity which would be binding on everyone, including the President, the Congress, and the state governments.

Marshall's famous decisions establishing these principles (*Marbury v. Madison, McCulloch v. Maryland, Cohens v. Virginia, Gibbons v. Ogden*) remain today as firm cornerstones of the American fabric of government. While it was Thomas Jefferson and James Madison who supplied us with the keystone of civil liberty, this, too, like the remainder of the structure, rests for support and effectiveness on

Marshall's doctrine that the Constitution is the supreme law of the land.

Before Marshall's appointment as Chief Justice in 1801, the Constitution was in many respects no more than a controversial piece of parchment; when, in 1835, he transmitted it to his successor, it had become a vital, operative method of government. Before 1801, the Supreme Court was feeble and ineffectual; when Marshall departed, even his opponents recognized that he had elevated the Court to be — what it has been ever since — the most powerful judicial tribunal in the history of civilized government.

When, even in our own time, Congress decides to adopt some advanced plan of social or economic legislation, it is exercising federal powers that Marshall staked out and made available for use. As the Constitution is great and enduring, so is John Marshall's work.

Yet when all the grateful tributes have been paid, one may still wonder how John Marshall became fit to deserve them. It is much easier to admire the man's visible achievements than to understand the inner man. It is easier because our own knowledge of subsequent history clarifies his decisions and emphasizes the enormous scope of their influence. But if we wish to appreciate the qualities that made him preeminent, we must discard our hindsight and see his problems, hopes and tribulations as he saw them — not retrospectively but prospectively. Though this way will be difficult, it may also be revealing.

Suppose we place ourselves in the political scene as it looked to John Marshall around 1798 when he was in his early forties. The American people were then divided between two antagonistic political parties: the Federalist and the Republicans. The Federalist leaders were George Washington, President John Adams, and Secretary of the Treasury Alexander Hamilton; the Republicans were led by Thomas Jefferson and James Madison.

Marshall belonged to the Federalists, who spoke for a strong central government, stability and order, and the interests of landowners and businessmen. Federalists had framed the Constitution and, over strong popular opposition, had secured its adoption.

The Republicans (later, the designation was changed, first to "Democratic-Republican," then to "Democratic") were the party who advocated "strict construction" of the Constitution to limit the powers of the national government. They denounced the Federalist administration for exceeding its delegated authority. Under the circumstances, they tended to espouse the political rights of the several states. Inspired by Jefferson's ideals, they demanded a national administration which would be more responsive to popular democracy. Whereas the Federalists sympathized with British conservatism, the Republicans applauded Revolutionary France and the "rights of man."

To many a conservative observer of events the Republicans seemed obnoxious, if not dangerous. Their rank and file were noisy and turbulent. And their leaders, what were they but irresponsible theorists and preachers of sedition? In contrast to this distasteful faction, the Federalists appeared quite warranted in styling themselves the party of "the rich, wise, and well-born."

Marshall had early attached himself to the Federalist cause. He had served with distinction as a young officer in Washington's army at Valley Forge. In 1788 at the Virginia convention to ratify the Constitution and later in the state legislature Marshall's voice had been raised ably and courageously on behalf of the Federalist philosophy.

Then, in 1797, he had gone as member of a three-man official mission to Directoire France; and when President Adams proceeded to publish Marshall's dispatches, which showed how steadfastly he had resisted Talleyrand's bribes and threats, the Virginia Federalist became something of a national hero. On his return, in 1798, he was feted, flattered and toasted in several cities. It was easy and comfortable to assume that the people were applauding the Adams administration and its policies as well as John Marshall, the courageous envoy.

There occurred then what might have been a most instructive episode. In August 1798, at the very crest of this wave of popularity, Marshall, being in Fredericksburg on business, went to a performance at the local theater. Recognizing him, a Philadelphia Federalist who happened to be there directed the band to honor Marshall by playing the new Federalist Party march, "Hail Columbia!"

The audience heard the opening strains, burst into a hostile tumult, insulted Marshall and ended the evening's program with a riot. Though momentarily a very disagreeable experience, the incident did not seem particularly important to Marshall.

Marshall, the bronze statue at the courthouse, and Marshall, the impassive portrait on the library wall, may somehow be made to anticipate everything we have learned from the pages of subsequent history. The statue or the picture may anticipate all the ominous meaning behind that uproar in Fredericksburg. But Marshall, the living man, had excellent reasons for believing that the ground on which he stood was perfectly solid and firm.

In September General Washington himself extended, for the first time, an invitation to Mount Vernon. There Marshall was at length persuaded to run for Congress. In April 1799, after a bitter and close campaign, he won the election. Despite Fredericksburg, the political ground felt firm.

For purposes of Marshall's career, the ground proved positively springy. By June 1800, he had left Congress to become Secretary of State. Then, in January 1801, President Adams named him Chief Justice of the United States, and the astonished Senate, though it grumbled a bit, confirmed the appointment. Chief Justice of the United States at the age of forty-five: was not this the zenith of a lawyer's dream, enough and to spare for John Marshall's complete happiness?

No, under the circumstances it was not enough. There were two drawbacks. For one thing, as we have seen, the Supreme Court in 1801 possessed none of the authority, respect and power that Marshall would win for it.

The second disadvantage was graver. The historic election of 1800 had taken place, Jefferson and his Republican followers had prevailed, and the Federalist administration had been swept away. Not long before the debacle, George Washington had died.

For a while, perhaps, his virulent hatred of Thomas Jefferson helped to sustain Marshall's spirit. Yet what must have he thought when some of the New England Federalists, impelled by the same hatred, shortly began preaching nullification of Federal embargo laws and secession from the Union? One after another, the main pillars of his political house crumbled.

If in this plight Marshall turned to his private life and looked for solace, we can only hope he found it. There, too, destiny seemed to have resolved against him. In 1801, whatever he might suspect, he could not know yet that the Federalist Party had been injured irreparably. On the other hand, he probably did realize by then that his wife's nervous illness, which affected her both physically and mentally, would remain permanent and incurable.

Marshall remembered they had fallen in love at first sight when he was a gangling soldier and she was a shy girl of fourteen. He could continue to serve and help and cheer her, which he did most patiently. But to all appearances, the man's own cosmos had collapsed about him.

It was easy in those times to underestimate John Marshall. The word for his outward aspect would be "shaggy." You saw a large head of hair, matted and disheveled, a body that was tall but loose-jointed and ungainly, a coat that very likely looked secondhand, legs in old, ill-fitting breeches, and a pair of dirty boots. Instead of walking, the man shambled. When he spoke, you heard a hard, dry voice. It would be accompanied by extremely awkward gestures.

His forehead was certainly not high, and the only features that gave a hint of inner genius were his eyes and his chin. The chin stood out like a solid forward wall. Anyone who saw it would believe readily what Marshall remarked many years later: "I could not conquer a stubbornness of temper which determines a man to make head against and struggle with injustice."

But his true excellence was manifest in his eyes. They were dark brown, so dark many people thought they were black. They were almost hypnotically brilliant; when they fastened on you, you found somehow it would be very pleasant to agree with whatever Marshall might be saying, and that it would be quite unpleasant to raise objections.

Marshall's was not the complicated, subtle glance of a scholar — he was never a scholar — but the simple, lucid, insistent gaze of a practical man filled with faith in an interior vision. He summarized the vision in a single phrase — "the American nation" — which he may have been the first to use. As he said, "I was confirmed in the habit of considering America as my country, and Congress as my Government."

John Marshall and Thomas Jefferson were of opposing, yet complementary, natures. Where Jefferson turned to philosophy and political theory and put them to the service of individual liberty, Marshall paid little or no attention to any theory unless it was to be found in the language of the Constitution. In the text of the fundamental charter were all the premises his reasoning needed.

While Jefferson disseminated the arts and experimented in the sciences, Marshall drew freely on Alexander Hamilton's writings, laughed with convivial judges and lawyers, and played hard at quoits. If the mold of Jefferson's temperament was Hellenic, Marshall's was Roman. The two men were cousins, and hated each other as cousins can.

Then again, while Jefferson loved humanity in general but was rather discriminating in the company he chose for himself, Marshall was antidemocratic and property-minded in politics, yet enjoyed mixing with unpretentious people and sharing their commonplace experiences. His jokes were so traditional and representative that they could be attributed just as plausibly to any judge in any country.

For example, on one occasion a young lawyer having asked the Chief Justice's personal advice because he had "reached the acme of judicial distinction," Marshall interrupted, "Let me tell you what that means, young man. The acme of judicial distinction means the ability to look a lawyer straight in the eyes for two hours and not hear a damned word he says."

If the Federalist Party lost elections, Marshall at least won constitutional arguments. No one could have been better endowed to express and defend an unpopular doctrine. Free as he was of the cumbersome paraphernalia of technical learning, he virtually never became tangled in ancient precedents. No American jurist has been less bound by the past.

He seems to have followed two main policies: (1) identify the exact goal of your reasoning, start your exposition very far away from it, get your adversary to admit to some apparently self-evident and innocuous proposition, and then move step by step from there to the goal, never relaxing your show of absolute, inevitable certitude; (2) among reasonable men "yes" is to be said briefly, "no" is to be said at length.

In a republic, therefore, unpopular decisions should be very elaborate and prolix, thus showing that every possible objection has been considered and that the unpopular outcome is logically inescapable. Hence, let there be a flood of words. Nevertheless, it is helpful to drop a quotable legal aphorism here and there in the verbal sea, for use as a buoy or life raft.

These were Marshall's talents. With them he undertook a seemingly hopeless resistance to the current of his times. For thirty-four years, from 1801 to 1835, the majority of Americans consistently rejected his nationalism. He was attacked scandalously in succeeding Congresses and denounced in state legislatures. The Jeffersonians reviled him until Jefferson died in 1826, whereupon Jackson and the Jacksonians took over with at least equal virulence. During all these years Marshall utterly refused to "follow the election returns." How he would have roared with laughter if there had been public-opinion polls in his day and someone had urged him to chart his course by them!

During the first few years he built slowly, with occasional signs of understandable nervousness. From the beginning he led and dominated his associates on the bench. Before he became Chief Justice it had been the practice for each member of the Court to prepare and announce his individual judgment of every case. Marshall saw to it that the Court spoke with a single voice (the "opinion of the Court"), and, to make certain that the voice said precisely what he wanted it to say, he composed 519 of the 1106 opinions handed down during his long Chief Justiceship.

A strong national government with a single national economy; faithful performance of treaties: supremacy of the central government over the states in the areas where national and uniform action was contemplated by the Constitution; respect for rights under contracts; obedience by the President, the Congress and the organs of state government to the Constitution as expounded by the Supreme Court —

these were the articles of his faith and the ruling principles of his decisions.

When vacancies occurred from time to time on the Court, Presidents Jefferson, Madison and Monroe in turn would select new associate justices to vote against John Marshall. The new justices almost invariably would succumb; they voted in support of the Chief Justice and his philosophy.

Whole decades passed. The American people did not become receptive to Marshall's national patriotism. His ideas continued to be disapproved, distrusted and reviled. Meanwhile he persisted with his work. He waited, forbore, used the materials that chance might bring his way. As Justice Holmes once said, "There fell to Marshall perhaps the greatest place that ever was filled by a judge. . . . When we celebrate Marshall we celebrate at the same time and indivisibly the inevitable fact that the oneness of the nation and the supremacy of the national Constitution were declared to govern the dealings of man with man by the judgments and decrees of the most august of courts."

This constitutional edifice, magnificent as we now see it is, would never have been established if Marshall had been the kind of judge who trembles before the shifts and gusts, much less the tempests, of popular excitement. In the center of the storms he persevered without dismay. I suggest that in this very practical sense John Marshall should be appreciated as our *greatest judicial dissenter*.

Even today there are several respects in which Marshall's vision remains unfulfilled. For instance, in the matter of school segregation, certain state and local authorities still show recalcitrance and contumacy. John Marshall would not countenance any such resistance to federal judicial supremacy. He might say now to the officials of his beloved Virginia what he did say to their predecessors in 1821:

"America has chosen to be, in many respects, and to many purposes, a nation; and for all these purposes, her government is complete; to all these objects, it is competent. The people have declared that in the exercise of all powers given for these objects it is supreme. It can, then, in effecting these objects legitimately control all individuals or governments within the American territory. The Constitution and laws of a state, so far as they are repugnant to the Constitution and laws of the United States, are absolutely void. These states are constituent parts of the United States; they are members of one great empire — for some purposes sovereign, for some purposes subordinate."

Despite his distrust of popular democracy, John Marshall deserves well of the people of this country. As congressman he defied his own party by voting against the detested Sedition Law. As Chief Justice he gave full scope to the constitutional privilege against self-incrimination. He placed the American future high above vested property rights when, in the interest of federal control over navigation, he struck down monopoly steamboat franchises which had been granted by New York and other states.

And he fought on to the last of his life without a reassuring omen or a single sign of popular acceptance. His fear for the safety of the Constitution — courage is not the absence but the conquest of fear — continued to the very end. When he closed his eyes the country was drifting a bit faster in the wrong direction and was headed toward the eventual calamity of the Civil War.

For us today, "the American nation" of 1955, the constitutional scene is infinitely brighter. Now, as patriots honor the two-hundredth anniversary of John Marshall's birth, it would be hard to doubt that he has long since reached an understanding with Thomas Jefferson. Surely the two have become friends and kindred spirits. For one of their birthday toasts in the Elysian Fields Jefferson may be counted on to quote the conciliatory words of his First Inaugural Address: "We are all Republicans — we are all Federalists." And Marshall may respond with this, the steadfast credo of his life:

"In heart and sentiment, as well as by birth and interest, I am an American, attached to the genuine principles of the Constitution, as sanctioned by the will of the people, for their general liberty, prosperity and happiness. I consider that Constitution as the rock of our political salvation, which has preserved us from misery, division and civil wars; and which will yet preserve us if we value it rightly and support it firmly."

From the New York Times Magazine, *August 21, 1955.*

Hamiltonians and Jeffersonians

FOR some fifteen years, two philosophers have been clashing against each other in the decisions of the Supreme Court, and with this significant book* they break into open warfare. Up to now, the struggle has resembled a more or less polite duel of ironies and sarcastic allusions, which may have entertained the initiate but certainly left the general public in a state of mystification. Henceforth it will not be necessary for anyone to remain mystified. Justice William O. Douglas,

* *The Right of the People* by William O. Douglas (1958).

one of our few great liberals, discloses just what the war is about and how much is at stake. As he sees it, the stake is nothing else than the entire First Amendment in the Bill of Rights.

Little wonder, then, that Justice Douglas felt constrained to submit the case to the people themselves, to whom the First Amendment guarantees (1) separation of church and state, (2) freedom of religion, (3) freedom of speech, (4) freedom of the press, and (5) freedom of assembly. These are, of course, the most basic constitutional rights that Americans possess against government.

At the start of the republic, it was over these rights that the Jeffersonian philosophy split with the Hamiltonian and thus compelled the adoption of our Bill of Rights. In our own day, disciples of Alexander Hamilton have resumed the struggle and have inflicted important losses. Foremost among modern Hamiltonians are the brilliant Justice Felix Frankfurter and the venerable Judge Learned Hand.

There are no sly insults or oblique cuts to mar *The Right of the People,* which embodies a series of lively and eloquent lectures delivered to the students at Franklin and Marshall College in the spring of 1957. The author's concern is with principles. He begins by declaring the classic Jeffersonian creed and contrasting it with the old and new Hamiltonian: "Hamilton had argued against the need for a Bill of Rights. He maintained that freedom of the press, for example, 'must altogether depend on public opinion; and on the general spirit of the people and of the government,' particularly on 'legislative discretion.' . . . There were those who did not trust the people, who felt that government need keep a firm hand on the citizen if the nation was to survive.

"Jefferson, the spiritual father of the Bill of Rights, and Madison, the astute politician who steered the Bill of Rights through Congress, were of a different school of thought. They recognized the risk of tyranny of the majority. But they had confidence in popular rule and confidence in a Bill of Rights as a restraint on 'the tyranny of the Legislatures' and as an aid to the judiciary in preventing encroachments on the liberty of the citizen."

The verdict of the American people and of history ran in favor of the Jeffersonians. It is demonstrable that the Constitution would never have been adopted without the First Amendment. In more recent times, the Amendment has received new infusions of vigor and dignity from Justices Holmes, Hughes, Brandeis, Stone, Murphy, Black, Douglas and Warren.

What, then, of Justice Frankfurter and Judge Hand, the latter-day Hamiltonians? Surely Justice Douglas does not contend they are personally opposed to separation of church and state, freedom of speech and the rest of the basic guarantees? Obviously not. What he does claim is that their Hamiltonian philosophy has enervated the First Amendment and that, under the influence of their views, the Supreme Court has diminished, compromised, or surrendered various parts of our elementary rights.

If Congress enacts a law which abridges a First Amendment freedom, judges of the Hamiltonian persuasion will hold it valid provided it appears "reasonable," and they will go on to say that the very fact that Congress has passed it shows presumptively that it must be "reasonable." This is tantamount to resurrecting Hamilton's maxim of "legislative discretion."

Modern Hamiltonians and modern Jeffersonians agree in saying that the American people must themselves provide the ultimate protection for First Amendment freedoms. To this both sides subscribe. Where they disagree is in defining the duties of judges. The Jeffersonians believe the judges should honor the mandate of the First Amendment and enforce its prohibitions; the Hamiltonians believe the judges should let the legislative judgment prevail in order that the people may learn to rely only on themselves and their own spirit of moderation.

Judge Learned Hand, revered as one of our national sages, takes a Hamiltonian position which, if not more radical, is at least more candid than Justice Frankfurter's. Again and again, Judge Hand has declared that the guarantees of the First Amendment and most of the remainder of the Bill of Rights are not really law at all. He says they are only "admonitions of moderation," "moral adjurations," "a mood rather than a command," "not jural concepts at all, in the ordinary sense."

There is no denying that Judge Hand's candid advocacy of his view has exerted a pervasive influence. With matching candor, Justice Douglas comments: "I disagree with the view of Judge Learned Hand that the prohibitions of the First Amendment, in terms absolute, are 'no more than admonitions of moderation.' The idea that they are no more than that has done more to undermine liberty in this country than any other single force. That notion is, indeed, at the root of the forces of disintegration that have been eroding the democratic ideal in this country."

Thus the issue is joined between the rival philosophies and, as in 1787, it goes to a jury of the whole people. Seeking to restore the full force of Jeffersonian faith, Justice Douglas presents an extraordinarily readable and popular balance sheet of freedom's assets and liabilities under three main headings: Freedom of Expression, The Right to Be Let Alone, and The Civilian Authority. Like Justice Brandeis before him, he feels a special attachment to "the right to be let alone." Brandeis called it "the most comprehensive of rights and the right most valued by civilized men." To Douglas, it is "a sturdy part of our heritage, more American than European, more Western than Eastern. . . . It will always be one of our great rallying points."

Rallying points are necessary, for almost every page of the book shows how callously various legislative, executive and administrative authorities have encroached and continue to encroach on First Amendment rights. Though the courts, as guardians of the Amendment, have occasionally yielded or retreated, it is clear that without their intervention fundamental liberties would have been stripped bare. One does not enjoy contemplating what might happen to nonconformists, religious minorities, ethnic minorities and freedom of the press if Hamiltonian philosophy should induce the judges to lay down their shields.

Recognizing the danger, Justice Douglas declares: "The philosophy of the First Amendment is that man must have full freedom to search the world and the universe for the answers to the puzzles of life. . . . Unless the horizons are unlimited, we risk being governed by a set of prejudices of a bygone day. If we are restricted in art, religion, economics, political theory or any other great field of knowledge, we may become victims of conformity in an age where salvation can be won only by nonconformity."

From the New York Times Book Review,
January 19, 1958.

Brief for the Supreme Court

THE United States Supreme Court is in the party platforms again. Ever since 1954 when the school segregation cases were decided, the Court has become a target of severe criticism. Decisions of minor legal points that would ordinarily pass without special notice are suddenly seen to possess deep and lasting significance. If a dissenting justice writes tartly of his colleagues' learning or wisdom, he may rely on a large, attentive audience. As before in its history, the Court is passing through a hostile phase when criticism becomes strident enough to seem substantial and extreme enough to suggest alarm.

While Americans argue and squabble about the Court, other nations are emulating it in every quarter of the globe. The latest disciple is Italy. In June 1956, the Italian Constitutional Court held that censorship laws inherited from the old Fascist regime were unconstitutional. In this, the very first decision of the new tribunal, freedom of the press was at issue, and it won a momentous victory. Leading Italian jurists hailed the decree as marking a new chapter for democracy. It was, they declared, their country's counterpart of *Marbury v. Madison*, in which Chief Justice Marshall established that a law contrary to the Constitution was void in our courts.

On every continent there have been judicial performances of this kind, in behalf of freedom and equality. For example, the judges of the Supreme Court of India endeavor courageously to enforce the guarantees of personal liberty which are set down in India's Constitution and, in doing so, they pay suitable attention to American sources and precedents. It is good tidings for the world that judges in New Delhi are reading Jefferson, Madison, Marshall, Holmes and Hughes.

Nevertheless, "judicial review," developed through one hundred fifty years of American experience, seems to be poorly understood at home. There are quite a number at home who assume that a native American does not need to read Jefferson, Madison, Marshall and the rest before expounding the Constitution and admonishing the justices. Perhaps that is why so many recent comments on Supreme Court decisions have been full of heat and noise. That the current state of misinformation and confused opinion can eventually become dangerous, I think no one will deny. It is high time to confront two basic fallacies about our Supreme Court.

Fallacy Number One. That contrary to what our more liberal Founding Fathers (such as Jefferson and Madison) intended at the time the Constitution was adopted, Chief Justice Marshall and his Court later usurped the right to decide questions of constitutionality.

Many Americans feel a vague unease about the Supreme Court's role in our government. Remembering from student days that John Marshall belonged to the Federalist Party, that the Federalists emphasized stability and conservatism, and that Marshall and Jefferson eventually became bitter antagonists, good citizens are liable to find themselves distrusting Marshall's accomplishments.

Did not Jefferson, as President and ex-President, frequently lash out at the Supreme Court? Even if one grants that today, after a century and a half, it is too late to reopen the question of whether the Court ought to determine constitutional issues, Americans who believe that the power was usurped in the first place are likely to examine the current of decisions with a suspicious eye. When we accept "judicial review," are we betraying the ideals of Jefferson?

The historical record is easy to consult. Since Jefferson was representing the United States in Paris through the entire period of framing and adopting the Constitution and framing and submitting the Bill of Rights, we have his letters to his friends, which conveyed his wishes and anxieties during this critical epoch. . . .

What were his remarks on the provision for a federal judiciary? He said he would prefer that the judges either participate in the President's veto power or possess a separate veto power of their own. In effect, Jefferson suggested that the judges determine not only the constitutionality but also the political wisdom and desirability of laws passed by Congress. The suggestion, which proved stillborn, would have vested the Supreme Court with more power than anyone has dared claim for it during all the subsequent generations.

In 1788, the several states ratified the Constitution, but only on the understanding that it would be amended forthwith to add a bill of rights. The new United States government got under way in New York City during the spring of 1789. . . .

The initial United States Congress, which voted to submit the Bill of Rights for ratification, was frankly and explicitly informed that the illustrious sponsors of the bill desired the judges to consider themselves active guardians of our fundamental freedoms.

If Jefferson could advise us today, he would be the first to insist that we in the twentieth century are not bound by anything he may have intended in the eighteenth. To the end of his life, he reiterated boldly that the Constitution belongs not to the dead but to every successive generation of living Americans. This has been the very life of the Constitution. To agree now with what Jefferson or Madison may have intended or may have communicated to the First Congress is only a comfort, not an obligation.

Nevertheless, this time we are entitled to the comfort. As we have seen, the foremost liberal minds among the Founding Fathers joined with the foremost conservatives in expecting the Supreme Court to enforce the Constitution and Bill of Rights. Concededly, no statesman ever assumed that the Court could perform the function alone, without cooperation from the President, the Congress, the states, or — most necessary of all — the American people.

"Judicial review" is only one of many apt devices for converting promises on parchment into living liberties, and there are obvious limits to what a single device can achieve. But the historical record is evident; "judicial review" was no usurpation. The Court's authority is not something stolen by lawyers' wiles. Historically it is legitimate.

Fallacy Number Two. That contrary to the principle of majority rule, the Supreme Court has been thwarting the will of the people's representatives in Congress.

Twenty years have passed since Franklin D. Roosevelt's major controversy with the Supreme Court, years so compact with wars, changes and crises that even during Roosevelt's lifetime the outlines of the controversy had begun to fade in our memories. In retrospect, the twenty years seem like twenty distinct eras and the issues of 1936–1937 like the small and simple issues of some outgrown, almost quaint society. The distance in time from 1937 is as nothing compared with the difference in historical conditions. Yet almost daily we hear the voices of lawyers, congressmen and governors assailing the Supreme Court in the nomenclature of that obsolete conflict. How they exert themselves to call up the spirit of 1937!

Twenty years ago, the conflict between legislative and judicial authority was real, profound and crucial. For decades, the Court majority had been reading their own economic and social predilections into the text of the Constitution. In 1936 the process reached its climax. New Deal statutes, state and federal, were falling like withered leaves in the glare of the judges' disapproval. The decisions of that year left enormous gaps in the powers of government, areas where urgently necessary action was forbidden to the nation and the states alike.

Conflict between the two departments became inevitable. Even if one combines the New Deal period with all the preceding years back to 1865, one finds the Supreme Court striking down an average of more than one act of Congress for every year from 1865 through 1936. Many of the invalidated statutes were essential in the highest degree; many of the decisions left impassable blocks on the road to social and economic reform. Public discontent cumulated and became peremptory. No wonder that today we witness such strenuous attempts to summon the ghost of 1937!

Here again, the historical record is quite manifest. Ever since 1937, the Supreme Court has followed a deliberate, consistent policy of reducing and withholding its jurisdiction. It has employed every known device in the tool chest of procedure to avoid friction with Congress. When the present Court has erred — as it has in the opinion of liberals — the error has served invariably to favor and sustain congressional action.

With invalidations at the rate of more than one a year from 1865 to 1936, it is impressive to contrast the average from 1937 to 1956: one act of Congress held invalid every six or seven years. Moreover, as even hostile critics would concede, not a single one of the post-1937 instances has affected an important legislative power.

Our Constitution is not proffered to individual or local option; it binds everyone, legislators and judges, the governors as well as the governed. It protects and, by like token, controls all persons, officials and departments.

It establishes principles that do not always bow to a majority vote; as a nation we have resolved that, just as there are fields of human experience where the popular majority is entitled to have its way even when it is wrong, there are other fields (e.g., religion) where it is not entitled to have its way even when it is right. To the Supreme Court we have committed a part — by no means all — of the responsibility for preserving the fabric of government and our own civic freedoms.

Yet what of the fact that the judges are appointed to life tenure? Surely they cannot pretend to respond promptly, as elected representatives may, to the currents of popular opinion. The judges cannot so pretend; they know, or ought to know, that their duty may require them to disregard the people's wishes. They are judges, not delegates. Theirs is the obligation to expound the Constitution objectively, impartially and justly — to the utmost limits of human capacity and individual endowment.

Popular majorities are volatile aggregations, they melt and reassemble, shift and change. The Constitution was conceived advisedly to channel the majority's temporary impulses in the interest of the historic tradition, the social conscience and the future welfare of the country. To enforce the Constitution, though at the cost of nullifying an act of Congress that clearly conflicts with it, is to keep America's covenant with the *abiding* majority.

Who of us would be naive enough to confide the Supreme Court's vast authority to nine lawyers in robes if they were required to compete at the polls for election and reelection? Suppose, for a moment, that a justice's future tenure were to depend on continued support from party leaders or from the President who appointed him. The supposition is worth making. It explains demonstratively why, like the Founding Fathers, we are determined to have thoroughly independent judges who will fulfill their conscientious duty, no matter whom they antagonize.

Independence does not necessarily imply aggressiveness or conflict. Continuing as it does to deal very tenderly with congressional legislation, the present Supreme Court deserves none of 1937's anachronistic charges and epithets. These days, if a congressman wishes to discover some pretext for discontent, he can no longer charge that the Court arrogantly nullifies acts of Congress. At worst, he can only complain that the Court misunderstands and misinterprets them.

In a few cases, the complaint seems right, in most it seems baseless. But, right or wrong, it can scarcely justify a very livid display of resentment, for if the Court does happen to misinterpret a piece of federal legislation, Congress need only pass another act to make its intent explicit, and the justices will accept the correction graciously. Nevertheless, when incidents of the kind do occur, they may provoke as much rhetoric and clamor as though the judiciary had collided head-on with the Congress.

In consequence, the public receives a distorted picture of the Court's work. One simply cannot compose a true mosaic of the Supreme Court out of episodes of conflict and sporadic clashes. Fragments like these are bright enough, but too discrete, too often untypical.

Even to begin understanding the Court's role in our government, one must at least observe how frequently and usefully the Court cooperates with the Congress. And one must also notice how the Court serves to educate the Congress. When the process of education succeeds, it may provide the subtlest dramas and the most gratifying denouements.

At bottom, the Supreme Court is the nation's exemplar and disseminator of democratic values. The role has been thrust on it. Americans have become accustomed to look to the Court for symbols and emblems, standards and ideals, lines below which communal action ought not to sink, goals toward which communal action ought to strive. Though, like other preceptors, this one has committed some sorry blunders and has occasionally underestimated its audience, its prestige remains indubitable.

Let me present one specimen to show how the educative process develops.

Act I (1929). Rosika Schwimmer, Hungarian-born radical and pacifist, seeks to become a naturalized American citizen. The naturalization law, passed by Congress in 1906, requires every applicant to swear to "support and defend the Constitution." Though the law says nothing about bearing arms in defense of the country, the official examiners ask her, as they ask all other applicants, whether she would be willing to do so.

On her negative answer and pacifist reasoning, the Supreme Court decides she is not entitled to citizenship. Three justices dissent, including Holmes, who says, "Some of her answers might excite popular prejudice, but if there is any principle of the Constitution that more imperatively calls for attachment than any other it is the principle of free thought — not free thought for those who agree with us but freedom for the thought that we hate."

Act II (1931). Douglas C. Macintosh, Canadian-born Chaplain of Yale Graduate School and Dwight Professor of Theology, applies for naturalization. He is willing to swear that he would bear arms in defense of the country, except in any war which might be unjust and contrary to his higher duty to God. The Supreme Court holds against him.

This time four justices dissent — Hughes, Holmes, Brandeis and Stone. Chief Justice Hughes writes a noble dissenting opinion. He insists Congress never intended to authorize an oath that violated the spirit of our institutions. Laws for military draft have always recognized religious scruples. "The essence of religion is belief in a relation to God involving duties superior to those arising from any human relation." The great Chief Justice calls this "our happy tradition."

Act III (interlude to 1946). In six successive Congresses, bills are proposed to reverse the Schwimmer and Macintosh holdings by providing expressly for religious objections. All such efforts fail. In 1940 Congress codifies the naturalization laws and leaves the oath as silent as before on the entire question of bearing arms. Meanwhile, Holmes, Brandeis and Hughes retire from the Court; Stone remains and becomes Chief Justice.

Act IV (1946). James L. Girouard, Canadian-born Seventh-day Adventist, applies for naturalization. In his registration for the draft, he has claimed exemption from combatant service only. Many Seventh-day Adventists serve as noncombatants in the medical corps; they object on religious grounds to combatant service. In the Supreme Court, Chief Justice Stone — to the astonishment of many — becomes spokesman for the denial of naturalization. In all sincerity, he reasons that the events in Act III show Congress's approval of the Macintosh decision as correctly interpreting the intent of the statute. Hence, he concludes, the Court is bound.

To this Justices Reed and Frankfurter agree. But Justice William O. Douglas, speaking for the majority of the Court, holds in favor of Girouard. Eloquently he supplements the earlier arguments of Holmes and Hughes. As for the circumstances in Act III, what did they prove? We ought not, he said, "place on the shoulders of Congress the burden of the Court's own error." Thus, at long last, the ethical ensign is raised too high for Congress to overlook it.

Act V (1952). In a new naturalization statute, Congress finally discharges its duty. It expressly requires applicants to take an oath to bear arms in defense of the United States and makes exception for those who object on grounds of "religious training and belief." Objectors of this type can promise to do noncombatant work or other work of national importance.

But, under the new law, what shall be considered "religious training and belief"? A very subtle and nebulous phrase, yet Congress easily finds a definition: it is "belief in a relation to a Supreme Being involving duties superior to those arising from any human relation."

(Whoever was alert during Act II will recognize the source of these words.) Thus, in respect of the naturalization oath, we return proudly to what Chief Justice Hughes called "our happy tradition."

The voices of the republic are not mere discord. Conflicts there must be from time to time, for when all conflicts cease, the spirit of political institutions dies. Yet amid the quiet harmonies, the rasps and the strange dissonances that accompany the American system, conflicts should not be confused with the principal theme. The theme is liberty and justice and compassion.

From the New York Times Magazine,
October 7, 1956.

Justice Frankfurter's "Dominating Humility"

THERE are many Felix Frankfurters, and this book introduces you to most of them.* It collects the essays and addresses of Justice Frankfurter since 1939, when he was appointed to the Supreme Court. In one selection he resumes his old role of law professor and beguiles a group of students with a suave, impromptu talk on "Chief Justices I Have Known." The more important chapters show him as a judge reflecting brightly on his predecessors' careers and uneasily on his own functions. Through the final portion he speaks as a mourning, eulogizing friend. In various aspects the reader meets Felix Frankfurter, a personage extraordinarily charming, brilliant — and controversial.

Among lawyers Justice Frankfurter's style has long been considered almost dangerously attractive. They catch themselves quoting his judicial sentences, even the ones they disagree with, because the way he says whatever he says is so invitingly quotable. In his phrasing they find precision and tidiness as well as elegance. Moreover, he has a special talent for ringing changes on the same idea (as judges must when successive cases are cognate) without appearing so to do. To see the gift at work one need only turn to the eulogies at the end of this book. They are very graceful tributes to interesting and superior personalities, yet (how shall I put it?) thirty-four eulogies do make quite a number of eulogies.

What does Justice Frankfurter believe about the function of the

---

* *Of Law and Men: Papers and Addresses of Felix Frankfurter, 1939–1956* (1956).

Supreme Court? General readers have good reasons for feeling curious. In 1939, when he was appointed, they knew mainly that he had been a scintillating figure on the Harvard law faculty; that in the Sacco-Vanzetti case he had contended bravely for fair play; and that for many years his friendly interest and personal prestige had provided bright young men with desirable chances for employment, which after 1933 were often connected with the New Deal.

Under the circumstances Justice Frankfurter was expected to become one of the Court's outstanding liberals. The expectation has been disappointed in large part. Frequently Frankfurter has voted to sustain laws that restrict freedom of speech, of the press, or of religion; occasionally he has appeared to lapse even on basic issues of procedural fairness, like the right to assistance of counsel. Why?

In an essay on Chief Justice Stone, the author provides a possible clue. "As is true in every calling," he writes, "men vary greatly in the temperaments they bring to judging. Some decide without great inner turmoil and others suffer anguish in the process. Some are serene once the inner debate is concluded; with some the throes of conflict linger long and are easily revived." Is it a mistake to conjecture that Justice Frankfurter's inner temperament may be of the latter kind? Otherwise, why on so many pages of this book do we find intimations like "the agony of a judge's duty," "the anguish of judgment," "the treacherous nature of the rational process," and "self-searching disinterestedness almost beyond the lot of men"?

Distrust of self may not be the only factor. Another may be identified in the author's rather enthusiastic preference for British legal methods and practices. (In Britain, the enacted will of Parliament is supreme, judges having neither the right nor the duty to determine constitutionality.) We can only conjecture; one reads at his risk between the lines of a judge's speeches and opinions. "Few speculations," Justice Frankfurter admonishes, "are more treacherous than diagnosis of motives or genetic explanations of the position taken by judges in Supreme Court decisions." Quite true; yet speculation may become less treacherous to the extent one adheres to the subject's own text.

Recurrently in this book, Justice Frankfurter repeats and underlines a theme already made conspicuous in his judicial opinions. His name for the theme is "dominating humility." By this he means that he does not and must not follow his own conviction but must derive his judgment as a spokesman, vicar, or proxy of some authoritative outside voice.

Liberals are distressed that, in exhibiting humility on the bench, Justice Frankfurter admits no distinction between laws regulating property and laws regulating the most elemental human rights. In either case, he insists, the only proper judicial posture is one of deference and acquiescence. If repression or injustice should result, he would let the responsibility rest with Congress, the state's legislature, the local school board, the state's court, the hysteria of the populace, the dullness of the public conscience — almost anywhere as long as it is elsewhere.

As the intellectuals of Alexandria once looked to Athens and Jerusalem, so Justice Frankfurter has searched the thoughts of Holmes and Brandeis. On occasion he writes as though he possessed no personal commission of office and could merely wield the continued authority of theirs; with the passing of years, he has found it less and less satisfying to ask, "How would Holmes (or Brandeis) have coped with this or that issue, which never arose in his lifetime?"

During the last few years Justice Frankfurter has turned toward one of the oracles of his youth, Professor James Bradley Thayer (1831–1902), a wise jurist and great scholar. Yet unless Thayer's observations about the Supreme Court are to be taken as eternal absolutes it is relevant that he expressed them in the eighteen nineties, when the Court was so reactionary and property-minded that it held the federal government could not levy an income tax. Thayer died seventeen years before the Supreme Court rendered its first important decision on freedom of speech. The whole context has changed since he wrote, and will never cease changing.

Felix Frankfurter has awakened and inspired a multitude of creative minds, and it is a public boon to have access to his urbanity and sparkle in these pages. With respect, one can submit the wish that he would put more trust in his own deliberate judgment. Fundamental freedoms are still in jeopardy.

From the New York Times Book Review,
May 27, 1956

Madison and the Pursuit of Happiness

O N October 24, 1787, James Madison wrote a long letter to Thomas Jefferson, who was then in France on business of state. Madison enclosed a copy of the Constitution which had just been drafted in Philadelphia, and modestly added that he would "take the liberty of making some observations on the subject, which will help to make up a letter, if they should answer no other purpose." The observations did considerably more than "make up a letter," for they embraced the whole framework of the author's republican ideal. Madison wrote from New York where he had come to join Hamilton and Jay in the series of newspaper articles which were called *The Federalist*. His own first contribution to *The Federalist* appeared in print a month later and is the justly famous number 10 of that series. So closely did the letter to Jefferson anticipate the style and content of the 10th *Federalist*, that it may be regarded as a thoughtful preliminary draft.

All this creates a fascinating historical focus. Here was Madison, fresh from the Constitutional Convention to which he had contributed so very much, on the one hand expounding his political philosophy to Jefferson, and on the other hand collaborating as a colleague with the Federalists Hamilton and Jay. The focus is made all the sharper by the close similarity between the letter to Jefferson and the composition prepared at Hamilton's urging. It is fair to infer that the 10th *Federalist* embodies the republican political philosophy of the American Constitution at least as forcefully and compactly as any other expression emanating from a single pen.

My purpose here is to submit a philosophic thesis for the consideration of Americans concerned with the postulates of their government. The thesis is that Madison's *political* philosophy of republicanism corresponds to the *ethical* doctrines and convictions which are epitomized in a single phrase of the Declaration of Independence. And the phrase is "the pursuit of happiness."

In order to sustain this thesis, it will first be necessary to try to ascertain what "the pursuit of happiness" connoted to the author or authors of the Declaration of Independence and their more cultivated companions such as Madison. My own conclusions on this subject are so different from generally prevalent notions, that I advance them only because I think I understand how such notions have come to be accepted. I believe that errors have been committed because most historians and philosophers, when they came to interpret the thinking of the Revolutionary leaders, have tended to concentrate on the political sources these men were familiar with and have tended to neglect the philosophical works that nurtured their thinking. Errors of this kind can be avoided if we remember the vast and varied interests of Jefferson, Adams, Madison, Franklin and company, the versatility of their talents and the richness of their reading, and if we bear in mind their universal conviction that however important government may be, its principal purpose is to make possible the flowering of a creative and many-sided personality. To understand the thoughts behind the Constitution, the best and noblest that the literature of political science has to offer is not quite enough.

THE MEANING OF "THE PURSUIT OF HAPPINESS"

In the first quarter of the twentieth century valuable studies were made, notably by John Hazelton and Carl Becker, of the sources and implications of the Declaration of Independence; but no particular attention was paid to the phrase in which we are interested — "the pursuit of happiness." Apparently it was assumed that just as one has no right to expect a beautiful woman to be endowed with brains, so felicitous a phrase as this need not convey any very concrete meaning. American scholarship of that time reiterated the familiar fact that Jefferson's greatest debt was to John Locke's *Second Treatise of Civil Government,* and Carl Becker was astute enough to add that the theory of knowledge advanced in John Locke's *Essay Concerning Human Understanding* was likewise part of the intellectual apparatus of the Revolutionary era.

The mistaken turn was made in 1927 with the publication of Vernon Louis Parrington's *Main Currents in American Thought* and with the enthusiastic reception of Parrington's heavy emphasis on economic influences. After mentioning the devotion of the Founding Fathers to Locke, and particularly to Locke's phrase "life, liberty and property," Parrington went on to say, ". . . in Jefferson's hands the English doctrine was given a revolutionary shift. The substitution of 'pursuit of happiness' for 'property' marks a complete break with the Whiggish doctrine of property rights that Locke had bequeathed to the English middle class, and the substitution of a broader sociological conception; and it was this substitution that gave to the document the note of idealism which was to make its appeal so perennially human and vital. . . . If the fact that he set the pursuit of happiness above abstract property rights is to be taken as proof that Jefferson was an impractical French theorist, the critic may take what comfort he can from his deduction." This historical myth, that is the myth that Jefferson had abandoned Locke and preoccupation with property rights when he substituted "the pursuit of happiness," has won wide acceptance. In fact, when in 1948 a magazine bearing the modest name of *Life* held a symposium on the meaning of "the pursuit of happiness" and published the discourse of the eminent historians and philosophers who participated, Parrington's myth was repeated as a basic assumption of their discussion.

It must be admitted that Locke gave considerable assistance to the misunderstanding of his own message. For example, in the *Second Treatise of Civil Government* he says: "The great and chief end therefore of men uniting into commonwealths, and putting themselves under government, is the preservation of their property. . . ." This sounds very much like Parrington's interpretation if one reads it out of context (context may be defined as that which the other fellow always fails to read). But if we examine the preceding sentence in Locke's *Treatise* we learn exactly what he means when he says "property." He tells us that men "unite for the mutual preservation of their lives, liberties and estates, which I call by the general name — property." Later on he says again: "By property I must be understood here as in other places to mean that property which men have in their persons as well as goods." In other words, Locke informs us at least twice that when he uses the word "property" he means everything that belongs to a man, not only the physical goods that he owns, but his life, his freedom, and his stake in society. As Locke sees it, government is under a duty to protect "property," but the word "property" is only an abbreviation for all the varied interests and rights that men value and wish to safeguard in a politically organized community. What confused Parrington, I think, is that Locke like most of us was not faithful to his own definition and from time to time used the word "property" in its narrower and more conventional sense.

Of course, if Parrington had been right, July 4, 1776, would have been an even busier day than it was. Jefferson's draft was subjected to all sorts of criticism in the Congress, and Jefferson sat there suffering and squirming like any author in the ordeal of multiple editing. But the attacks were confined to that part of the Declaration which dealt with the grievances against George III. No one criticized the statement of fundamental principles with which the Declaration began. "The pursuit of happiness" was in the text from the beginning and held its place unchanged to the end. If it had been a novel and momentous departure from the Lockean phrases in which these men were steeped, they would hardly have acquiesced so easily. Moreover, although in Jefferson's later years considerable controversy arose as to whether he had written anything original at all and as to the extent of his indebtedness to George Mason and others, everyone accepted John Adams's verdict that the content of the Declaration of Independence was made up of what had been "hackneyed about" for months if not years, and agreed that Jefferson's contribution consisted in the accuracy and felicity with which he expressed the American mind of the time. I think we can take it for granted that the phrase "the pursuit of happiness" and the source which it called to mind were reasonably familiar to Jefferson's cultivated contemporaries.[1]

What was that source? Suppose we turn to Locke's *Essay Concerning Human Understanding,* consulting it in any of the editions accessible to that generation of Americans.[2] If we examine the table of contents we find one chapter which could not possibly have escaped Jefferson's interest. It is entitled "Of Power." Then if we go on to read the chapter through, we find the phrase "the pursuit of happiness" or its close equivalent approximately a dozen times! In a single important paragraph, we find "a careful and constant pursuit of true and solid happiness," "an unalterable pursuit of happiness," and a third version, "pursuing true happiness." Other variations are "pursuit of our happiness," "pursue happiness," and — in so many words — "the pursuit of happiness." Does it not appear likely that this is our source? We have always felt safe in attributing the balance of the Declaration's creed to Locke's *Second Treatise of Civil Government,* and by like token may we not attribute "the pursuit of happiness" to the reiteration of those words in another work by the same revered author? And it is noteworthy that such evidence as we have[3] of Madison's familiarity with the *Essay Concerning Human Understanding* shows that this chapter "Of Power" was the one that seemed to interest him most.

What did Locke have to say here? When he first wrote the chapter (dealing mainly with the subject of human freedom), he said that the preferences of our minds are always determined for us by the appearance of good or greater good. After the first edition was published he reconsidered the matter from beginning to end, rejected his early views, and rewrote almost the entire chapter. He said he was neither "so vain as to fancy infallibility nor so disingenuous as to dissemble [his] mistakes," and so he frankly changed his analysis. It is the later wisdom, the revised analysis that Jefferson and Madison studied and that I propose to recapitulate briefly.

Locke begins by saying that the philosophical question whether men's *wills* are free is a mistaken question. The real question is whether *men* are free. Our wills, he says, are immediately determined from time to time to every voluntary action by the uneasiness of desire, that is, the desire for some good that is absent. At this stage of Locke's presentation we have an out-and-out determinism and one that is attached to a nonrational cause. Desire leads to uneasiness, uneasiness determines the will. What is it that moves desire? Happiness, he answers, "happiness, and that alone." The lowest degree of happiness is the absence of pain; the highest degree is the utmost pleasure we are capable of. Our freedom as human beings consists in and only in our power to suspend the execution and satisfaction of any of our desires, that is, to consider the objects which we seek and to weigh them along with others. And he adds, "When upon due examination we have judged, we have done our duty, all that we can or ought to do in pursuit of our happiness." What then is the way to human liberty? Locke replies, "As therefore the highest perfection of intellectual nature lies in a careful and constant pursuit of true and solid happiness, so the care of ourselves that we mistake not imaginary for real happiness is the necessary foundation of our liberty." His final thought — one that we should consider of paramount importance — is that though all men seek happiness, they do not all seek the same sort of happiness. He says, "Men may choose different things, and yet all choose right." Variety and self-determination in what men pursue as their happiness is a dominant motif of Locke's doctrine.

These passages in Locke gave the Revolutionary period three basic philosophic notions and three corresponding ethical ideals. The first philosophic notion is that our wills are at least partly determined and impelled by nonrational factors. From this Locke inferred the ethical ideal of intellectual modesty: if reason is no absolute sovereign it cannot expect men to stand in ranks like stiff lead soldiers with painted smiles. The second philosophic notion is that our desires — short-term and long-term, lofty and earthy — compete eternally with one another in an unremitting contentiousness. The corresponding ethical ideal is diversity and variety in the individual's right to pursue his happiness. The third philosophic notion is that we have the power to suspend the execution of our desires and to exercise discriminating judgment as among them. The ethical principle based on this notion is that in their pursuit of happiness men must undertake moral responsibility for their choices. These philosophic concepts and these ethical ideals can be epitomized in the words that Jefferson selected for his Declaration. They depict the human wayfarer as he presses forward in a hopeful but everlastingly precarious pursuit. They describe the political forces in what he may justly call his "inner republic."

HAPPINESS AND THE CONSTITUTIONAL REPUBLIC

It is evident that we are dealing here not with a slice out of the biographies of Jefferson and Madison, but with the concomitance between a body of ethical doctrine on the one hand and a body of political doctrine on the other. No one is able to demonstrate that in those hot June days in Philadelphia when Jefferson was composing the Declaration of Independence he mentally rehearsed the twenty-first chapter of the second book of Locke's *Essay*. Conjecture on the subject would be futile, for Jefferson's own later recollection of the circumstances proved to be only partly accurate. As for Madison, he was probably too busy in the spring of 1787 with political studies and constitutional projects to turn his conscious mind toward the philosophic propositions that had absorbed him in the years following his graduation from college and that remained unchallenged among the postulates of his thinking. However that may be, here amid the anxieties of the twentieth century where all our charts seem blurred and obscure, the reassurance we seek is not so much biographical as philosophic. And I believe there is profound reassurance to be gained in perceiving that *Madison's national political republic is Locke's individual inner republic "writ large."*

What was the basic problem of a free society as Madison saw it? The problem was what he called "factions," that is, groups of citizens held together by some common interest or impulsion which they endeavor to realize, to the detriment of the general welfare.[4] Today we should call them "special interest groups." Madison saw these various streams of interest cascading like spring freshets over the political terrain of his time and threatening to inundate the rights and welfare of the whole society. It has often been said that in the movement of these factions Madison identified only economic forces, and in truth there is some strong current of economic determinism in all of Madison's thinking. But the man was too intelligent to be guilty of the oversimplification that seduced later economic determinists; he was explicitly aware of at least two other vectors in the formation of factions. The first of these consisted in distinctions according to national origin, for Madison had witnessed with shame the oppression of German and Irish settlers in his own Virginia. The second and more important source of factional dissension was religious sectarianism and clerical arrogance. Madison had waged a brilliantly successful struggle in the Virginia legislature on behalf of Jefferson's bill for religious liberty, and on achieving victory had expressed the boast that its provisions "have in this country extinguished forever the ambitious hope of making laws for the human mind." But he could not forget the persecutions that marred our early history or the inhuman treatment of the Baptists, who had stood at one and the same time for political independence and freedom of worship. And so in the 10th *Federalist* he listed these along with the conspicuously important economic causes of factionalism, and he attributed all such causes to an irreducible variety in the opinions and passions of men and to an irreducible diversity in their faculties. "The latent causes of faction," he said, "are thus sown in the nature of man."

Factions present the same menace to the political republic that passionate desires present to the inner republic. If not dammed or stemmed in some rational fashion, if not converted into useful and constructive forces, they will overwhelm and destroy the whole landscape. Their impulses are recklessly blind and they know no regard for the inevitable reckoning.

What then is to be the cure? He said there are two ways of removing the causes of faction: one is to take away liberty and the other is to give every citizen the same opinions, passions, and interests. Several nations in our own time have chosen to employ both of these; but Madison had little fear that his countrymen would be willing to stomach either. "Liberty," he said, "is to faction what air is to fire, an aliment without which it instantly expires. But it could not be less folly to abolish liberty, which is essential to political life, because it nourishes faction, than it would be to wish the annihilation of air, which is essential to animal life, because it imparts to fire its destructive agency." Shall we then give every citizen the same opinions, passions, and interests? That, he replied, would be utterly impracticable. "As long as the reason of man continues fallible, and he is at liberty to exercise it, different opinions will be formed." Factions are the expression of elemental and ineradicable diversities. Therefore, he concluded, the *causes* of faction cannot be removed; our remedy must consist in the means of controlling faction's *effects*.

History had convinced him that no lasting remedy could be devised in a pure, that is, a direct democracy. The solution must be what he called "a republican remedy for the diseases most incident to republican government." And the republican remedy, as he saw it, corresponds to that faculty of suspension, deliberation, refinement, and responsible decision which Locke had attributed to every fallible human being.

A few men elected to represent the whole mass of the citizenry are bound to balance the factional interests of the mass with more comprehensiveness and equilibrium than their constituents could hope to attain. The majority in a republican legislature can act so as to represent the needs and rights not only of its own interest but of the minority as well. If the representatives are chosen from large geographic areas, then the very diversity of interests among their constituents will prompt them to compose and integrate conflicting claims into a rational program. Possibly the representatives will have enlightened views and virtuous sentiments superior to local prejudices; possibly the great variety of factions represented in the legislature will prevent any one group from outnumbering and oppressing the rest; possibly faction which burns like a prairie fire in a single state will be unable to spread its flames throughout the union. The experience under the Articles of Confederation had shown a desperate need for a national government of stability and vigor. Stability and vigor, indispensable as they were, must yet be reconciled with the faculty of reflective wisdom. A representative republic was the answer. It could assure both the power to act and the duty to reflect before acting.

Locke had seen the contentious desires in the human individual determining his will with largely nonrational drives. These corresponded to Madison's ominous factions. Locke had insisted on an incorrigible diversity in the desires of men. Madison likewise insisted that opinions, passions, and interests could never be made uniform. Locke had pointed hopefully to the faculty of suspending the execution of our desires until we weigh their consequences and choose among them. In Madison's republic this faculty epitomized the function of the people's representatives.

Probably it would have been better if Locke's analysis had gone a step further, that is, if he had recognized the extent to which the social relationships of an individual serve to mediate, compromise, and incarnate desires which must otherwise destroy one another. For example, sexual gratification, personal vanity, the demand for companionship, economic advantage, and a number of other apparently conflicting needs may all be integrated and fulfilled within the relation between a man and a woman. By the same token, Madison, writing his 10th *Federalist* long before American political parties assumed their ultimate shape, did not foresee the extent to which otherwise mutually destructive factions might be combined and somehow reconciled within the ranks of one of our major parties. It is a peculiar attribute of the major political party in the United States that instead of representing one interest and one legislative program as against all others, it combines and amalgamates many diverse groups, who must within the ranks of the party begin their education in the processes of compromise and rationalization. Thus, the movement of a major political party follows the drives of many contradictory segments. It may be called a dynamism of dissidence.

But we have not yet completed the parallel between Locke's ethical appraisal and Madison's republican ideal. Locke in his exposition of the moral qualities of man had taken the most important of all for granted. He said that we have the power to suspend the execution of our desires, to weigh their consequences, and to make a responsible choice. What he assumed was that that choice might by and large and in the greater number of human instances become a wise and virtuous one. Mature choice, he assumed, would be moral and conducive to a higher and more constant happiness. This, I believe, he took on faith, and I think that we too must take it on faith if we are to have any hope in a life refined by reason and purified by moral principle. If our second thoughts are not better than our first impulses then we are brutish indeed.

What Locke believed as to the individual human molecule Madison most categorically affirmed as to the whole American people. It was in the people that he found the ultimate protector of the Constitution, the ultimate judge of the competition for power between state and federal authorities, and the ultimate safeguard — as well as the ultimate menace — to all fundamental rights. The leaders who oppose the new Constitution, he said, lack confidence in the wisdom of the people. And that wisdom, he went so far as to say, was such that no bill of rights was necessary in the formation of the federal government. For a whole year, while Jefferson was insisting on a bill of rights as indispensable to the adoption of the Constitution, Madison continued to resist what he called "these parchment barriers."

History has established that Jefferson and Madison were both right. Jefferson was right only because Madison was right. In every country where the people were not such as to deserve Madison's faith, bills of rights have in truth proved to be mere parchment barriers. When Madison finally yielded to Jefferson's inflexible determination, he yielded to reason not to his friend. He became satisfied to advocate the adoption of a bill of rights because "1. The political truths declared in that solemn manner acquire by degrees the character of fundamental maxims of free Government, and as they become incorporated with the national sentiments, counteract the impulses of interest and passion. 2. Although it be generally true . . . that the danger of oppression lies in the interested majorities of the people rather than in usurped acts of the Government, yet there may be occasions on which the evil may spring from the latter source; and on such, a bill of rights will be a good ground for an appeal to the sense of the community." These are the convictions of a true democratic republican.

As long as men read the Declaration of Independence, that incandescent phrase "the pursuit of happiness" will illumine their minds. Some few will recognize the fecundity of those words and their richness of ethical content, and they may pause to accord a moment of gratitude to Locke who spoke them as a philosopher, to Jefferson who proclaimed them as a statesman, and to Madison who animated them with political reality. Perhaps it will be enough for the rest to know that a government can be founded on reverence for the integral man, the man to whom all the statutes and decisions, the ordinances and administrative licenses are mere ministers and body servants. It will be enough for Americans to carry on the work of Madison in a proud faith that "Men may choose different things, and yet all choose right."

Address at the James Madison Bicentennial Celebration, New York University Law Center, 1951, published in the New York University Law Review, *1952.*

Supreme Court and Supreme Law: An American Contribution

BEGINNING with Oliver Cromwell's "Instrument of Government" adopted in 1653, the modern history of written constitutions covers a period of some three centuries. At the precise halfway point in 1803, John Marshall delivered his judgment in *Marbury v. Madison*. Now after the lapse of another century and a half we propose to take stock of the various consequences his doctrine has brought about; and by way of prologue this chapter will suggest why the decision itself represented an important departure in the progress of American government.

For some time it has been fashionable to disparage *Marbury v. Madison* on the ground that there was nothing particularly new about it. Recent American scholarship grants that the decision raised the Supreme Court's prestige from a very low plane and that it linked John Marshall's powerful personality to the institution of judicial review; in all other respects the case is usually dismissed with a rather patronizing shrug. Legal historians have pointed to earlier judgments in the state courts, precedents in the British Privy Council on appeals from the colonies, and passages in *The Federalist* papers — as demonstrative proof that John Marshall borrowed and did not invent. But unless our philosophy of government is to be controlled by the rules of a patent office, novelty can hardly be accepted as the sole or decisive test of merit. In point of fact, a mature understanding — far from identifying the important with the novel — would attribute greater value to *Marbury v. Madison* precisely because it formalized and installed political conceptions which had already gained some measure of general support.

It is interesting to note how American treatises on the theory of constitutionalism have been influenced by the British experience of the seventeenth century. To this day our scholars tend to concentrate on supremacy of law as the central problem of the subject. The basic antithesis, as most of them see it, remains substantially what it was in the period between Coke and Locke, that is, the antithesis between government by laws and government by men, between legal precept and executive prerogative, between wise rules and exercise of wise discretion. In this sense the issues of constitutionalism are fully as old as Plato, whose thought moved in successive stages from the unfettered discretion which he favored in the *Republic* to the particularized statutes which he set down in his final work, the *Laws*.

However, the selfsame struggle against the Stuarts which focused attention on this classic problem of constitutionalism also inspired resort to the expedient of a written constitution. Thus there arose a cognate yet competing problem in the philosophy of government, a problem with antecedents even older than Plato. Its origins can be traced to the period in Greek philosophy when men like Parmenides were preaching that all was sameness and unity and men like Heraclitus were insisting that all was flux and change. In short, it was the antithesis between *permanence* and *change* that became one of the characteristic and magistral problems of constitutionalism as soon as men attempted to embody the constitution in a written document.

There is nothing abstruse about the way this antithesis presents itself in concrete experience. Let us suppose that, in a time of great public disturbance, the leaders of the people determine that certain fundamental institutions are indispensable to the survival of their political principles. Accordingly they compose a written constitution which describes the framework of government, defines the several political organs, and establishes certain lines of relation not only between one organ and another but also between the government and the citizenry. This is the fabric they desire to endure, this is to be the fundamental and permanent structure of government. But even if no extraneous cause should intervene to destroy the structure, the lapse of time most assuredly and inevitably will. For though we assume that the founders' wisdom has been entirely adequate to the needs of their society and the sentiments of their fellow-citizens, nevertheless social, economic, and technological changes will sooner or later make what was appropriate obsolete, what was modern archaic, and what was enlightened oppressive. If the constitution is drafted in loose and flexible terms, it may last somewhat longer, but the framers hardly dare draft it in terms so elastic as to imperil their own purposes. The minimum degree of rigidity necessary for the preservation of social order eventually becomes a political straitjacket.

In the experience of the Anglo-Americans from the middle of the seventeenth century down to the time of *Marbury v. Madison,* written constitutions proved very short-lived. Of course, many adopted since 1803 have likewise fallen into history's wastebasket. But the naked fact that the United States Constitution has survived for more than a century and a half implies that something special was accomplished between 1787 and 1803 to make it an exception. Somehow or other, a sufficient balance was attained in the tension between the principle of permanence and the principle of change. If such was the case, the

American solution, although it may or may not be suitable to the government of other countries, certainly merits careful study. It may constitute a major contribution to the technique of successful government. Let me therefore suggest the outlines of the historic turn which I see initiated in 1787 at the Constitutional Convention and consummated in 1803 by *Marbury v. Madison*. It was a turn in the theory of the written constitution, which may be summarized:

	As to Objective	As to Content	As to Sanction
from	perpetuity	immutability	appeal to heaven
to	efficacy	adaptation	appeal to the courts

II

Suppose we take ourselves back to the Constitutional Period (1784–1803) and consider the concept of a written constitution as it must have appeared to educated Americans of the time. Surely, it presented a strange, almost baffling history, streaked with confusion in theory and utopianism in practice. In point of fact, if the leaders of American thought had felt a wholehearted respect for the indications of that history, they might never have attempted a written charter. As it was, they were astute enough to consult the history mainly for negative purposes: from it they ascertained some of the things a wise draftsman should *not* do.

Rarely in any department of human interest has theory been so obscured by errors and ineptitudes of practice. Among the ancients, for example, a few keen observers like Plato, Aristotle, and Polybius seem to have perceived that a "constitution" should be identified rather by its content and political function than by the source which promulgated it. Their works offered highly instructive reading on the level of theory. When, however, one turned to the concrete texts in the various ancient polities, what did one find? Code after code, without exception, deemed to be a fundamental law for no other reason than its inspired, preternatural, or divine authorship. The authoritative differentia was not the content but the source, not the function but the charisma of the legislator. Hence only a confirmed heretic would feel disposed to suggest that this command deserved a higher rank than the other; that this prohibition could be enforced by jural sanctions and that could not; that certain provisions had only ceremonial value; or that dispositions fixing the general fabric of government might be distinguished from conventional, transitory, and particularized regulations. To everyone but the heretics, it seemed fairly obvious that if these classifications and distinctions had been worth making, the divine or divinely inspired legislator would have made them.

It is easy to smile at the vagaries of ancient political practice, and to reflect with pleasure on modern superiority — but perhaps not wholly justified. For we are about to see a strange phenomenon: the typical political theorist of seventeenth-century England proceeds in a sensible fashion to secularize and naturalize the process of drafting a fundamental law; he transmutes the obsolete supernatural code into a product of human ingenuity and intellect; yet — the moment the draft has been formulated — incontinently he assumes the prostrate attitude of the ancients, invests the document with the same reverential awe he feels for its source, and declares — in terms suitable for a doxology — that every part and the whole of it shall remain immutable forever and in perpetuity!

Here again, our reluctance to criticize can be overcome only by the exigencies of our theme and the obligation to deal justly with the accomplishments of the Constitutional Period. In the first place, we know that we stand on a height of vantage which three intervening centuries of historical experience have provided for us. There are propositions that have become so obvious in the course of these centuries that we are likely to confuse our own fund of empirical information with a superior endowment of wisdom and judgment. For example, when in his last years Mr. Justice Brandeis remarked, "A code of law that makes no provision for its amendment provides for its ultimate rejection," he merely asserted, in a neat rhetorical form, what the modern history of written constitutions has taught Americans to accept as palpably evident, if not truistic; but who of us has sufficient pride of intellect to claim that he could have excogitated this simple maxim *a priori*, without knowing anything about our ancestors' efforts and failures? In the second place, the American indebtedness to England's Classical Republicans, to the statesmen of the "Glorious Revolution," and especially to John Locke is so enormous that any disparagement — however justified — suggests an unworthy ingratitude or, at best, a chauvinistic attempt to minimize our national obligation. When of all men it is John Locke that I feel compelled to single out for criticism, my consolations seem hardly adequate. Yet even they have been provided by him, for he too cared more for truth than for John Locke's stated opinions and, when he would discover error in his own work, he did not hesitate to acknowledge it and to recast his thinking.

Locke's example is the one we must select, not only because his intellectual eminence is beyond cavil but also because he drafted his written constitution with the conscious expectation that it would be put into prompt and practical effect. Unlike various other charters — intended rather for edification than for application — his was designed to serve the day-to-day government of a specific country, covering a specific area, inhabited or to be inhabited by colonists of known origins and customs. This was no figment of a willful dream, destined to live only in the still air of a philosopher's study. Quite the contrary; when the young Locke drafted and redrafted his "Fundamental Constitutions," he knew very well that they were commissioned expressly for the government of Carolina.

There is no need to comment on the detailed provisions of the fantastically baroque document that Locke concocted. The Carolina colonists of the time commented more or less conclusively by resisting adoption of the plan for nearly fifty years until, despite continued support from the lords proprietors, it was finally abandoned in its entirety. If we turn back to Locke's text today, the scheme proposed seems bizarre and unrealistic almost beyond belief. It is like one of the White Knight's inventions in *Through the Looking Glass,* which he described to Alice:

> "Now the cleverest thing of the sort that I ever did," he went on after a pause, "was inventing a new pudding during the meat-course."
> "In time to have it cooked for the next course?" said Alice. "Well, that *was* quick work, certainly!"
> "Well, not the *next* course," the Knight said in a slow, thoughtful tone: "no, certainly not the next *course.*"
> "Then it would have to be the next day. I suppose you wouldn't have two pudding-courses in one dinner?"
> "Well, not the *next* day," the Knight repeated as before: "not the next *day.* In fact," he went on, holding his head down, and his voice getting lower and lower, "I don't believe that pudding ever *was* cooked! In fact, I don't believe that pudding ever *will* be cooked! And yet it was a very clever pudding to invent."

But could not the Carolina colonists have been induced to experiment with Locke's document and then remedy its defects by resorting to a prescribed method of amendment? We have no way of telling. For although the draft of the "Fundamental Laws" went through various revisions at Locke's own hands, it concluded by providing categorically that: "These fundamental constitutions, in* number* a hundred and twenty, and every part thereof, shall be and remain the sacred and unalterable form and rule of government of Carolina forever."

I wish Locke had done no more. If he had been content to ordain that no one must ever alter his handiwork, he would merely have followed the accustomed path of seventeenth- and eighteenth-century framers. (For instance, in the 1689 Bill of Rights, without a pretense of discrimination between general and specific, lasting and temporary provisions, it is laid down that "All . . . shall stand, remain, and be the law of this realm for ever. . . .") But since Locke was a philosopher of the new enlightenment, he surpassed the lawyerlike parliamentary draftsmen — even in the dimensions of his error. Apparently, immutability and perpetuity were not enough to claim; he felt impelled to kick harder against the pricks of history's teachings. And so, imitating the fatuous example of Justinian, who had attempted in vain to prohibit commentaries on his *Corpus Juris,* our great democratic philosopher inserted an additional clause reading: "Since multiplicity of comments, as well as of laws, have great inconveniences, and serve only to obscure and perplex, all manner of comments and expositions on any part of these fundamental constitutions, or on any part of the common or statute laws of Carolina, are absolutely prohibited." As the physicians of Locke's time would have expressed it, there must be something about sitting down to prepare a constitution which induces the "humors" to become excessively sanguine. Indeed, the most modest instance I have come upon was that of ancient Solon, who was satisfied to state that his legislation should endure for only a hundred years. (Of course, like so many others, he lived to see it subverted after a decade or so.) In the seventeenth and eighteenth centuries, eminent draftsmen would accept nothing less than a provision for unqualified perpetuity.

Yet some of these were very wise and thoughtful men, at least in many other respects. I do not feel we ought to leave them here in a posture that borders on the ridiculous. We ought, on the contrary, to take note of the premises implicit in their thinking; for if we do, we shall readily see that — given the premises which were generally accepted in those times — a claim of immutability and perpetuity was neither so implausible nor so pretentious in their eyes as it appears to us. We should remember that although they succeeded to a considerable degree in secularizing the process of constitution-making, they were intimately familiar with the Bible and the series of solemn covenants and compacts reported in it. Understandably, therefore, they were led to assume that fundamental arrangements of this kind would have to be immutable and perpetual. The religious influence continued in the background of their thinking.

In the foreground there were cogent factors derived from the law, the politics, and the philosophy of the situation. In its legal appearance, the early modern written constitution followed the technical form of a charter or land grant; it resembled the customary deed of real property, which was assumed to be binding on the grantor and his heirs forever. Politically speaking, the charters had served, as far back as the time of Magna Carta, to provide rallying points for the assertion of various civil rights; whether in England or America, the men who claimed "imprescriptible rights" would be prone to insist that the documents had eternal validity. And in the philosophic aspect of the matter, a written constitution was deemed to possess superior dignity and force because it mirrored the principles of the natural law, which everyone agreed were fixed, immutable, and permanent. All these assumptions were exceedingly easy to credit at least during the seventeenth century and the greater part of the eighteenth. Soon the full impact of the Industrial Revolution would be felt; soon the paw of accelerated technological change would brush aside everything that appeared so continuous, disciplined, and static in those simpler days; but at the time even the most gifted and enlightened statesmen might fairly suppose that the social relations with which they were familiar would continue or could be made to continue indefinitely without material disruption.

When the American Continental Congress undertook in 1777 to consider "Articles of Confederation and Perpetual Union," the assumptions we have just described were still in full vigor and more or less unchallenged. Obviously, in that particular setting they must have seemed valid and expedient in the highest conceivable degree; else why had the Americans resolved to revolt at the risk of life and honor? Immutability of charters and rights under them was one of the American maxims against George III, just as it had been an English maxim against Charles I and later against James II. But in 1777 the Americans had additional good reasons to impose immutability on their "Articles of Confederation and Perpetual Union." From the positive aspect, they knew that they had no chance of military success unless the newborn states would act unanimously, that is, they must without exception "hang together or hang separately." From the negative aspect, no delegation, no state trusted the others sufficiently to commit itself to an instrument of confederation which might be amended without its approval.

In the Articles of Confederation these considerations, theoretical and practical, political and military, all converged to induce a reiteration of the weary yet magical word "perpetual" (What wry smiles that word must bring to the lips of heavenly observers!) as well as a prohibition of "any alteration at any time hereafter" except by *unanimous* consent of the thirteen states.

It was in the teeth of these provisions, of course, that the members of the Constitutional Convention proposed a completely new charter in 1787. What they did amounted to nothing less than a coup d'état —

an overturn not merely in the form but likewise in the theory of American government. For suddenly, the states were told that the principle of immutability had been abandoned. No longer would a single state be able to veto the process of growth and adaptation, because Article V of the new Constitution provided boldly that amendments binding on *all* could be adopted by action of *three-fourths* of the states.

It seems that in England during the preceding century one states-man had been endowed with such a happy combination of practical wisdom and intellectual modesty that he had hit upon the prototype of this remarkable device. When William Penn in 1682 issued his "Frame of Government of Pennsylvania," he wrote a preface explain-ing the purposes and objectives he had in mind. It is clear that he had reflected long on the subject. His reflections taught him that, in the long run, change and chance will not be subdued by any static framework the mind of man can devise. Therefore, having said in his preface, "I do not find a model in the world, that time, place, and some singular emergences have not necessarily altered . . ." he went on to provide that his charter might be amended whenever the governor and six-sevenths of the freemen in the Provincial Council and General Assembly would consent. Thus to William Penn we owe the invaluable expedient of permitting amendment by a vote less than unanimous yet large enough to ensure extended deliberation and lasting approval.

In the fall of 1776, Pennsylvania adopted its first constitution as a new state. Guided by Benjamin Franklin, the state convention not only accepted but considerably elaborated the device it had inherited from Penn. It framed a plan for the periodic election of "censors," who would be charged simultaneously with (1) seeing that the state consti-tution was obeyed scrupulously, and (2) recommending any amend-ments that might appear to be necessary. Here was a sure omen that American statesmen were beginning to recognize the inherent relation between efficacy and progressive adaptation in the life of a constitu-tion. But, as we have seen, an attempt at that juncture to apply this perception on the level of federal government would have met enor-mous and probably insuperable obstacles. In relation to federal struc-ture, Penn's guidance was required to wait another decade for a riper and wiser gathering — held, fittingly, in Penn's own city.

To the men at Philadelphia in 1787 an amendment clause must have seemed an absolute necessity. Behind the closed doors of their convention they had struck one ingenious compromise after another in order to achieve approximate unanimity among the delegates. All of them realized that because of these compromises the document they had signed probably contained a number of imperfections. Most of them must have speculated at least privately whether the compromises would work to their satisfaction in actual practice and whether experience would show that one interest had yielded too much or the other had acquiesced in an unrealistic solution. In arguing for ratification, even Hamilton was not willing to say more than "that the system, though it may not be perfect in every part, is, upon the whole, a good one [and] is the best that the present views and circumstances of the country will permit." I suspect the statesmen of 1787 would be astonished to learn that at this remote date the Constitution remains in force at all and would scarcely believe that since 1804, when their generation finally rested content with the document, it has been amended only ten times. (From these ten, two may be subtracted because the Twenty-first Amendment did little if anything more than repeal the Eighteenth.) Could we consult them today, I think the framers would inquire why we have not exercised the power of amendment more frequently and extensively.

If they looked upon the amendment clause as a necessity, what a virtue they forthwith made of it! It became one of the standard arguments in the campaign for ratification, a big gun which was reserved for use after every other debating weapon had failed to repel the opposition, then wheeled systematically into place, loaded with the ammunition of ostensible reasonableness, and discharged pointblank in the adversary's face — to his discomfort at least, often to his devastation. Does this or that provision in the draft seem unwise? Does the gentleman persist in his objection? Very well, since the times do not admit of delay, let us proceed to ratify in haste, then we can go about amending at leisure.

When Madison wrote *The Federalist* number 43, he was satisfied to expound Article V and to find in it "every mark of propriety"; but by the time Hamilton was ready to compose number 85, which would serve as the peroration and ultimate epitome of the whole Federalist case in New York, he found himself compelled to endow Article V with supreme practical importance. For his opponents had largely consolidated behind the argument that the process of corrective amendment should precede, not follow, the act of ratification. Then did Hamilton prove his virtuosity. He took Article V out of its modest position, burnished it until it fairly shone, and displayed it to America as an incomparably easy and expeditious arrangement for the remedying of errors, compared to which an attempt to improve the instrument before it was ratified would be desperately difficult, inept, and divisive.

The Virginia scene was not different. Objecting vehemently to the lack of a bill of rights in the document Madison had sent overseas to him, Thomas Jefferson acknowledged that the draftsmen's mistake could be corrected by resorting to the amendment clause. And in the Virginia ratification convention, which largely determined the destiny of the Constitution, the Federalists repeatedly pointed to Article V by way of answer to Patrick Henry's and George Mason's indignant criticisms. Yet even after the Federalists had solemnly promised to support amendments which would supply the missing bill of rights, the motion for ratification squeezed through by the very barest of margins; it is therefore an understatement to say that without Article V the Constitution would never have been adopted.

What a fascinating reversal we have here! How the tune has changed in that brief decade from 1777 (when a power to amend without unanimous approval was denied by way of reassurance) to 1787 (when just such a power made it possible for the new pattern of government to come into existence)!

Once the Constitution had been ratified, Article V was given immediate exercise. By the time Marshall rendered his judgment in *Marbury v. Madison,* the first ten amendments had been added to establish a bill of rights, the Eleventh had been adopted to reverse a decision of the Supreme Court, and the Twelfth was under way to correct defects in the original plan exposed by the presidential election of 1800. It is fair to conclude that, by 1803, the American theory of a written constitution (1) had begun to subordinate perpetuity to practical efficacy, (2) had completely discarded the false notion of immutability, and in its place (3) had approved a policy of seeking stability through progressive adaptation.

Much however remained to be done. The slow and cumbersome mechanism of Article V can at most produce a needed change in the literal text of the Constitution; the goal of adaptation requires more than that, the goal of efficacy requires considerably more. How can we discover just what the broad, sweeping phrases of the text signify as concrete legal mandates unless they should be interpreted by some authoritative organ? How can their meaning reflect the shift and flux of social conditions, economic interests, and political ideals unless the organ which interprets should likewise be equipped to reinterpret? And finally what pragmatic value can either the text or the successive interpretations retain unless the process of adapting the Constitution should be somehow combined with a concomitant process of effectuating it by force of law? These concernments lead us to the import of *Marbury v. Madison.*

III

If the objective and content of the written constitution were transformed during the course of the Constitutional Period, there was an even sharper turn in theory on the subject of effectual enforcement. No political problem perplexed the leading American statesmen so deeply and continually. To them it seemed inevitable that from time to time one official organ or another would attempt to infringe the Constitution; they were perfectly familiar with the way power brings out arrogance and ruthlessness in men, and the way personal ambition or fanatical enthusiasm can exacerbate the process. They knew that often the most redoubtable enemies of a free society are very sincere individuals obsessed with a belief that destiny has singled them out and anointed them to protect liberty by defining its limits. Clearly, against dangers and inroads like these, "parchment barriers" — to adopt Madison's phrase — would be futile without effective sanctions.

The sanctions they found available when they consulted previous history can be grouped under the heading of "appeal to heaven." In ancient times — Livy, Herodotus, and similar sources tell us — the technique for enforcing fidelity to a treaty, compact, or charter consisted in exacting a sacramental oath from the person who undertook the obligation. (These were strictly promissory oaths, relating only to acts to be performed in the future. They should not be confused with iniquitous "test oaths" which relate to one's past conduct and past opinions.) When a vow was taken in ceremonious circumstances, it involved a great deal more than merely promising to perform. It amounted in effect to a sort of conditional imprecation, because the oath-taker agreed either expressly or by religious implication that his promise might be considered as having been made to the celestial powers, who, if he should violate it, would evince their displeasure in some characteristically divine fashion. In seventeenth- and eighteenth-century England, statesmen set great store on the precise wording of all official oaths; what the king would or would not be willing to swear might well determine whether he or some other candidate would be found present at the coronation. The constitutional sanction consisted in invoking *lex coeli,* the law of heaven.

Not long after the close of our Constitutional Period, Jeremy Bentham wrote a devastating critique of this belief in the efficacy of promissory oaths. In it he said:

> . . . The arm pressed into service is that of the invisible and supreme ruler of the universe.

The oath being taken, the formularies involved in it being pronounced, is or is not the Almighty bound to do what is expected of Him?
Of the two contradictory propositions, which one do you believe? If He is
NOT bound, then the security, the sanction, the obligation amounts to
nothing. If He IS bound, then observe what follows: the Almighty is
bound, and by whom? Of all the worms that crawl about the earth in the
shape of men there is not one who may not thus impose conditions on
the supreme ruler of the universe.

And to what is He bound? To any number of contradictory and
incompatible observances, which legislators, tyrants, madmen, may, in the
shape of an oath, be pleased to assign Him.

As usual, Bentham was correct. For sheer, unmitigated insolence,
men who presume they have God's power at their beck and call to
enforce their paltry engagements can hardly be surpassed — except
perhaps by men who purport to "demonstrate" syllogistically that God
exists.

Yet likewise as usual, Bentham was not quite wholly correct. There
is a genuine moral cogency in an oath of office when it is taken in
solemn form by a man of radical integrity. In the forum of conscience,
he feels committed, no longer free as he was before but tethered to the
obligations he has assumed. Thus it was that when in 1766 Edmund
Pendleton — sitting as a judge in the colony of Virginia — resolved
intrepidly to disregard the Stamp Act because he considered it unconstitutional, he referred very simply and movingly to his "having taken
an oath to decide according to law." So also if one turns to *Marbury v.
Madison* and reads Marshall's justification of judicial review: it all
seems inspired by Hamilton's analysis in *The Federalist* — until one
comes to the conclusion. And there with rather eloquent indignation
Marshall insists on the oath he has taken to discharge his duties
"agreeably to the Constitution." These factors seem to have changed
very little since his day: I have known quite a register of trial and
appellate judges but never one who doubted that the solemn assumption of office had somehow fettered his will. Even in the case of
executive and representative officials this is sometimes true, particularly where the influence of some professional or corporate tradition
can be felt. However, these considerations have no pretentious connection with appeals to heaven or conditional imprecations. The official
oath is now only a solemn type of promise, the penalties involved in a
breach are strictly secular. Perhaps without intending to, we of the
twentieth century manifest a more seemly reverence in this regard.

I do not mean to imply that the issue presented itself in any such
aspect during the Constitutional Period. Quite the contrary: when the
American statesmen of the time decided they could not put their trust

in oaths as the working warranties of the Constitution, it was simply because human experience, including their own, had established beyond question that an oath would be a sadly feeble kind of tether. Their generation had first sworn fealty to King George, then they had sworn it to the cause of independence; they had vowed a perpetual allegiance to the Articles of Confederation, then they had agreed to disregard them at the Philadelphia Convention. If egregiously honorable men like themselves were susceptible to awkward shifts like these, how could they expect a mere oath to restrain the ordinary run of politicians who might succeed them, much less the morally perverse? The Constitution clearly could not be left dependent on the efficacy of ceremonious oaths.

"Appeal to heaven" had, however, a second and possibly more familiar connotation to the Founding Fathers. John Locke had taught them to associate it with a people's resort to revolution. If major provisions of the Constitution should be violated arbitrarily and persistently, the people were entitled to consider that the political compact had been dissolved, that they had been thrown into a state of nature in relation to the sovereign, and that their taking up arms in defense of their rights constituted an appeal to *lex coeli*. Of course, the framers of the Constitution were constrained to endorse everything in these propositions; how else could they justify their own participation in the Revolutionary War? But now that an American government was in contemplation to restore confidence and stabilize the social order, Locke's maxims, however valid they may have been when they were needed, must be laid aside as irrelevant. In '76 there had been a time to tear down; that time had passed. In '87 "the good people," "the right-minded people" agreed that the time to build up had long since arrived. In their judgment, "appeal to heaven," having served its historic purpose, had nothing to offer toward meeting the need of the new era, i.e., the day-to-day enforcement of a written constitution. (Consider moreover the infamous behavior of this Daniel Shays!)

In respect of sanctions, it was clear that *lex coeli* could never provide an acceptable solution. What was needed was a change to the law of the land or *lex terrae,* a change from higher-than-positive law to higher, positive law. This, of course, is the very change that Marshall consummated in *Marbury v. Madison:* by legitimizing the appeal to the courts he presumedly bastardized any possible "appeal to heaven."

Where did he learn the method of solution? I should like to suggest that his indoctrination in judicial review came several years prior to the issuance of *The Federalist* — to be precise, on November 2, 1782. If I am correct, then Marshall's intellectual debt to Hamilton was considerably smaller than most of us have assumed. Hamilton's arguments in the 78th *Federalist* did in all likelihood provide Marshall with a ready-made model of exposition for the *Marbury* opinion; and considering the intrinsic qualities of the model, its prestige as a factor in bringing about ratification, and the superbly ironic twist that the present defendant — Jefferson's own Madison — had collaborated actively with Hamilton in writing *The Federalist,* Marshall would have been either more or less than human if he had not availed himself of such a tempting opportunity. Since he was intensely human, he did adapt and paraphrase Hamilton's line of presentation. But his understanding of judicial review and his faith in its efficacy he owed to others.

I have found no indication that Marshall became acquainted with judicial review before November 1782. His formal education in the law consisted in attending George Wythe's lectures at William and Mary College "for perhaps six weeks" beginning about May 1, 1780, during which time the jottings in his notebook show he was profoundly preoccupied with thoughts of the young lady whom he was to marry in January 1783. The notebook records Wythe's lectures, but these appear to have related to topics of private law only. Then, in 1782 having been elected to the Virginia legislature, Marshall came to Richmond for the purpose of taking his seat and establishing a law practice in the city.

For lack of a quorum, the opening of the House was delayed for eighteen days until November 9, 1782, and Marshall seems to have been entirely at leisure during this interval.

Now, anyone arriving in Richmond in the fall of 1782 would have found the city agog over one of the most dramatic and celebrated cases of its history. Three alleged traitors had been convicted and condemned to death. The Virginia Assembly had passed a bill pardoning them, but the Senate had refused to concur. They were respited just as they were about to be hanged. (I may say here at the outset by way of easing the reader's mind that if any of them was eventually hanged, it was not because of the crime of treason.) The issue of the validity of their pardon was finally remitted to the Virginia Court of Appeals. One of the great questions in the case was whether the legislation passed by the House had conformed to the requirements of the Virginia constitution governing the subject of pardons. At the unprecedented invitation of Edmund Pendleton, who was presiding over the Court of Appeals, many leading lawyers in the State of Virginia voiced their opinions in order to assist the judges.

On November 2, 1782, each of the judges delivered his views to the assembled public. There was Pendleton. (It will be remembered that when he was a colonial judge he had not feared to declare the Stamp

Act unconstitutional.) Now he could be heard to emphasize the desirability of avoiding affront to a coordinate branch of the government; he could also be heard to declare if he were ever compelled to face the issue, he would not shrink from the performance of his judicial duty. There was Judge Mercer, who flatly pronounced the legislation unconstitutional — the first such occasion in the annals of the State of Virginia. And on the same bench there sat none other than Marshall's only law teacher, George Wythe, revered for the profundity of his scholarship and the brilliance of his reasoning. Wythe proceeded to hold the pardon invalid without having to reach the question of constitutionality. But these are the words he spoke concerning the obligations of judicial office:

> I have heard of an English chancellor who said, and it was nobly said, that it was his duty to protect the rights of the subject against the encroachments of the crown; and that he would do it at every hazard. But if it was his duty to protect a solitary individual against the rapacity of the sovereign, surely it is equally mine to protect one branch of the legislature and consequently the whole community against the usurpations of the other: and whenever the proper occasion occurs, I shall feel the duty; and fearlessly perform it. Whenever traitors shall be fairly convicted by the verdict of their peers before the competent tribunal, if one branch of the legislature without the concurrence of the other shall attempt to rescue the offenders from the sentence of the law, I shall not hesitate, sitting in this place, to say to the general court, *Fiat justitia, ruat coelum;* and to the usurping branch of the legislature, you attempt worse than a vain thing; for although you cannot succeed, you set an example which may convulse society to its centre. Nay more, if the whole legislature, an event to be deprecated, should attempt to overleap the bounds prescribed to them by the people, I, in administering the public justice of the country, will meet the united powers at my seat in this tribunal; and pointing to the constitution, will say to them, here is the limit of your authority; and hither shall you go, but no further.

It seems safe to conclude that on November 2, 1782, the principles were first planted which would bear fruit twenty years later in *Marbury v. Madison,* and that Wythe, Pendleton, and Mercer deserve to rank with Hamilton as Marshall's intellectual coadjutors in installing the institution of judicial review. On him destiny conferred the role it reserves for its special favorites — the role of converting essence into existence. In the *Marbury* case, applying his mentors' teachings, Marshall equipped the United States Constitution with an efficacious sanction. Thus he gave it an opportunity to maintain its legal vigor and preserve its identity through all subsequent vicissitudes. I think even those of us who are not fond of Marshall's personality or his politics must recognize that he received little more than a piece of parchment and finally transmitted a viable organism.

In terms of our theme, it is exceedingly important that when we call judicial review an efficacious sanction, we detect the bivalence of the word "efficacious." Judicial review is always more than pure and simple enforcement of the Constitution; in addition, it always comprises express or tacit interpretation of the Constitution, or — in other words — a continual process of adjusting and adapting the fundamental fabric. The sanction which Marshall installed in *Marbury v. Madison* should be seen as having served both purposes; it has maintained the Constitution not only by giving it legal force but also by providing in a substantial measure for continual reshaping and development. That is why our theme has linked Article III concerning the judicial power with Article V concerning the power of amendment. I believe their functions link them of necessity.

Yet when we have reached this point in our analysis, it is strange to discover that what William James used to call "the sentiment of rationality" seems somehow to elude us. We have traced the turn from perpetuity to efficacy, from immutability to adaptation, and from heavenly to judicial sanctions; yet some element, some strand appears to be missing without which there is only an abstract pattern. Oddly enough, it seems as though we have lost sight of the country while describing its government. If our account was adequate and satisfactory, why has there been little or no room in it for the American *people?*

The *Marbury* opinion has a comment to contribute on this very subject. In a paragraph that has attracted comparatively little notice, Marshall refers to the people's exercise of their right to establish a constitution as "a very great exertion; nor can it nor ought it to be frequently repeated." The people, he reiterates insistently in the same paragraph, "can seldom act." A rather enigmatic sort of reference, this; what might Marshall have intended by it?

IV

I think the meaning — in an objective sense, of course — should not be difficult to reach, if only we place ourselves in the circumstances of the time and recall that the *Marbury* opinion represented an attempt on Marshall's part to rebuke his arch-adversary, Thomas Jefferson. Under the thin guise of an impersonal utterance, the Chief Justice was really engaged in admonishing the President and challenging his political creed. At least that is the way the opinion was understood by contemporary readers in both camps. In the setting of February 1803 where Jefferson was far and away the outstanding advocate of popularism, to say — as Marshall did — that "the people . . . can seldom act" was equivalent to firing a shot in his direction. Which is, I think, the right direction for us.

To follow it, one must begin with an accurate picture of Jefferson's contribution to the development of judicial review, which has often been distorted by anachronisms of emphasis. For example, it has become usual to quote from an informal letter he addressed to Mrs. John Adams in 1804, where, justifying the pardons he had granted to persons convicted under the Sedition Law, he asserted that the judges were entitled to decide on constitutionality "for themselves in their own sphere of action" but not for the executive and (presumably) not for the legislature. This remark did constitute a portion of Jefferson's doctrine; it has subsequently been vindicated at least to the extent the Supreme Court has refused to adjudicate so-called "political issues"; nevertheless, just because it dealt only with power relations inside the structure of government, it remained a more or less subordinate element in the Jeffersonian philosophy. It was hardly the kind of contention that would put John Marshall in a febrile state.

Jefferson's more fundamental doctrine was the outcome of long and thoughtful study. As early as June of '76, he had tried his hand at drawing up a constitution for the emerging State of Virginia. In a few weeks' time he produced three successive drafts. The first of them prohibited amendments except with the unanimous consent of both legislative houses. Then Jefferson's thinking advanced very rapidly: the second and third versions permitted adoption of amendments by a majority vote of the people in two-thirds of the state's counties. Unfortunately, although the state convention made considerable use of Jefferson's draft, it ignored his amendment section. As adopted the Virginia charter contained no provision on the subject.

In Jefferson's intellectual advance, these steps proved to be merely preliminary. Lodging in Philadelphia until September and conversing often with men like Franklin, he enjoyed a fine opportunity to observe the preparation of the Pennsylvania state constitution of 1776. This, as we have seen, was the constitution which provided for a periodic choice of "censors" who would report on breaches of the constitution and on desirable amendments.

Though he must have been intrigued by the Pennsylvania device, Jefferson apparently let his ideas incubate for as long as seven years, or until the advent of peace afforded a more propitious occasion to improve Virginia's charter. In 1783 he composed a new plan. For the pertinent clause of this plan he set out to build upon the model that Pennsylvania had furnished, but since his philosophy would not permit him to touch anything — any institution, expedient, or arrangement — without democratizing it, he finally produced a clause that was altogether Jeffersonian because it was so firmly bottomed on the people's good judgment and their right of ultimate decision.

In effect, the 1783 draft provides that whenever any two of the three branches of government shall determine (by two-thirds vote) that "a Convention is necessary for altering this Constitution or correcting breaches of it," delegates shall be elected by the people, to convene within three months and to exercise the same powers as the convention that adopted the original constitution. Thus where Pennsylvania had recognized the connection between enforcing a charter and amending it, Jefferson went a great deal further: he converted the Pennsylvania device into an effectual nexus between the operations of government and the desires of the governed. According to his plan, final jurisdiction over every constitutional controversy would reside in the minds of the people. In regard to fundamental issues, the people would be more than the passive source of the constitution, they would intervene actively and enforce or construe or amend it as they might see fit; in short, it would at all times remain theirs and express their genius.

It is very important to discern Jefferson's position clearly. Far from objecting to judicial review of constitutionality, he frequently proposed that the judiciary share with the executive in exercising the veto power. If his proposal had been accepted, the judges would have been concerned not only with questions of constitutionality but also, quite avowedly, with the desirability and wisdom of legislative acts. And, as we saw, he conceded the courts' right and duty to pass on constitutionality at least "in their own sphere of action." It was not judicial review that he opposed, but the assumption that its results would be final and beyond further appeal. Not so, he submitted; if the judges should err so egregiously that the executive and legislature might have cause to fear for the constitution, then there must be provision for a further appeal — to the whole people as ultimate arbiters. This looks like a stride beyond the Declaration of Independence. In the Declaration he had described governments as *deriving* their powers from the consent of the governed; in 1783 he would further require that the very fabric of government be subjected to continual reassessment and reshaping in conformity with the judgment of the governed. For the balance of his days, Jefferson was to preach that the Constitution of the United States belonged only to the living generation.

The Federalists felt no difficulty in accepting what Jefferson had written in '76; in point of fact, so consistently were they persuaded of the people's status as the sovereign fountainhead of legitimacy that they were willing to invite opposition to the Constitution by beginning it with "We the People" instead of "We the States." But they found Jefferson's subsequent, more advanced attitude entirely unacceptable. It would leave a constitution tentative like a power of attorney issued by an officious and meddlesome principal; they understood that a constitution should be rather like an irrevocable and immutable grant or, if the need of some slight possibility of amendment must be admitted, then like a nearly irrevocable and immutable grant.

One of the authors of *The Federalist* (whom we shall call by his pseudonym "Publius" because it is not certain whether the relevant passages were Hamilton's or Madison's) was astute enough to recognize that Jefferson's 1783 proposal might epitomize the entire philosophy of popular rule. He appears to have given much care to the strategy of refuting it. The means employed were well chosen: Publius began by lavishing compliments on the author of the proposal; abstained from any suggestion of false or improper motives; conceded the proposal's plausibility and consistency *in theory;* showed however that it was idealistic to a fault, utopian, and impractical; and finally, having analogized it to the device in the Pennsylvania constitution, went on to demonstrate that Pennsylvania's experience with periodic conventions had been very unsatisfactory. Two complete papers (numbers 49 and 50) of *The Federalist* were devoted to this refutation — which indicates the importance Publius attached to it.

With considerable adroitness he manipulated his readers' anxieties, pointing out that "frequent appeals" to the people would deprive the government of "veneration" and would involve a "danger of disturbing the public tranquillity by interesting too strongly the public passions." Sadly he added that "it must be confessed that the [constitutional] experiments are of too ticklish a nature to be unnecessarily multiplied." "The *passions,* therefore, not the *reason,* of the public would sit in judgment." Things would, of course, be different in "a nation of philosophers." But as matters stood, the people's decision "could never be expected to turn on the true merits of the question." There was therefore no possibility of enforcing the Constitution by "occasional appeals to the people."

Now, Publius's eloquent and ingenious argument in the 49th *Federalist* would of itself sufficiently explain what John Marshall was referring to when he insisted redundantly that "the people . . . can seldom act." If the balance of the *Marbury* opinion derived its inspiration from *The Federalist* number 78, the phrases we have been tracing seem unmistakably to echo not only the reasoning but also the emotional overtones of number 49. And considering the events and developments between 1788 (when number 49 was issued) and 1803 (when Marshall drew upon it), the only wonder is that the Chief Justice was able to exercise so much restraint. The mere thought of popularly elected conventions would cause him to suffer; thirty years after *Marbury v. Madison* he still described the process of ratifying the Constitution as though it had been an almost traumatic experience. To him, Publius's "too ticklish" must have appeared an extreme understatement.

The frequent use of Article V to amend the Constitution may well have troubled the Chief Justice; he could scarcely have regarded the Eleventh Amendment, which reversed a decision of the Supreme Court, with complete equanimity. But these matters appeared like child's play when he recalled certain other events — as recent as February of 1801. At that time, despite the popular mandate expressed in the tumultuous campaign of 1800, Marshall's party had come exceedingly close to frustrating Jefferson's victory; the electoral stalemate they had decided to contrive seemed reasonably certain; and there was considerable talk (or perhaps a concerted plan) that, since no President would be elected by the end of Adams's term on March 3, 1801, the Congress could choose a sort of Provisional President, a Federalist of course, who would necessarily assume semidictatorial powers. Many of Marshall's persuasion thought that a firm, Federalist hand could yet bring the country back to sanity. And then —

And then the searing bolt had fallen. Let me describe the climax in Jefferson's words, written while the outcome still remained uncertain:

> . . . If they could have been permitted to pass a law for putting the government into the hands of an officer, they would certainly have prevented an election. But we thought it best to declare openly and firmly, one and all, that the day such an act passed, the Middle States would arm, and that no such usurpation, even for a single day, should be submitted to. This first shook them; and they were completely alarmed at the resource for which we declared, to wit, a convention to reorganize the government, and to amend it. The very word convention gives them the horrors, as in the present democratical spirit of America, they fear they should lose some of the favorite morsels of the Constitution.

Within two days, Jefferson was duly elected President of the United States. The Federalist rank and file had at last agreed to emulate the example of Henri IV; they had concluded that the Constitution was well worth stomaching a "democratical" President. At worst, dangerous though he was, he presented a lesser menace than amendment or revision by a popularly controlled convention.

Two brief years after this feverish melodrama, was it not natural that Marshall should attempt in the *Marbury* case to foreclose consideration of "appeals to the people"? He did make the attempt and, by doing so, he joined the most fundamental issue affecting the concept of a written constitution and the process of judicial review.

Jefferson had proposed that whenever indications of a constitutional crisis might arise, the development and reshaping of the charter should be confided to the discretion of the people. In opposition, Marshall declared for the Court as the ultimate place of judgment, permitting exception only by means of the formal and cumbrous machinery of Article V. The *Marbury* opinion would have been vastly important to constitutional law and political theory if it had done no more than place this elemental conflict at issue and thus invoke the arbitrament of the future. Indeed, without anticipating my colleagues' analyses, I venture to predict that, in every ensuing chapter of our stocktaking, the reader will be able to discern various subtle manifestations of the two opposing philosophies, and that at some points he may be tempted to wonder whether Jefferson's system, which the builders thought they had refused, has not become the headstone of the corner.

Marbury v. Madison has proved to be one of those very special occurrences that mark an epoch in the life of the republic. Culminating the great achievements of the Constitutional Period, it accomplished the transition from perpetuity to efficacy, from immutability to adaptation, and from heavenly to judicial sanctions. Finally, it introduced an unending colloquy between the Supreme Court and the people of the United States, in which the Court continually asserts, "You live under a Constitution but the Constitution is what *we* say it is," and the people incessantly reply, "As long as your version of the Constitution enables us to live with pride in what *we* consider a free and just society, you may continue exercising this august, awesome, and altogether revocable authority."

From Supreme Court and Supreme Law,
Indiana University Press, 1954.

The Firstness of the First Amendment

ONE's sympathy goes out to young James Madison in the fall of 1788. After the strenuous labors of the Constitutional Convention, he had traversed a series of anxious stages on the road to ratification. The state conventions (except in North Carolina and Rhode Island) had ultimately voted approval, but several of them —

including his own Virginia — had exacted a promise that amendments would be adopted promptly to declare the people's fundamental liberties. When the initial Congress under the new Constitution convened in the spring of 1789, Madison knew, it would be watched with suspicion and distrust until the pledge was redeemed and the amendments submitted to the states. The enterprise was to be his, as leader in the House of Representatives — to assemble the multifarious state proposals, organize them in rational order and guide them through. He understood that some reassuring action was inevitable: to this he was bound in honor and reconciled in thought. But a vague, general expectation was scarcely enough for a mind as analytical as his. He foresaw that while the Constitution's adversaries might wreck the whole fabric by submitting destructive amendments, the arrogant and intransigent among the Federalist group might refuse to consider amendments which were entirely reasonable. To steer through this perilous strait, he must study his course carefully, critically, in advance.

WHY SHOULD THE RIGHTS BE DECLARED?

During the previous year, Madison had often exchanged views of the subject with Thomas Jefferson, who was representing the United States in Paris. From the first, Jefferson had insisted that "a bill of rights is what the people are entitled to against every government on earth. . . ."[1] Now it was fitting to tell him that his demand would be met. Under these circumstances, on October 17, 1788, Madison composed a letter of self-examination and self-revelation. In it he announced the withdrawal of his early objections to a declaration of rights, and proceeded to conduct a conscious search for the doctrines and practical criteria he would use to guide his course in the Congress.

Madison still believed — as he had from the beginning of the correspondence — that since the real power in a republic resides in the people, it is they who are the main source of danger to freedom. Solemn declarations still seemed to him like "parchment barriers," for "in Virginia, I have seen the [state] bill of rights violated in every instance where it has been opposed to a popular current." Well, then, was it all to be a pious fraud, which he would only compound by proposing solemn amendments to the forthcoming Congress? No, Madison said, addressing simultaneously his distant friend and his own conscience:

What use, then, it may be asked, can a bill of rights serve in popular Governments? I answer, the two following which, though less essential than in other Governments, sufficiently recommend the precaution: 1.

The political truths declared in that solemn manner acquire by degrees the character of fundamental maxims of free Government, and as they become incorporated with the National sentiment, counteract the impulses of interest and passion. 2. Although it be generally true, as above stated, that the danger of oppression lies in the interested majorities of the people rather than in usurped acts of the Government, yet there may be occasions on which the evil may spring from the latter source; and on such, a bill of rights will be a good ground for an appeal to the sense of the community. Perhaps, too, there may be a certain degree of danger, that a succession of artful and ambitious rulers may by gradual and well-timed advances, finally erect an independent Government on the subversion of liberty. Should this danger exist at all, it is prudent to guard against it, especially when the precaution can do no injury.

This letter, which was delayed in some strange fashion, gave Jefferson rather less comfort than the prevailing party may expect in an argument between friends. He seems to have wondered why Madison had paraded so much subtlety to refute a list of obviously false objections. On March 15, 1789, Jefferson replied. Somewhat lightly, he complimented Madison for conceiving bright answers to what he apparently considered very dull questions. He added several summary answer — or rather, retorts — of his own. Here is a sample:

4. "Experience proves the inefficacy of a bill of rights." True. But though it is not absolutely efficacious under all circumstances, it is of great potency always, and rarely inefficacious. A brace the more will often keep up the building which would have fallen, with that brace the less. There is a remarkable difference between the characters of the inconveniences which attend a declaration of rights, and those which attend the want of it. The inconveniences of the declaration are, that it may cramp government in its useful exertions. But the evil of this is short-lived, moderate and reparable. The inconveniences of the want of a declaration are permanent, afflicting and irreparable.

Not satisfied with merely elaborating Madison's defenses and replies, Jefferson went on to urge what he considered the affirmative side of the case. For the first time in the course of the transatlantic dialogue, he came to assert:

In the arguments in favor of a declaration of rights, you omit one which has great weight with me; the legal check which it puts into the hands of the judiciary. This is a body, which, if rendered independent and kept strictly to their own department, merits great confidence for their learning and integrity. In fact, what degree of confidence would be too much, for a body composed of such men as Wythe, Blair and Pendleton? On characters like these, the *"civium ardor prava jubentium"* [frenzy of the citizens bidding what is wrong] would make no impression.

Thus Jefferson opened his mind. First, an explicit declaration of rights was indispensable because it would furnish the judiciary with a "legal check" on aggressions against liberty. Second, to perform their function, judges must be "rendered independent." Third, the judges must be kept "strictly to their own department."[2] Fourth, good judges would be men of "learning and integrity" (like Wythe, Blair and Pendleton), whose characters would stand firm amid the storms of popular passion.

How fortunate for the constitutional dignity and efficacy of the Bill of Rights that Madison was required to wait until June 8, 1789, before addressing the Congress on the subject! By that time, when the House of Representatives at long last turned its attention to the proposed amendments, Jefferson's critically important letter had arrived in New York.[3]

In his principal speech, Madison told the House candidly that he still considered the popular community as the locus of greatest power, hence of greatest danger, in a republic. Nevertheless, he said, even if constitutional guarantees would be only "paper barriers," they might at least enlighten public opinion and inculcate respect for individual rights. With these mild currents running through it, his speech was bound to be a tepid one. It was one thing to paraphrase Jefferson and quite another to share his felt convictions.[4] Madison sounded conciliatory, reasonable, and rather detached. He seemed to doubt that even a limited protection could be devised against the people's unreasoning heat and violence. While it was quite intelligent of him to suggest that constitutional guarantees might serve as educational precepts for the community, he apparently failed to recognize that the precepts would be driven home only if court decisions would enforce them. For if the guarantees were destined to be ignored in court, they would become very ineffectual pedagogues of republican ideals; worse yet, they would provoke mockery and cynicism. At bottom, I think, Madison tended during this period of his development to underestimate — as Jefferson did not — the profound adverseness of interest between the governors and the governed in *any* political society (except only the direct, participating self-government of a town meeting).

Nevertheless, in presenting the proposed amendments to Congress, Madison did declare the momentous doctrine he had derived from

Jefferson's letter. Not having assimilated it entirely, he expressed it on this occasion with a mechanical absoluteness which was not characteristic of him. He mentioned no qualifications. The First Congress was frankly and explicitly informed that the sponsors of the Bill of Rights expected the judges to "consider themselves in a peculiar manner the guardians of those rights." Madison told the House:

> If they [the rights] are incorporated into the constitution, independent tribunals of justice will consider themselves in a peculiar manner the guardians of those rights; they will be an impenetrable bulwark against every assumption of power in the legislative or executive; they will be naturally led to resist every encroachment upon rights expressly stipulated for in the constitution by the declaration of rights.

A CURIOUS DEBATE: SHOULD THERE BE A BILL OF RIGHTS?

At this stage, one might expect that chance, having postponed Madison's principal address until Jefferson's letter arrived, had fulfilled its role and would withdraw from the narrative. But there was another unpredictable happening ahead, which would have momentous consequences in constitutional law. The episode was as brief as it was strange.

In view of the novelty of the amendment provisions in Article V of the Constitution, Madison may well have entertained doubts as to the proper mode of proceeding.[5] Nevertheless, by June 8 when he addressed the Congress, he had a definite method to propose: The way to amend the Constitution was to insert new matter in the appropriate places of the existing text and simply replace old words and phrases with new words and phrases that would supersede them. People had been complaining that certain safeguards should have been included in the Philadelphia document; very well, let that be done now by incorporating the provisions where it was claimed they had belonged from the start. This was Madison's interpretation of the amending procedure contemplated under Article V.

In the episode Madison's chief adversary was to be old Roger Sherman, experienced, skillful, "as cunning as the Devil." On June 8, 1789, Judge Sherman was satisfied to take the floor briefly and express his general opposition to a bill of rights. He saw no need for one; moreover, only time and experience would show what specific amendments were desirable. Since Connecticut, his state, had not insisted on a bill of rights as a condition to ratifying the Constitution, Sherman's position was entirely comfortable. He let matters take their course until August 13, when the committee appointed in June to consider proposed amendments brought in its report.

At this juncture, Sherman rose to insist, "We ought not to interweave our propositions into the work itself, because it will be destructive of the whole fabric"; and he moved that all amendments be made by way of addition and supplement to the existing constitutional text. The motion precipitated a long and intricate debate. Madison's chief interest was in avoiding further delay; the difference between the two procedures, he insisted, was only a matter of form; Sherman's motion would "so far unhinge the business, as to occasion alterations in every article and clause of the report." Some very penetrating arguments having been exchanged, Sherman's motion was voted on and defeated. Apparently this setback did not dismay the old judge, who knew well that the first vote is not always the decisive one. When on August 19 the House again considered the amendments as a committee of the whole, Sherman renewed his motion. After what amounted to a repetition of the earlier debate, the motion was carried by two-thirds of the House. Madison acquiesced, and the Sherman procedure became a permanently established constitutional practice.

In certain respects, the episode could hardly have been more paradoxical. Had it not been for Roger Sherman's insistence, our basic guarantees would have been sprayed over the constitutional text instead of being assembled in a single, integrated bill of rights. One would think it fairly apparent that a declaration of rights could exert greater educational influence on the general population if it was adopted in a unitary and consecutive form. Yet Madison, expounder of the importance of community opinion and the educational value of written guarantees, did not perceive this at all. On the opposite side, we find equal incongruity. Roger Sherman, who declared himself opposed to the libertarian amendments, nevertheless recommended — and achieved — the very amendatory procedure best suited to invest them with life and force. I suggest that, in Sherman's case, it was the pull of professional experience and craftsmanship that overcame competing motivations. He seems to have reasoned, in effect, that if the laymen were resolved to have their written guarantees, the lawyers must at least show them the proper and artificial way to go about it.

As we know, the assembling of the guarantees in a unified bill did considerably more than increase their educational value. In constitutional law, the impact of Roger Sherman's motion was to prove momentous and permanent. It introduced a new factor in the theory of civil liberties, for it conferred *contextuality* on the first ten amendments.

This attribute of contextuality has influenced whole areas of later constitutional doctrine. Consider, for example, the long period during which the Supreme Court used the Tenth Amendment as the avenue of approach to other portions of the Bill of Rights. (Under Madison's proposal, the basic guarantees would have been tucked away in sections 6, 9 and 10 of Article I and section 2 of Article III; and what was to become the Tenth Amendment would have stood far away from them in an Article VII.) Again, consider the decisions of the most recent years, those of the decade since World War II. In several of these, the specific prohibitions of the Bill of Rights have been treated as though they were mere adjuncts to the Due Process Clause's overall requirement of reasonableness. Whether it was the arm of destiny or the finger of partisanship or only the impulse of professional competence that prevailed in Congress along with Roger Sherman, the forces he set moving in the summer of 1789 are more active and prominent today than ever. The *laissez faire* jurists of our time choose the Due Process Clause as their habitual perspective position, while the libertarian jurists usually prefer a much firmer point of vantage; nevertheless, both groups follow the practice of construing the first ten amendments as a unified, organic text. That is how, within the framework of the Bill of Rights, it has become possible to speak of the functional "firstness" of this or that particular amendment.

MAY THE RIGHTS BE GRADED?

Point by point, we have so far identified historical archetypes for articles in the libertarian creed of our own time: (a) the declaration of explicit constitutional guarantees, (b) the reliance on judges for enforcement within the orbit of their competence, and (c) the adherence to a unified Bill of Rights. Except for one important element, our picture shows that a libertarian jurist of the present day — for example, Justice Hugo L. Black — may claim continuity with the original republican tradition. A critical element, however, remains for testing. The question is: Are there also eighteenth-century precedents to sanction modern libertarians in *grading* the respective guarantees?

Here we have the central battleground where current philosophies meet and clash. If a judge responds to the contextuality of the Bill of Rights by reading the whole bill in terms of the Due Process Clause, he may construe other clauses, which contain absolute prohibitions, as though they merely specified and illustrated an overall criterion of reasonableness; and he may go much further. His approach will prompt him to conclude that that is reasonable which the legislature has, by enacting it, found to be reasonable. Of course, this conclusion is not at all incompatible with bewailing what, in a particular instance, the legislature has seen fit to do; judicial opinions of the *laissez faire* school are often accompanied by hand-wringing, some of which is quite sincere. But the result is nonetheless to make the texture of First Amendment rights look just as porous as the Due Process Clause.

For several years past, Justice Black has struggled resolutely against the *laissez faire* trend. Like other libertarian judges, he believes the Constitution confers a "preferred position" on certain guaranteed rights as against others. When governmental action restricts freedom of religion, or speech, or the press, or assembly, he refuses to let it pour at will through the wide meshes of due process. He too has been affected by the contextuality of the Bill of Rights, but with results very different from those of the *laissez faire* school. Since his attitude toward personal liberty is formed by the flat prohibitory language of the First Amendment, he approaches even the subordinate provisions of other amendments in a stiffer mood. For example, in Justice Black's axiology, the privilege against self-incrimination, instead of being linked to the Due Process Clause, its Fifth Amendment neighbor, is valued as a defense and practical implement for First Amendment freedoms. The whole philosophy rests on assigning the various guarantees to distinct classes and grades. Does the tradition furnish any precedent for this process of grading?

Before attempting an answer, it would be advisable to pause for a moment and take counsel. Suppose the answer should be affirmative. Suppose we should find some clear and persuasive eighteenth-century precedents. Would that circumstance control the Court's jurisprudence today, over a century and a half later? I should say, assuredly not. I do not think the American people unseated George III with a view to putting history in his place. The Bill of Rights is a national inheritance precisely because it has passed again and again from the dead to the living — to be used as the living find best, reinterpreted in the using, then passed along to the succeeding generation. . . . If, in the considered judgment of our time, the process of grading the rights is found to fill the immediate and the long-term needs of civil freedom, we certainly ought to grade them, whatever the eighteenth century would have done.

But to say these things does not amount to dismissing the past. If a libertarian ought not to brandish the history of the Bill of Rights like a sword or recline on it like a couch, he may at least present it before him like a shield. If he should be charged with inventing a new constitutional doctrine, he may properly show that he is only maintaining a very old one; and even if he should be convicted of deviating from Brandeis, he may still make bold to submit that he is returning to Jefferson. *Laissez faire* jurists have assigned historical arguments, among others, for treating all the rights as though they had a uniform texture. The idea of grading, they contend, ought to be abandoned because it is a recent innovation in the theory of civil liberties. By way of comment on the argument, it is worthwhile to look at three quick tableaux.

First Tableau. The year is 1787 or 1788; the place is Paris. Thomas Paine has just returned to his quarters after a long talk with Jefferson. Too excited to rest, he sits down and writes:

> After I got home, being alone and wanting amusement I sat down to explain to myself (for there is such a thing) my Ideals of natural and civil rights and the distinction between them — I send them to you to see how nearly we agree.
>
> Suppose 20 persons, strangers to each other, to meet in a country not before inhabited. Each would be a sovereign in his own natural right. His will would be his Law, — but his power, in many cases, inadequate to his right, and the consequence would be that each might be exposed, not only to each other but to the other nineteen.
>
> It would then occur to them that their condition would be much improved, if a way could be devised to exchange that quantity of danger into so much protection, so that each individual should possess the strength of the whole number. As all their rights, in the first case, are natural rights, and the exercise of those rights supported only by their own natural individual power, they would begin by distinguishing between these rights they could individually exercise fully and perfectly and those they could not.
>
> Of the first kind are the rights of thinking, speaking, forming and giving opinions, and perhaps all those which can be fully exercised by the individual without the aid of exterior assistance — or in other words, rights of personal competency — Of the second kind are those of personal protection of acquiring and possessing property, in the exercise of which the individual natural power is less than the natural right.
>
> Having drawn this line they agree to retain individually the first Class of Rights or those of personal Competency; and to detach from their personal possession the second Class, or those of defective power and to accept in lieu thereof a right to the whole power produced by a condensation of all the parts. These I conceive to be civil rights or rights of Compact, and are distinguishable from Natural rights, because in the one we act wholly in our own person, in the other we agree not to do so, but act under the guarantee of society.

The notions Paine expressed were not nearly so novel as he imagined. I should suggest that it was John Locke who transmitted the pattern — not in his *Second Treatise of Civil Government,* where scholars have searched in vain for any grading of basic rights, but in his *Essay Concerning Human Understanding.* In the latter, Locke (who may have been prompted in turn by Robert Boyle, the eminent chemist and philosopher of nature) had supplied a model of physical and metaphysical classification which his eighteenth-century American admirers could easily adopt and use for their political theories. According to Locke the qualities of any body are either "primary," like solidity, extension, figure and mobility, which "are utterly inseparable from the body, in what estate soever it be"; or "secondary," like colors, sounds and tastes, which are only "powers to produce various sensations in us by their *primary qualities*." For the educated men of the Enlightenment, it would be a short leap from Locke's grade of "primary" and "inseparable" qualities to Paine's corresponding "natural rights of personal competence"; or from Locke's grade of "secondary" and affective qualities to Paine's corresponding "rights of compact" which arise in civil society. One need only change "any body" in Locke's text to "anybody," and the rest of the pattern emerges.

Second Tableau. We are back in New York on June 8, 1789, where Madison is expounding the Bill of Rights to the House of Representatives. Far from considering the rights all of one piece, grade and texture, he classifies and reclassifies them like a virtuoso of the taxonomic art. First, he classifies the rights in order to distinguish the American problem from the English experience with Magna Carta. Magna Carta, he says, furnishes no answer because it "does not contain any one provision for the security of those rights, respecting which the people of America are most alarmed." He refers here to "the freedom of the press and rights of conscience" as "those choicest privileges of the people."

Then he reclassifies the various rights in terms of their origins. If one analyzes bills of rights, one will find:

> In some instances they assert those rights which are exercised by the people in forming and establishing a plan of Government. In other instances, they specify those rights which are retained when particular powers are given up to be exercised by the Legislature. In other instances, they specify positive rights, which may seem to result from the nature of the compact. Trial by jury cannot be considered as a natural right, but a right resulting from a social compact which regulates the action of the community, but is as essential to secure the liberty of the people as any one of the pre-existent rights of nature.

A few minutes later, he proposes still another order for grading the rights. Some guarantees are asserted against the executive, others against the legislative branch; some against the federal government as a whole, others against the state governments. Since however the greatest danger, as he believed, lay in the democratic community, the "prescriptions in favor of liberty ought to be levelled in that quarter." This third method of classifying, based on the sources and directions from which civil liberties may be menaced, is probably more representative of Madison's personal thinking than the other two. Yet, in his judgment, the result would not vary: the freedoms embodied in the First Amendment must always secure paramountcy.[6]

Third Tableau. A year and a half later. Having assumed the office of Secretary of State, Jefferson is now in Philadelphia. From Hartford, Noah Webster has sent copies of his *Essays,* one for the Secretary of State to file for copyright protection, one for Jefferson to add to his personal library. On reading the *Essays,* which are dated "New York 1788," Jefferson finds that Webster has taken him to task for advocating the adoption of a bill of rights. On December 4, 1790, in a letter replete with tact and thoughtfulness, Jefferson writes:

> A desire of being set right in your opinion, which I respect too much not to entertain that desire, induces me to hazard to you the following observations. It had become an universal and almost uncontroverted position in the several States, that the purposes of society do not require a surrender of all our rights to our ordinary governors; that there are certain portions of right not necessary to enable them to carry on an effective government, and which experience has nevertheless proved they will be constantly encroaching on, if submitted to them; that there are also certain fences which experience has proved peculiarly efficacious against wrong, and rarely obstructive of right, which yet the governing powers have ever shown a disposition to weaken and remove. Of the first kind, for instance, is freedom of religion; of the second, trial by jury, habeas corpus laws, free presses. These were the settled opinions of all the States, — of that of Virginia, of which I was writing, as well as of the others.

He went on to call the first class "unceded portions of right" and the second class "fences against wrong."

In classifying freedom of the press along with other "fences against wrong," it is not likely that Jefferson intended to derogate from the press's station and dignity as a means of free personal expression. In any case, we need not inquire now whether Jefferson's mode of grading was valid in 1790. For our purposes, it is enough to record that like others of his era he did grade the various guarantees and that, in grading them, he awarded primacy to the freedoms of conscience and personal expression.

Thus the judicial libertarianism of the American present is securely linked with a very old and genuine tradition. In insisting on the firstness of the First Amendment, modern thinkers like Hugo Black are continuing and advancing the American vision of a good society. Popular majorities being what they often are and acting as they often do, the libertarian tradition requires an extraordinarily patient, if not obstinate, fortitude. Recently Justice Black summarized the credo: "In my judgment, the very heart of the Bill of Rights is the First Amendment. Unless people can freely exercise those liberties, without loss of good name, job, property, liberty or life, a good society cannot exist. That is my faith."[7]

THE AMENDMENT IN BLACK LETTER, WRIT LARGE

It is time now to consider Hugo Black's personal contribution. Has he given anything of his own to the tradition; in what respects, if any, has he moved it forward? Before attempting to list the answers, let us first summon his sense of humor and native clemency, for if we are about to misread or misconstrue his thinking, only the former will console him and only the latter will rescue us. With these our guardians, we proceed to epitomize.

Emphasis on Text and Texture. Not very many years ago, it was modish in sophisticated liberal circles to insist that the Court ought to apply the literal text of the Constitution, as distinguished from various judge-made phrases, concepts and glosses. Only by adhering to the text, liberals were wont to argue, could the Court reconcile its own power of judicial review with the democratic postulate of majority rule; only thus could it exercise the self-discipline needed for wise adjudication. No one has taken these once-popular admonitions more seriously than Hugo Black. To him the language of the Constitution is more than a source of law, it is the only authentic commission of his office. Hence, when he comes to consider the Bill of Rights, he insists that the Court pay due regard to differences of tenor and mood in the several provisions — in short, that contextuality must not prevail to the extent of eliminating textuality.

On this reasoning, none of the schemes we have mentioned for classifying and grading the guarantees would quite suit his purpose. He would be inclined to prefer a more textual criterion for grading. And he has found one in Madison's famous phrase, likewise in the speech of June 8, 1789, distinguishing fields "in which the Government ought not to act" from fields in which it ought "to act only in a particular mode." According to Justice Black, the language of the First Amendment belongs unmistakably to the former category: it tells the authorities not to act at all. By way of contrast, the prohibition of "unreasonable" searches (Fourth Amendment) and the Due Process Clause (Fifth Amendment) contemplate that the authorities may act if only they act reasonably. To exclude absolutely is one thing; to admit yet require reasonableness is another.

Against these views of Justice Black's, it has been objected that the First Amendment's guarantee of free expression has never been taken so literally as to grant immunity from civil liability for libel or slander. If there are conceded "exceptions" of this kind, do they not prove that the seemingly rigid First Amendment must be subjected to an emollient of "reasonableness"? Does not "reasonableness" pervade our entire juridical order? Certainly Justice Black has not contended that the sponsors of the First Amendment expected it to end civil actions for defamation. I understand he would freely grant the existence of this "exception."

He would probably go on to respond that civil remedies for defamation are not only consistent with but were considered by the founding libertarians as virtually essential to the maintenance of free speech and press. Exceptions of this type, existing and recognized in 1789, may be allowed as implicit in the First Amendment so long as, on reexamination in later epochs, they can be found still compatible with the main guarantees of the text. But — he would likely add — the operation of "reasonableness" factors was exhausted by exceptions of vintage 1789. Save only for these, the solemn text of the Amendment declares precisely what the American commonwealth has decided to call "reasonable." The decision having been made and declared once for all, there remains no further factor of "reasonableness" for the Congress or the Court to evaluate. It follows that what may have been a litigable question of reasonableness *ante* the First Amendment has been taken out of the judicial province *post* the Amendment. The judges' commissions simply do not authorize them to conduct inquiries within this area. If they reopen the closed question of reasonableness, they become chargeable with a usurpation.

Emphasis on the Hither Side of the "Fences." As has been noticed, Thomas Jefferson, writing to Noah Webster, classified the basic guarantees into "unceded portions of right" and "fences against wrong," and mentioned trial by jury, habeas corpus and free presses as examples of the "fences." Here he expressed quite fairly the libertarian mind of his time. In that era, the press — which twentieth-century thought tends to associate with other forms of free personal expression

— was valued primarily for its function as political censor. Free presses were desired because they supplied the community with independent critics and censors of the government. With all their faults, they could nevertheless act like barriers against official tramps, trespassers and arsonists. This was the libertarian attitude that Jefferson espoused. As trial by jury and habeas corpus stood like fences to ward off official abuses, so too might the institution of press freedom. The fact that the governors were roving about on the far side of the fences was sufficient for him.

From the beginning, it has been evident that the "fences" themselves need unremitting attention and defense. In every generation they are gashed and rammed and undermined, often under a pretext of mending or modernizing them. As long as the fences continue to be appreciated only in a negative sense — as stockades *against* the forces on the far side instead of safeguards *for* the values on the hither side — popular support for them will probably remain flabby, uninformed, and at best spasmodic. Our generation has had ample opportunity to observe that when an administration (like Franklin D. Roosevelt's or Dwight D. Eisenhower's) gains popular approval of its major objectives, the majority of Americans do not understand why they need feel concern about inherited rules of court procedure or other refinements of method. If, as libertarians insist, the First Amendment guarantees are the really vital ones, have not these been separated and distinguished from the list of procedural "fences"? Even should the fences sway and sag here and there, civil liberty does not inhere in them but in the "unceded portions of right." By such reasoning, people who feel deeply attached to the First Amendment may come to vilipend one or another provision in the Fifth, Sixth, or Eighth. Does the firstness of the First Amendment imply unimportance of the remainder?

Hugo Black has given his answer by turning attention to the inner side of the fences. We have understood what it is the fences are intended to exclude; he asks that we also appreciate what they are placed there to protect. In his view, the firstness of the First Amendment, far from diminishing the others, works to enhance their importance. He explains:

> The first of the ten amendments erected a Constitutional shelter for the people's liberties of religion, speech, press, and assembly. This amendment reflects the faith that a good society is not static but advancing, and that the fullest possible interchange of ideas and beliefs is essential to attainment of this goal. The proponents of the First Amendment, committed to this faith, were determined that every

American should possess an unrestrained freedom to express his views, however odious they might be to vested interests whose power they might challenge.

But these men were not satisfied that the First Amendment would make this right sufficiently secure. As they well knew, history teaches that attempted exercises of the freedoms of religion, speech, press, and assembly have been the commonest occasions for oppression and persecution. Inevitably such persecutions have involved secret arrests, unlawful detentions, forced confessions, secret trials, and arbitrary punishments under oppressive laws. Therefore it is not surprising that the men behind the First Amendment also insisted upon the Fifth, Sixth, and Eighth Amendments, designed to protect all individuals against arbitrary punishment by definite procedural provisions guaranteeing fair public trials by juries. They sought by these provisions to assure that no individual could be punished except according to "due process," by which they certainly intended that no person could be punished except for a violation of definite and validly enacted laws of the land, and after a trial conducted in accordance with the specific procedural safeguards written in the Bill of Rights. If occasionally these safeguards worked to the advantage of an ordinary criminal, that was a price they were willing to pay for the freedom they cherished.[8]

Here the Bill of Rights is revealed anew, in a fresh and original perspective. Suddenly the sections fall into their destined places, and a grand organic design stands out. The "fences," we see, do much more than channel, control or obstruct the currents of official action. They constitute the indispensable ministers and defenders of First Amendment freedom. Without them, the promises of free worship, speech and press become a mockery. In Justice Black's view, a legislative, executive or judicial mandate that impairs the guarantee of trial by jury or the privilege against self-incrimination puts every substantive liberty — including liberty of conscience — in jeopardy. If Americans are resolved to remain free, they will defend these fences as uncompromisingly as, in former times, citizens would defend their city walls.

The Ideal of an Edified Society. Now we have reached Justice Black's most creative contribution to the theory of the First Amendment. In the course of the great dialogue between Madison and Jefferson about the desirability of a bill of rights, neither correspondent took a naively exalted view of the democratic community. Madison saw in it the chief source of danger to civil liberty; Jefferson, while urging the people's case for guarantees against official oppression, was concerned more with safeguarding the elementary rights of individuals than with raising the level of the social group.[9] Dwelling as he did in Paris and attending successive stages of the incipient French Revolution, he fully recognized the risks and evils of democracy. He referred to them in Horace's tidy phrase, *"civium ardor prava jubentium"* (frenzy of the citizens bidding what is wrong), and when he quoted Horace to Madison, it was not French but American behavior that was under consideration. In Jefferson's outlook of 1788–1790, a nation's claim to a declaration of rights could not be made to depend on the people's proving their discipline, wisdom or judgment. Since every government tended in some degree to encroach on basic liberties, all should be required to subscribe to solemn guarantees. Barricades in the Paris streets and Shays' Rebellion in Massachusetts were lively incidents, true, but any American who considered them impediments to a bill of rights must be either congenitally timorous or disingenuous. The focus ought to be placed and kept on the faults and wrongdoings of the *governors*.

It has been very difficult for First Amendment theory to move beyond this point. From the beginning, the Supreme Court has declined to determine questions of constitutionality unless the person seeking the decision could show he had legal standing to sue. When the rights in issue pertain to the First Amendment, the Court has expected to hear appeals from the individuals who were molested in their worship, or arrested for their speech or censored or impeded in their printing, or prevented from assembling to petition for redress of grievances. If a person's own rights had been injured, he could sue; otherwise not.

How, then, was the general community likely to come into view under this system? In only two ways: (a) in the course of denying a plea for some First Amendment freedom, the community might be pictured as susceptible to provocation, or seditious influence, or corruption; or (b) the community, represented by its duly constituted officials, might be before the court to argue for the validity of a law regulating or repressing some claimed First Amendment right. In either event, it would always be the individual or group of individuals on one side, speaking on behalf of freedom, and the community officially or tacitly on the other side, speaking at best for orderliness, quietness or unlittered streets, and at worst for persecution of unpopular cults and causes.

These circumstances, proper though they were for *jurisdictional* purposes, established a badly distorted *social* background for First Amendment litigations. Various *laissez faire* jurists proceeded to exploit the distortion. They took his extraneous datum, which the Court's own doctrines had manufactured, and purported to discover in it a preestablished, inflexible hierarchy of interests. Whoever might come before them as spokesman of First Amendment freedom was required to be an individual; ergo, his interest was to be labeled "an individual interest" of one kind or another. On the other hand, whoever might appear for the government was automatically dubbed the spokesman of "a public or social interest." Thus, in a typical opinion composed by a *laissez faire* judge — despite the parade of precedents and the show of reluctance and the business of weighing one interest against another — the whole question would be begged from the start and the result would be a foregone conclusion. Rare instances there have been when even such judges have allowed the so-called "individual interest" to prevail; but in these exceptional cases one generally finds that ulterior, corrupt motives impelling the prosecution were simply too obvious to be ignored. In sum, a purported "jurisprudence of interests," read anachronistically into the First Amendment, has become a familiar tool of *laissez faire*. It is quite analogous in its use to the purported "natural law" that stodgy minds of past eras were accustomed to read into the Due Process Clause. But while lawyers are generally able today to see through the old reactionary nomenclature of "natural law" immutables, a jargon of "weighing the interests" can still take them in. The truth of the matter is that even if two conflicting or competing interests could somehow be weighed against each other, a judge might "fix" his own scale in half a dozen different ways before the alleged "weighing" began.

Justice Black has furnished the answer to this game of false balances. In the celebrated *Marsh* and *Tucker* opinions, among others,[10] he presents the libertarian ideal of an edified and advancing community. Where would we really find the principal danger to civil liberty in a republic? Not in the governors as governors, not in the governed as governed, but in the governed unequipped to function as governors. The chief enemies of republican freedom are mental sloth, conformity, bigotry, superstition, credulity, monopoly in the market of ideas, and utter, benighted ignorance. Relying as it does on the consent of the governed, representative government cannot succeed unless the community receives enough information to grasp public issues and make sensible decisions. As lights which may have been enough for the past do not meet the needs of the present, so present lights will not suffice for the more extensive and complex problems of the future. Heretofore public enlightenment may have been only a manifest desideratum; today it constitutes an imperative necessity. The First Amendment, says Justice Black, "reflects the faith that a good society is not static but advancing, and that the fullest possible interchange of ideas and beliefs is essential to attainment of this goal."[11]

If, therefore, judges should still insist on using the nomenclature of "interests," what higher *public* interest is there than enlightenment of the electors, and what higher *social* interest than the intellectual advancement of the community? Not alone the speaker, missionary, writer or printer, has a stake in the First Amendment; the whole conglomerate mass of the community audience is involved,[12] including those who are almost sure they will never wish to speak and those who are completely sure they do not wish to listen. Under Black's doctrine, no one is required to listen, but even a unanimous unwillingness to listen does not justify repression, for an advancing society must be free to revise its judgment on this score as well as on others. The audience has the indefinitely continuing right to be exposed to an ideological variety; it will not be heard at any one period of time to renounce exercising the right in other, future periods.

Justice Black's ideal carries an ambitious compliment for the democratic audience. He assumes, in effect, that if given access to the various facts and contentions, the members of the audience are generally rational enough to identify, and well-intentioned enough to choose the better, wiser, more beneficial of alternative courses. Or at least, that though this method of political decision may be faulty, any other method would prove disastrously worse. Since ancient days when the stubborn backsliding Israelites made life difficult for Moses, no nation has ever complied satisfactorily with the ordinances of its finest preceptors; nor, for that matter, has any of the preceptors lived with perfect consistency on the plane of his own teachings. Yet considerations like these need not cloud a sincere democratic faith. They only demonstrate that social progress involves continual striving and that men strive for what lies beyond them rather than for what they already possess. In Justice Black's hands, the Bill of Rights is directed toward the values that lie beyond. He reads it as a people's charter of edification, and postulates the kind of national community whose practices would do daily honor to the First Amendment. It would be an American community not unworthy of Madison's and Jefferson's best aspirations.

The practical fulfillment requires certain cultivated traits of mind and character. They are the traits Jefferson specified to Madison when he recommended looking to the judges to enforce a bill of rights. He cited the names of Pendleton, Blair and Wythe. The consummate qualities they exemplified in their generation, Hugo Black exemplifies in ours. When, after mentioning those great figures, Jefferson went on to quote a phrase out of Horace, he probably intended to invoke the remainder of the strophe. It sings of justice and integrity:

Iustum et tenacem propositi virum	*The just man firm of purpose turns*
non civium ardor prava iubentium	*aside*
non vultus instantis tyranni	*Neither for fury of the mob in power,*
mente quatit solida, neque Auster. . . .	*Nor in the presence of the tyrant's*
	pride;
	Nor can the stormy South wind make
	him cower. . . .[13]

It is these classic republican virtues that will ultimately maintain the firstness of the First Amendment.

From the Yale Law Journal, *1956.*

The Parchment Barriers

THERE is no denying that the twentieth century has been almost continually in contempt of court. With little tact and less mercy, it has disclosed one after another of the seamy aspects of judicial office and the judicial process. It continues its revelations relentlessly. Unfolding immediately before our eyes is one of its greatest dramas — I might almost say, one of its greatest tragedies — the degradation of law, the courts and the judiciary in the Republic of South Africa.

Most of us are acquainted with the South African government's general policy of apartheid, with some of its practical details, and with its blighting effect on the social, economic, political and moral status of the country. But few of us have attempted to put ourselves in the position of a decent South African judge whose very office calls on him to enforce the laws and regulations of apartheid hour by hour and day by day.

For Americans, it is important to remember that apartheid does not even pretend equivalence to the doctrine of "separate but equal" that our Supreme Court repudiated once and for all in 1954. Apartheid is a throwback well enough, but not to the early part of the twentieth century or the later part of the nineteenth; if we desire an analogy in American history, we must term it a throwback to the period before the Civil War. In short, what has befallen the South African native is a status not merely of segregation but also of peonage and involuntary servitude.

Every native is required to have with him at all times a so-called "reference book" or "passbook" with an identity card, data covering his employment, and information about his agricultural classification, plus a whole dossier of permits and official certificates. Every year many thousands of natives are arrested under the regulations, incarcerated in private jails built by the farmers' associations, summarily sentenced to prison terms, and then rented out by the farmers' associations or by the Prisons Department at a price that, according to a recent study, ranged from nine pence to two shillings per day per convict.

Ten years ago the government extended the "reference book" or "passbook" system to include women. Showing the kind of spirit we should expect of women, spontaneous demonstrations and passbook bonfires broke out in all parts of the Union. Thereupon the government canceled the old-age pensions of the protesting women and even the pensions of their husbands and fathers. It refused to accept tax payments from the husbands and fathers, thus leaving them open to criminal prosecution for failing to pay taxes. Women without passes could not participate in legal marriage. They were denied the right to medical care. In addition the courts sent the women to jail on the theory that in burning the passbooks they had destroyed government property.

The apartheid policy reaches implacably into every aspect of social life. The churches of the country were instructed to enforce it and when all protested except the Nationalists' Church, the law shifted the main burden of enforcement to the natives, under criminal penalties. According to a recent statute, a court may punish a clergyman, even to the extent of whipping, if, actuated by religious faith and conscience, he advises his flock not to let apartheid hold sway within the walls of the church.

By now there is not an institution of society or area of activity that apartheid has not infected. One might imagine, for example, that taxation at least would be the same for the natives as for the whites; after all, pounds, shillings and pence mean as much and as little to the government, whoever may pay them. Money does not know differences between races; nor does it share the nightmare fears that can drive a government to racial persecution. If anything is neutral, it is money.

But not in South Africa! In South Africa even money and government taxes are race-conscious. A white man pays his income tax on net income while a native pays his on gross income without deductions or exemptions. I suppose there are two possible reasons for this: one is that the natives may as well give their money to the government because they are not permitted to do much else with it; the other is that they ought to pay higher taxes because they get so many special favors, benefits and protections from the government. Whoever can believe that this system makes sense can believe anything; he can even believe that South Africa, alone in the world, is somehow exempt from the laws of retribution that govern the destinies of men and nations.

While the persecution continues and the regulations become more inhumane, cruel and sadistic year by year, what have the judges of South Africa been doing? Let me say at the outset that although the judges have furnished no instance or token of true egalitarianism, they have made a general record of fairness, decency and moderation. Some observers tell us that recent appointments to the bench have been confined to extreme Nationalists and have impaired the previous quality of the courts. Whatever this may augur for the future, it is only fair to say that during the past crucial decade most of the judges have done what they could.

The Nationalist government came into power in 1948. Since the overwhelming majority of the natives had long since been deprived of the right to vote, the only important impediment that remained on the scene consisted in the limited voting rights of the so-called "coloured" group, the descendants of unions between Malays or Europeans and Hottentots or Bantus. The qualified males among the "coloured" group had good reason to feel secure in their right to vote, since the South Africa Act guaranteed this right. The South Africa Act also provided that only a two-thirds majority of both houses of Parliament sitting together could amend the clause that contained the guarantee.

In 1951 the Nationalists pushed an act through Parliament to disenfranchise the "coloured" voters. The highest court (which they call their "appellate division") unanimously struck down the law as unconstitutional because it had not been passed by the required two-thirds vote of the combined houses of Parliament. Infuriated by the decision, the Parliament passed a law declaring itself to be the highest court in the land, dubbing itself "the High Court of Parliament," and claiming the right to reverse what the appellate division had decided. The judges of the appellate division responded like men. They held this law to be unconstitutional.

It was an unequal contest, and the judges must have sensed that sooner or later they would have to retreat before the Nationalist juggernaut. The Nationalists' next step was predictably obvious. They simply passed a law that greatly increased the membership of the South African Senate, then packed the Senate with a flood of Nationalist additions, and thus obtained the two-thirds vote in the combined houses that was constitutionally indispensable. In 1957, when this maneuver came before the appellate division, the judges, with a single dissent, yielded to it. It was a transparent fraud, a grave political injustice and an insult to the spirit of their constitution. But it did conform to the letter of the law and, when one considers how long the appellate division offered the example of an inspiring resistance and how dismally the majority of the white population failed to rise to the occasion and rally behind the example, one can only bemoan the demise of the rule of law in South Africa.

What is a decent man in a judicial robe to do under circumstances like these? Almost everything that could be done was done. For example, particularly in the early years of apartheid the judges assumed that the government meant to treat the natives fairly and humanely, and if a statute said nothing on the subject, the judges interpreted it as imposing such requirements and standards. But this never succeeded long. The government invariably responded by amending the law in such a way as to make perfectly clear that they did not intend any such restraint as the judges had inferred. On the contrary, they explicitly announced an opposite purpose.

For a while, when a government bureaucrat threatened to remove a native from his place and home or from the neighborhood in which he earned his living, the judges would issue an injunction forbidding the removal until a court hearing could be held on its legality. This help too was soon stifled. In 1956 the Nationalist Parliament passed a law prohibiting all natives who were threatened with ejection, removal or arrest for the purpose of ejection or removal from obtaining any injunction that might interfere with the execution of the administrator's order.

What is a judge to do? For hundreds of years the tradition that these judges inherited had been admonishing them that the voice of Parliament was the law, and the only legitimate law, of the land. Ever since the sixteenth and seventeenth centuries, the struggle for political liberty had taken the form of a struggle for parliamentary supremacy. A parliament was the only offset, the only counterweight to the absolute power of Tudors, Stuarts or the House of Hanover.

The judge's function, they had been told a thousand times, was not to legislate, but only to enforce the statutes he received from the Parliament. To set up his own ideals and standards against those furnished by the legislature not only would be undemocratic, it would be a breach of ethics, a violation of duty, a usurpation.

At first the Nationalist storm — like Hitler's and Mussolini's too — did not seem so very ominous. Exercising a judicious moderation, the judges must have assumed that they could weather it. They must have believed that it would subside, that campaign slogans would be moderated in the Nationalists' practical actions and that equilibrium and sobriety would soon return. But what can the judges believe now?

What are they to do? Some — probably an increasing number — experience no pangs of conscience or moral dilemma, since they are themselves products of the apartheid policy. Others may remain mute out of sheer anxiety, conscious that the nation has embarked on a suicidal course and that they and their families are being swept to a general destruction. If they resign from the bench, the government will replace them with its rabid zealots. Perhaps, if they remain at their posts, they may find opportunities to temper the harshness of decrees. But even as they reassure themselves in this fashion, they must wonder whether the reassurance is not mere rationalization and turpitude of conscience. Meanwhile, new laws and regulations close in on them from day to day. For example, under the so-called Sabotage Act of 1962, a native who only goes on strike for better wages or living conditions can be held to have committed sabotage, which is punishable by death. At what point does one halt and refuse when one has already gone so far and acquiesced in so much?

In this condition of affairs the usual voices will be heard advocating that we return to natural law and rely on it to cure the maladies of the age. They will recommend that the South African judges resolve the dilemma simply by declaring that the apartheid legislation, in all its roots and branches, violates natural law and is therefore no law at all. Natural law, they tell us, is the panacea.

The sad truth is that natural law is no more dependable than other widely advertised panaceas. It boasts an old and noteworthy tradition, going back at least as far as the ancient Stoics. In Grotius's version it helped to rationalize the beginnings of international law. In John Locke's version it furnished our Founding Fathers with the ideology they needed to justify the Declaration of Independence. We owe gratitude to the long line of libertarians and egalitarians who expressed their ideals in the language of natural law.

But gratitude, becoming though it is, is no substitute for honest and realistic thinking. History shows us that natural law is a flag that anyone can nail to his mast. It has been used to justify slavery as well as freedom, persecution as well as fairness, exploitation as well as equality. In ancient Athens the Sophists contended that nothing conformed so much to natural law as homosexuality, else why would so many men and women practice it? As for the apartheid program in South Africa, cannot the Nationalists contend, as Plato did, that only those whom nature has endowed with superior ethnic stock and qualified to rule should exercise political power? How often have tyrants boasted that the strong are designed by nature to dominate the weak? Aristotle in his day, Cicero in his and John C. Calhoun in his were willing to defend the institution of slavery on the ground that some men and some nations were slaves by nature. The history of the tradition proves that natural law will vouch for any proposition in the whole register of moral values — from the saintly all the way down to the very worst.

Since natural law systems are so numerous and diverse, one wonders how they dare lay claim, as they do, to being fixed, eternal and immutable. On certain psychological types the effect of the mere claim is curiously soothing. The sequence of verbal sedatives — words like "fixed, eternal and immutable" — seems to bring an almost hypnotic repose to minds that are troubled in a world of flux. If you are desperately unsure about your convictions, it may relax and comfort you to call them laws of nature and thereby summon the whole physical universe to their support. Oddly enough, at the other extreme, if you feel quite dogmatic about your convictions, you are likely to do much the same thing, that is, insist that whatever you believe the entire cosmos is required to practice. Thus, at least in our time, many statements of natural law theory amount to a sort of cosmic imperialism, taking in more territory than the Russian claims to the moon. It makes no difference whether what they cloak is an extreme incertitude or an extreme certitude, for both of these may be symptoms of one and the same pathological condition.

The only natural law precepts that possess even a specious certainty and stability are those proclaimed by the Roman Catholic Church. As anyone can see, when the church gives doctrinal status to so-called propositions of natural law, what looks like certainty and uniformity is due not at all to natural law but to the church, the authority of the church and the discipline of the church. Non-Catholics also accept many of these propositions, like the contents of the Ten Commandments — not as doctrines of the church or of natural law, but as good, sound moral principles. On the other hand, non-Catholics may vehemently reject some of them, such as the proposition that the law of nature and sound morals forbid the use of contraceptives. The uniformity does not reside in natural law but in the specific ecclesiastical institution that declares it. Outside the Catholic Church there are countless competing natural law systems, as many, in fact, as there are writers on the subject. Hence the only sensible way for a secular judge to ascertain whether the claims of natural law have any worth is to take a practical test case and see what it shows. Putting the matter concretely: If, as its adherents contend, natural law could solve the judges' problem in South Africa, how did it solve the similar problem of Catholic judges in Nazi Germany and Fascist Italy? Let us look at the record.

What use did the German judges, Catholic or non-Catholic, make of natural law? What did they do with natural law when they were confronted with the cruel legislation of the Hitler regime? A German expert reports: "Two groups deserve the place of honor among those who made their scholarship subservient to the Nazi ends: the . . . biologists and the jurists. . . . The jurists . . . spared no effort in molding the abstruse ideas of the new rulers into clear-cut articles of law and directives and in defending the legality of the measures taken." Another German expert says: "The whole profession is to be blamed for a high degree of guilt and for having brought great disaster upon itself and the German people." A third expert writes: "They acted as 'yes-men.' Instead of leading in the field of at least intellectual resistance to a criminal system, they readily joined it as followers and in quite a few instances even as activists. In all the prolific literature of the German Resistance, little if anything can be read about the members of the legal profession. Most, if not all, German jurists of the Hitler period were far from becoming martyrs in the defense of justice. Quite a few of them acted as hangman's assistants in the extermination of justice. . . ."

Suppose we turn our eyes to Fascist Italy where it can be said that all of the judges were fully conversant with the doctrine of natural law. What do we find there? As you will recall, Mussolini eventually installed the entire fabric of the infamous Nazi Nuremberg laws. According to a prominent Italian jurist, Professor Paolo Barile of the University of Siena, no one can remember a single instance of a judge's offering his resignation or making any other gesture that might have served the purpose of protest. No single judge refused to apply a Fascist law on the ground that it violated the law of nature. Professor Barile concludes: "It does not seem to me that the Italian judges made a better showing than the German judges." Yet had not the education of these judges, at least in its philosophical and ethical aspects, been saturated with natural law? It is a woeful record, in Italy as in Germany, and a humiliating commentary on the pretensions of natural law. The entire episode proves that Judge Jerome Frank was right when he remarked, "Man does not find his 'oughts' spelled out for him in nature, he puts them there."

If natural law furnishes no remedy for the South African judges, what about the common law? Did not Lord Coke say in a famous dictum that an act of Parliament that violated the common law would be pronounced null and void? Yes, he did utter such a dictum, but for the ensuing three hundred years the law of England has uniformly contradicted it. To the British judge the voice of Parliament has long since become the voice of God. Whatever Parliament may ordain, no matter how repressive or unjust, becomes the law of the land. British judges have allowed themselves to become subservient to every passing majority in Parliament.

This subservience is so extreme in England that the judges will not even move the common law forward by reconsidering and overruling any of their old decisions that were mistaken in the first place or became obsolete. If Parliament does not correct them, the old unsuitable precedents must go on forever. Recently Lord Justice Devlin summarized the situation as follows: "The common law has now, I think, no longer the strength to provide any satisfactory solution to the problem of keeping the executive . . . under appropriate control." He recognized that the attitude of the British judges provided what he called "nothing but a death certificate" for the common law. If the common law of England cannot even survive, how can it furnish judges with the intellectual principles and moral courage that they would need to defy an act of legislation?

Shortly before our nation was founded, a Swiss political scientist named Delolme uttered an aphorism that has been repeated ever since. He said, "The English Parliament can do everything, except making a woman a man, or a man a woman." As though this statement did not go far enough, twentieth-century English jurists protest against Delolme's exception because, they insist, the legislation of Parliament can treat a woman like a man and a man like a woman. Quite a thought! If *this* is what Parliament has been attempting in recent years, it may account for the interesting confusion we observe in certain social relationships. It may also explain the themes of many current books and dramas. Parliament omnicompetent? Nonsense; like the American Congress, it is often so incompetent that one is tempted to exclaim, as Horace Walpole did shortly after Delolme's statement, "There is nothing a majority in Parliament can do, but outvote a minority."

There are several important respects in which the English notion of freedom would be sorely inadequate for Americans. Of course it was inadequate in 1776 when we declared our independence, in 1787 when we drafted our Constitution, and in 1789 when we drafted our Bill of Rights. Despite England's subsequent advances and various shortcomings of our own, the standards of liberty that Englishmen seem to accept are not high enough for us.

Let me take a few elementary examples. The fact that England has an officially established church, together with all its practical implications, is a condition obnoxious to American principles. We should regard any form of establishment as violating the rights of conscience of all citizens, Christians and Jews, Protestants and Catholics, believers, unbelievers and doubters. Establishment is so oppressive an institution that it does not even spare those persons who belong to the established church. It wrongs everyone, every conscience. Not many years ago the clergy of the Church of England, after spending some fourteen years in preparing a revised prayer book, submitted the revisions to Parliament, which English law required them to do. Naturally, many of the members of Parliament did not belong to the established church; many were Protestant Dissenters, Catholics, Jews, atheists. In two successive Parliaments the House of Commons, so constituted, rejected the revisions that had been solemnly approved by the Church's House of Bishops, House of Clergy and House of Laity. This sort of political interference in the very means of worship would be intolerable to Americans.

Consider other freedoms. In England it is still necessary to obtain the Lord Chamberlain's license before one can present a play to the public. In the United States all such previous restraints on the performance of a drama are unconstitutional.

The authority of the English judges has succumbed not only to Parliament but also to any executive official whom Parliament may choose to clothe with irresponsible power. For example, in 1939 by authority of Parliament it was decreed that if the Home Secretary had reasonable cause to believe any person to be of hostile origin or associations and that it was necessary to exercise control over him, the person could be arrested and held in prison or wherever the Home Secretary might choose to detain him. Various persons having been imprisoned in this cavalier way, one of them, a man by the name of Liversidge, applied to the courts, claiming that he was held illegally and asking merely to be told the grounds on which the Home Secretary thought he had reasonable cause to hold him. Liversidge lost his case in the King's Bench Division, lost again in the Court of Appeal and lost (four to one) in the House of Lords. The House of Lords decided that an English court could not even request the grounds of the Home Secretary's belief, much less ascertain whether they were reasonable. The lone dissenter, Lord Atkin, protested that the arguments in the case "might have been addressed acceptably to the Court of King's Bench in the time of Charles I." And these were the arguments that prevailed.

Civil liberties are not dead or moribund in England. But since Parliament can ignore Magna Carta whenever it chooses, they are neither robust nor secure enough to provide a standard for others to emulate. Not by the natural law, not by the common law, will judges rescue their integrity in our time.

Surely we cannot leave the judicial office in such a slough of despond, nor can we hope to obtain conscientious judges if we subject them to the performance of morally repulsive duties. There must be some way out.

I believe that there is and that the essence of the matter begins to emerge as soon as we ask how American judges have managed to escape this sort of moral dilemma. American judges have indeed escaped it, and the means is quite plain. It consists in what the men of the eighteenth century described condescendingly as "parchment barriers." We have gradually learned to prize the parchment barriers as our most vital possessions, vital in the sense that our national life depends on them, equally vital in the sense that we must be prepared, if necessary, to lay down our lives for them. We call these parchment barriers our Bill of Rights.

Four men at the beginning of our history did all that was needful to make the office of the twentieth-century American judge morally viable as the office of the South African judge cannot be. It is pleasant to note that these four were not of one political faction or party, but that two of them were Federalists and conservatives, and the other two Democratic-Republicans and libertarians.

Suppose we consider the conservatives first. The Constitution having been drafted in Philadelphia in 1787, Hamilton, Madison and Jay advocated its adoption in *The Federalist* papers. In May 1788, Hamilton published the famous *Federalist* number 78, which expounded the American doctrine of judicial review in terms that hold true to this day. Pointing out that the Constitution forbade Congress to pass bills of attainder and *ex post facto* laws, he said, "Limitations of this kind can be preserved in practice no other way than through the medium of the courts of justice; whose duty it must be to declare all acts contrary to the manifest tenor of the constitution void. Without this, all the reservations of particular rights or privileges would amount to nothing." Years later, in 1803, Chief Justice Marshall would follow the line of Hamilton's reasoning in the 78th *Federalist* and issue the landmark decision of *Marbury v. Madison*.

On the libertarian side the record is equally clear. As soon as Jefferson, who was serving as American Minister in Paris, received a copy of the draft Constitution, he demanded that it be corrected to include a bill of rights. . . . Spurred by Jefferson's incessant demand, the supporters of the Philadelphia draft pledged themselves to add a bill of rights immediately after ratification, and the task of redeeming the pledge fell on James Madison. Madison's letters show that he understood a bill of rights would be "a standard for trying the validity of public acts, and a signal for rousing and uniting the superior forces of the community"; but, possibly because he was not a lawyer, Madison did not at first perceive that the judges might play a leading role in enforcing the Bill of Rights. . . . In a letter dated March 15, 1789, Jefferson called Madison's attention to this all-important factor. . . .

When Madison rose to address the House and submit the Bill of Rights, he was prepared to depend on the judges. He told Congress, "If [the basic rights] are incorporated into the constitution, independent tribunals of justice will consider themselves in a peculiar manner the guardians of those rights; they will be an impenetrable bulwark against every assumption of power in the legislative or executive; they will be naturally led to resist every encroachment upon rights expressly stipulated for in the constitution by the declaration of rights." Jefferson, who demanded the Bill of Rights, and Madison, who composed it, relied explicitly on the judges to make it a living reality.

In fairness I should also mention an important incident during the Constitutional Convention of 1787 that scholars have generally overlooked. When the convention took up the famous clause that forbids *ex post facto* laws (laws making an act criminal after it is done although it was innocent when it was done), several delegates objected that the provision would be ineffectual and futile. But Hugh Williamson of North Carolina swung a majority of seven states to three in favor of the clause. How did he convince them that it would have practical value? He said, "The judges can take hold of it." Here, in this incident of August 22, 1787, even before the time of *The Federalist* papers and the Bill of Rights, we see Americans depending on the judges and consciously furnishing them with an authoritative text.

Now the critical difference becomes evident between the decent American judge and his South African counterpart. It does not consist of a difference of convictions or principles; it consists rather in the plain fact that the American judge who desires to preserve liberty and equality has been provided with a constitutional text, and the South African has not.

Why should a text be so important to a judge? This is one of the most interesting questions in the philosophy of law. Without an authoritative text the modern democratic judge may or may not be willing to overrule an earlier *judicial* decision; he will certainly decline to overrule or annul a *legislative* decision.

The modern democratic judge shrinks from the burden of unlimited authority that the advocates of a so-called higher natural law would confer on him. Since there is no authoritative secular text in which he can find the rules of natural law, the proposed authority would be boundless. It would leave him at large, free to convert his whims and prejudices into the supreme law of the land. He knows enough about the prejudices of his brothers on the bench to mistrust his own. He needs a text as a chart to control their will and his.

Once he receives a formal text, the judge's position is entirely different. He feels equipped with legitimate standards of decision and ready to perform his functions independently and manfully.

To the judge the text represents both authority and responsibility. It is his authority not only for what he undertakes to decide, but also for how he ultimately decides it. It is the criterion of his responsibility because it enables the parties before him and the general public to ascertain whether he has decided correctly, reasonably, rightly. Thus the text is the beginning and also the end of his process of judging. As he judges by it, he knows he will be judged by it. Gladly he welcomes parchment barriers.

Although America's parchment barriers have not always succeeded (neither Jefferson nor Madison believed that they always would), they have served so well that they need no extraneous justification. It is enough that the people need and will continue to need them. Nevertheless we discover now that they do have a justification beyond anything contemplated by the Founding Fathers. The twentieth century has demonstrated that the judges as well as the people require them. Humane judges must have the authority of a bill of rights.

If this is so (and surely the evidence of current history shows that it is), then every democratic nation owes its judges a bill of rights with which they can safeguard basic human privileges and immunities. In the deepest moral sense, it is no longer optional to adopt or not to adopt a national bill of rights; it has become a categorical duty. The American judge can look compassionately at his brother on the South African bench and say, "There, but for the Bill of Rights, go I."

The twentieth century impels us beyond even Jefferson's position. In his time it was enough to say, "The people are entitled to a bill of rights against every government on earth." Facing the inhumanities of our own day we must add, "and judges too are entitled to a bill of rights against every democratic legislature and executive on earth." The experience of the South African judges points an unmistakable moral: Every democratic nation owes a solemn obligation to its judges to adopt a written bill of rights beyond the reach of legislature and executive. In the years since World War II most of the new democratic nations in Europe and Asia have acknowledged the obligation and followed the American lead. Parchment barriers, indeed! Yes, they are only parchment barriers, these guarantees and bills of rights, never perfect, never self-executing, always precarious as all human arrangements must be; but in them the judge can find his textual authority and personal valor and moral salvation.

It is time to examine the home scene. How firm are our own parchment barriers and how clear are the freedoms that were inscribed on them? Are the guarantees still black and bold and sharp as ever on the parchment of the Bill of Rights?

One would expect the answer to be a resounding "yes" — not only because so many of us care deeply about our liberties; not only because America stands at the bar of destiny in our time, to prevail if we retain our freedoms and to succumb ignominiously if we part with them; but also because no nation in all history has been so richly endowed with liberty-loving judges on its highest tribunal. Think of the judicial libertarians we had during recent decades — Holmes, Brandeis, Stone, Hughes, Murphy, Rutledge; and those now on the bench — Black, Douglas, Warren, Brennan! Not being ashamed of freedom, they are able to enforce the Bill of Rights with the vigor it deserves. As we need the text, so too do we need men like them. The personal element is always consequential in the exercise of judgment. Hence the superiority of our jurists has given us a significant national advantage.

Yet, notwithstanding the quality of our libertarian judges, there is no denying that nowadays the civil liberties of Americans stand in grave jeopardy. I do not think that the Bill of Rights ever faced a more serious menace. The threat does not come from overseas or from any foreign source — would that it did; we could easily repel it. It comes from within our own borders and from certain of our own judges, who are widely echoed by various lawyers, professors and journalists. It is the threat of the "ink-eradicator" philosophy.

What is the "ink-eradicator" philosophy and what does it propose to accomplish? Its immediate objective is simple to state. It aims to erase the words of the First Amendment from the parchment of our Bill of Rights. The First Amendment guarantees us separation of church and state, freedom of religion, freedom of speech, freedom of the press, freedom of peaceable assembly and — by implication — freedom of association. The "ink-eradicators" have long since served notice that they disapprove of the whole notion of a written Bill of Rights and would prefer to eliminate the entire document. But at the moment they are concentrating their efforts on the First Amendment, shrewdly recognizing that if that goes, the rest will quickly follow. After all, if the people do not fight to defend guarantees of religious freedom and press freedom, they will scarcely cavil over a few other deletions.

The "eradicator" school evidently believe they are making substantial progress, for they have recently intensified their campaign. They used to be content with disparaging the First Amendment as "doctrinaire"; now their epithet for it is "obsolete." In all apparent seriousness, they expect us to believe that the First Amendment guarantees of our liberties have somehow become obsolete.

How they do argue! One would imagine that all the Sophists of ancient Hellas had been resurrected and had begun forthwith to display their skills. Equipped with every solvent known to modern semantics and communications theory, they tell and keep telling us that the language of the First Amendment is the least and last of our serious concerns. They insist that all words are too imprecise to be taken for what they say, that every affirmative may just as well be a negative and every negative an affirmative, and that only the naive among us will permit a categorical prohibition to stand in the way of what seems expedient at any given moment. Words have so little meaning in their view that one wonders how they can use words to tell us so.

What do the "ink-eradicators" say about the First Amendment? The Amendment itself is couched in what the rest of us might consider rather direct terms. It provides that "Congress shall make no law" on certain subjects that the Founding Fathers considered sacred and indispensable to human dignity. Although the Amendment says precisely that "Congress shall make *no* law" in these fields, the "ink-eradicators" claim that it means something quite different. They claim that when it says "Congress shall make no law," it means "Congress shall make no *unreasonable* law."

So far, so ominous. But the next question is: What is an unreasonable law? They have a quick answer: A law, they insist, is unreasonable only if a majority of the judges decide it is. Suppose, then, that Congress proceeds to flout the First Amendment and abridge our freedom of religion or speech or press, how are the judges to determine whether the law is reasonable or unreasonable? This, they reply, is easy: The law *must* be reasonable or Congress would not have enacted it. It would be an insult to the members of Congress, for whom all patriotic Americans feel a reverence bordering on idolatry, were the judges to take the First Amendment literally and nullify such a law.

By this sort of reasoning the words of the First Amendment can be made pale and shadowy indeed. Some of us cannot acquiesce. We protest that the guarantees in the Bill of Rights are still meaningful, still worth the struggles, sacrifices and martyrdoms our ancestors underwent for them. Consequently, they label us as naive and doctrinaire, and charge that we hold a heretical belief in "absolutes."

It is well known that our "eradicator" friends experience shudders of terror at the mere sound of that wicked word "absolute," which, as we have learned to expect, they habitually use without attempting to define it. They do not even distinguish between "absolute" in abstract theology or theoretical ethics, on the one hand, and "absolute" in the concrete, working dispositions of law, on the other. "Absolute" — what an incantation they make of it! If the rest of us are accepting "absolutes" because we believe that a solemn legal prohibition *can* mean literally and precisely what it says, what else would they have us do? What kind of society would there be without some modicum of fixed legal commands, positive and negative? When the law forbids bribing a judge, does it mean only "unreasonable" bribes; when it forbids assassinating a senator, does it mean only "unreasonable" assassinations? When it frowns on rapes, does it mean only "unreasonable" rapes? Words, our modern Sophists tell us, never convey precise meaning; prohibitions, they say, must never be taken literally; how, then, would they enjoy a trip by plane if the pilot up front and the technician in the control tower adopted their philosophy?

One would imagine that the "ink-eradicators" might take warning from the desperate spectacle of the South African judges — textless, helpless, chartless, adrift on a sea of individual and social injustice. Yet the example seems to have taught them nothing; on the contrary, as the plight of South African freedom has steadily worsened, the Sophists have increased their scoffings and intensified their propaganda against the First Amendment. Why? What are their motives? In truth, we do not know. We know only that their philosophy, whatever may be its psychological springs, is cynical in approach, corrosive in effect, in all unwholesome.

America is not South Africa; let it not become South Africa. Through no effort or merit of our own, we, the people of this fortunate country, have inherited the radiant text of our Bill of Rights. For nearly two hundred years it has been our proudest possession, the supreme convenant that binds all of us to enlightenment and justice. Without it our dream, the age-old libertarian dream, is lost and we are nothing. With it we can rise from the bed of doubt, gird ourselves with hope and show the world what it means to be free.

Address at the annual banquet of Phi Beta Kappa Associates, 1962, published in the American Scholar, *1962–1963.*

3

FREEDOM OF THE PRESS

*M*ANY men have spoken eloquently of the First Amendment's guarantees of free speech and press. Of Edmond Cahn, however, it can be truly said that he erected a complete philosophy of justice around these freedoms. The bonds of friendship and intellectual understanding between Edmond Cahn and Supreme Court Justice Hugo L. Black were formed out of a mutual dedication to a civil libertarian goal. Drawing primarily from an exhaustive study of the history of the First Amendment and of governments' attempts to supress free expression, Justice Black interpreted the commands of the First Amendment as judicial "absolutes" to be defended vigorously against the claim that free speech must be "balanced" against governmental interest in suppression.

While Justice Black's frame of reference was essentially a judicial one, Edmond Cahn probed the moral values of a democratic legal order and sought to define the responsibilities and rewards of individual participation in a free society. His philosophical search, like Black's judicial one, returned again and again to the First Amendment for the bedrock values upon which all else rests. If government restricts freedom of expression, not only the speaker but all of the national audience is robbed of its rightful participation in the democratic process. And if the people may not be heard, either in forming the democratic decision or in protesting the actions of government, then a vital moral link between the governors and the governed is broken, and democracy loses its claim to moral superiority. In short, to paraphrase the titles of Edmond Cahn's books, the "sense of injustice" is dulled, there can be no "moral decision" of government, and the "predicament of democratic man" remains unresolved if free thought and expression are curtailed.

The universality of Edmond Cahn's message is apparent in this chapter. His letters to Mr. Ben-Gurion and the lectures delivered in Israel demonstrate that the moral values and political relationships which our First Amendment were designed to secure are the property — or at least the hope — of democratic man wherever he may be found.

N. R.

Correspondence with David Ben-Gurion:
A Debate

THE following letters are published with the permission of Mr. David Ben-Gurion, former Prime Minister of the State of Israel. Together they constitute a candid debate on one of the perennial issues of political democracy, i.e., whether the aim to prevent defamation justifies a government in restricting the freedom of the press.

Although the immediate issues covered by these letters arose in the State of Israel, recent libel verdicts in English and American courts prove that the problem is not local but may emerge in any free nation. Those who view it in one perspective or another are likely to differ widely. For example, the reader will notice that at the end of our exchanges neither Mr. Ben-Gurion nor I had budged an inch. In point of fact, Mr. Ben-Gurion reiterated his original position in the very letter that graciously gave leave to publish.

BACKGROUND OF THE CORRESPONDENCE

In March 1962, the *New York Times* reported that the government of Israel had offered a defamation bill in the Knesset (Parliament) which would sharply abridge the freedom of the Israeli press. Disturbed by this dispatch, which was to prove entirely accurate, I wrote a letter of protest to Mr. Ben-Gurion.

On March 19, 1962, *The Times* of London assailed the bill in an editorial which summarized its most objectionable features:

A SHOCKING LAW

The Government of Israel proposes to alter the law of libel and slander in a way which must shock all those who care for freedom of speech and who have until now liked to think that the rulers of Israel were among their numbers. Most of the draft Bill, which has already received its first reading in the Knesset, concerns the press, and if it became law Israel would join the ranks of countries where the press operates in a twilight of open and concealed censorship. This is especially shameful because most of Israel's press is lively and responsible. Perhaps the worst of many bad clauses is that which makes it possible for a newspaper to be closed down for any period if two convictions for libel are made against the newspaper or any member of its staff within a period of two years. As the definitions of libel and slander are drawn as widely as possible the door could thus be opened for a Government to silence for ever an irksome critic. For, although the preamble of the Bill talks of protecting the individual, this is not its only — indeed, perhaps not its main — interest. Slander can be against a sect or a religion "or any other community or group of people," which would presumably give political parties, trade unions — and Governments? — new grounds for legal action in the courts. The dead as well as the living can be slandered. And in one strange clause any Israeli citizen or foreign resident in Israel who publishes abroad a libel against the state of Israel (not against individuals) is liable to prosecution in Israel. This could, in spite of the assurances of the Ministry of Justice, make conditions for foreign correspondents intolerable. What chance would there be for Israeli journalists?

Of course it will be explained that the law will be interpreted with reason, that it is designed to deal only with abuses, that fair criticism will be respected, and so forth. These are the excuses always offered in similar circumstances. They have never yet turned a bad law into a good one. The proposed Israeli law has other aggravating elements. No reports of libel and slander trials can be published unless the court gives its special permission. Nor may the judgment be published. Printers are made responsible as well as journalists, editors, and publishers, unless they can prove they took every reasonable step to stop publication of the offending passage — thus censorship by printer is created.

It may be wondered why the Government of Israel, which can in the name of security already exercise wide control over the press, should seek these extra extravagant powers. One reason is the exposed position of the country emphasized by Saturday's clashes on the Syrian border. Another may be the so-called "Lavon affair" last year, which not only threatened *Mr. Ben-Gurion's* authority but also, as he felt, exposed men and institutions to unjustified attack. Whatever lies behind the law, it is a bludgeon attack on liberties which, in the Middle East, have all too few footholds.

A few days later, Mr. Ben-Gurion responded to my initial letter. Exchanges of correspondence continued between us until May 1962, by which time tension over the issue had at least temporarily abated. Meanwhile, the government's announcement that it was withdrawing the bill in order to revise it reassured the Israeli public, but Mr. Ben-Gurion's letters showed that his purpose was adamant.

The State of Israel is a democracy of the parliamentary type. It has no constitutional provision for judicial review of legislation enacted by the Knesset. When the new state came into being in 1948, it inherited exceedingly repressive ordinances and regulations governing the licensing and distribution of newspapers, which the English Mandatory government had adopted during the 1920's. Thus in the juristic antecedents of the nation, there was nothing parallel to the American libertarian tradition of Thomas Jefferson (at his worthiest) and James Madison.

Born in warfare and menaced at all times by the unrelenting hostility of its neighbors, the State of Israel has nevertheless maintained a highly creditable plane of freedom for a lively and critical press. Even without the textual tools which a written bill of rights might afford, the Supreme Court of Israel has protected the press from unwarranted administrative interference and has bravely emulated English and American precedents. Nevertheless, the Court would have no power to nullify a clear legislative mandate, such as the Defamation Bill of 1962 was intended to supply.

DEVELOPMENTS AFTER THE CORRESPONDENCE

Though the bill was withdrawn for revision, Mr. Ben-Gurion's letters left no doubt of his eventual intentions. When, therefore, the Hebrew University Law Faculty invited me to lecture on freedom of the press, I readily accepted the opportunity. During the month of December 1962, I delivered a lecture in Tel Aviv on the general theory of a free press (under joint auspices of the university and the Association of Journalists, who published a Hebrew translation in their yearbook) and a second lecture in Jerusalem, on the special problem of defamation. The lectures are not appended here[1] in order not to exaggerate their slight influence on the course of events. According to various Israeli jurists they at least served to ease the task of liberal judges and officials: Israelis who had previously been considered extremists in liberalism could thenceforth claim to be moderates.

Early in 1963 the government offered a different and much more liberal Press Bill, which the newspapers welcomed with outspoken relief. At this writing, the Press Bill of 1963 has not yet been debated in the Knesset and there is no way to predict what ultimate form it will take. When Mr. Ben-Gurion retired as Prime Minister in June 1963, new and imponderable factors entered the political situation.

So much for the objective data. Perhaps the reader will permit two subjective remarks before turning to the letters. For one thing, let me attest my admiration for Mr. Ben-Gurion, who deserves to rank with the ablest and most astute statesmen of the age. For another, let me pay due respect to the people and press of the State of Israel, who in this incident took an unequivocal stand for freedom. We must not forget that Americans were required to oppose Jefferson himself on the rare, unhappy occasions when he sought to silence newspaper criticism that he rightly considered unfair: they opposed him and brought his attempts to a halt. Even so the Israeli people opposed and halted their most gifted leader when he advocated the Defamation Bill of 1962. It was a heartening episode in each instance and a firm ground for faith in popular government.

[1]

12th March 1962

The Prime Minister
The Knesset
Jerusalem, Israel

DEAR MR. BEN-GURION:

When I visited Israel and gave some lectures at the Hebrew University four years ago, the opportunity was proffered to have an interview with you. I declined on the ground that your time was far too valuable to be parceled out on visiting American scholars. Now, however, the situation is different and I feel compelled to address you.

If we can give credence to a dispatch by Lawrence Fellows in yesterday's *New York Times,* your government has offered a bill which would, among other things, enable it to close a newspaper "found guilty of publishing two libelous statements in the course of two years." Almost every particular of the bill as summarized by Mr. Fellows is totally incompatible with the existence of a free press.

The news of this bill comes like a blow between the eyes to those of us who have always associated the State of Israel with liberty and enlightenment. Repressive measures of the kind that Mr. Fellows describes are not expected of democracies. Nor are they expected of you, who have never been one to quail before adverse criticism.

I still believe that Israel is too proud to accept such a bill and that your government is too proud to support it.

Respectfully yours,

EDMOND CAHN
Professor of Law
New York University

[2]

25 March 1962
Jerusalem

DEAR PROFESSOR CAHN,

Many thanks for your letter of March 12th. I have not seen Fellows' report in the *New York Times* of March 11th. I am aware that this correspondent has already in the past supplied his paper with inaccurate information, when he reported my speech at the last Zionist Congress in a distorted fashion. The *New York Times* was quite fair about the matter and corrected the mistake by publishing the full and accurate text of my speech.

I do not believe that freedom of the press entails freedom to slander people, and the Bill submitted to the Knesset aims at preventing just this. According to the Bill: "It will be considered adequate defense in a criminal or civil charge of defamation, if according to information in the possession of the accused or the defendant before publication of the statement, he had a reasonable basis for belief that the said statement was true."

The law defines defamation as follows: The publication of a statement which injures a man or damages his good name in one of the following ways:

1. Accuses him of a crime or misdemeanour;
2. Accuses him of behavior unfitting his public position;
3. Is liable to cause him harm in his profession, occupation, or his position;
4. Is liable to make him the object of hatred, scorn or contempt;
5. Is liable to cause people to avoid his company.

Do you believe that in the case of a paper which has no reasonable basis before publication for believing that the statement which it is about to publish is true, but nevertheless publishes the slander, punishment for defamation would be a violation of freedom of the press?

We believe that the freedom of every individual is limited by the freedom of rights of others and that no individual or a newspaper has the right to humiliate his fellow man or to make him the object of hatred and contempt if he has no reasonable basis for believing that the statement which he wishes to publish against him is true.

We distinguish between freedom of the press and licence of the press, and believe that it is the duty of a democracy to defend its citizens against unjustified attacks, and that one of these is the publication of a slander when he who publishes it has no reasonable justification for believing that the statement is true.

There may be differing opinions regarding the punishment to be meted out to a newspaper repeatedly publishing slanders without having a reasonable basis for believing in the truth of its statements — but the authority granted to a Court to close a newspaper for such a recurrent misdemeanour — authority and not obligation — in no way violates democratic principles.

Several months ago I read that the *Daily Telegraph* had been sentenced by an English Court to pay a fine of £ stg. 100,000 (close to 300,000 dollars) for a trifling insult to the good name of a certain group of people. No one then claimed that England was not a democratic country.

Yours sincerely,

D. BEN-GURION

Professor Edmond Cahn
New York University School of Law
Washington Square, New York 3
U.S.A.

[3]

30th March 1962

The Prime Minister
The Knesset
Jerusalem, Israel

DEAR MR. BEN-GURION:

I appreciate the great courtesy of your letter of March 25 about the Defamation Bill. Since you doubtless had seen the London *Times* editorial of March 19 before writing me, it seems fair to infer that mere overseas objections and protests will not avail as long as you are convinced that the bill is right. On this assumption, I request your leave to discuss the merits.

In order to show a proper respect for your time, I shall limit this letter to the two points that seem most fundamental.

I

Prior restraint is "the essence of censorship." It is one thing to hold defamatory publishers liable for civil damages or even, when they provoke an imminent breach of the peace, for criminal penalties; it is — as more than two centuries of the struggle for Enlightenment attest — a wholly different and impermissible thing to suspend or suppress newspapers and thereby close the people's sources of opinion and information.

How I wish your Ministry of Justice would provide you with a copy of Chief Justice Charles Evans Hughes's judgment on behalf of the United States Supreme Court in the landmark case of *Near v. Minnesota*, 283 U.S. 697 (1931)! The judgment held unconstitutional a statute that authorized courts to forbid and enjoin the business of publishing "a malicious, scandalous, and defamatory newspaper." The same statute provided that a publisher could defeat such an action by showing "that the truth was published with good motives and for justifiable ends."

In this case, Chief Justice Hughes confronted as worthless, scandalous, and defamatory a newspaper as one is likely to find anywhere. Yet he held that the press of the country could not be free if publishers were put in the position of having to satisfy any official, including a judge, that their motives in publishing were good and justifiable, at the peril of having their papers suspended or closed. No matter how often a defamatory publisher might incur civil or criminal penalties for *past* actions, the press could not be free if the law imposed a *previous* restraint on him. Said Chief Justice Hughes for the Court, "This is the essence of censorship."

Obviously, the question cannot depend on the measure of confidence that ought to be reposed in a particular minister or particular government, even a government as meritorious as yours, for a meritorious government will be followed sooner or later by less trustworthy successors. Even under the best of ministers, the mere availability of a power of suspension — regardless of the discretion and care with which it is exercised — constitutes a sword of Damocles, a perennial threat to the freedom of the press. Most publishers are not such Nathans or Jeremiahs that they will risk the existence of their papers in order to issue disagreeable or unpopular information. You and I know, Mr. Prime Minister, that important truths are often disagreeable and sometimes repulsive.

Then there is the simple, massive fact that the people of your country are the ultimate consumers of its law and government. If they cannot eventually judge between political true and political false, the blunders of choice they may commit are the very ones they must consume. Even if they did not learn from their mistakes, no one could rightly dispute their title to have the facts and make the ultimate political decisions. Thus, what will, at the final outcome, prove a true use and what will prove a false abuse of press freedom can scarcely be known before the unfolding of the event. The community of Israel has the fundamental right to read and receive publications and to determine the extent of their political truth or falsity for itself without prior restraint.

II

Under a "group libel" law, it is not possible to allow the accused to plead either truth or a reasonable basis for belief as a defense. Your letter of March 25 emphasizes that proof of "a reasonable basis for belief" would constitute an "adequate defense" under the proposed legislation. If it could, the bill would be *pro tanto* less ominous. That is why I wish you to realize that allowing this defense in "group libel" cases would generally be out of the question.

My opposition to "group libel" law rests on a number of factors, of which I shall take your time to describe only one. Any "group libel" law is bound to be incompatible with press freedom because in the most significant applications it automatically precludes the defense of truth or of reasonable basis for belief. Permit me to illustrate.

Suppose a newspaper made a disparaging remark about Jews who had come to Israel from a certain African country, say, that they were lazy and dishonest. In a civil suit or criminal prosecution for "group libel," is it thinkable that an Israeli court would receive the accused's evidence to prove either truth or "a reasonable basis for belief that the said statement was true"?

Surely not. The people of Israel have not established courts to pass judgment on the general merits of any group among them. Courts cannot vindicate a whole group any more than they can condemn one. It would be an impertinence for an Israeli judge to receive the defendant's evidence even for the purpose of holding it inadequate. In the really consequential cases, therefore, where "group libel" is charged, the supposed defense of truth or reasonable belief is a chimera, and without this feature to rationalize it, the prosecution becomes pure oppression.

One thing is clear, sir. In the end you will do what, after due deliberation, you consider enlightened and right, and these are the criteria to which I appeal.

Respectfully yours,

EDMOND CAHN

[4]

Jerusalem, April 22, 1962

DEAR PROFESSOR CAHN,

I have read your second letter with great interest.

I am well aware that I cannot hold my own in an argument with a distinguished jurist like yourself. In a democracy, however, even laymen have the right to their opinions, and if I venture to continue this discussion it is by right of democracy and not by virtue of juridical expertise. From the practical point of view the argument may be premature, for the bill of which you have read was drafted by the previous Minister of Justice, who was the leader of the Progressive Party, and the present Minister of Justice has proposed to the Government that the draft should be reconsidered before being submitted to the Knesset (for it has never been presented to the legislature). It is now under consideration.

I venture, however, to make a few remarks in reply to your letter. I have not read the London *Times* editorial — and I do not regard that paper as Holy Writ. In the four-volume history of the *Times,* we can read that in the days of Hitler its editor forbade all criticism of the Nazis. The paper deserves credit for acknowledging its error, but this shows that it cannot always be taken as a guide. I will refer only to a few of your remarks.

As it happens, I knew Chief Justice Hughes, and I remember the election day in 1916, when the papers announced Hughes' election, and he went to sleep in the confidence that he was President of the United States, though this does not minimize his importance as a jurist. In my opinion, however, the article in your constitution which authorizes a court to annul an Act of Congress is undemocratic, although I understand the historic reasons that have led to such a position in the United States, and I doubt whether the Supreme Court will use this power often in our day. If, however, you value so highly the rights and status of the courts, I find it somewhat surprising that you should oppose one of the clauses of the draft bill which has been withdrawn for the time being, under which not the Government but the Court would be empowered to close down a newspaper if it had for the second time published a libel without its author having any basis to assume that it was well founded.

In our country we have confidence in our courts, and I am sure that they deserve it, though I am not so simple as to imagine that a judge can never make a mistake — that is why there is a right of appeal. And if one of your courts has the right to annul a decision by the majority of the people's representatives — the Senate, the House of Representatives and the President as well — I cannot grasp why a court should not be entitled to close a paper that makes a habit of disseminating libels. Such a publication does not deserve the name of newspaper, and fortunately our newspapers are not suspected of making a habit of this practice. Supreme Court Justice Hughes' words, with all due respect to his personality, are not the words of the deity and it is permissible to differ from him — if it is permissible to differ from the decisions of the people's representatives and annul their laws.

It is not only a libelous newspaper that has rights — the citizen has a right not to be slandered, and it is not the Government that decides these matters, but independent judges. There is a fundamental difference between "disagreeable or unpopular information" and slander. It seems to me that you demand that the reader himself should be able to distinguish correct information from libel. This is an exaggerated demand — it should be addressed first of all to the newspaper.

You also defend collective libel in the name of liberty of the press. The defamation of a group is worse than the defamation of an individual — especially in our country where the problem of integrating the communities is acute and the education of all sections to respect citizens of all origins is a primary duty.

There are things no less sacred than the "liberty" of the press, which it is sometimes difficult to distinguish from licence. We must implant in the hearts of our people an attitude of respect to every group, territorial or communal. I regard it — I am expressing my personal opinion and not the attitude of the Government — as a dangerous crime to inflame emotions of communal hatred or scorn, a crime which the independent judge should prevent and punish with the full rigour of the law.

I have no doubt that almost all the Israel press would support your view, but I, who hold precious the honour of the press — and even more the honour of the individual and the honour of the public — cannot, to my regret, agree to all that you say.

Yours sincerely,

D. BEN-GURION

[5]

7th May 1962

The Prime Minister
Jerusalem, Israel

DEAR MR. BEN-GURION:

I hope I may say that your letter of April 22 about the Defamation Bill charms me. As a sample of polemical skill, it would be more instructive to my students than anything they could find in Aristotle's *Rhetoric;* never have I been invited up so many seductive bypaths. I count myself fortunate in not having to engage in debate with you in a parliamentary forum, for if I did, I should be severely drubbed. I also count Israel fortunate in having your unique gifts and capacities in its service.

Of course, Mr. Prime Minister, I should deservedly forfeit your attention if I succumbed to temptation and discussed tangential subjects. Let me, therefore, confine this letter closely to the issues.

First, may I narrow the issues by indicating the points on which we agree? I think we are equally concerned with protecting private reputations and deterring newspapers from false and slanderous charges against private individuals. Though the law of defamation has its shortcomings in both principle and application, I agree that a democratic society requires it in order to safeguard reputations. In point of fact, you and I take reputations so seriously that one of our main concerns in this correspondence is *the reputation of the State of Israel* as a land of liberty.

Furthermore, we have no occasion to debate the propriety of punishing a newspaper publisher for an offense against public order *after* he has committed it. Our discussion relates only to *previous* restraint in the form of administrative or judicial authority to suspend or close newspapers. To close a newspaper has only one practical significance for the community, i.e., to stifle future expression. Such authority, I submit, is irreconcilable with freedom.

In any libertarian view, the freedom of the press is not a mere formula to summarize jural relations between a publisher and a government. While granting that the publisher is the usual proponent of the right, I should deny that he alone owns it or that his behavior can determine its status. On the contrary, freedom of the press belongs to the people. It is as inherent and indestructible a possession of the people of Israel as the land itself.

While there are several good reasons for holding that press freedom belongs to the people, I shall mention only one here, that is, the factor of representative government. Because they are citizens whose chosen representatives act in their name and on their behalf, Israelis are put under a moral obligation to protest against official misdeeds that may come to their notice. Representative government implicates the people. Like the age-old Jewish tradition, it leaves no option about protesting against injustice; it compels citizens to come forward and raise their voices. Hence, a press free of prior restraint, though desirable anywhere, becomes a moral necessity in a democracy. The very fact that your government is a representative one obliges it to avoid previous restraints of the press. Because the people are responsible for what the government does in their name, they are entitled to have uncensored channels of protest.

Is it not clear, Mr. Prime Minister, that the institution of "parliamentary immunity" rests on the selfsame popular base? Under the law, a legislator is exempt not only from prior restraints but also from civil liability after the event; why? Surely the immunity is not provided for his sake; not for his sake do we permit him to injure reputations with impunity. We do it for the people's sake, in the interest of uninhibited democratic debate. All of us have, in part, socialized our reputations in order to clothe high executive officials and elected representatives with an immunity that they may — and sometimes, as in Senator McCarthy's case, do — abuse. Nevertheless, we pay the price willingly and appreciate what it purchases for the general good. According to the democratic consensus, the same considerations apply to the press. Is not its mere exemption from previous restraint a much smaller price, relative to the social values it purchases?

Concerning your reference to "group libel" laws, I have already made clear why they cannot contribute to the coalescence of the people of Israel. The coalescence will come from association in the school system, the labor unions, the military service and similar enterprises.

It will also come from a common pride in the freedom of the citizenry. In the end, every government gets the kind of citizenry it expects, for every official prediction about the people is largely self-validating. If your government distrusts the people and the press freedom that belongs to them, it is likely that, sooner or later, they will justify the distrust. But if your government thinks of the people as grateful though often ignorant, sensible though often garrulous, and decent though often irritating, you will have no use for previous restraints. Do not the people of Israel, who had judgment enough to make you their Prime Minister, deserve a reciprocal vote of confidence?

Respectfully yours,
EDMOND CAHN

From the journal of Public Law, *1964.*

Freedom of the Press:*
The Libertarian Standard

FREEDOM of the press is far too important to leave in the hands of lawyers and publishers. No other institution affects the shape and nature of a society so directly, no other civil liberty penetrates community life so pervasively, and — since freedom of the press is at

* The following two addresses were delivered in Israel.

bottom a mutual covenant among all the people — no other covenant they undertake displays so precisely the people's estimate of their own intelligence, critical judgment, and moral worth. To consider the law of press freedom is to consider the social quality and future hopes of democracy itself. From the seventeenth century to our own day, many brave men have been willing to suffer persecution, ostracism, imprisonment, and death in the cause. It is they who bought us the freedom.

What would they say of our present-day press? Let us be realistic about it. Of course, having so little acquaintance with your newspapers, I do not intend to refer to them. I take it for granted that *your* newspapers, unlike those in the United States, are always scientifically accurate and perfectly objective; that they never misquote a speaker or misrepresent an incident; that Israeli publishers are never influenced by the attitudes of their stockholders and bankers much less their advertisers; that Israeli reporters always allot the same space and mode of treatment to a news item regardless of the subject's political ties and affiliations; that in Israel it is no advantage to be related by marriage to the publisher's wife; that editorial writers in Israeli papers never fail to investigate thoroughly and reflect profoundly before expressing an opinion; that all their opinions are gentle and compassionate; that no Israeli newspaper would feature crimes of violence or sex scandals, well knowing that readers in this country find such accounts boring; and generally that Israeli newspapers evince the reliability of the *Encyclopaedia Britannica* and the wisdom of the Book of Proverbs.

Nor do I doubt that every Israeli reader, appreciating the editor's infinite wisdom, votes precisely as his newspaper tells him to. This may be the reason why political life in Israel is so much simpler than in America. Americans — curiously enough — persisted in electing and reelecting Franklin D. Roosevelt for their President though at one time as many as eighty-five per cent of the country's newspapers opposed him. Be that as it may, when we come to postulate one standard or another of press freedom, we should be candid about the quality of the daily and weekly press. In the United States, with a few praiseworthy exceptions, the quality of newspapers and newsmagazines generally ranges from mediocre to contemptible. It is not the press but the legally established freedom of the press that deserves our dedication.

What do we mean by freedom of the press? In modern democratic societies one can observe three different standards or levels of press freedom. Granted that no society is always consistent either in its legal dispositions or in its daily practices, there are wide and significant differences among the respective standards.

The lowest democratic standard can be called "constricted" freedom of the press. It may also be called "colonial" because it confers the same authority to censor and suspend newspapers that imperial powers have been wont to confer on governors or commissioners in the colonies. People who prefer this standard usually defend it by invoking a long procession of horrors and disasters that would inevitably befall if newspapers could publish without restriction. Their arguments are replete with imaginary disorders, insults that never quite get published, and blood that somehow never gets shed. They live in a superstitious dread of mere words, firmly believing that if the press should utter a disrespectful thought, the ceiling would fall in the House of Parliament or the army would refuse to fight. They actually feel safer when they see the police drive lorries up to a newspaper plant and cart away entire editions of a paper; they relax in their easy chairs and enjoy gazing at the blank spaces which the censor has imposed. To them, there is nothing uncongenial about decrees that suspend newspapers either for a limited time or permanently.

Like Goethe, men of this kind frankly prefer an injustice to a disorder and even to the remote risk of a disorder. They have what I call a Roman type of mentality, eager for system and efficiency at any cost in human values. One can find their standard set forth in the French Revolution's Declaration of the Rights of Man and of the Citizen. Article 11 of the Declaration contains the strongest statement that the government of Revolutionary France could be induced to utter on freedom of the press, a farcical anticlimax if ever there was one. It read: "Free communication of thought and of opinion is one of the most precious rights of man: therefore every citizen may speak, write, and print freely, *taking into account the abuse of this liberty in such cases as are determined by the law.*" As anyone can see, this was tantamount to no guarantee whatever — which the ensuing events of French history proceeded to demonstrate forthwith.

The second standard or level we may call "abridged" freedom of the press. Another label for it would be "prudential" because, while it is a genuine and authentic measure of freedom, it remains always subject to the demands of caution. Abridged freedom is the standard that England has maintained for use at home. None of the great charters of British liberty contains a guarantee of freedom of the press. In England, to this day, the freedom remains, as it was at the time of the American Revolution, a popular slogan, a political ideal, a rhetorical motto — but not an explicit legal mandate secured by a formal, authoritative text. Though Parliament and the courts have generally been reasonable in limiting the British press, no press can attain a maximum level of freedom as long as government possesses constitutional power to censor or suspend, nor as long as judges employ the contempt power as aggressively as they do in Britain to curtail press comment on their proceedings.

It is easy to identify the men who are satisfied with an abridged standard of press freedom; they are always assuring us unctuously that they believe in the "liberty" of the press but abhor the "license" of the press. As long ago as 1798 James Madison, the father of the American Constitution and Bill of Rights, exposed this "liberty-license" cliché for the fraud that it was and still is, and a few years later Jeremy Bentham castigated it as a transparent political fallacy. It deserves to rank among the shoddiest of semantic tricks. If you happen to like what the press is saying because it attacks your adversaries, you stoutly defend its "liberty"; but if it turns and attacks your party, you indignantly denounce its "license"; and this you call "legal reasoning." Come now! Though the freedom of the press does have rational bounds and limits, we shall never find them in talk about "liberty and license."

The third level of press freedom I shall call "maximum" or "libertarian." This is the standard proclaimed at the end of the eighteenth century by the American statesmen Thomas Jefferson and James Madison, and in the middle decades of the twentieth century by a number of eminent jurists, foremost among whom have been Justices Holmes, Brandeis, Hughes, Black, Douglas, Warren, and Brennan. Theirs is the libertarian standard which premises a free, open, and advancing society. They submit that the proper function of government is to regulate men's conduct, not the expression of their opinions and beliefs; that a press is not free unless we respect its right to publish thoughts that we disapprove, reject, and detest; and that a free people will never permit government officials — their hired servants and employees — to tell them what they can or cannot read. What the men in office believe to be error has as much right to plead its case at the bar of public judgment as what they believe to be truth. According to the libertarian view, freedom of the press necessarily involves risks but abridgment of the freedom necessarily involves greater risks.

One of the curious things about these brilliant American libertarians, of both the eighteenth and twentieth centuries, is that their careers and biographies prove so disobliging to those who disagree with them. If you disagree with the French *philosophes* of the eighteenth century, it is easy to brush them aside by commenting that they had no experience in political affairs, never assumed the responsibilities of public office, but habitually concocted their theories in some philosopher's chamber, some wooded retreat, or some duchess's boudoir; how then could they be expected to develop a rational standard of law? But the American libertarians, at least the great ones whom I have named, were not obliging enough to disqualify themselves in this way. On the contrary, all have been men of long and extensive experience in public affairs, all successful political leaders, administrators, and practitioners. The libertarian standard is not the product of an academic institution or a foundation grant; nor is it a mere motto or utopian ideal. In both the eighteenth and twentieth centuries, sensible and experienced men proclaimed it in their writings, enacted it into constitutional law, and effectuated it in practice, occasionally under circumstances that tested their sincerity to the utmost. Though the total American record may contain aberrations and grave lapses, the libertarians have demonstrated that maximum freedom is not only right in theory but also workable and successful in practice.

II

The time has come to ask a certain question candidly, that is, why do I emphasize the American history of the subject and American cases? The question is a proper one and deserves an answer. For one thing, the history and cases that we deal with here do not have a peculiarly American reference, do not turn on technicalities of American law. The history has its parallel in every new and emerging democracy. As for the cases, they are American only in the sense that the trial of Socrates was a Greek case or the trial of Captain Dreyfus a French case. It is not their local but their universal democratic meaning which draws us to them. Moreover, the libertarian standard that I lay before you is surely the highest and best on the face of the earth. If I thought any other standard worthy of the State of Israel, I should be happy to expound it.

How did it happen that the American libertarians of the eighteenth century conceived such an ambitious plan for freedom of the press? Their own statements tell us that they intended consciously to surpass the level of freedom existing in England. What were the forces that impelled them?

I think that if one examines the voluminous records and correspondence of the period, it is possible to identify four consistent themes or influences. The first of these, and by no means the least important, was religious. From the very beginning and on recurrent occasions to this day, freedom of expression in America has been linked with free exercise of religion. The press whose freedom was to be made secure was not only an implement for disseminating secular news, it was also an implement for spreading religious beliefs. Jefferson, the most eloquent, and Madison, the most profound of the Founding Fathers, came from Virginia where they witnessed considerable religious persecution though they suffered none personally. In Virginia, they waged a magnificent and eventually victorious struggle for freedom of religion and the separation of church and state. Thus they developed an intense devotion to freedom and an inveterate hatred of censorship that they proceeded to apply to every other realm of social existence. As Thomas Jefferson said, "I have sworn upon the altar of God eternal hostility against every form of tyranny over the mind of man."

So much for the religious factor. The secular impulsions to freedom were equally strong. There was the natural pride and self-esteem of men who had settled in the wilderness, had defied the hostile neighbors who continually threatened to slaughter them, had trusted to their own valor and resourcefulness, and had built the foundations of a new and hopeful society. Their pride had a negative side as well. They could not believe that one of their fellow-citizens was metamorphosed into some sort of superior being just because he had assumed the robes of public office. They were suspicious of governors who claimed absolute wisdom, and they abhorred every manifestation of official arrogance. Finally, these early libertarians insisted that government censorship could have no place in a republic because the people were no longer servants but masters. "If we advert to the nature of republican government," said James Madison, "we shall find that the censorial power is in the people over the government, and not in the government over the people." Here is the proud spirit behind the libertarian standard.

It produced a fixed dichotomy in their philosophy between speech and writing, on one side, where they resolved that official power ought not to operate, and overt conduct, on the other, where, of course, it ought. Even before the libertarians produced the American Bill of Rights with its formal guarantee of free speech and free press, they had marked the boundary line between words and conduct in the Constitution of their new republic. Being aware that under the law of England the crime of treason could be stretched and expanded by analogy to condemn a man for what he had merely said or written or believed, they ordained that nothing so dangerous to liberty should be permitted to their government. In the Constitution they provided as follows: "Treason against the United States shall consist only in levying War against them, or in adhering to their Enemies, giving them Aid and Comfort. No Person shall be convicted of Treason unless on the Testimony of two Witnesses to the same overt Act, or on Confession in open Court." No overt act, no treason.

This brings us to an aspect of the problem of free expression that did not become evident or explicit until our own day and time. Not until our time did the libertarian jurists see the necessity of inquiring: Whose freedom is freedom of the press? To whom does freedom of the press belong?

Much depends on the answer a legal order may give to this question. If freedom of the press belongs to the state and is merely granted or leased or licensed by the state (as some have been heard to contend, even in Israel), then it can never rise above what we have called the "constricted" or colonial level. If, on the other hand, it belongs merely to the writer, editor, or publisher, it must remain a purely individual right and will be required to retreat and yield on every occasion of public pressure or apparent emergency. In short, when we might need it most, we should have it least. Moreover, if the publisher is regarded as the sole and exclusive owner of the freedom, his behavior can be availed of to impair, compromise, or even destroy it. On such a postulate, the freedom can never rise above what we have called the "abridged" or prudential standard. But if we consider the freedom as belonging not only to the publisher and writer but also to the consumer and reader, we may find a sound basis for raising it all the way to the "libertarian" level. Consequently, in order to define freedom of the press in a democratic society, we must first ask: Whose freedom?

In 1946, the question came explicitly before the Supreme Court of the United States. Grace Marsh and Arthur Tucker, members of the religious sect called "Jehovah's Witnesses," considered themselves ordained to promulgate the doctrines of that sect by distributing its booklets and magazines. Every Saturday afternoon, Grace Marsh would stand on the sidewalk and display the magazines to passersby. Arthur Tucker would call on people from door to door, present his religious views, and distribute the magazines to those who were willing to receive them. Grace and Arthur conducted themselves in an orderly manner. It was the peculiar legal status of the respective localities where they operated that eventually involved them in trouble with the police.

Grace's station was on the only business block in a so-called "company town" in the State of Alabama. The very sidewalk on which she stood and the street she faced belonged to the private manufacturing company that owned the entire town. She was warned several times that she could not distribute the magazines without a company permit and was told that no permit would be issued to her. When she refused to leave, she was arrested and convicted under an Alabama law which made it a crime to enter or remain on the premises of another after being warned not to do so.

Arthur's endeavors took him to a village located in the State of Texas. The United States government owned the entire village and used it to provide housing for workers in national defense projects. The village manager, appointed by the appropriate agency of the United States, ordered Arthur to cease all religious activities in the village. On the ground that the manager had no right to suppress the exercise of religion, he refused. He was arrested and convicted under a Texas law which made it an offense for a peddler to remain on any premises after the owner or possessor had told him to leave.

On appeal, the United States Supreme Court (5 to 3) reversed and set aside both convictions as unconstitutional. Freedom of the press forbade that either the state or the company completely bar the distribution of political or religious literature on public streets. Legal title to the town, the streets, and the sidewalks was not decisive, said Justice Hugo Black for the Court. Regardless of technical ownership, the public had a paramount interest in keeping the channels of communication free and open. The people who live in company towns or government-owned towns must, like all other citizens, "make decisions which affect the welfare of community and nation. To act as good citizens they must be informed . . . their information must be uncensored."

The reasoning of the Court was incandescent. Justice Black made it clear that in reversing the convictions of the Jehovah's Witnesses the Court meant to uphold the basic rights of the people they were addressing. From a technical point of view, this was a bold departure because the residents of the company town in Alabama and of the federal project in Texas did not appear before the Supreme Court, nor did they voice any claim that their rights had been violated. No one spoke to the Court on their behalf, except perhaps the states' attorneys who were contending that the Jehovah's Witnesses should not be allowed to address them. Nevertheless, the Court declared that it was they whose rights were at stake and whose access to information must not be abridged. Freedom of speech and press belong not merely to the speaker and writer but also to the audience, the readers, the democratic community.

Why is it necessary to hold that freedom of the press inheres in the entire community? There are many excellent reasons which were familiar to libertarians of the eighteenth century. Freedom of the press is requisite for the advancement of science, the development of literature, the mutual and reciprocal communications among citizens, the uniting and knitting-together of the people, and the admonishing and guiding of public officials. A community needs freedom of the press not only in order to express community opinion but also to form and refine individual opinions into community opinion and, even more fundamentally, to draw together and become a consolidated and unified society.

These are the contentions that leaders of democratic thought have used since ancient times to support and justify freedom of expression. No one should be naive enough to believe that a society can enjoy freedom of expression without some incidental annoyance, whether in the form of impudence, fanaticism, stupid error, malicious mischief, or mere undesirable delay. Freedom of the press cannot be maintained without price. On the contrary, if the press were always to say what we considered opportune and agreeable, it would have little social value.

Despite the power and persuasive force of these considerations, the age-old literature of free expression somehow failed to satisfy the psychological demands of our century. It failed, I believe, because it overlooked a certain essential factor, one that may eventually surpass all others in impact on the morale of the individual citizen. In demanding freedom of expression, the classic libertarians followed the practice of insisting on the people's civil *rights;* this they did with undeniable eloquence. The difficulty was that they said nothing about the people's civil *obligations.* Displaying impressive gifts of rhetoric, they based the claims of liberty on every philosophic foundation that ingenuity could suggest or imagination create — *except* the people's sense of injustice or social conscience. (This lack, I believe, helps to explain the apparent gap between the typical themes of libertarian literature and those of Jewish literature. Jewish literature becomes pertinent to our subject only when we invoke moral duty as a foundation stone of freedom.)

It was only in very recent times that some of us began to understand democratic citizenship as involving something beyond rights and privileges, claims and pressing demands. We began to perceive that representative government had introduced a new factor into our moral existence. We, the citizens of the democratic nations, have long insisted that we alone are the sovereigns by whose name and under whose authority every official act of government is performed. Through the exercise of our franchise and by our consent, legislators, executives and administrators wield the immense powers of modern government. Representative government implicates us in their acts, their misdeeds and oppressions. It makes us participants — accomplices if you will — in the deeds that are done in our name and by our authority. Unexpectedly, we find that we have wandered into the circle of moral responsibility. For millennia, we have been accustomed to connecting ourselves only with the victim of wrong. As citizens living in a representative democracy, we suddenly find ourselves connected also with the inflicter of wrong.

Because representative government involves us vicariously in its shortcomings, lapses and misdeeds, we can no longer debate our title to freedom of the press. Nor can we share the title with government. If government implicates us in its operations, as it does, it must acknowledge our indefeasible freedom to protest, to object, to denounce. We have lost whatever option of silence we ever had in the presence of social injustice. Representative government acts upon our consciences as the divine message acted upon the consciences of the ancient prophets. The prophets were not asked whether they desired to convey God's message, whether they found it convenient or even safe to criticize and admonish. They do not seem to have enjoyed fulfilling their unpopular missions. Nor need we, in our day, welcome the vicarious responsibilities and guilts that official laxity, bigotry, or corruption can impose on us. Freedom of the press belongs to us not only because we have rights to assert but also because we have inescapable obligations to perform in a democratic polity.

III

The moment we perceive that freedom of the press belongs as much to a democratic people as the traditions of their history and the very land on which they live, every rule of law appears in a new and different light. We become less concerned with some administrator's temporary convenience or some publisher's petty misbehavior and turn our primary attention to the interests of the community. In the process we find ourselves reshaping the old, established rules of public law.

For example, under the traditional English version of press freedom, a newspaper was expected to be exempt from what was called "prior restraint," which meant that, whatever the government might do to the publisher or the paper *after* publication, it would not attempt to license or censor the contents of the paper *before* publication. On this basic point, English law of the eighteenth century was entirely acceptable to American libertarians. The Americans, however, always insisted that freedom of the press must extend far beyond the rule against "prior restraint" and must comprise an extensive immunity from interference after as well as before publication. At least as to prior restraints, the doctrine has been the same on both sides of the Atlantic. A press could not begin to be free unless they were excluded.

But if prior restraints are forbidden, the question remains: What is a prior restraint? One of the most interesting struggles of the twentieth century has emerged from the efforts of ingenious officials to impose prior restraints and censor the press without appearing to do so. Some of the regulations they devise may seem well intentioned and innocuous in their impact on freedom of the press. Only when one reminds himself that the freedom is the people's heritage and not solely the publisher's does one recognize that the regulation is in practical effect a form of control and censorship, a prior restraint, and therefore impermissible.

Let me submit an example. Take the case of J. M. Near, a man who appears to have made a checkered career for himself out of publishing defamatory and scurrilous weekly newspapers. The *Saturday Press*, which he published for a while in the city of Minneapolis, featured articles attacking the Jews. Somehow one gathers the impression that Near was one of those who pander to anti-Semitism mainly because they think it is a profitable way to make a living and because, as they explain, others would do it if they did not. There are individuals everywhere who seem born for this kind of career. While still in the carefree years of high school, they begin by purveying advance copies of examination answers, obscene pictures, and narcotic cigarettes; then they graduate to more ambitious varieties of merchandise. To please the kind of following it had, the *Saturday Press* would probably have engaged in attacks on Catholics, Negroes, Japanese, or Arabs with the same ratio of logic to zeal that it exhibited against Jews.

In a series of weekly issues, Near, who admitted to a reputation tainted with suspicion of blackmail, chose to vilify and bespatter the mayor of Minneapolis, the county attorney, the chief of police, the representative of the citizens' law-enforcement league, certain members of the current grand jury, and, of course the "Jewish Race." If one could credit the *Saturday Press*, all of these, including the "Jewish Race," were conspiring to protect a Jewish gangster who was supposed to control local gambling and racketeering. Though using the foul phrases that are typical of such papers, the *Saturday Press* did not incite its readers to riot against the alleged conspirators but merely to abhor and revile them.

At length, the county attorney brought a civil suit against J. M. Near and the *Saturday Press* to have the newspaper abated and closed as a public nuisance. A state statute authorized the court to forbid the business of publishing "a malicious, scandalous and defamatory newspaper." The statute also provided that a publisher could defeat such a proceeding by showing "that the truth was published with good motives and for justifiable ends."

At the trial of the case against him, Near offered no evidence at all. The trial court decided that he had in fact made a business of publishing a malicious, scandalous, and defamatory newspaper, and it forbade and enjoined him from continuing the nuisance. After a unanimous affirmance in the Supreme Court of the State, Near appealed to the Supreme Court of the United States.

It can fairly be said that if ever the circumstances might tempt a court to impose a prior restraint, this was the case. Near's way of exercising the freedom of the press had virtually no social value. If anything, it was harmful. On the other hand, a decision suppressing his paper might not only serve to reduce religious and other tensions; it might also protect honorable officials against false scandals and thus help the community to recruit better candidates for municipal service. It was a hard case for the constitutional guarantee of freedom.

Yet the United States Supreme Court decided (5 to 4) that the state statute and the injunction against Near were unconstitutional. Near might be subject to pay civil damages for libel; but in no event could he be enjoined *before* publication. No publisher in a free society could be put in the position of having to satisfy any official, including a judge, that his motives in publishing were good and justifiable, at the peril of having his newspaper abated as a public nuisance. The state statute attempted to impose a prior restraint on publishers, and this, said Chief Justice Hughes for the Court, "This is of the essence of censorship."

Yet were not Near's accusations scandalous? Yes, they assuredly were, said the Chief Justice. "Charges of reprehensible conduct, and in particular of official malfeasance, unquestionably create a public scandal, but the theory of the constitutional guaranty is that even a more serious public evil would be caused by authority to prevent publication." Yet were not these accusations of Near's also totally false? Granted that they were, there would still be no ground for a decree of prior restraint. The community was entitled to hear any accusations that might be published and to determine the extent of their truth or falsity for itself. It could not legislate to strip itself of that right. Whether or not Near's freedom of expression protected him from damage suits after the fact, a restraint before publication would deprive not only Near but the community as well. For how could one know before publication that what he would print was totally false? Thus the Court majority adhered to the classic libertarian assumptions about the common people's good sense, practical acumen, and capacity to recognize a fraud when they see one.

Obviously, in every society the people will err from time to time, for they are no more infallible than their elected representatives. When they do err, it is to be hoped that they may learn from their mistakes and make wiser and safer decisions. In any event, since they are the ultimate consumers of law and government, it is they who must live with the products of their own choices and judgments. As for government, what is there in its long and varied history — with all its gross injustices, blunders, brutalities, and savage persecutions — that could warrant it in disparaging the good sense of the common people?

Mr. Near and his newspaper have long since faded away. Of course, they have their successors and loathesome counterparts in every time and generation. But, lest you draw the inference that freedom from prior restraint in America always means freedom to attack Jews, Negroes and other ethnic minorities, let me mention an instance with the contrary effect. In the critical year 1946 when Israel's future was hanging precariously in the balance, an organization styling itself the "League for Peace with Justice in Palestine" tried to get the New York courts to enjoin a liberal newspaper from publishing an article that contained grave charges against the League. According to the article, the League had been charged with being "anti-Semitic" and "warmly sympathetic toward the pro-Nazi leaders of the Arab League." The New York court categorically dismissed the suit for an injunction because it was "repugnant to the democratic tradition" and "unprecedented in our jurisprudence." The exposé continued effectively. Thus the rule against imposing prior restraints on the press can work both ways.

Let us confess on behalf of every free people that some of us do annoy and exasperate the man who holds the reins of office, however high or low his post may be. Day by day, while he strives and struggles with the reins, he sees that some of the people are indifferent, some pompously officious, and some nastily hostile. Likely enough the newspapers remain silent when he does well, and burst into shouts of abuse when he slips or they think he slips. Particularly in times of crises, he feels the stings of envy and invective. Some citizens grumble because, though he does his very best, he is only a man with a man's limitations; others grumble because they enjoy grumbling. There must be times when the criticism and unfairness seem too much for him, and in such hours he can only pray for an added store of humility, patience and endurance; he can only call to mind that he is not really greater than Moses, who was barred from the Promised Land because he let the people provoke him to a momentary explosion. No wonder that officials feel moved to raise questions about freedom of the press. A free press can never provide a courteous, deferential, or dainty society; it can only provide openness, self-respect, and social justice.

According to the libertarian standard, what we owe our government is allegiance but never idolatry; what we owe our representatives and administrators is respect but never reverence; and what we owe ourselves is a political life consonant with the demands of conscience. We owe ourselves emancipation from the fear of printed words and from trembling before mere epithets. A certain small dosage of error and malice such as we may get in our daily paper can gradually immunize us against the disease of credulity. "Credulous" is scarcely the word one would use for the people of Israel.

It would be truer to call them inquisitive, critical, proud, brave, and stiff-necked like their ancestors. Being inquisitive they will not long tolerate attempts to censor their reading; being critical they will not accept misrepresentations and falsehoods, whether purveyed by officials or by publishers; and being proud, brave and stiff-necked they will ultimately insist that the press of Israel be as free from government restraint as any on the face of the earth.

Freedom of the Press: Responsibility for Defamation

I F one desires to understand the true value of freedom of the press, one need only consider what our lives might be without it. Without it, every other social expectation would become doubtful, every formal guarantee of official fairness would be imperiled, and every procedural safeguard which respects human dignity would be exposed to arbitrary deprivation. The classic libertarians regarded due process of law and fair administrative procedure as fences and protections around freedom of expression. This was correct. But it is equally correct to say that free expression is a fence and protection around all other rights. Deny freedom of the press and sooner or later you find yourself denying all the other elements of legal liberty; abridge one and you inevitably abridge the others; defend one and you are equipped to defend all the others.

Let us return to the main themes of my initial lecture. In it we began by identifying three distinct levels for democratic freedom of the press: first, the level of "constricted" freedom, where the courts, the ministers, and the police may take what they call preventive measures such as carting away an entire edition of a newspaper or suspending its publication; second, the level of "abridged" freedom, where, though preventive measures and prior restraints are frowned upon, publishers and editors may still be imprisoned for commenting imprudently on certain official proceedings; and third, the level of "maximum or libertarian" freedom, where the newspapers are regarded as independent tribunes of the people and unofficial censors of government.

According to the libertarian philosophy, freedom of the press belongs not merely to the publisher or editor but also, quite fundamentally, to the people themselves. It is a part of their social birthright. Living as we do under a representative form of government, we find ourselves continually implicated in the wrongs and misdeeds that officials commit in our name and by our authority. Since, then, we have an inescapable moral duty to object and protest, by like token we have an incontestable moral right to maximum freedom of the press.

What does maximum freedom mean? It means at least that we exclude prior restraints on the press and forbid the suspending or closing of newspapers. Suspending a newspaper, even for a single day, is an offense against freedom. The offense is unlimited in its consequences because no one can know how much of inspiration and truth or how much of social action might have resulted from that day's paper. To suppress and destroy a printed book, as John Milton said, is like killing a man. Yet to prevent a book or newspaper from ever coming into being may be worse; it is like killing an unborn child, for we can never know what creative potentialities have been lost. In the mysterious processes of human imagination and experimentation, it is often error alone that can suggest the path to truth.

Prior restraint is censorship in its most obnoxious form. It cannot be made acceptable by assuring the people that it will be exercised wisely or that it will be exercised seldom or that newspapers will be suspended only when the judges give their permission. The mere presence of such a power on the statute books — no matter how discreetly or seldom it may be used — is a threat to the existence of newspapers and a prior restraint on their freedom. A free people should be too proud to grant the authority and their government too proud to desire it.

What then are the free societies to do by law about the evil of defamation? I say "by law" because it would be unfair to assume that the problem of defamation does not pertain primarily to other social institutions and activities. The main lines of defense against defamation are in the family home, the synagogue and church, the elementary and secondary schools, the social club, the army, the labor union, the professional bodies, the agricultural community, and the business organization. These are the places where most people can be taught not to defame and not to lend credence to defamers. Ideally, the remedy for defamation would be a broad, all-pervasive generosity; realistically, the remedy is a sharp, wholesome skepticism.

Defamation, as Jewish tradition has always taught, is a vicious, wicked, and cruel practice. The rabbis could scarcely find words angry and bitter enough to condemn it. Though some of their strictures related primarily to delators and informers (a special breed of slanderers who might imperil a person's life by accusing him before the non-Jewish ruling powers), they condemned each and every form of defamation as a moral offense and social outrage. One cannot but admire their moral sensibility.

For our purpose, the problem of defamation falls into two main divisions, that is, the libel of public officials and the libel of groups. These are currently the main areas of controversy. When a newspaper happens to defame a private individual, whether out of malice or by mistake, he can generally find adequate provision in the law to compel retraction, payment of pecuniary damages, or both. Thus, though the law governing liability for strictly private defamations would probably benefit from detailed reexamination and modernization, it is not one of our main concerns here. We are concerned with what is immediately controversial: the libel of officials and the libel of groups. Ought the law to punish these by inflicting imprisonment?

II

It is time to consider a concrete case. There are occasions when a trial in a court of law can assume national and even international significance. Most cases, important though they may be to the individuals involved, are mere statistics for everyone else. Yet once in a long while, even the simplest trial occurs at such a decisive moment in a nation's history and discloses the people's goals so dramatically that it becomes an episode or chapter in the national myth. Such was the trial, in the year 1735, of an obscure printer by the name of John Peter Zenger, a native of the Palatinate who had settled in New York and found himself in serious trouble because he published frank and harsh criticisms of Colonel William S. Cosby, royal governor of the province.

Determined to suppress this impertinence, Governor Cosby arranged to have Zenger formally accused of the crime of seditious libel. In those days as now, it was the regular procedure to conduct a criminal trial before a judge, who would decide any questions of law, and a jury of twelve ordinary citizens, who would decide any questions of fact after hearing the evidence on both sides as presented by the Attorney General and counsel for the accused. Of course, the public were entitled to attend.

Though Governor Cosby was a haughty, pompous, irascible, oppressive, arrogant, greedy, and tyrannical man, no one can say that he was careless. By the time the trial began, he had the following arrangements to depend on:

First, he tore up the commisison of the Chief Justice who had decided another case in a way he did not like, and appointed a new Chief Justice who would do his will.

Second, to make certain that the new Chief Justice remembered to whom he owed his office, Cosby gave him a commission only "during pleasure," not, as customary practice required, "during good behaviour."

Third, when two lawyers who represented Zenger and supported his newspaper dared to question the form of the commission, the new Chief Justice summarily disbarred them, leaving Zenger without assistance of counsel. Then the Chief Justice appointed a lawyer of his own selection to defend Zenger, carefully choosing one who was not only young and inexperienced but also a known supporter of Governor Cosby.

Fourth, when Zenger asked to be released on bail until the day of the trial and swore that he was not worth forty pounds, the Chief Justice fixed the amount of bail at four hundred pounds and thus held Zenger in jail for ten months awaiting trial. During these months the accused was allowed to speak to his wife through a hole in the door. These conditions are not considered ideal for purposes of preparing one's evidence and defense.

Fifth, under the English law of the time, Cosby knew that the Chief Justice would not permit Zenger to prove that his criticisms of the governor were true. Evidence to that effect would not even be entertained. Under the law, truth, far from being a defense, would only aggravate the crime. English lawyers had a maxim for cases like this one, "The greater the truth, the greater the libel."

Sixth, Cosby also knew that the only question which the jury would be permitted to answer was, "Did the accused actually publish this libel?" The question whether his statements constituted a libel was not for them but for the court to decide. Thus the jury too seemed safe. (Incidentally, when the trial began, the governor's officials attempted to violate the law by choosing their own supporters for the jury instead of selecting the jurymen by lot. But here they had gone a bit too far, and the attempt was abandoned when it was discovered and protested.) Everything considered, there are few lawyers who prepare for trial as carefully as Governor Cosby did.

But, as the governor soon learned, virtue, even the virtue of painstaking preparation, must often be its own reward. Things did not happen as any reasonable person would have expected. Hardly had the trial begun when an elderly man entered the court, approached the bench, and announced that he was joining counsel for the accused. It was none other than Andrew Hamilton, venerable leader of the Philadelphia Bar, who had come to New York despite poor health and poorer roads to defend the freedom of the press. Zenger's own lawyers, disbarred by the Chief Justice, had journeyed to Philadelphia and induced him to enter the case. Hamilton, who counted the great Quaker and landowner William Penn among his clients, was easily one of the ablest and best-known lawyers in the American colonies.

Nevertheless, Zenger's dilemma still seemed grave. Though he now had eminent counsel, the rules of law seemed to condemn him. What could even an Andrew Hamilton accomplish against the existing law and a Chief Justice determined to enforce it to the hilt? Though the jury might sympathize with the accused, their function was narrowly restricted. They were authorized to decide only whether Zenger had published the paper, a fact that Mr. Hamilton proceeded immediately to concede. (Why should he risk antagonizing the jury by contesting what all New York knew to be true?) Prospects still seemed bright for Governor Cosby and dark for John Peter Zenger.

All the same, there was a way out and Hamilton found it. First he made the jury realize that the case had momentous implications, saying, "The question before the Court and you, gentlemen of the jury, is not of small or private concern; it is not the cause of a poor printer, nor of New York alone, which you are now trying. No! It may, in its consequence, affect every freeman that lives. . . . It is the best cause; it is the cause of liberty!"

The problem, of course, was how to give the jurymen an excuse for holding Zenger not guilty, which they were clearly willing to do, without openly proposing, as no lawyer could, that they disregard the Chief Justice's statement of the law. How did Hamilton solve it?

Let me condense the long series of colloquies, arguments, and retorts into a few phrases that contain the gist of the solution. It amounted to a mere shift in emphasis on words. In effect, the customary question, the question everyone knew the Chief Justice must ask the jury at the end of the trial was, "Did the accused *publish* this libel?" But by employing hints, suggestions, and sly innuendoes, Hamilton made the jury understand that they might answer a quite different question couched in precisely the same words. They might answer the question, "Did the accused publish this *libel?*" If they did not believe that the paper before them was a libel, why need they answer the question affirmatively? The jurymen nodded their comprehension, conferred together, and returned an immediate verdict of "not guilty." Instantly, the courtroom exploded in an uproar of shouts, embraces, rejoicings, and noisy happiness. Generations later, men would say that the seeds of the American Revolution took root on that day. The news of Zenger's vindication spread throughout the American colonies and even to England where some few were liberal enough to acclaim it. A member of the British Parliament remarked, "If it is not the law, it is better than law, it ought to be law and will always be law wherever justice prevails."

The New York jury's defiant spirit in the Zenger case showed how bravely a free people could respond to the libertarian standard. True, there have been times in American history when the government strayed ignobly from the standard. One such occasion was in 1798 when certain Americans feared the French Revolution as passionately as some of their descendants in our century fear the Russian. In a brief fit of hysteria which lasted from 1798 to 1800, the government enacted a so-called Sedition Act, making it a crime to publish any false and malicious statement that might bring the government, the Congress, or the President into disrepute. Even this repressive legislation allowed an accused to prove the truth of his utterance as a defense.

The sponsors of the Sedition Act claimed it was consistent with freedom of the press because it imposed punishment only after publication of a seditious libel, it involved no prior or previous restraint. The argument probably convinced some Americans. But the libertarians, led by Thomas Jefferson and James Madison, rejected it as totally fallacious. Madison, himself the father of the United States Constitution and Bill of Rights, declared, "A law inflicting penalties on printed publications would have a similar effect with a law authorizing a previous restraint on them. It would seem a mockery to say that no laws should be passed preventing publications from being made, but that laws might be passed for punishing them in case they should be made." With characteristic penetration, Madison perceived the pith of the matter. Every law that authorizes imprisonment of publishers, editors, and reporters after publication is necessarily a species of restraint on them before publication and an abridgment of freedom of the press.

Incidentally, the American people reacted vehemently against the Sedition Act and elected Jefferson President in 1800; he forthwith pardoned and released everyone who had been imprisoned under the act. In the twentieth century, though libertarians may justly criticize some aspects of the American record, it is gratifying that publishers and editors are no longer prosecuted for criticizing our contemporary Governor Cosbys. As far as I have been able to find, the last instance of an attempted prosecution occurred in 1908 when President Theodore Roosevelt lost his temper because the *New York World* and the *Indianapolis News* asserted that a Wall Street group had profited in millions from the transactions in which the United States acquired control over the Panama Canal Zone. Forgetting the lessons of history, Mr. Roosevelt had his subordinates institute criminal prosecutions against the publishers. The courts, however, proceeded to rescue him and the country. After delaying matters long enough for all parties except Theodore Roosevelt to cool off, they dismissed the charges against the publishers on technical grounds which, by leaving the merits forever unadjudicated, saved everyone's face. Meanwhile, Mr. Roosevelt's term of office having expired, his successor was delighted to let the episode slide into deserved oblivion. And there may it remain.

Does the defense of truth make a difference? Is a state justified in imprisoning men of the press for criminal libel if it allows them to exonerate themselves by proving their utterances true? I suppose the answer will vary according to what men think about freedom of the press and to whom they think it belongs. Those who favor a constricted freedom because they believe it belongs to the state will be ill-disposed toward the defense of truth. If they grant it at all, and some of them will, they will insist that the accused must prove not only that what he published was true but also that he published it "with good motives and for justifiable ends" or "that it was for the public's benefit that it should be published." In practical effect, this makes the state, acting through a court, a jury, or a cabinet minister, the judge and ultimate master of the freedom.

Then there are those who, desiring an extensive though somewhat abridged standard of freedom, insist that the defense of truth should be made unconditional and absolute. Rightly they urge that the state should never inflict imprisonment for publishing unpleasant facts except, of course, secret military and security data. Be the motives good or bad, generous or sinister, the press should always enjoy immunity when it publishes the truth. An attractive position this, but is it adequate? It too acknowledges the personnel, the mechanisms and the organs of the state as ultimate arbiters of what is and what is not true.

James Madison saw that it was incumbent on libertarians to go further. He noted that the truth is often difficult for the accused to prove in a prosecution for criminal libel. The tribunal is generally hostile and reluctant to believe him. Moreover, the documents he needs to justify himself are usually in the custody of government officials, including the very ones he is charged with libeling. To make matters worse, the truth so often consists in an amalgam of opinions and facts, mixed confusedly together. As Madison said, "It must be obvious to the plainest minds why opinions and inferences and conjectural observations are not only in many cases inseparable from the facts, but may often be more the object of the prosecution than the facts themselves; or may even be altogether abstracted from particular facts; and that opinions, and inferences, and conjectural observations, cannot be subjects of that kind of proof which appertains to facts, before a court of law."

For all these reasons, libertarians are not content with the defense of truth. Believing as we do that freedom of the press inheres fundamentally in the people, we oppose any device for abridging it. Whether a publisher's charge against a public official is true or false may, for the internal purposes of government, be a question for other officials to decide. But we cannot agree to let their decision result in imprisoning the publisher and thereby imposing a prior restraint on freedom that belongs to the whole citizenry. We need to hear all voices, even those that sound the worst, so that we may find our own way and judge for ourselves. Frequently, in public affairs, we cannot appreciate what the prophet Elijah is trying to achieve with his altar at Carmel unless we first watch the vain efforts and foolish antics of the prophets of Baal.

That truth, though precious, is likewise slippery Emile Zola would learn to his dismay when he published his immortal *J'Accuse*. Yes, his accusations were totally, utterly, and absolutely true. Nevertheless, in making them, he challenged the entire military and clerical establishment that was ruling his country and disgracing it. The defense of truth proved worthless, for truth is not truth in court unless judges open their eyes to it. Zola was convicted of criminal libel, the appellate court affirmed his conviction, and his only recourse was to flee the country and go into exile.

How then was the monstrous fraud of the case against Dreyfus exposed? Not by criminal libel prosecutions, not by trials in either military or civil courts; it was exposed only because men like Zola in writing *J'Accuse* and Clemenceau in publishing it appealed to the highest of all human tribunals, the conscience of the civilized world. Long after that conscience had vindicated Dreyfus and condemned both his persecutors and the military and clerical forces behind them (so long after, in fact, that it seemed more like a vain afterthought than a triumph of justice), the state and the army finally acknowledged the wrong they had committed.

Surely the leaders of every free nation ought never forget the ordeals of Alfred Dreyfus and Emile Zola. If they remember, they will observe the maxim laid down for them by Mr. (now Attorney General) Gideon Hausner. Recognizing an exception only for national security, Mr. Hausner said, "A democratic leader would rather give his back to the smiters and hide not his face from shame and spitting than muzzle the press."

Of course, we free citizens have never left our public officials without means of defense against any smitings or spittings which may come their way. It is not our habit to choose a collection of Bontche Shweigs for public office. (Though I love Bontche, I have always suspected that he was just a bit persecution-prone.) Far from desiring our representatives to submit to vilification, we have provided the most powerful of weapons by which they can defend themselves, fight back, and assume the offensive. The weapon is called "parliamentary immunity."

Parliamentary privilege or immunity is absolute in law. A representative cannot be touched by criminal prosecution or civil suit for anything he may say on the floor, no matter how false, malicious, and destructive of private reputations. Moreover, the immunity extends to outside reports of his remarks. Thus the safest and most unrestricted defamation in any free society is the defamation that the people's own representatives may utter.

To put it another way: we have all partly socialized our reputations and put them at the risk of defamation in the legislature. It is entirely right that we have done so. Nevertheless, if anyone naively assumes that the risk involved is slight, he need only consider how the late United States Senator Joseph McCarthy infamously abused his privilege and ruthlessly destroyed reputations and lives.

In some countries, notably the United States, there has been a constant trend toward conferring an absolute privilege of defamation first on chief executive officers, then on executive department heads, and now on executive officials of distinctly subordinate rank. While the privilege of executive officials may not be quite so broad as parliamentary immunity, it is nonetheless absolute in immunizing both the false and the malicious. If one consults the signs of the time, one is disposed to fear the increasing defamatory privileges and immunities of government officials rather than those of newspapers and private citizens. At least, democratic law offers no shield of civil immunity to the newspaper such as it offers to the representative and high executive. Does it not seem evident that public officials need no greater protection than we have already furnished? A free society will not consent to jail the worst of its publishers in order to soothe the best of its officials.

III

We come now to the question of group libel, that is, whether a democratic government ought to make it a crime to publish defamatory statements about unincorporated social groups. Some people argue that group-libel laws would prevent the growth of ill-will toward minorities in the population and would thus produce not only social harmony but also legal equality. They believe that if incidentally the group-libel laws should abridge freedom of speech and of the press, the gain would be well worth the cost. Yielding to these arguments, a very few of the American states, including the State of Illinois but not the State of New York, have adopted such a law.

The typical group-libel law makes it an offense to publish a statement or picture which portrays "depravity, criminality, unchastity, or lack of virtue of a class of citizens, of any race, color, creed, or religion, or exposes them to contempt, derision, or obloquy." Let me make it plain that a group-libel law is not a law against causing breach of the peace or against inciting to riot or against forming a mob to perpetrate some sort of violent action. Illinois, like every other state, had laws of these types on its statute books, and no one questioned their propriety. But a group-libel law attempts much more; it seeks to control words without any necessary reference to deeds. It seeks to proscribe the implanting of certain ideas that are considered vicious but that may or may not ever engender a resort to violence. A group-libel law makes a crime of mere publication.

The record of enforcement shows how deficient and ineffectual these laws really are. Anyone acquainted in the slightest with American society knows that groups of one kind or another are being defamed countless times a day in every part of the country. Yet, although Illinois enacted its group-libel law as early as 1917, I have found only one instance of enforcement reported in an appellate court. It was the case of Joseph Beauharnais.

Shortly after World War II, Beauharnais, a venomous bigot, was convicted for violating the Illinois group-libel law and appealed to the United States Supreme Court on the ground, among others, that it infringed his constitutional right to freedom of the press. The trial record in Beauharnais's case contained nothing about violence or breach of the peace. All it showed was that, at a meeting of a so-called White Circle League, he had distributed bundles of a leaflet which, in disgusting terms, defamed the Negroes of Chicago and petitioned the mayor and city council to stop them from encroaching on white residential neighborhoods.

When Beauharnais came to trial in Chicago, he offered to prove that the leaflet's nauseating statements about the Negroes, their rapes and robberies, were factually true, but the judge rejected the evidence. On this record, the United States Supreme Court held, by a vote of five to four, that the Illinois group-libel statute and Beauharnais's conviction were not forbidden by the constitutional guarantee of freedom of the press. As the Court went on to remark with unusual explicitness, it was not ruling on the desirability of group-libel laws but only on Illinois's constitutional power to enact one.

To libertarians it seems clear that the five justices of the majority were mistaken in upholding the statute and that the four dissenting justices were right. Some observers disapprove of the decision as soon as they learn that Beauharnais was not permitted to defend himself by attempting to prove the truth of his statements. They reason that if he was telling the truth, the community's interest in what he had to say would be the same whether he spoke in good faith and for a benevolent purpose or in bad faith and for a detestable purpose. Allegations and opinions which may contribute to the shaping of public policy are not less true and meaningful when they emerge from a vicious mouth. If we cannot trust our citizens to discriminate between truth and falsehood, then we cannot say that they are morally responsible for the disposition of public affairs. If they are responsible as representative government makes them, they must have the opportunity to decide what is social meat and what is social poison.

Yet could anyone seriously urge that a trial judge ought to entertain evidence of the kind that Beauharnais was offering? Ought a judge allow testimony to be introduced which, whether or not it be believed, must serve to humiliate and degrade a whole segment of the population? Ought the law authorize him to decide whether Beauharnais's insults to the Negroes of Chicago were true or false in fact? Nothing could be worse to contemplate. Imagine, if you please, a judge who reads in the statute that groups must not be accused of "lack of virtue" and then after listening to the evidence on both sides proceeds to announce a decision concerning "virtue" or "lack of virtue" of Jews, Catholics, Protestants, Moslems, bankers, lawyers, university professors, or any other pertinent group.

Suppose, for example, that the defamatory statement is to the effect that the Jews who have come to Israel from a certain country in Africa are lazy and dishonest. Picture, if you like, submitting the truth or falseness of such a statement to a court, any court at all! Manifestly, the very notion would be intolerable. A free people does not establish courts to pass judgment on the *general* merit of any of its constituent groups. Judges cannot vindicate a whole group because they cannot condemn a whole group. For a judge to acquit a group of "lack of virtue" would be as impertinent as to convict them of it.

Thus the laws against group libel are equally unacceptable whether the court admits evidence to support a defense of truth or excludes it. A court is simply not the forum in which to contest and determine questions of wholesale or general desert. The function of a court is to determine particular desert, that is, the desert attached by law to some specific overt act or some specific incident of default or negligence. A court's business is to assess men's particular transactions, not their overall human worth, and no secular tribunal possesses authority to judge an entire social group.

There are other reasons why group-libel laws simply do not work. Suppose we test the Illinois statute by assuming that the state officials would apply it quite literally, allow no exceptions, and prosecute every publication which "portrays depravity, criminality, unchastity, or lack of virtue of a class of citizens." The consequences would be fascinating to behold. The officials could begin by prosecuting anyone who distributed the Christian Gospels, because they contain many defamatory statements not only about Jews but also about Christians; they show Christians failing Jesus in his hour of deepest tragedy. Then the officials could ban Greek literature for calling the rest of the world "barbarians." Roman authors would be suppressed because when they were not defaming the Gallic and Teutonic tribes they were disparaging the Italians. For obvious reasons, all Christian writers of the Middle Ages and quite a few modern ones could meet a similar fate. Even if an exceptional Catholic should fail to mention the Jews, the officials would have to proceed against his works for what he said about the Protestants, and, of course, the same would apply to Protestant views on the subject of Catholics. Then there is Shakespeare who openly affronted the French, the Welsh, the Danes, and sundry important residents of the fairy kingdom. Dozens of British writers from Sheridan and Dickens to Shaw and Joyce insulted the Irish. Finally, almost every worthwhile item of prose and poetry published by an American Negro would fall under the ban because it either whispered, spoke, or shouted unkind statements about the group called "white." Literally applied, a group-libel law would leave our bookshelves empty and us without desire to fill them.

It is easy to anticipate that those who support group-libel laws must try to defend their position by saying, "This literal application is not what we intend, not at all. The judges know quite well that a group-libel law is enacted to protect minorities, not to muzzle them or censor classical literature. We can trust the judges to avert any undesirable consequences. The judges will interpret the statute suitably in each case that comes before them. Depend on the judges!" And here, in this reply of theirs, they have exposed the worst and most pervasive defect of group-libel legislation. For notice, please, the paradox that they have constructed for themselves. They propose that we enact group-libel laws in order to advance the cause of equality; yet when they have to face the practical consequences of their proposal, they can only recommend that we diminish not only our liberty (our liberty of expression) but also a priceless portion of equality itself (our equality before the law). They ask not only that we restrict the freedom of the press but also that we confide our fates and our neighbors' fates to the unpredictable will of prosecutors and the uncontrolled discretion of judges. They would have us give every court a sort of roving commission to decide for itself and for us whether this book, that leaflet, or that picture insults more than it informs, informs more than it insults, or — being extremely ancient and inaccessible to hoi polloi — has acquired an immemorial license to insult with impunity.

Taking these considerations into account, it is easy to understand the enforcement record, or rather the absence of an enforcement record, of group-libel laws. Though the Beauharnais case, holding group-libel laws permissible, was decided ten years ago, not a single American state has subsequently enacted such a statute. Moreover, as far as I have found, not a single prosecution has been instituted since Beauharnais's. Thoughtful people who care deeply for the rights of minorities and for harmony among social groups have recognized the ineffectuality, if not the harmfulness, of the proposal. The only time Beauharnais ever secured a brief place in the limelight was when Illinois prosecuted him under its group-libel statute.

Let us learn something from the millennial history of the Jewish people. Where can one find sharper, more critical, more caustic statements about the lack of virtue of the Jewish people than in our own Sacred Scriptures? Where can one find a more candid portrayal of group errors, lapses, and backslidings, each instance reported by eye-witnesses and certified by unimpeachable authority? We do not abandon the Bible or the Talmud because anti-Semites have frequently distorted and misused them to attack us. On the contrary, when ignorant or vicious men seek to turn some passage or other against us, we respond sensibly as our ancient sages did when they were asked why God did not destroy the heathen idols. They replied, "Misguided men also worship the sun, the moon and stars, and ought God destroy all the beauties of the universe because some men fall into error and adore the creation instead of the Creator?" We know there is no proposition, no principle, no truth that evil minds cannot twist to their purpose, and shall we therefore ban the whole universe of literature?

Far from hiding invidious facts, the Bible and Talmud explicitly record every disagreement, no matter how bitter, and every dispute, no matter how charged with defamation. Our classical sages seem to have understood perfectly that if men can listen to good statements, good commandments, and good exhortations without automatically becoming good, they can be exposed to bad ones without automatically becoming bad. For good or ill, words simply do not have the magical efficacy that fearsome people attribute to them. If they did, would the world be what it is today after millennia of religious and ethical preaching? It is the mark of a free and open society to be able to hear and read words of error without following them or imprisoning their authors.

This is the libertarian standard, the best and highest that political man has ever produced. It summons all citizens to rise to their full intellectual and moral stature. It invites them to hold themselves erect, gird themselves with dignity, and declare that the officials whom they have chosen to administer their common affairs owe the people a reciprocal vote of confidence.

Lectures delivered in Israel, December 1962, under the joint auspices of the Hebrew University of Jerusalem and the Association of Journalists.

4

CHURCH AND STATE

WHILE believing that the ethical and moral principles of religion were important ingredients of a free society, Edmond Cahn believed with equal fervor that religion could be free only if it was completely independent of the state. It was not enough to guarantee individuals the right to practice their religions without government interference. History has taught the powerful lesson that if governments provide financial assistance to religions, even on a seemingly nondiscriminatory basis, numerically superior religious faiths with large numbers of schools, hospitals, welfare programs, and antipoverty projects will grow stronger at the expense of those religions which insist only on following the will of God by catering to the spirit of Man. Because he understood the importance to religious freedom of strong independent religious organizations, free from government support or control, Edmond Cahn was in the forefront of those who tried to explain the original meaning and modern significance of that clause in the Constitution which forbids government from passing any law "respecting an establishment of religion."

He regarded the growing governmental support of religious institutions as one of the gravest threats to the liberties of Americans in our age. In this chapter religious belief, historical scholarship, and perceptive satire are blended toward the goal of preserving the principle of separation of church and state. This uniquely American institution — so fundamental to the Founding Fathers that it was the very first right guaranteed in the Bill of Rights — may yet withstand the pressures of an expanding federal beneficence if these words of Edmond Cahn are heeded.

N. R.

How to Destroy the Churches

SEPARATION of church and state in recent months has become an uncomfortably timely issue. There are controversies about Bible-reading, prayers, and Christmas observances in public schools; about Sunday closing ordinances and state laws that penalize atheism in one manner or another. The latest storm has raged around the question of federal loans or grants to schools under ecclesiastical control.

Whenever public discussion turns to such subjects, it is fashionable to stress the moral defects of the state, the politicians, and the voters and unfashionable to tell home truths about the church, the clergy, and their congregations. Democracy has rightly taught us to be tolerant and mindful of the sensibilities of our neighbors of other faiths. We have learned the lesson so well that many of us, including our movie-makers, no longer feel free to say "Elmer Gantry" when we meet an ecclesiastical charlatan.

If you describe or even exaggerate the imperfections of democratic government you will command respect. But mention a few obvious facts about the behavior of the church (or the synagogue, which I mean always to include) and in certain circles you will be branded an enemy of religion, a bigot, and perhaps a crypto-Communist. By these means, the state is made to appear irredeemably corrupt, while an uncritical silence cloaks the church in righteousness, sagacity, and idealism. Thus it would seem to follow that the church, which abounds in virtue, should utilize if not direct the state, which is amoral. With the logic of the matter so badly askew, no wonder that separation of church and state is misunderstood and in jeopardy.

Those of us who believe in organized religion have a duty to restore the equilibrium of truth. We are the ones who comprehend the church from within. In stating the truth, we can confine our comments to the all-too-human attributes of *all* churches. Then no one need feel that his denomination has been singled out for criticism.

What are the simple facts? Not about creeds, dogmas, and theological beliefs, which, however bizarre or irrational, are matters of private conscience, but about the extent of righteousness, wisdom, and altruism inside the churches. What shall we say of them?

Now, perhaps the specific congregation or parish to which you belong is very close to perfect; all gifts for its support are made anonymously, and the donors, in order to enjoy the full beauty of religious sacrifice, do not deduct their contributions for tax purposes. Your own clergyman may be a saintly man who spurns rich people and prefers the poor; he is so pure in fact that the most vicious malefactors, coming within his aura, tearfully assign a reasonable percentage of their net gains, both past and future, to holy causes. The ladies of your congregation are ascetically indifferent to clothes, material possessions, and social status; they steadfastly decline to gossip. The children in your religious school are all dainty little pre-Freudian disseminators of sweetness and light. All this we can grant. But what of the other congregations and parishes in your denomination, and what of all the other denominations?

Looking back at the role of the churches in relation to the great ethical issues in our time, one must confess that, with a few commendable and even heroic exceptions, the clergy have failed to furnish the nation with moral leadership. Most churches have lagged behind the moral progress of secular law and many of them have not yet begun to close the gap. On the question of racial equality, for example, the Supreme Court has moved far ahead of organized religion. On that of free speech and association, we find that the ugly disease of McCarthyism, which still infects our democracy, has met more principled and courageous opposition among the jurists than among the clergy. It is true that in resisting McCarthyism the Supreme Court has been firm in some respects, weak in others. The judges needed — and generally lacked — the support of libertarian voices in the major pulpits of the country. Nor can we blame radio or television for the reduced importance of weekly sermons in American life. The new media could provide unprecedented new opportunities. But the pulpit itself has diminished in virile courage, spiritual profundity, and prophetic vision.

Almost every day clergymen appear and testify before state commissions, local school boards, congressional committees, and other official bodies. Their views as presumably informed and responsible civic leaders are entitled to respectful and serious consideration. But this is not true of the pretense that some of them make of controlling the votes of the laymen of their denomination; indeed this pretension and the promises or threats that may accompany it should be dismissed as presumptuous, undemocratic, and factually false.

There once was a time when ecclesiastical politicians could direct large blocs of votes, dispensing plums to their political friends and punishments to their opponents. Even today there are a few areas of the country where ignorance and political illiteracy still permit this sort of abuse. But it is a rarity, and a fading one.

Presidents, governors, and legislators have in fact discovered that they need not tremble when political clergymen scowl menacingly. Experience has taught most public officials what we may call the Law of Inverse Pretension. According to this principle, the less a clergyman happens to know about his communicants' or congregants' views on any given subject, the safer he will feel in pretending to declare them.

Many of us recall the lurid years of National Prohibition when Bishop James Cannon, a Methodist, was able to terrorize congressmen by threatening disaster at the polls if they did not vote as he demanded. Eventually they discovered that the bishop's threat was thunder without lightning. Similarly, the Catholic bishops of Puerto Rico last year called on their faithful to defeat Governor Muñoz-Marín. Despite Puerto Rico's high ratio of Catholic voters, Muñoz-Marín prevailed by a wide margin. (Bishop Cannon had one advantage over the Puerto Rican prelates. Being a *Methodist* bishop, he could at least deliver his wife's vote.)

Aggressive clerics present their case in terms of a choice between "God and Caesar," implying that a decision against their claims would be tantamount to a decision against God. This is completely fallacious. Our American principle of separation gives the true picture. It designates the separated entities not as "God and Caesar" but as "church and state." A free government is never so bad as Caesar and a church administered by mortal men is never so good as God.

The Founding Fathers, particularly Thomas Jefferson and James Madison, defined two distinct aspects of the American doctrine of separation: one negative and legal, the other positive and religious. They formalized the legal aspect through the First Amendment, which not only guaranteed the "free exercise" of religion but also prescribed that government "shall make no law respecting an establishment of religion." What does the latter provision mean today? Speaking for the United States Supreme Court, Justice Hugo L. Black answered in the following celebrated passage:

> [It] means at least this: Neither a state nor the federal government can set up a church. Neither can pass laws which aid one religion, aid all religions, or prefer one religion over another. Neither can force nor influence a person to go to or to remain away from church against his will or force him to profess a belief or disbelief in any religion. No

person can be punished for entertaining or professing religious beliefs or disbeliefs, for church attendance or nonattendance. No tax in any amount, large or small, can be levied to support any religious activities or institutions, whatever they may be called, or whatever form they may adopt to teach or practice religion. Neither a state nor the federal government can, openly or secretly, participate in the affairs of any religious organizations or groups and vice versa. In the words of Jefferson, the clause against establishment of religion by law was intended to erect "a wall of separation between church and state."

This much, at least, is what separation means in terms of constitutional law. However, the law of the subject utters only prohibitions. In effect, it directs the government to attend to its own affairs and avoid intruding into the realm of religion.

Outside the margin of the law, however, one finds a wholly different aspect of the matter, that is, the positive or religious side. According to the American tradition, churches separated from the state are a religious necessity. We hold it self-evident that as long as a church speaks God's message and exemplifies God's way, it can require no assistance from the political power. If, then, the church seeks political help, it demonstrates to that extent that it deserves none.

To the believing church member, the separation of church and state is more than a barrier erected to restrain arrogant clergymen. It is also a solemn affirmation of confidence and pride in the independence of his church. The firm trust which our ancestors declared in the self-sustaining efficacy of the church was the proudest philosophy religion had ever evoked in a political society. It was a radically new idea not borrowed from England, which maintained an established church.

The new American nation embraced this new concept not only because its founders desired freedom of worship, not only because they detested the meannesses and dreaded the hostilities of sectarian conflict but—above all else—because they believed with complete fervor that religion, as Madison said, "flourishes in greater purity without than with the aid of government."

Coming now to the current scene, I must ask you to help me by imagining—for only a few pages—a condition of affairs that is entirely fictitious, namely: If, for whatever reason, you and I were determined to destroy organized religion in the United States of America, how would we go about it? Our hypothesis is that instead of feeling devoted to our respective churches we are so bitterly hostile to them that we are resolved to extirpate them from American life. Precisely how would we proceed? In seeking an answer let us invite Mephistopheles to join us, and see what advice he would give.

He would, I believe, begin by reminding us that Americans have a curious emotional attitude toward their churches. No matter how irregularly they attend them, no matter how inadequately they support them, no matter how rarely they heed them, nevertheless at the very first sign of a frontal attack, they rally stanchly to the churches' defense. Mephistopheles insists therefore that the demolition be planned along devious and oblique lines. He recommends starting modestly: by persuading the Congress and the people that, to preserve the separation of church and state, they need only refer all controversies on the subject to the United States Supreme Court. The notion sounds respectable: it has the added attraction of relieving everyone except the judges of the unpleasant duty of thinking. Send it to the judges and forget it!

Of course, Mephistopheles, being well-versed in the decisions of the Supreme Court, knows that, under certain old precedents, the judges may flatly decline to rule on some of the most important church-and-state issues. This is because the Court — to avoid interfering with functions that the Constitution confides to other branches of government — will not consider an issue of constitutionality unless the party appearing before it has sustained or is in immediate danger of direct injury from the law he seeks to challenge. No matter how dubious the measure may be, he will not be permitted to attack it if he merely suffers from it in some indefinite way in common with everyone else.

Back in 1923, the Court went further and held that the mere fact that a person could show he paid federal taxes made no difference in this respect and gave him no standing to challenge an act of Congress appropriating public funds. The Court recognized that an unconstitutional spending of public money might conceivably necessitate a rise in subsequent tax levies. Nevertheless it held that the causal connection between any specific expenditure and future tax rates would be too remote and uncertain to constitute an immediate personal injury to a taxpayer. Hence he would have no more to complain about than others.

Rulings of this kind, designed to keep peace among the departments of government, are eminently sensible as overall policies. Yet they also provide a way to immunize a bad law from attack in the courts: one need only frame the law in such a way as to violate the basic rights of nobody in particular but everybody in general, that is, of the *entire* American people. Then, since no one can point to an injury that is distinguishable from his neighbors', no one can come into court and challenge the legislation!

For example, if the Congress were to appropriate a billion dollars for direct grants to schools under ecclesiastical direction, some of the judges would decline to entertain the question of constitutionality;

they would hold that no citizen or taxpayer could challenge the appropriation in court. Some of them would take the same position even though the very statute which appropriated the money required the Attorney General to obtain a ruling from the Supreme Court before the money was distributed.

Nevertheless, Mephistopheles has had too rich an experience with lawyers to depend entirely on any technicality of law, even one that appeals to his taste as much as this one. He knows that what one lawyer may knit, another lawyer may find a way to unravel. Though Mephistopheles relishes the fictions and refinements of the law, he has found that too often truth and common sense have a way of breaking through. And they may do it again. In the case of direct federal grants to church schools, he suspects that a procedure will be developed that would induce the Court to decide the question of constitutionality.

He hopes of course that in that event, the majority of the judges would uphold the validity of the grant to church schools. But he does not care very much how any particular case comes out. For *his* purpose in this initial stage does not relate to the courts. It is rather to accustom the American people to regard church-and-state relationships as strictly legal and political issues, fit for judges and lawyers to wrangle about, too esoteric and technical for other citizens to comprehend. If he can only get the people used to considering separation of church and state in terms of qualifications, conditions, reasonable adjustments, and practical exceptions, Mephistopheles can rejoice. Aware that Thomas Jefferson solemnly dubbed it a "wall of separation," he hopes that the people will become accustomed to seeing a few exceptions here and there, a few doors or gaps in the wall. How can one hope to erode an obviously beneficial rule if one is not permitted to introduce exceptions?

Heretofore, when called on to maintain the wall of separation, the Court has made a rather mediocre record, failing more often than it succeeded. If Mephistopheles can convince the judges that the American people care so little about the solidity of the wall that they are willing to leave its fate to any five justices who happen to compose the Court majority of the day, the wall will soon crumble away. The first destructive step is to teach the people that separation of church and state is not their affair but the Court's.

The second stage follows. It consists in persuading church members that the cost of maintaining their own sectarian institutions has become too onerous for them. Here Mephistopheles has a powerful ally in human selfishness and cupidity, not to mention the joy we all take in feeling sorry for ourselves. Self-pity is the occupational disease of modern man. Anyone who appeals to it is certain of a receptive hearing.

In the past, when most church members were much less prosperous than they are today, they discovered a special pride and religious exaltation in contributing to the construction and maintenance of churches, missions, funds for the sick and poor, and other religious causes. Granted that some of the donors were actuated by an unworthy expectation that they could, as it were, bribe their way into heaven; there were plenty of others who gave for the sake of social conscience. In fact, according to our view of things, some gave too much to ecclesiastical uses. At any rate, every section of the United States is studded with imposing cathedrals, churches, synagogues, seminaries, monasteries, nunneries, institutes, and clerically directed universities, which would have been impossible if millions of Americans in every generation had not attested their faith by donating billions of dollars.

In the face of such conspicuous proof that every church can take care of its own and that its own can take care of every church, it would seem hard to picture the church schools and universities nowadays as victims of abject poverty. Yet Mephistopheles finds it rather easy. True, the communicants may be more prosperous than ever before in history, secure and sleek and obese; but think of the cost of keeping two cars these days. Consider the income taxes one must pay, even at the popular capital-gains rates. Mephistopheles fairly weeps as he recounts how inflation has increased the cost of scientific equipment for the church schools. Of course, he finds no need to mention how inflation has increased the gifts and contributions, the income from the churches' real estate, securities, and bingo games, and the schools' fees. It is easy to convince men that they cannot afford to pay what they do not desire to pay; tell them how heavy their burdens are and they will greet your every word as a sagacious understatement.

Now for the third stage, the decisive one. Here Mephistopheles can use his favorite instruments of destruction, those most ancient and efficacious temptations — power and money. Power and money can work like salt water on a shipwrecked mariner — the more he takes, the more he requires, till death alone can slake his thirst. If you want to kill him, you need only persuade him to swallow the first draught.

That is why Mephistopheles would be elated to see us bloat the churches with political power and gorge them with public grants. He understands that — unlike the church in the Middle Ages — the modern church can no longer use the state as it chooses; on the contrary today when the two play the game of power and money, it is the state that ultimately calls the tune and makes use of the church.

Grant the churches all the political influence they desire, he urges —

only make sure to attach a single, entirely plausible condition to its exercise. Give them their way; enact into law any regulation, no matter how censorious or repressive, which the loudest clerical voices in the community may demand — only require them first to lay their hands on their hearts and solemnly aver that the regulation has nothing to do with religion but is merely an ordinance for social welfare, community comfort, or administrative convenience. You will be amazed to see how readily some of the clergy will succumb to this stratagem. In order to impose their own sectarian ways on the remainder of the population, certain clergymen — speaking either for themselves or through state officials who share their views — seem willing to erase all lines between sacred and profane, and to demote the most precious inheritances of faith to the plane of mere secular arrangements. Some of these clergymen are the very ones we hear continually denouncing the trend toward secularism; yet when they see a chance to wield political power, they enter the front ranks of the secularizers.

One example will suffice. Thirty-four of our fifty states had general laws prohibiting business, gainful work, and commerce on Sunday. Twenty-one of these states are considerate enough to provide exemptions for persons like Seventh-day Adventists and Orthodox Jews who in good faith observe a different day as the Sabbath. The Pennsylvania law which makes Sunday work a criminal offense allows no exemptions for such persons, no matter how devout they may be.

A few months ago, the United States Supreme Court held that it was constitutional for Pennsylvania to prosecute some Orthodox Jewish merchants who opened their shops on Sunday. They claimed they could not remain in business if they were permitted to work only five days a week. No one questioned their religious sincerity. (The factor of sincerity is important because in other debates about Sunday closing laws nothing more sacred has been at stake than commercial rivalry between urban merchants and highway merchants.) The Supreme Court offered them no comfort. It told them that under Pennsylvania law they must either suffer the inevitable losses or find "some other commercial activity which does not call for either Saturday or Sunday labor." Justices Douglas, Brennan, and Stewart dissented indignantly.

Why did the majority uphold the Pennsylvania statute (and similar ones in Massachusetts and Maryland) in the face of the First Amendment? Because the Attorney General of the state insisted that Sunday laws were not connected with the Christian Sabbath but were mere secular provisions for rest, relaxation, and recreation. True, he had to concede, the laws were orginally enacted for religious purposes; true, as they stood on the statute books, they were still couched in religious phrases, referring to Sunday as "the Lord's day" and to commerce as "worldly employment"; true, the Supreme Court of Pennsylvania had recently declared that "Sunday is the holy day among Christians"; nevertheless, the Attorney General submitted, the mores have changed in recent years, and many people, instead of going to church, use Sunday for visiting and entertainment. In this curious fashion, some Christians, by merely staying away from their churches, have — it would seem — changed the meaning of Sunday not only for other Christians, but even for Orthodox Jews; such was the contention and such was the decision. Rather than allow a few devout Seventh-day Adventists and Orthodox Jews the same exemption that twenty-one other states have granted without ill effect, good Christians in Pennsylvania, Massachusetts, and Maryland appear prepared to politicalize, secularize, and downgrade their own sacred day. No wonder Mephistopheles takes courage! If they are prepared to deny their Sabbath, who knows what they may deny next?

On the other hand, the best bait to ensnare the churches may not be political power, but loans or grants of public money. On this score, Mephistopheles points out that, for the purpose of destroying churches and church institutions, certain types of public assistance are much more efficacious than others because they create a condition of financial dependence. Among the more destructive types, for example, are assistance in expanding personnel and capacity, or in purchasing equipment that will soon become obsolete, or in paying teachers' salaries or the cost of school-bus transportation — any assistance, in fact, that can trap an institution into a commitment of long-term outlay. If a church can solve its financial problems by merely explaining that every observance that appears to be religious — and has always been considered so — is really secular in essence, well then, secular all of them must be!

This much accomplished, we hasten to the stage of open demolition. The church being no longer in a position to question that so-called "religious" education, "religious" observance, and "religious" creed are essentially secular, it is manifestly incumbent on the state to organize and regulate these activities in the public interest.

Perhaps it would be well, Mephistopheles suggests, to begin with matters of external observance and adapt them to modern engineering standards. In order to reduce congestion on the highways and increase the utility of recreational and resort facilities, the day of rest heretofore observed on Sunday will be distributed throughout the week, the population being divided for the purpose into seven categories assigned to the respective days, with leave to apply for transfer in the event of marriage or divorce. Moreover, the dates of Christmas and

Easter will be fixed annually by a majority vote of the retail merchants subject to veto by a majority vote of milliners.

Next, at the instance of the pork-packing industry and its many loyal friends in the right places, all kosher shops and restaurants will be ruled against public policy and summarily banned. Something must also be done for the real estate interests. As it is uneconomic and wasteful for the various religious denominations to conduct worship services in different edifices (some of them located on very choice corners), they will be required by law to share a specified list of church buildings at hours to be arranged. The remaining parcels will be condemned to provide municipal parking lots. In addition, since the so-called "religious" practice of lifelong celibacy is manifestly disadvantageous to several different professions and industries, a commission will be appointed to investigate the practice and recommend appropriate remedial legislation.

Furthermore, Mephistopheles calls attention to certain doctrines and modes of behavior, formerly considered to have "religious" import but now discovered to be strictly secular in nature. These require no preliminary investigation; they are so obviously deleterious. It will be made a serious crime to advocate or knowingly join, assist, or conspire with any group or organization that advocates poverty, abstinence, or self-denial — all of which the Congress finds inimical to and subversive of American business. Similarly, since competent authorities have reported that the preaching of peace and universal brotherhood is injurious to military discipline and national security, institutions which permit this activity and all related and associated schools will become ineligible to receive public grants and will be required to repay any grants received during the preceding twenty years.

It may be that this legislative program will require a certain period of adjustment. Hotheads may criticize and a few may even oppose the dawn of the new, secularized era. Mephistopheles is ready with a strikingly simple device to eliminate all friction or conflict.

This is the final phase of his program, a plan of beautiful simplicity. He recommends that the power of appointing — or, as it used to be called, "ordaining" — the clergymen of any and all denominations and religions be vested in the President of the United States subject to confirmation by the United States Senate.

For all its brilliance, the idea may involve a few difficulties. For a while, there may be a few strains between the major political parties and even between senators and local district leaders in filling the more desirable posts. But since Francisco Franco solved the problem in Spain by obtaining personal control over the selection and appointment of bishops, why doubt that American know-how will do at least as well? To consummate the entire program, Congress need only confer on the President the ex-officio title of Supreme Head of *All* Churches and Defender of *All* Faiths.

It is time to return soberly to the wisdom of the Founding Fathers. The churches which so many of us cherish are in grave jeopardy. Since their beginnings when our ancestors suffered and sacrificed to build them, they have faced no deadlier threat. The outlook is not a bit less ominous because those who propose to intermingle the church with the political state happen to be well intentioned. Regardless of denominations, creeds, and intentions, they are dangerously misguided. All church members — Catholics and Protestants, Jews and Christians — have the same interest in resisting them. As Elihu Root said, "It is not a question of religion, or of creed, or of party; it is a question of declaring and maintaining the great American principle of eternal separation between church and state."

True, maintaining the principle may cost us inconvenience, misunderstanding, and even hostility. But did fear of embarrassment silence Jefferson or Madison? Like them, we consider the wall of separation indispensable to both church and state, and to our country's freedom.

Indispensable we know it is to the welfare of the churches; but why is it equally indispensable to the political state? Because today, more than ever before, the government of the most powerful democracy on earth needs the critical scrutiny of independent churches, their visions, exhortations, and unsparing rebukes. Organized religion knows no higher duty than to maintain the enduring ideals and universal values that exceed the jurisdiction of any earthly power, transcend the widest political boundaries, and defy the currents of popular opinion. The louder the voice of the people in a society, the more it requires the inner monitions of religious conscience.

In recent years, the inroads and encroachments have grown serious. If we do not speak out for principle today, we or our children may later have to fight for it. A little retreat, a little delay, a little appeasement — these will only encourage the misguided to attempt further aggressions. Silence has become too costly; we can no longer afford it. A little candor, a little courage, a little intransigence exhibited openly here and now — these will surely preserve the integrity of our religious institutions. The times have summoned us.

Adapted from the North Lecture at Franklin and Marshall College, 1961, and published in Harper's *magazine, November 1961.*

The "Establishment of Religion" Puzzle

IN publishing the sixth and final volume[1] of his great life of James Madison, Irving Brant has just completed the most influential American biography of the century. The work has gradually compelled the abler among our judges, lawyers, historians, and political scientists to revise their previous estimates and to appreciate Madison's full eminence of intellect and statesmanship. Chapter by chapter, it has stretched his image from the level of dependable competence to that of authentic greatness. It has proved beyond doubt that the man we used to picture as a mere disciple and lieutenant of Thomas Jefferson was, in fact, an independent, creative, and tough-minded thinker, a forceful personality, and a bold leader at several critical junctures of the nation's destiny.

But this is by no means the whole of Mr. Brant's achievement. The biography has likewise prompted us to confront and reassess Madison's political concepts, to probe again into the fundamental postulates of free government, and to raise in the twentieth century some of the same unsparingly realistic questions that Madison raised in the eighteenth. More and more often, when first principles are at stake, it is Madison whom we find the justices of the Supreme Court quoting, citing, and contending with. He has become one of the most interesting, most contemporary of our interlocutors. In some respects, his notions are so timely that judges find it hard to keep pace with them.

A PUZZLE

There are several instances — one or two, at least, in each of Mr. Brant's volumes — where, with admirable depth of research and brilliance of reasoning, he corrects previous popular misapprehensions, generally held fallacies, and mistaken historical estimates. Drawing on the wealth of information he provides, I should like to discuss one of the most baffling aspects of recent constitutional doctrine in the Supreme Court. The cases I find so puzzling have arisen under a clause of the Bill of Rights that concerned Madison deeply throughout the busy years of his life, that is, the clause forbidding any law "respecting an establishment of religion." Taking into account the whole train of recent "establishment of religion" cases, what one faces is quite a juristic enigma.

In fairness, let me make my own approach plain. It is the same as that of the leading civil liberties organizations who have uniformly advocated a total separation of church and state and have contended that all of the instances of state action which were challenged in recent litigations before the Supreme Court were unconstitutional. The puzzle does not arise merely because the Court has drifted away from a libertarian position; when the Court drifts, one can usually discern a direction. It arises rather because observers see no way to reconcile the voting policy of distinguished justices in one case with their policy in other cases involving the same clause.

The leading cases on the subject have been *Everson* (permitting state reimbursement of school bus expenses to parents of parochial school pupils), *McCollum* (prohibiting religious instruction on public school premises), *Zorach* (permitting released time for religious instruction elsewhere), and *McGowan* (the 1961 decisions permitting states to enforce general Sunday laws against merchants who were devout observers of a different sabbath day).[2] Where in them is one to seek a consistent pattern of doctrine or analysis? Perhaps, if Justices Jackson and Rutledge had survived to participate in all four decisions, their votes might have provided us with examples of continuity. But this is mere speculation. Moreover, Justice Jackson himself contributed to the general confusion by employing the word "absolute" (usually anathema to him) with approval in his *Everson* dissent, as, for that matter, did Justice Frankfurter (to whom the word is likewise an epithet) in his *McCollum* opinion.

The Sunday law decisions of 1961 provide a typical illustration of the puzzle. Two of the libertarian justices (Warren and Black) voted to uphold the Sunday laws while the other two (Douglas and Brennan) dissented indignantly. Even between the two libertarian dissenters there was a grave difference. Only Justice Douglas saw the Sunday laws as violating the "establishment of religion" clause as well as the "free exercise" clause.

Three members of the court — Justices Black, Frankfurter, and Douglas — have been on the bench long enough to participate in all of these "establishment" decisions. Seeking to understand their views, one may be tempted to emphasize the opinions handed down in *McCollum* because the outcome was not only correct but also closest of all the decisions to unanimity. Yet even *McCollum* provides no firm footing, for its authority has been compromised, at least in some eyes, by the later decisions in *Zorach* and *McGowan*. If we put *McCollum* aside as a safe and dependable criterion, we are left with the frustrating patterns established in the other cases. Justice Black voted for constitutionality in *Everson,* for unconstitutionality in *Zorach,* and for constitutionality in *McGowan.* Justice Frankfurter voted for unconstitutionality in *Everson* and *Zorach,* only to shift to constitutionality in

McGowan. Justice Douglas voted for constitutionality in the first two cases and for unconstitutionality in the third.

One might try to dismiss the puzzle by simply insisting that every "establishment" controversy depends on its own facts and circumstances, that judges appraise the diverse facts and circumstances according to their best lights, and that no two types of state legislation touching the subject of religion are quite identical. Did not Justice Black show how close the *Everson* case was by saying that in it the state had approached the very verge of its constitutional power? Did not Justice Jackson, dissenting in the same case, say that his first inclination was to vote for constitutionality and only continued reflection had driven him to the opposite conclusion? Perhaps, in "establishment" contests, the Court has become something like a jury, with a jury's measure of predictability.

I for one find any such exit illusory. While substantial differences of fact might help to account for shifting majorities of the whole Court and shifting votes of a single justice, they do not adequately explain why justices like Black and Douglas, whose votes in cases involving freedom of religion, freedom of speech and press, and freedom of association have consistently been on the libertarian side, should fail to provide an intelligible pattern when "establishment of religion" is at issue. Similarly, it is odd that Justice Frankfurter, whose votes in cases falling within the same categories have been rather consistently majoritarian, should oscillate so widely in "establishment" cases. It is not unfair to say that "establishment of religion" is the *only* provision of the First Amendment where the respective working premises of the three justices seem so volatile.

BACKGROUND OF THE "ESTABLISHMENT" CLAUSE

In 1776, while Jefferson was in Philadelphia with the Continental Congress, George Mason headed a committee to frame the Virginia Declaration of Rights and Madison rendered decisive service on the committee. Mason drafted a clause which went no further than to reflect John Locke's ideal of "toleration" for those who did not belong to the Established Church. Madison succeeded in converting this into a guarantee of freedom of religion, to which "all men are equally entitled . . . according to the dictates of conscience." He also attempted but did not succeed in inserting an explicit condemnation of "peculiar emoluments or privileges" for those who belonged to a particular church.[3]

An unremitting debate ensued between the supporters of establishment, led from time to time by Patrick Henry and Edmund Pendleton, and the disestablishmentarians, led by Mason, Jefferson, and

Madison. At almost every session of the Virginia legislature the former proposed to extend the legal and economic privileges of the church, the latter to remove the remaining vestiges of its special position. In 1779, Jefferson drafted and submitted his celebrated "Bill for Religious Freedom,"[4] which at that time failed even to reach a third reading in the Assembly. Jefferson's *Notes on Virginia* (written in 1782 and published in France in 1785) contained a further moving appeal for disestablishment.[5]

In 1784 the sponsors of establishment pressed for enactment of their bill, which would require all persons to pay an annual contribution for the support of the Christian religion or of some Christian church or denomination which the taxpayer might designate. The bill contended, in its preamble, that since organized religion was beneficial to the general welfare, all citizens should be required to participate in supporting it. Thus, the contention which would be put forward in the twentieth century in support of school bus assistance and general Sunday laws (that is, that sectarian education and the sectarian sabbath possessed a strictly secular utility) was advanced, considered, and — as we shall see — rejected in the struggle that led to the First Amendment.

At this stage, George Mason, George Nicholas, and others asked Madison to prepare a statement of the full case for separation of church and state. He produced the epochal "Memorial and Remonstrance Against Religious Assessments"[6] which was circulated in 1785 and evoked a mighty wave of support for disestablishment. Taking advantage of the tide, Madison called up Jefferson's Bill for Religious Freedom and in 1786 obtained its enactment. Even then, the establishment forces endeavored to enervate the Jefferson bill by changing the word "Lord" in the preamble to "Lord Jesus Christ," only to receive a sharp rebuke from Madison for using such a name as a means of abridging "the natural and equal rights of all men." Jefferson's Bill was adopted without material amendment of its scope. Reporting the struggle and its outcome to Jefferson, who had been serving as American minister to France since 1784, Madison wrote that he flattered himself that the provisions of the Bill "have in this country extinguished forever the ambitious hope of making laws for the human mind." Would that he had been right!

In 1785 Madison showed that he was already committed to total separation of church and state as a *national* principle. A committee of Congress had proposed, in a plan for certain Western territories, to set aside one section in each township for support of public schools and one section for religion. When Congress struck out the provision for religion, Madison expressed his amazement that a committee had even proposed a principle "so unjust in itself . . . and smelling so strongly of an antiquated bigotry."

During and after the Philadelphia Convention of 1787, Madison stood against the formulation of a federal bill of rights. One of his chief reasons was the fear that no verbal prohibition of religious establishment could be found quite categorical enough to prevent a narrow interpretation, which in turn would invite further encroachments by aggressive clergymen. Yielding eventually on all other counts, he never felt wholly at ease on this one.[7] Perhaps his misgivings had originated in his 1776 experience with the text of the Virginia Declaration of Rights. At any rate, the debates recorded in the legislative annals of 1789 proved that Madison's semantic anxieties were not imaginary. Various formulations were toyed with to prohibit governmental action in the religious realm, but none seemed entirely free of ambiguity. The experience of the twentieth century has further exposed the semantic complexities of the matter.

In processing the First Amendment's "establishment" clause, Congress furnished only one completely explicit and illuminating episode. In September of 1789, certain senators who were supporters of the established churches in New England, backed by Senator Lee of Virginia, who had been a partisan of the 1784 assessment bill, attempted a bold coup. They proposed to begin the First Amendment as follows: "Congress shall make no law establishing articles of faith or a mode of worship or prohibiting the free exercise of religion." This, of course, would have opened the way for government support of churches and church schools. Madison, as chairman of the House conferees, succeeded in defeating the maneuver.

On September 25, 1789, Congress formally submitted the Bill of Rights for ratification. The establishment clause of the First Amendment declared: "Congress shall make no law respecting an establishment of religion." If words can ever confer an absolute tenor on a constitutional prohibition, these were such words.

There is direct proof that when Madison inserted absolute prohibitions in the federal Bill of Rights, he acted with full awareness of what he was doing. On October 17, 1788, only a few months before preparing the document, he had written Jefferson an elaborate statement of his principles and policies. In the final paragraph of his letter, Madison expressed reluctance to frame *"absolute restrictions in cases that are doubtful, or where emergencies may overrule them."* The examples he gave were well chosen, consisting of proposed absolute restrictions against (a) suspension of the writ of habeas corpus, (b) maintenance of a peacetime army, and (c) government grants of monopolies. As his correspondent must agree, none of these ought to be made "absolute." (Madison actually underscored "absolute," as though to wink at the judges and law professors of the twentieth century.) In view of this passage, it is plain that when he drafted and sponsored certain "absolute restrictions" a few months later, he acted advisedly.

How much weight should we attach to Jefferson's and Madison's official behavior when church-and-state issues arose after 1789? This is still a highly debatable question. Obviously, though the subsequent conduct of the two Presidents is pertinent as a kind of practical construction, the people of the United States cannot be said to have adopted it in advance when they ratified the Bill of Rights. Suffice it to say that both men, during their respective administrations, sedulously maintained the libertarian stand for which they had fought in the 1780's.[8] Jefferson's felicitous phrase, "a wall of separation between Church and State," uttered during this period,[9] aptly characterizes it. Nevertheless, it seems less controversial for us to concentrate on the two deliberate expositions of their philosophy that were familiar to the congressmen who submitted and the state legislatures who formally ratified the Bill of Rights. These were Jefferson's Bill for Religious Freedom and Madison's Memorial and Remonstrance.

EXPLANATION BEGUN: THE BIOGRAPHICAL FACTORS

With this outline of the record before us, it may be possible now to explain why the Supreme Court's decisions and the justices' votes in "establishment of religion" cases seem to lack a consistent pattern. The explanation I am about to offer has nothing to do with reconciling the respective decisions or votes with one another. Believing that by and large they are not really reconcilable, I shall not even make the attempt. My purpose is quite modest; I aim not to dispel but merely to explain the state of confusion.

At the outset, let me say that I do not think the main cause is a conflict of views about the intended meaning of the word "establishment" in the First Amendment. Although once in a while some zealous writer may contend that the First Amendment does not forbid government support of organized religion but only government preference of one religious sect over the others, we may dismiss the argument as summarily as the Supreme Court has. It does not deserve serious consideration if only because in effect it puts forward the same proposal (on nondiscriminatory support for all sects) that provoked Madison's Memorial and Remonstrance of 1785.

If not in the meaning of "establishment," where then does the confusion originate? Let me summarize what I believe is the explanation:

The Court and the individual justices have been working with two different understandings of the scope of "religion" in the "establishment of religion" clause. The narrower understanding may be called the Jeffersonian or Enlightenment view; the broader may be called the Madisonian or Dissenter view. If one adopts the Jeffersonian or Enlightenment view, one treats the establishment clause as an adjunct or auxiliary to the clause guaranteeing the "free exercise of religion"; if one adopts the Madisonian or Dissenter view, one treats the establishment clause not only as an implement of other guarantees but also as a self-sufficient and independent imperative, meriting the most scrupulous obedience because it safeguards the purity of organized religion itself. Though the difference between the two views is merely one of degree and emphasis, it is quite important enough to determine how a judge will cast his vote in a close case. Consequently, any judge who does not distinguish one view of "religion" from the other is quite likely to oscillate between them in a series of "establishment of religion" litigations.

In offering this explanation, I draw encouragement from Mr. Brant, who likewise seems to sense an underlying difference between the two great Americans in their attitudes toward religion. He says, "In his paramount emphasis upon religious liberty as the core of all freedoms, Madison differed somewhat from Jefferson, whose mind centered on freedom of the press, trial by jury and habeas corpus, and from Mason, who was steeped in generalities about the original principles of government."[10] The data of Madison's biography illustrate this difference rather clearly.

Whereas Jefferson obtained a strictly secular education, Madison spent his formative years at the College of New Jersey (Princeton), an institution that was at least as Presbyterian in general atmosphere as it was liberal and democratic in political influence. His family seems to have been attached to religious interests; a cousin and devoted friend, the Reverend James Madison, became the first Episcopal bishop in Virginia — in 1790, after the church had been disestablished. If during his Princeton stay the young Madison had not developed a vocal disability that permanently limited his oratorical powers, he himself might have followed the then popular vocation of Princeton graduates — the pulpit. (Was the disability merely a psychosomatic proof that he heard the yet-uncertain voice of a different calling? If it was, we can only render thanks that his body knew what his mind was not yet ready to declare.)

At Princeton as at home, establishment appeared not only as an enemy of religious freedom but also as an engine and instrument of British imperial policy. The established clergy held a vested interest in

espousing the cause of the Royalists. No wonder, then, that disestablishment seemed so imperative to the young Madison. In Virginia, he
had observed, as Jefferson had, how an established church inevitably
violates the freedom of the individual; at Princeton, he could not fail
to learn something further, i.e., how it also violates the freedom of
other churches and sects.

All this explains the boldness verging on temerity with which
Madison, then only twenty-five years of age, attempted to revise
George Mason's article on religious freedom in the Virginia Declaration of Rights of 1776. As we noted, he proposed two drastic changes:
(1) the radical advance from Mason's (and Locke's) "toleration" to
genuine religious freedom to which "all men are equally entitled," and
(2) the abolition of all special privileges enjoyed by the established
church, its clergy, or its members. That he succeeded with the first
item was, of itself, a historic achievement. As for the second, though
rejected at the time, it demonstrated that as early as 1776 Madison was
viewing disestablishment not merely as an adjunct to religious freedom but as an independent prerequisite to a free society.

It was three years later that Jefferson introduced his Bill for
Religious Freedom as a part or element in an extensive program of
statutory reform. The Bill was not enacted until 1786 — when Madison, seeing that his own Memorial of 1785 had overwhelmed the
supporters of establishment, brought it forward for action. The Bill
for Religious Freedom is a noble and beautiful statement, displaying
Jefferson's finest gifts of mind and pen.

Yet would it be unfair to suggest that the Bill has occasionally
acquired a status that is anachronistic? It is unquestionably more
eloquent than Madison's Memorial; moreover, it glows with Jefferson's
great charismatic name; of these advantages there can be no doubt.
But to regard it as the culminating statement of the disestablish-
mentarian movement is, I think, anachronistic. Though enacted into
law a year after Madison drafted the Memorial, it was actually
prepared six years before. The Bill spoke Jefferson's reaction to the
scene of 1779. Madison, using much less colorful rhetoric in the
Memorial, absorbed all of Jefferson's arguments and added several
important ones of his own. The Memorial is the authentic culminative
text not merely because Madison who wrote it also prepared the Bill
of Rights; it is definitive because it is both later in date and more
comprehensive in scope.

EXPLANATION CONTINUED: THE INTELLECTUAL FACTORS

The intellectual factors are those I had in mind when using "Enlightenment" as a crude label to characterize Jefferson's understanding

of religion (reflected in his Bill) and "Dissenter" as an equally crude label to characterize Madison's understanding (reflected in his Memorial). Both understandings have intellectual merit. The two have coincided in application where the free exercise of religion is at issue; their influences have differed only in "establishment" cases. Madison's understanding of religion, being broader in scope than Jefferson's, necessarily leaves less room for state support of church activities.

What were the chief factors that defined religion's scope according to the two views?

A. The Enlightenment Approach:

1. *Influence of the Speech-Conduct Dichotomy.* First among them was the basic Enlightenment theme that political liberty required the drawing of a boundary line between thought and speech, on one side, where official power ought not to operate, and overt conduct, on the other side, where it ought.

One can rightly say that this was and is the most precious boundary line that political man ever staked out. Even fearful old Hobbes had recommended making a distinction between thoughts and physical conduct — without indicating to which side he would assign the right of speaking. From Spinoza and Locke to Montesquieu and Voltaire, the whole thrust of Enlightenment doctrine was directed toward the speech-conduct dichotomy. During the seventeenth century, the drive had borrowed a goodly part of religion's zeal, which it never bothered to return. (For example, freedom of speech, which later periods would link automatically with freedom of the press, was historically an offshoot of the demand for free exercise of religion.)[11]

Accordingly, it would seem quite reasonable to the men of the Enlightenment that the speech-conduct dichotomy might likewise govern when church and state were to be kept apart. Surely, one could not expect the state to respect the immunity of speech unless one conceded it a full right to regulate overt behavior.[12] Thus, if a judge should be presented with a regulation affecting overt behavior only (for example, one of our state Sunday laws), he would feel obliged to inquire merely whether the regulation was reasonable. If it was and if it did not appear to abridge the free exercise of religion, he would be warranted in holding it valid.

2. *Distrust of Corporations.* The Enlightenment's political program was as individualistic and molecular as its psychology. Associations it viewed with the distrust and hostility that eventaully found expression in Revolutionary France's *Loi Le Chapelier* (1791), dissolving all corporate bodies, whether ecclesiastical or secular, as organs of oppression and feudal privilege.[13] Why was disestablishment deemed im-

perative? Precisely in order to secure religious freedom for the *individual*.

Some of the Enlightenment leaders were atheists, scoffing at religion in all of its forms; some were deists, who by consigning God to an emeritus status had left little room for churches in their scheme of things; some, like Jefferson, were sincerely religious and even more sincerely anticlerical. None of them was likely to see disestablishment as a right to which *groups* or sects were entitled. One set of organized superstitions, they would say, or another; it was all the same. On this reasoning, the "establishment of religion" clause would never become a cogent imperative except as an auxiliary to the "free exercise" clause.

3. *Equating the Holy with the True.* Standing in awe before the grandeur and symmetry of the Newtonian cosmos, many of the atheistic leaders of the Enlightenment evinced a reverence like Plato's for the True. Deistic leaders, on the other hand, would be more likely to equate the Holy with the True, and certain Protestant theologians of the era, who really ought to have known better, seem to have strayed in the same direction. Seen in this shallow fashion, religion could be defined as a specific way of searching for truth. A man's religious "opinions" were comparable to the rest of his opinions; he ought to be free to hold and express them for the same reason that he ought to be free to hold and express aesthetic, scientific, and political views. (Of course, the churches had been inviting some such reductive reaction as this for centuries; they had made it a "religious" proposition that the world was flat, that it stood still, that it was the center of the universe, etc.)

If, then, one assumed that the whole religious enterprise was only a way of searching for truth, one would feel entitled to reduce the role and radius of religion whenever physical science or empirical technique might disclose some new area in which they could do a better job of searching. Ultimately, by applying the formula with consistency, it would be possible to do just what the senators proposed in vain when the "establishment" clause was being shaped, that is, shrink "religion" to nothing more than "articles of faith or a mode of worship." This accomplished, support for church schools might readily follow.

How remote such a result would be from Jefferson's purpose! Yet, while intending to assert the utmost religious freedom and denounce every conceivable kind of clerical aggression, his Bill for Religious Freedom did postulate a dangerously narrow understanding of "religion." Notice, if you please, how often in our times people extract mottoes and apt maxims from its text when the stake they are concerned with is not religion at all but controversial political speech. Eloquent though it is, it offers too meager a criterion of religion for cases under the "establishment" clause.

B. The Dissenter Approach:

1. *Reliance on Multiplicity.* In order not to exaggerate the difference between the two approaches, we shall begin with the points at which they were closest. Madison matched Jefferson perfectly in a lifelong devotion to the religious freedom of the individual and what he repeatedly called "the rights of conscience." The first five paragraphs of the Memorial offer little more than a vigorous paraphrase of Jefferson's statements in the Bill for Religious Freedom.[14] They leave the purport of the Bill entirely intact. Madison's distinctive achievement consisted in superimposing an *institutional* acceptance of "religion" on Jefferson's monadic acceptation of the term.

For another thing, since like other educated men of the epoch, Madison was conversant with the writings of the *philosophes,* he undoubtedly learned a good deal from them. Madison followed Voltaire in insisting, as he frequently did, that the best possible safeguard of religious freedom was not in legal guarantees but in the sheer multiplicity of religious sects. This conviction Madison retained from early youth to the end of his life; even in old age, he saw fit to regard separation of church and state as a pertinent topic in an essay on the general theme of monopolies!

Though he may have come across the reliance on multiplicity of sects in Voltaire[15] or, for that matter, in the manuscript of Jefferson's *Notes on Virginia,* Madison made it wholly his own, fitting it with skill into his pluralistic philosophy of society. He saw that the religious sphere had attributes of its own that made it essentially unlike the spheres of economics and of political structure. Granted that in any sphere of human activity the processes of competition, rivalry, and reciprocal checks and balances would serve to restrain monopoly and preserve liberty; nevertheless, when an activity was religious in nature, the government possessed no jurisdiction or warrantable power over it. It had no more right to aid than to hinder the competing sects.

In America, Madison submitted most astutely, the rights of conscience must be kept not only free but *equal* as well. And in view of the endless variations — not only among the numerous sects, but also among the organized activities they pursued and the relative emotional values they attached to their activities — how could any species of government assistance be considered genuinely equal from sect to sect? If, for example, a state should attempt to subsidize all sectarian schools without discrimination, it would necessarily violate the principle of equality because certain sects felt impelled to conduct a large number of such schools, others few, others none. How could the officers of government begin to measure the intangible factors that a true equality of treatment would involve, i.e., the relative intensity of religious attachment to parochial education that the respective groups required of their lay and clerical members? It would be presumptuous even to inquire.[16] Thus, just as in matters of race our belated recognition of intangible factors has finally led us to the maxim "separate therefore unequal," so in matters of religion Madison's immediate recognition of intangible factors led us promptly to the maxim "equal therefore separate." Equality was out of the question without total separation. While, therefore, under Jefferson's individualistic approach it would be extremely difficult to reconcile religious subsidies with the principle of equality, under Madison's institutional approach it would be quite impossible.

2. *The Dissenter Need for Association.* Of course, when one attaches a Dissenter label to Madison's approach, one does not mean that the Virginia struggle for religious liberty belonged exclusively to the Baptists or any other group. Reading the text of the Memorial, one catches echoes of many noble voices — John Knox and Andrew Melville in Scotland, Peter Wentworth and John Lilburne in England, not to mention the Hebrew prophets who were their common source and inspiration. During the Virginia contest, the Presbyterians of the state were among those who provided significant support for Madison's efforts. All of these would have rejected a narrow or circumscribed notion of religion's role.

Yet, after we have awarded due credit to the general climate of American thought and Madison's own libertarian genius, there is still much in the particular history of the Baptists that confers depth on the 1785 Memorial and poignancy on the role of religious associations. One understands nothing about so-called "voluntary" associations or their human significance unless one grasps what they mean to the members of a persecuted group. Often, to such a group, church-affiliation is "voluntary" only in the sense that life itself is, or if not life, then the keeping of self-respect. In Revolutionary Virginia, the Baptists were the ones to whom persecution had disclosed not merely the personal but also the corporate value of religion, not merely its individual function as a search but also its group function as a refuge.

The keynote of seventeenth- and eighteenth-century Baptist experience was sounded at the start. Significantly enough, the first English Baptist Church was organized not by free men in England but by religious exiles in Amsterdam. Their initial confession of faith contained a splendid article on religious liberty and separation of church and state, declaring that "the magistrate is not to meddle with religion, or matters of conscience nor to compel men to this or that form of religion." This, be it noted, as early as the year 1611! The subsequent ordeal of almost unremitting persecution, both in England and in America, only served to reinforce these sound principles and increase the number of adherents.[17] When Madison wrote in his Memorial about the rise of the Christian Church, its independence of government support, and its growth in the face of official persecution, other readers probably recalled the events of the first and second centuries; the Baptists probably recalled those of the seventeenth and eighteenth. Thus the Memorial evoked ideals and loyalties that were not monadic but explicitly social and institutional.

A certain lack of sympathy is to be expected when one tries to convince a very superior mind that the people's understanding of religion does not fully coincide with his. He is likely to dismiss the people's view as merely superstitious. Nevertheless, to the common man and to quite a few uncommon men, religion does possess emotional, ethnic, and cultural aspects — both desirable and undesirable — which cannot be severed from its corporate and communal operations. A church is far more than a search. Concededly, a temperament like Jefferson's may have needed no fellow-communicants; along with most other intellectuals, he would have approved Alfred North Whitehead's celebrated definition: "Religion is what the individual does with his own solitariness." But this is, at best, a definition suited to the Jeffersons and Whiteheads of the country if there are any, and to others of similar disposition. It is not fit for the remainder of us, or for the judicial enforcement of a clause forbidding "establishment of religion."

3. *Factors of the General Welfare.* Recognizing organized religion as an ongoing social institution, Madison was much too realistic to overlook the influence it can exert on the general welfare. He proceeded to argue an excellent secular case, proving that here too the establishmentarians were completely mistaken. Religion in a society could indeed serve the general welfare, but government support of religion could serve only the forces of resentment and hatred. Religion could be solidary, but government assistance could be only divisive. These hardheaded considerations, set forth in paragraphs 9 to 15 of the Memorial, have had a massive impact; in fact, they may constitute the main cause why religious liberty has survived in America. Madison warned that anything resembling an establishment would (a) deter persons oppressed in other countries from coming to America, (b) banish some of our citizens from their own land, (c) destroy the harmony we have endeavored to build among highly diverse groups,

(d) provoke bitter inter-group hostilities, and (e) weaken the general enforcement of the laws and "slacken the bands of Society."

The argument he concluded with was overwhelming. How could Americans yield on establishment without impairing all the rest of their fundamental rights? Having insisted earlier in the Memorial that even "three pence" for support of an establishment would imperil the people's religious liberty, he now drew the full register of consequences. Since all of our basic rights were held by the selfsame constitutional title as freedom of conscience, a compromise on the issue of establishment must jeopardize the entire "basis and foundation of Government."

RESPECTFULLY SUBMITTED

Only by applying Madison's broader understanding of "religion," which involves full recognition of the term's institutional as well as its individual references, can the Supreme Court realize the just purposes of the "establishment of religion" clause. Acquiescence in a narrower acceptation inevitably works an abridgment of the rights of conscience and a denial of justice. "Justice," wrote Madison, "is the end of government. It is the end of civil society. It ever has been, and ever will be pursued, until it be obtained, or until liberty be lost in the pursuit."[18]

From the 1961 Annual Survey of American Law.

On Government and Prayer

IT IS only now, almost two centuries after the event, that we are beginning to understand the full significance of 1776. Declaring our national independence was a great feat of political emancipation, but it was more than that. It liberated the mind and will of democratic man to fulfill themselves, but it did more than that. It cut certain bonds that inhibited our pursuit of happiness, but that was only a part of its work.

To grasp the whole import of 1776, one must notice that the Declaration of Independence, like the Constitution and every subsequent political instrument, was issued not by the people but on behalf of the people by their chosen representatives. This is typical of our system. Our government is based almost entirely on direct or indirect representation of the citizenry — a fact so familiar and obvious that philosophers have overlooked its serious moral implications. When the Founding Fathers installed a representative form of government, they not only caused democratic man to emerge from his former state but also lifted him to an entirely new plane in the evolution of human conscience.

With 1776 the American entered a higher moral condition. In some sense and degree, he, a member of the people, became morally responsible for what his representatives did in the people's name and by their authority. Government, which now belonged to him, might implicate him when it used authority wrongfully or unjustly or oppressively. For millennia, he, the common man, had been accustomed to identify himself in sympathy, interest, and conscience with the persecuted; now, in his radically new status, he might also be identified with the official persecutor.

Thus, the Declaration of Independence meant much more than an emancipation of man's mind and will; perforce it meant a concomitant emancipation of his social conscience. After 1776, if his mind and will could claim the right to exert and fulfill themselves, his conscience must possess a similar and equally cogent claim. Though he might let his mind use its new freedom merely to relax and lie dormant, he could not assume the same of his conscience. Democracy, even as it liberated conscience, thrust it into an entire series of fresh involvements. For democratic man, conscience became free in order to exert its force, perform its duty and engage itself for the common good. It had a new role in the world.

As early as 1776, Jefferson and Madison seem to have sensed that something novel was afoot in the evolution of morals, that with the advent of the new republic the human conscience was instituting a new phase. We see it in Madison's chief preoccupation during the spring of 1776. Working with George Mason in the state legislature, he obtained the adoption of a guarantee of religious freedom, to which "all men are equally entitled . . . according to the dictates of conscience." And Jefferson too, as soon as he returned from his immortal hour in Philadelphia, presented a sweeping program for social and political reform which, among other things, would secure freedom of religion in Virginia and end the establishment of the church. Though most of Jefferson's program took years to win approval (disestablishment, for example, was not fully achieved until 1786), it contained one item that even the religious conservatives were ready to accept, that the Virginia legislature enacted into law in December 1776, and that thus became a permanent portion of the American heritage and a harbinger of the future society.

What was this great early stirring of democratic conscience? It was the repeal of the old English and colonial laws that had made absence from the place of common prayer a criminal offense. Under the old laws, anyone who stayed away from church for one month could be committed to prison until he conformed. One of Jefferson's first concrete achievements on behalf of religious freedom consisted in wiping these provisions from the statute books. If there was any issue on which even the most pious defenders of establishment (patriots like Edmund Pendleton and Patrick Henry) could agree with the prophets of the new enlightened age (patriots like Jefferson and Madison), it was the issue of using state power to bring about attendance at prayer. This was considered obnoxious beyond possibility of debate.

THE NATURE OF THE AMERICAN PRINCIPLE

There are two aspects of the American principle of separation of church and state that are quite widely misunderstood. For one thing, many people believe that the motive behind separation is not religious but exclusively secular. For another, many believe that separation confers no benefits on the majority of the electorate but merely protects the minority. Both of these impressions are erroneous — erroneous and likewise dangerous, for they tend to invite erosion of the First Amendment. It is important to set the record straight.

Of course, separation does have many great secular advantages which would fully justify it as a principle of our political system. Secular government does not need to apologize when it gives consideration to secular advantages; it should apologize when it does not. Among the advantages, surely the most valuable is the truce that separation imposes on hostile religious sects. The history of organized religion in the Western world contains countless discreditable chapters stained with blood and torture, distrust and conspiracy, persecution and genocide. Some of the goriest and most shameful pages have been written in our own century.

Why are differences of religious doctrine able to cause so much hostility and ferocity between group and group? One of the reasons is the very nature of theological belief. Since by definition there is no scientific way to prove conclusively that any belief about the Deity, the source of revelation, the spiritual realm, or the afterlife is factually true, many zealously religious persons suffer from inner uncertainty, frustration, and subconscious doubt when they see that others do not share their theology. In this condition, they have two evident alternatives. The hard alternative is to validate one's faith as far as one can through righteous ethical behavior; the easy alternative, if one can use the authority of government for the purpose, is to compel one's neighbor to agree, by torturing or killing him if necessary. In the

Western world, man has rarely hesitated to choose the easier method. As Mark Twain said, "He is the only animal that loves his neighbor as himself, and cuts his throat if his theology isn't straight." At very least, the separation of church and state does keep certain citizens from periodically cutting other citizens' throats, and this, I suppose, we must classify as a merely secular advantage because it benefits not only the faithful, not only the heretics but even agnostics and atheists, who also possess throats.

Yet the American principle of separation has never rested on exclusively secular grounds. On the contrary, when Roger Williams first pronounced it in the seventeenth century, his concern was almost purely religious. Williams lived a life of rigorous piety. His dispute with the Puritan theocracy was theological in nature. The danger he saw and denounced in Massachusetts was not to the secular state but to religion itself. He solemnly averred that any law compelling men with diverse religious convictions to observe a uniform mode of prayer was nothing less than "spiritual rape."

In Thomas Jefferson too we meet this same solicitude for the purity and sanctity of religion. Remote as he became from any formally Christian belief, he always retained a lofty natural piety. His personal views, though heartily anticlerical, were not atheistic. They oscillated freely and inconsistently between the cool deism of the *philosophes* and a pious but creedless theism. Oscillation of this kind was not uncommon, and no one seems to have found it embarrassing. We meet it in the very text of the Declaration of Independence, which at the opening, using Jefferson's words, invokes "Nature's God" (a standard statement of deism) and at the end, using words inserted during debate in the Continental Congress, invokes "the protection of divine Providence" (an avowal of supernatural theism). When Jefferson returned to Virginia in 1776, and prepared to launch the campaign for disestablishment, he wrote in a private notebook: "External forms of religion, when against our belief, are hypocrisy and impiety." Thoughts like these show much more than a merely secular concern.

As for Madison, we know that when he was young, he was so attached to religion that he came close to taking the cloth. One need only examine his great Memorial and Remonstrance — or for that matter Jefferson's Bill for Religious Freedom — to recognize that the men who separated the church from the state in America believed that only thus could they preserve the purity and integrity of the clergy, the church and religion. As Justice Black said in *Engel v. Vitale,* "The Establishment Clause . . . stands as an expression of principle on the part of the Founders of our Constitution that religion is too personal, too sacred, too holy, to permit its 'unhallowed perversion' by a civil magistrate."[1] Let me add that considering the overwhelming power and resources of the modern state, the church and religion need the protecting shield of separation today much more than the state does.

We can turn now to the other mistaken notion, the notion that separating the church from the state confers no benefit on the majority of the people but only on the dissenters, heretics, atheists, in short, the various minority groups. To discuss this notion intelligently, we have to assume, as a sort of hypothesis, that in the United States today there exists some majority religious sect. (The census flatly refutes any such hypothesis.) We have further to assume that the postulated majority denomination displays a unanimity so monolithic and permanent that none among its members can ever be expected to disagree with the others on the slightest detail of religious belief or observance. (All ecclesiastical history is to the contrary.) Finally, we must assume, in the very teeth of the record, that today's sectarian majority — if such there be — will somehow never dwindle but remain proponderant for all time. Let us try to assume these palpable fictions.

If we do assume them, we only discover how farsighted James Madison and Thomas Jefferson were and how wisely they anticipated the moral consequences of the democratic revolution. Of course, the minorities need and will always need the legal shield of the First Amendment. It safeguards their elementary right not to suffer for believing or disbelieving, their right not to be persecuted. But the religious majority also have a certain right which the Founding Fathers were concerned to protect. Neither Madison nor Jefferson belonged to any disadvantaged or persecuted sect, neither was impelled by any personal suffering or deprivation to demand the separation of church and state. While they sympathized with the oppressed Virginia Baptists, they never thought of joining them. The legacy they intended for us is much more than the indispensable (minority) right not to be persecuted. It consists as well in the precious (majority) right not to participate in inflicting persecution. As representative government would implicate all citizens if it compelled uniformity of prayer — or, in Roger Williams's words, committed "spiritual rape," the majority as well as the minority draw protection from the prohibitions of the First Amendment. The Amendment makes it ethically safe to belong to the majority. By separating church and state, it assures the rarest, and perhaps the most excellent, of all civil rights: the constitutional right not to persecute.

THE SCHOOL PRAYER DECISION

Seen against this background, the Supreme Court's decision in *Engel v. Vitale* was about as close to predictable as the judicial process ever comes. The New York Board of Regents having composed a prayer and recommended its use in public schools, the Board of Education of New Hyde Park directed the school principal to cause it to be said aloud at the beginning of every school day. The parents of ten pupils claimed that these actions violated the constitutional guarantee against any "law respecting an establishment of religion." Speaking for the Supreme Court, Justice Black held, "We think that by using its public school system to encourage recitation of the Regents' prayer, the State of New York has adopted a practice wholly inconsistent with the Establishment Clause." Government, said the Court, "should stay out of the business of writing or sanctioning official prayers and leave that purely religious function to the people themselves and to those the people choose to look to for religious guidance."

To anyone conversant with the origins of the First Amendment and particularly with Madison's Memorial of 1785 which Justice Black cited repeatedly with telling force, the decision ought scarcely have been surprising. Of the seven justices who participated in the case, all except Justice Stewart agreed on the outcome. In a concurring opinion, Justice Douglas not only confirmed the rightness of the result but went on to announce that he now disapproved of the earlier *Everson* decision (the so-called *School Bus* holding). Like Justice Black, he noted, "The First Amendment teaches that a government neutral in the field of religion better serves all religious interests."

Among the arguments advanced to defend the Regents' action, I believe only two deserve mention. One is that since under the plan any pupil who so desires can remain silent or be excused from the room during the collective prayer, the participation is not coercive but merely optional. Justice Black disposes of this contention in two ways. First, on the *law*, he holds that the Establishment Clause does not depend on proving coercion; in America, government has no right to establish religion whether individuals are coerced or not. Second, on the *facts*, he holds that there is at least indirect coercion whenever "the power, prestige and financial support of government is placed behind a particular religious belief."

On this point, it is extremely difficult to understand the action of the New York Board of Regents. Even if one can overlook the curious presumptuousness implied in what they did, one must still try to explain their apparent unfamiliarity with the feelings and behavior patterns of school children. They were actually satisfied to tell a school child of normal sensibility, "If you want to be different from everyone else, you can remain silent while your classmates pray in unison to God; you can conspicuously absent yourself at the opening of school while they ask God to bless *their* parents and *their* country. No coercion, purely voluntary!" If one can believe *that,* one can believe anything.

The Regents had a further contention to advance. Though this one could hardly be called novel, James Madison having refuted it explicitly in his Memorial of 1785 and in various later writings, it is still heard often enough to require renewed refutation. It is the hackneyed old argument that, though the immediate proposal — for instance, a school prayer — may overstep the limits of the First Amendment, we should accept the trespass because it is relatively slight. The theme begins ingratiatingly: "Is not everything in life a matter of degree? The encroachment we are proposing is very small, and surely you are too sophisticated to believe in absolutes."

Plausible enough, but at this point the theme becomes less reassuring. It continues *sotto voce:* "If you do act pliably and yield on this occasion, you will not mind our returning next year to cite it as a precedent and propose some further trivial encroachment. Perhaps, for example, we should come forward with a Regents' Definition of God's Nature and Attributes which the children will memorize so they can understand whom they are addressing when they recite the Regents' Prayer. Everything is a matter of degree. Not having objected now, you will scarcely begin then. Clever of us — is it not? — to use every step, no matter how dubious when first proposed, as solid ground from which to project the next."

To the Founding Fathers, all this would have been familiar strategy; it was quite similar to what they had heard from the British Crown and Parliament. They answered it so well that when the argument bobbed up again in *Engel v. Vitale,* Justice Black dismissed it by merely quoting a famous passage in Madison's Memorial. Thirty-five years after he wrote the Memorial, in the evening of his life, Madison repeated the warning. "The people of the U.S.," he said, "owe their Independence & their liberty, to the wisdom of descrying in the minute tax of 3 pence on tea, the magnitude of the evil comprized in the precedent. Let them exert the same wisdom, in watching against every evil lurking under plausible disguises, and growing up from small beginnings. Obsta principiis."[2]

Why — unlike other litigations involving religion, such as the *School Bus* and *Sunday Law* cases — did *Engel v. Vitale* seem so clear to the Supreme Court, why was the decision almost unanimous? The answer is not hard to find. For one thing, the subject matter of *Engel v. Vitale* was purely and exclusively religious in. nature. Buses for parochial school children and Sunday closing laws partake not only of religion but also of secular concerns like highway safety, public convenience, rest and recreation; in the earlier litigations religious activity was mingled and tangled with secular interests. But how could anyone say the same of a school prayer? In *Engel v. Vitale,* even the Regents conceded the religious nature of the prayer.

For another thing, *Engel v. Vitale* involved nothing but religious belief and speech; it contained no element of overt physical conduct. Under the classic libertarian dichotomy,³ the State of New York had no conceivable authority for what it was attempting. Government can rightly encourage and even compel certain kinds of overt conduct — for example, submission to vaccination — despite anyone's conscientious objections. Other kinds of conduct — for example, distributing religious literature — it may or may not control depending on the circumstances. But when we come to religious belief and the mere avowal of belief, we are in a realm where government must never intrude. The decision in *Engel v. Vitale* was not only right but imperatively necessary.

If such it was, what shall we say about the anguished outcry that greeted it in many quarters? While President Kennedy, ex-President Truman, and a number of other personages gave informed and understanding comments to the press, while the bulk of the people treated the holding as an interesting conversation piece with a short life-expectancy, a number of individuals in public and private life reviled the decision with sulphurous epithets, denounced the justices of the Supreme Court, and predicted the imminent decline and total fall of the United States of America. Generally speaking, the more florid criticisms showed on their face that they were uninhibited by acquaintance with the Court's opinion. Some very curious pronouncements on God, prayer, worship, and religion were uttered by some patently amateur theologians. The whole performance made quite a spectacle. Perhaps the most charitable way to summarize it would be to quote a remark of Emerson's that fits the occasion. Emerson said, "I knew a humorist who, in a good deal of rattle, had a grain or two of sense. He shocked the company by maintaining that the attributes of God were two — power and risibility; and that it was the duty of every pious man to keep up the comedy."

PRESIDENTS JEFFERSON AND MADISON ON GOVERNMENT-SPONSORED PRAYER

For those of us who take democracy and religion very seriously, there is much to be learned from the example of Jefferson's and Madison's official behavior when church-and-state questions came before them during their respective administrations. Both of them firmly supported the libertarian standard they had struggled for since 1776.

It was during his presidency that Jefferson issued the happy metaphor, "a wall of separation between Church and State."

What does it mean for a statesman to take our democratic form of government seriously? Among other things, it means that he gives thorough and consistent attention to its *representative* character. Government has a special ethical import when it draws its authority from a popular mandate developed in free public discussion and formalized in free competitive ballots. A democratic government, simply because it represents the whole people, may find itself barred in conscience from doing certain acts that other governments would not hesitate to do. For example, government in this country must abstain from the vicious practice of racial discrimination because, in what it does, it represents, binds, and implicates the electorate. By like reasoning, if it intrudes into the forbidden realm of religion and offends the religious or antireligious convictions of a single citizen, it wrongs the entire people.

This was Jefferson's attitude. As President of the United States he consistently refused to proclaim a day for national prayer and fasting (which the clergy of the time considered appropriate for thanksgiving). "Fasting and prayer," he said, "are religious exercises." The government had no right to meddle with them, even to the extent of a mere recommendation. Presidents Madison and Andrew Jackson were of the same view.

But suppose an emergency situation. Suppose, after a long series of provocations, the country at the President's instance declares war on a harassing foreign power; suppose the people show that they are deeply divided in their support of the war; suppose the more patriotic elements display intense anxiety about its outcome; suppose the Congress, for reasons of partisanship and stubborn sectionalism, only talks and procrastinates, impedes the President's military measures, and delays or withholds money, ships and weapons that are critically necessary. Suppose finally, in the midst of such turmoil, the Congress passes a joint resolution formally requesting the President to recommend "a day of *Public Humiliation and Prayer*." What then ought the President do?

These were the extreme circumstances and this was the problem that James Madison had to confront as President during the War of 1812. It was no easy dilemma, for if he refused, Congress would surely retaliate — at the expense of the war effort. Many of the New England clergy, preaching open sedition, rejoiced in their pulpits because, as they put it, God had seen to it that the depredations and horrors of the war had fallen on the very parts of the United States that were loyal to the government.

We may possibly regard Madison's solution to the problem as marking the extreme outer verge beyond which government must never venture where prayer is concerned, no matter how imperious the demand or impelling the emergency. He issued a proclamation as follows: (1) while recommending a specific day for collective prayer, he restricted the recommendation to those who might feel disposed to come together for the purpose; (2) he made clear that even they were to assemble not under government auspices but "in their respective religious congregations"; (3) he offered no form or text of prayer; and (4) he solemnly insisted that only voluntary prayers "can be acceptable to Him whom no hypocrisy can deceive, and no forced sacrifices propitiate." The proclamation provided cold comfort to those who had expected to embarrass the President.

Yet in later years, when Madison considered the episode in calm retrospect, he recorded[4] an impressive list of reasons why the government should do nothing whatever to recommend prayer, not even the innocuous little he had done. He said that even if all American citizens were attached — as they are not — to the very same creed and all desired to unite in a universal and simultaneous act of prayer, it was the religious leaders who should effect the arrangement, not the people's political representatives. Then he added, "In a nation composed of various sects, some alienated widely from others, and where no agreement could take place thro' the former, the interposition of the latter is doubly wrong."[5]

As Jefferson and Madison perceived, the practice they opposed was as wrong for the church as for the state and considerably more harmful. It soon became evident that the misguided clergymen who demanded government sponsorship for an annual service of pious thanksgiving destroyed their own objective. They desired a day of solemnity, humiliation and prayer; they got one of merchants' parades, football games, and general frivolity. Once they enlisted government to coordinate their efforts, the degradation was inevitable. Today, if anyone remembers that the intended way for Americans to offer thanks was to fast, it must be the thanksgiving turkey.

THERE IS NO NONDENOMINATIONAL PRAYER

We turn to the current scene. Scarcely had the Supreme Court announced its decision on the Regents' Prayer when resolutions were offered to amend the Constitution of the United States, overrule the Court, and give sanction to government-sponsored school prayers provided only they were "nondenominational." Since these proposals so obviously imperil the fabric of American rights, violate the historic principles of American liberty, and endanger the religious lives of the people, it seems likely that they will find their way, sooner or later, to the dusty shelf where they belong. Americans owe too much to the First Amendment to begin tinkering with its text at this late date.

Of all conceivable forms of tinkering, what could be more imprudent than an amendment to confer legal status and constitutional dignity on the term "nondenominational prayer"? The term is self-contradictory; it is a chimera. A nondenominational prayer does not, and cannot be made to, exist. It is as impossible as the progeny of a mule.

But did not the New York Regents label their prayer "nondenominational"? So they did. The time has come to question and test the accuracy of that label. If we do, we shall soon see how many denominations and religious consciences the so-called "nondenominational" prayer must affront.

Before beginning the test, I wish to make one simple, preliminary point — a matter of ordinary human psychology. That is: If, in the text of a service or prayer in my own church or synagogue, my child happens to meet some phrase that I do not find quite consonant with the ideals of my faith, I shall probably shrug off the incident and rely on the total tradition, doctrine and discipline of my religion to counteract the questionable detail. No one sits in his own church and scans the prayers critically, literally, suspiciously — unless, of course, he is preparing to leave it. All prayer books contain phrases that worshipers have to condone on grounds of familiarity and custom. One makes allowances and tries not to hear too distinctly.

But suppose you put our children in the "captive audience"[6] of a public school alongside children of other faiths and impose an unknown, alien prayer on them; will you not find us less indulgent? Now we become wary, critical, distrustful; we suspect that every line of the text is replete with ethical flaws and theological traps.[7] The closer we look, the more of them we find. Having been affronted by the school board's impertinence,[8] we are likely to examine the official prayer the way an experienced housewife in the market examines a box of strawberries, and we have as much right as she not to be duped.

The Regents' Prayer reads as follows: "Almighty God, we acknowledge our dependence upon Thee, and we beg Thy blessings upon us, our parents, our teachers and our country."

Let us describe just a few of the denominations and types of religious conscience[9] to whom the text of the Regents' "nondenominational" Prayer would be unacceptable. (Of course, the Regents' mistakes were not confined to text; they disregarded the well-known fact that some sects instruct their children to genuflect when they pray or to pray only in silence or not to pray with uncovered heads; but the text is bad enough.) We can list the following offended denominations:

First, all who believe in nontheistic religions. These would include Ethical Culture, Buddhism and Confucianism.

Second, all who believe in pantheistic religions, as exemplified by Spinoza and Einstein.

Third, all who believe in polytheistic religions. In *The Varieties of Religious Experience,* William James, one of our deepest students of the subject, said that every practical theism has been more or less polytheistic, and his own thought tended in that direction.

Fourth, all of us who believe in a God who is not "almighty." This was the basis of Judge Jerome Frank's religious faith in his last years. To put it gently, the concept of an almighty God does not readily comport with man's ethical freedom and personal responsibility.

Fifth, all whose religion excludes prayer from its assemblies and services. Ethical Culture is such a religion.

Sixth, all who believe that it is irreverent for anyone to pray unless he turns his heart and intention to God,[10] and that coerced or mechanical prayers are mere "vain repetitions"[11] which desecrate the communion between spirit and spirit. As Professor A. J. Heschel says, "To pray with *kavanah* (inner devotion) may be difficult; to pray without it is ludicrous."

Seventh, all who, while they approve of prayer, believe it should express glorification, gratitude, humility and so forth — but should never ask, petition, or beg anything of God, who they believe knows already what is best for men.

Eighth, all who believe that since God has irrevocably elected them at their birth among the few whom He will save from general perdition, prayers from the remainder of mankind are bound to be futile and void.

Ninth, all who believe that God, being just, may disapprove of a prayer that asks Him to confer His blessings indiscriminately on parents and teachers. He may not feel disposed to reward a parent who abandoned the child or a teacher who treated it meanly. And

Tenth, all of us who believe that religion's first duty in our time is to inculcate understanding, kindness, harmony and compassion among the men of all lands. It seems inexcusable that the Regents' Prayer does not continue beyond the words "our country." It teaches children to invoke divine blessings only on one nation within a single set of political boundaries. Thus the prayer reverts to early, tribal concepts of the Deity, discards the highest ideals of Judaism, Christianity, Unitarianism, Ethical Culture and other universal faiths, and shrinks the children's horizons to a smug and narrow nationalism. No wonder

Father Robert E. Hood, a Protestant Episcopal priest, contemned the Regents' Prayer as "non-Christian" and "sub-cultural"![12]

The whole notion of a nondenominational prayer is fallacious; it is much too primitive for the moral plane of democratic man. It can never be reconciled with equal freedom of religious conscience.

From the 1962 Annual Survey of American Law.

5

LAW AND RELIGION

*E*DMOND CAHN *was concerned over the state of religion in America. It was the concern of a religious man who believed that the great Western religions, if true to their original faiths, could be a powerful force impelling our legal order toward the goals of freedom, equality and social justice. When he wrote that in the mid-twentieth century the law was in many respects in advance of the religious faiths in its concern for ethical values and the rights of man, he was not extolling the state of the law but lamenting the state of religion.*

He was one of the few modern thinkers who tried to bridge the gap between law and religion. Despite the common concern of both disciplines for human values, the scholars attracted to one rarely have any interest in the other. He found in religious sources — particularly the Bible and Talmud — profound moral insights, and by combining a strong faith with a lawyer's analytical skills, he made ancient words do the job they were always intended to do, for, as he wrote, ". . . the very first place for grace to shine is within the practical workings of the law."

N. R.

A Lawyer Looks at Religion

WHAT is the very first provision one meets on reading the First Amendment in the American Bill of Rights? It is not the constitutional right to free speech or a free press, not the right to assemble and petition the government for redress of grievances, not even the right to free exercise of religion. Ahead of all these, there appears the solemn determination that in America church and state shall be forever distinct, independent, and separate. Believing this principle indispensable to a free society, Jefferson and Madison built it into the fabric of their new nation. The practical separation of church and state was invented in America, and it bears the identifying marks of American political genius.

But separating the church from the state does not automatically divorce religion from the law. Since the church and the state are corporate institutions, ingenuity and determination can draw rather precise lines between the jurisdiction of one and the jurisdiction of the other. It is not equally feasible to separate religion from the law. After all, the man who attends services in his church is the same man who exercises the rights and privileges of citizenship. When religious ideals and practices are generated in the church and disseminated through the community, how can they fail sooner or later to influence the law of the country? Conversely, when ideals of liberty, equality, and justice are announced and practiced in the legislatures and the law courts, how can churchmen who are also citizens avoid responding to the inspiration? However strong the wall of separation between church and state as independent institutions, nevertheless there will be a continual flow of ideals, values, and even of methods between the two distinct domains. In the language of constitutional law, this is a stream of civic and moral "interstate" commerce, commerce that moves back and forth in countless subtle and indirect currents.

I

To map the course of the stream and its present influence, let me begin with *some ancient insights*. In ancient literature, the Babylonian Talmud presents a sagacious and sophisticated account of the commerce between law and religion. The account begins with the proposition that man must be free to exercise his mind and reason as he may see fit, independently, self-reliantly, and without interference from anyone, even from a Heavenly Voice. The following paragraphs are a fair paraphrase of an episode in the Talmud.

When the scene opens, we find ourselves attending a court conference of the rabbinical sages; and we observe that one of the most distinguished among them, Rabbi Eliezer by name, is engaged in heated argument with his colleagues over a delicate, technical point in the interpretation of the law.

After exhausting all his resources of precedent, distinction, analogy, and citation of textual authority without convincing any of them, Rabbi Eliezer becomes desperate and cries out, "If the law agrees with me, let this tree prove it!" Thereupon the tree leaps a hundred cubits from its place, some say four hundred cubits. But the other judges calmly retort, "No proof can be adduced from a tree." Then he says, "If the law agrees with me, let this stream of water prove it!" At this the stream of water flows backwards. The others rejoin however, "No proof can be adduced from a stream of water." Again he calls out, "If the law agrees with me, let the walls of the house prove it!" Whereupon the walls begin to fall. But Rabbi Joshua, one of the sages present, rebukes the walls, saying, "When scholars are engaged in a legal dispute, what right have you to interfere?" And so they do not fall, out of respect for Rabbi Joshua, nor do they resume the upright, out of respect for Rabbi Eliezer, but remain standing and inclined. Finally Rabbi Eliezer says, "If the law agrees with me, let it be proved from heaven!" At that moment a Heavenly Voice cries out, "Why do you dispute with Rabbi Eliezer, seeing that in all matters the law agrees with him?" For a space the assembly sits transfixed, but then Rabbi Joshua rises from his seat and exclaims, "The law is not in heaven! It was given on Mount Sinai. We pay no attention to a Heavenly Voice."

Soon thereafter one of the rabbis happens to meet the prophet Elijah, who, having been alive when he was transported into the celestial regions, remains able to converse with mortals. The prophet is asked, "What did the Holy One, blessed be He, do at that point?" Elijah replies, "He laughed with joy, saying, 'My sons have defeated Me, My sons have defeated Me.' "

The incident was a splendid one and the Heavenly Voice was treated just as it deserved. But anyone even slightly acquainted with the Talmud knows this is by no means the only passage in which a Heavenly Voice was reported. According to the beliefs of that time, since direct inspiration had come to an end with the last writings in the Old Testament, the only remaining supramundane source of guidance would be the sound of a Heavenly Voice. There are about forty occasions in the Babylonian Talmud when a Heavenly Voice was heard, and they comprise a wonderfully rich variety of episode and legend. A Heavenly Voice warns this one, rebukes that one, promises, commends, issues proclamations, and even assists in interpreting an obscure verse of the Bible. On one occasion, a Heavenly Voice brought the distant news that the Roman emperor Caligula had been slain and his decrees against the Temple annulled. This time, in order to reach the general population with the glad tidings, the Heavenly Voice deigned to speak in Aramaic.

The significant point about the numerous Heavenly Voice legends is that only three of them have anything to do with the law. All the others, charming and colorful as they may be, leave the law and the courts scrupulously alone. I have already presented one of the three exceptions, that is, the story of the attempted intervention on behalf of Rabbi Eliezer.

The second story shows the other side of the same coin. It seems that before the time of the classical rabbis, the men of the so-called Great Assembly were regarded as successors in the chain of tradition from Moses, and many religious institutions were deemed to have been founded by them. One day they were seated together considering who would and who would not have a portion in the world to come. They prepared an extensive list of those who would not have any such portion. We may imagine they took a keen pleasure in the process. Finally, without stopping to question the scope of their authority, they proposed to include King Solomon on the list of those who would have no portion in the future world.

At this point an apparition of his father, King David, appeared before them and prostrated itself, begging them not to add Solomon's name. This, however, they disregarded. Then a heavenly fire descended and its flames drew near and licked at the very seats of their chairs. This too they disregarded. Finally a Heavenly Voice cried out to them, saying that King Solomon had built God's house before he had built his own, that he had hastened to complete God's house in seven years and had taken thirteen years to build his own, and that he deserved to stand before kings in the world to come. Even to this they paid no heed. Whereupon even the divine patience was exhausted and the divine reason triumphed over human impudence. Paraphrasing the Book of Job, the Heavenly Voice cried scornfully, "Should it be according to *thy* mind? It is *he* who will recompense it, whether thou refuse or whether thou choose!"

Well said, Heavenly Voice, and high time! As the episode of Rabbi Eliezer authenticates the freedom of human reason, this story presents an obverse moral, for it marks the outer limits of human powers and pretensions.

We come now to the third episode, the only remaining intervention by a Heavenly Voice in a legal setting that I have been able to find. To those who, unlike myself, are genuine Talmudic scholars, this instance is the most familiar. We are told that, at an early stage in the development of the traditional law, there were two distinct and separate schools of interpretation, the School of Shammai and the School of Hillel. It seems that for three years there was a dispute between the two schools, each group asserting that the law was in agreement with their views. Thereupon a Heavenly Voice announced, "Both are the words of the living God, but the law is in agreement with the rulings of the School of Hillel!" The later rabbis pondered, if "both are the words of the living God," how was it that the School of Hillel were entitled to have the law fixed in agreement with their rulings. They gave three reasons for this state of affairs. First, the men of the School of Hillel were kindly and modest; second, they studied not only their own rulings but also those of the School of Shammai; and third, they were humble enough to mention the deeds of the School of Shammai before mentioning their own.

I suppose that, in subsequent literature, no statement by a Heavenly Voice has been quoted oftener than "Both are the words of the living God." It announces a philosophy of bold and candid pluralism. Since human judgments at their best are destined to be incomplete and partial, two or more entirely disparate judgments of the same trans- action may be equally rational and equally estimable. Nevertheless, as between two different and inevitably partial views, the view that has been informed with tolerance, modesty, and humility will generally prove truer, wiser, and altogether worthier. There is open pluralism here, at least on the intellectual level, yet it is a pluralism nourished by tolerance and humility on the religious level.

Thus if we combine and integrate the themes of the three episodes, we produce a rather impressive model of exchange and collaboration between religion and the law. The principles on which the model was built are: first, that man's mind ought to be independent; second, that man's will ought to acknowledge its proper limits; and third, that by the religious virtues of kindliness and humility, man can continually refine the quality of his judgments.

But these worthy principles were stated long ago in a distant land. Another thousand years must pass before Englishmen began to de- velop the common-law system which in turn provided the material of American legal institutions. Though the pattern of relation which we have seen in the Talmud may have been excellent, it exerted little or no influence on the current of thought in England and America. The Anglo-American attitude has been entirely different. It came from a different congeries of political, cultural, and religious developments. These developments began in ancient Palestine and continued through almost the entire Christian era in the Western world. To comprehend why the Talmudic pattern exercised so little influence and why the contemporary gap between law and religion constitutes an active threat to our society's future, we need to summarize this long, continuous movement.

II

Beginning at the time of St. Paul and continuing in large part down to our own epoch, law and religion have been living what may be called *the centuries of alienation*. In many respects, the alienation was both unnecessary and factitious. If we consider the beginnings of organized society as reported by the anthropologists, we find religion and law so closely entwined in the lives of primitive groups that it is hard to determine whether they are two separate social activities or only different ways of looking at the same activity. If we shift our gaze to the other end of the scale and examine law and religion in the United States or any other mature community, we are bound to find an immense and pervasive overlap between the concerns of religion and the concerns of law. While there are some acts that religion either encourages or forbids and law considers outside its jurisdiction, and while there are other acts that law either encourages or forbids and religion considers irrelevant to itself, almost all the primary events and relations in human life belong very properly within both jurisdictions. I mean matters like birth, family, sustenance, use of property, sharing of economic advantages, social harmony and peace, and the advent of death, whether from disease, accident, suicide, or murder. Law and religion have been habitually involved in each of these.

Intelligent men realize that religion is one of the supreme factors in human affairs. Intelligent jurists know that religious influences — whether good or pernicious — have continually affected the history and growth of the law. It is fair to say that a jurist who closes his mind to the role of religion in human affairs displays a serious defect of judgment, for how can he aspire to regulate political structure or prescribe social organization when he disregards one of mankind's greatest interests?

Suppose, instead of looking at the beginning through the eyes of the anthropologist or the current stage through the eyes of the modern jurist, we turn our attention to the experience recorded in the Bible; then, I think, we shall find overwhelming evidence of the overlap. The

Bible, among other things, is a constitution of government — organized according to the old, established functions of legislative, judicial, and executive. Throughout the Bible, God is presented as the Supreme Legislator who makes the laws by which men ought to live; he is presented as the Supreme Judge, deciding the conflicts and destinies of men and nations; and he is also presented as the Supreme Executive, who not only enforces his law by granting rewards and inflicting punishments but also exercises the ultimate prerogative of clemency, mercy, and pardon. In sum, according to the Bible, we might reasonably expect to find law and religion progressing together — at best in a harmonious cooperation, at worst in a sharp and enterprising competition for the allegiance of mankind. How then explain almost two millennia of alienation between law and religion in the Western world?

I suggest there have been four principal factors pushing the two apart. The first of these is *creedal,* and has to do with the implications of Pauline Christianity. Without repeating familiar themes of church history, I need only recall that, from Paul to and including Augustine, one of the dominant currents in Christian thought consisted in denigrating the political state and secular law. Having heard Paul denounce the law of Moses as a burden which sin had put on men and Jesus had lifted away, many pious Christians considered the excesses and brutalities of the Roman Empire and inferred quite understandably that Rome and its law were even more unfit for a Christian world. The Roman state could scarcely expect Christians to approve or admire it as long as it persecuted their religion and killed their saints. The statutes of the empire bore the marks of their pagan origin. Though in some respects the laws were wise, humane, and just, their sources were certainly not Christian. The best ethical influences in Roman law stemmed from the philosophy of the Stoics. Ultimately, the Stoic maxims would be given fresh labels and denominated Christian, but this adaptation had to wait until the blackguards and despots who ruled the empire found it profitable to become converted and baptized. Meanwhile, detestation for the state and secular law had struck deep roots in the soil of Christian theology.

During the Middle Ages — some countries of the Western world have only recently emerged from the Middle Ages, and some have not yet completely emerged — religion was further alienated from secular law by the *political* factor. Though the Roman state was often brutal, it did maintain civic peace and order with unparalleled competence. By way of contrast, the ruling authorities of the Middle Ages, cruel as the worst of the Caesars, could not even preserve order in their own petty fiefs and territories. The church rightly regarded most of them as ferocious gangsters, and the church wrongly employed most of them as hired gangsters. The victims of the Inquisition were usually turned over to the secular arm for the execution of judgment. It was secular authorities who would be assigned the task of torturing, hanging, disemboweling, or burning at the stake. Though the law and its officials who attended to these chores were clearly convenient, they were nevertheless repulsive. Nor was distaste of the law confined to Roman Catholics. When the Reformation made its appearance on the European scene, some of the most dedicated and zealous sects among the Protestants completely disavowed allegiance to law and the state. In point of fact, while responsibility in the conduct of human relations has long since matured, sophisticated, and refined Roman Catholic attitudes toward the law, antinomianism still tends to distort the Protestant perspective.

The trend of modern political philosophy has supplemented and reenforced these antinomian attitudes. On the level of theory, the secular state was amoralized progressively from Machiavelli to Hegel. On the level of action, the behavior of states in the twentieth century has often confirmed the very worst charges in antinomian literature.

During most of the centuries of alienation, the validity of law was attributed strictly to its imperative sources, that is, law was law because the emperor, king, or archduke had commended it. If the king chose to act with and through a parliament, then the people would have an assortment of rulers instead of one. Either way, the law would emerge as an alien imperative — alien to the people in source, form, and interest. Usually it was not even in their language. This imperative view was characteristic of our early New England Puritanism and the puritanism (Protestant, Catholic, and Jewish) in our own times. The early American Puritans identified the law with God's command and assumed that virtue could be imposed by merely uttering decrees and punishing people who failed to obey. Only a generation ago, the prohibitionists made a similar error. So, in our own day, do the censors of books, plays, and movies. Such people seek to exploit the law after the fashion of the medieval Inquisition; while they are using it, they cannot help despising it.

The third factor of alienation is *economic*. Since the beginning of the nineteenth century, the Industrial Revolution has been confronting Western law with innumerable new problems: problems of the factory system, the organization of unions, picketing and boycotts, trusts and industrial combinations, the control of banking and fiscal policy, the preservation and social use of natural resources, and inventions of titanic destructive power. To these problems the law's response has been irregular and spotty, often clumsy, on occasion retrograde. I say "spotty" because at certain periods (the New Deal was an example) members of the legal profession have exhibited exceptional vision, insight, and democratic idealism. These endowments have never been shared by the majority of lawyers, or for that matter of any other profession. In general, it is fair to admit that most judges and lawyers do not display the remotest understanding of social change or ethical trends. If American law deserves well of us, it is because in every generation it has been preserved, advanced, and inspired by what the ancient prophets would have called "a saving remnant."

But we should not expect laymen who suffer from outworn and unjust laws to take a long view while they fold their hands in pious resignation. Laborers, for example, who were prevented by law from organizing, striking, or picketing in the early days of this century, could not know that sooner or later some of Louis D. Brandeis's ideas would prevail. When social evils become acute, those who suffer them in patience may be strengthening the hand of the exploiter and oppressor. Consequently, many idealistic and religious Americans have always looked on the law as unforgivably slow in meeting social discontents. Some decades ago, they began speaking of "social lag" and "the lag in the law" to describe this state of tardiness. They were largely right, but their judgment was iconoclastic and rebellious rather than critical. It was easier to condemn the entire institution than to examine particular operations and decisions. It is still easier.

A fourth factor has alienated religion from the law. For purposes of politeness, we may call this one the *institutional* factor, but it will be quite a euphemism on our part, because what we are about to describe is really nothing else than the sum of three large and impressive ignorances. Add these three ignorances together and we have the total "institutional" factor.

Ignorance number one is the clergymen's ignorance of the law. Most clergymen do not know the law, and what one does not know one is likely to fear and distrust. Somehow, in almost every mature society, the lawyers seem to prosper in wealth and political authority. They are like Jack Horner, who pulls out a plum and joyously admires his own wisdom instead of the qualities of the pudding. On occasion this spectacle may affect a clergyman unpleasantly, yet it has long been the way of the Western world. In the beginning of modern times, Erasmus said, "With great unanimity the philosophers — not that I would say such a thing myself — are wont to ridicule the law as an ass. Yet great matters and little matters alike are settled by the arbitrament of these asses. They gather goodly freeholds with broad acres, while the theologian, after poring over chestfuls of the great corpus of divinity, gnaws on bitter beans, at the same time manfully waging war against lice and fleas."

Ignorance number two is the lawyers' ignorance of the functioning of their own institution. The majority of American lawyers still cling to primitive legends and fables about the nature of the judicial process. Despite everything written by Holmes, Cardozo, and Jerome Frank, they choose to believe that rules of law are self-operative in an impersonal, mechanical fashion and that by some occult magnetism the circumstances of a dispute are automatically governed by the foreordained doctrine. Really, however convinced you and I may be that the world is not flat and that the personal factor is indispensable to decision and cannot be banished from the judicial process, there are countless lawyers who assume that if one does not mention the personal factor, it may become discouraged and go off and disappear somewhere.

Ignorance number three is the lawyers' ignorance of moral philosophy. When a successful and prominent lawyer is asked to discuss a moral issue of general application (not a mere question of professional ethics or etiquette), the audience is usually in for a severe trial — a trial by ordeal of tedium. He is almost sure to dispense the kind of copybook analysis we have learned to expect at bar association meetings. Notice and admire his truly miraculous complacency — no suspicion of the depth of his subject, no acquaintance with the profound variety of its literature, no trace of intellectual humility, not even an inkling that his glassy-eyed auditors are being martyred to the cause of good form! As they inhale the stream of platitudes, each member of the audience beseeches divine grace for himself and his neighbors — some heavenly gift of hardness of hearing, sudden deep sleep, or at least a temporary obtuseness of intellect.

The institutional factor deserves to be taken very seriously. There are reasons for hoping that, if we could overcome the clergymen's misunderstanding of law and the lawyer's misunderstanding of judicial process and moral philosophy, we should be able to cope satisfactorily with the creedal, political, and economic factors. Our first step is manifest: we must develop a reciprocal understanding that both divine law and human law are in constant process of growth, change, and emergence. Religion and law will remain distant from each other, distrustful, and alienated until men reach the point of knowing as thoroughly as they know their own physical existence, that both creation and revelation in the cosmos and in the law are incomplete, ongoing, and continuous. Deprived as they are of the light of this knowledge, law and religion stand rigidly apart, and the gulf between them grows ominously wider.

III

Because of this gulf, religion is approaching and soon must confront *a great and unnoticed crisis*. At least in America and probably in most other parts of the Western world, religion has been entering an unnoticed crisis which appears to increase rapidly in scope and intensity. What is it that marks the crisis? *The fact that for the first time in the general course of Western history since the advent of Christianity, law often equals and occasionally surpasses religion in the quality of its announced faith and practical works.* If the trend is as I see it, that is, if the ethical and humanitarian implications of law have really begun to rival the messages and preachings of religion, then religion is indeed facing a challenge which makes its nineteenth-century anxiety about Darwinism and evolution seem relatively trivial.

The present trend may constitute a threat not only to the future of organized religion but likewise to law and the administration of justice. This anyone will understand who considers how much Roman law gained from Stoic-Christian influences or how much what we now call "equity" derived from the infiltration of Roman and Christian standards during the English Renaissance. In a democratic society like ours, law is tethered to the opinions and moral standards of the general public, and if religion fails to lead and edify these, the advancement of law will inevitably suffer.

What does the lawyer hear when he listens hopefully for the voice of religion? In answer to his concern for a national and international society of freedom, justice, and fraternity, he hears very little that he could not have heard a century ago. When he aspires to bring harmony and understanding between man and man and group and group, he often finds the teachers and textbooks of religious and private schools canceling his efforts by erecting barriers in the minds of the young. He sees the Supreme Court endeavoring continually to elevate the legal plane of human dignity and he sees most of the churches and synagogues complacently content to vouch for theological and ethical notions that would cause embarrassment if they were expressed and taken seriously in a secular setting.

Let me give an example which, since correction — like charity — begins at home, will have a strictly Jewish reference, for I know that sincere Christians will have no difficulty finding examples appropriate to their churches. In the early cultural background of the age when the people of Israel made their exodus from Egypt, they believed that God had slain all the first-born children of the Egyptians and even the first-born of the Egyptian cattle. Though it is entirely understandable that in their day they should have believed this thing, how can we continue to believe or teach it in the middle of the twentieth century? It is high time we refused. Surely this is not a matter of appeasing the villainous Mr. Nasser; it is not exclusively a matter of considering the sensibility of modern Egyptians — though I must say that if I were an Egyptian, I should find it hard to understand how a religious and reverent people could recite this part of the traditional story every year in the Passover ceremony (see Deut. 23: 7–8). The paramount reason for denying that God slew the first-born of the Egyptians and of their cattle is simply that we have passed the stage when we can accept such thoughts concerning God. I concede that, owing to poor hygienic conditions and similar causes, the rate of infant mortality in Egypt may have been high in those ancient days; for that matter, the Israelite children may have been better protected and thus escaped the plague; be that as it may, there is not the slightest doubt that the children who died and the children who escaped were of equal concern to their divine Father. As the instance illustrates, religion may impair whatever influence and meaning it still possesses in American society unless its leaders recognize a continuous demand for revaluation and progressive revelation.

Now, let me recall just a few of the many ethical and humanitarian issues with which the law has been struggling during recent years, in order to sketch the extent of the crisis and the dimensions of religious default. I begin with the most obvious example, that is, the whole complex and ramified problem of race relations in the United States. For twenty years or more, the courts, legislators, and executives have been advancing and supporting Negro rights to equality. Of course, they have not done nearly enough; not always have they done everything feasible under the circumstances; and deeply grievous wrongs remain to be righted. But whether we look at public school education, university education, transportation, economic opportunity and employment, or public housing, we find vast and accelerating movements toward equality and justice. In these movements, the churches have furnished little or no leadership. Though the Roman Catholic Church possesses the best interracial record of major denominations, it did not anticipate but followed the advance thrusts made by secular authority. Generally speaking, Southern Protestants and Southern Jews who favor desegregation can scarcely look to their ministers and rabbis for aid and direction. Thus, by and large, a noble movement which ought to show the white population bearing the banner of Judaeo-Christian ideals exhibits those ideals mainly in the forbearance and self-discipline of the Negroes.

For my second example, let me take the issues that rise under the First Amendment in the Bill of Rights. These are issues involving free speech, free association, free inquiry, and free communication. Behind the constitutional guarantees, there are certain magnanimous postulates about the capacities of man and the integrity of his inner being. The Supreme Court has been endeavoring to preserve these postulates during a period of unprecedented international tension and discreditable domestic hysteria. Here again, the law has performed its work imperfectly, and the eventual outcome cannot be predicted with confidence. In many aspects, intellectual freedom is still at bay, still in jeopardy. Nevertheless, if freedom retains a foothold today from which to move forward, how much of this can be attributed to the influence of organized religion? Amid the noise and clamor of shameful McCarthyism, there were probably fewer ecclesiastics on the side of freedom than on the side of obscurantism and repression. Yet is not man's liberty to think, to investigate, and to dissent one of religion's most central and fundamental concerns? The Jewish prophets and the Christian martyrs believed it was.

Likewise, the justices of the Supreme Court have done something, though not nearly enough, toward restricting the scope of so-called "guilt by association." The charges of guilt by association could have been expected to awaken the oldest of Christian memories, for Jesus himself had been attacked for associating with sinners (as though there were ever anyone else to associate with). Moreover, at least since the time of the prophet Ezekiel, guilt by association had been challenged by ethical Judaism.

Let me carry the process a step further. Both Judaism and Christianity have always taught that sincere repentance reduces or cancels the burden of transgression, that God is merciful and pardons abundantly, and that good Jews and Christians ought to follow the divine example and at least avoid actions of spite and vengeance. In the face of these gentle and humane teachings, there was no protest from the majority of religious voices when fathers of families who had lived in America for as long as twenty-five years and had given sons to its armed forces were taken from their homes and ordered deported to foreign lands because, forsooth, in their juvenile days during the 1920's they had briefly been members of the then-legal Communist Party. Who can doubt that a large volume of protests from religious sources would have stopped the deportations and caused Congress to alter the deportation statute? Dissenting when the Supreme Court permitted deportations of the kind, Justices Hugo L. Black and William O. Douglas showed they understood the demands of a genuine religious approach; so in their respective lifetimes had Justice Frank Murphy and Justice Louis D. Brandeis.

For a final illustration of the vacuum which religious inertia has left in our communal life and which the law, under secular proddings, is endeavoring to fill, there is that national infamy of ours called "capital punishment." Almost two millennia ago, the most enlightened Jewish rabbis stated their absolute opposition to the death penalty. At about the same time, Christian opposition was admirably ardent. For when the state takes human life, it violates the most excellent ethical ideals of the Western world, it brutalizes the spirits of the citizens, and it presumes to act irrevocably and irremediably, which is prohibited to it by the inherent fallibility of earthly judgments. The infliction of capital punishment is the typical instance of *hybris* or overweening arrogance in our society. Yet — need I remind you? — only a minority of religious leaders have dedicated themselves to the abolition of this uncivilized and antireligious practice. Though, in England, after endless efforts the death penalty has been almost abolished, we know that the heads of the established church did much to resist and retard the achievement. In the United States, we might have wiped the barbaric laws from our statute books long ago, if Christians and Jews in the twentieth century had not sunk below the ethical plane of Saints Ambrose and Augustine and Rabbis Tarfon and Akiba.

Sooner or later the cause of abolition will prevail in every country that dares call itself civilized. That is not the question; the question is whether religion will gird itself with its ancient power and hasten the day of humaneness and compassion. We are given no clear answer to this question. All we can say under present circumstances is that we see religion losing its status as conscience's helpmate and becoming a mere thing of rhetoric and ceremony, a background for weddings when the spirit is too happy for intellection, and for funerals when mind and social conscience are benumbed with grief. Such a religion would be prosperous, paunchy, popular — and inconsequential.

Meanwhile, under pressure of society's daily needs, secular law is beginning to fill the ethical vacuum. It is a dangerous function to leave entirely in the hands of legislators and judges, for if they need religion for no other purpose, they always need it to instruct them in the ways of humility, clemency, and compassion.

Yet there is considerably more at stake. Even if our legislators and judges were able to develop the wisest and most expedient corpus of law, they could not make it suitable to the infinitely varied circumstances of particular cases unless they perceived and acknowledged that a human being is not only a member of the species entitled as such to equal treatment but also a unique individual endowed by birth and environment with attributes that belong exclusively to him. Without its generic quality, law becomes unjust because it is unequal; without its individual quality, law becomes unjust because it is mechanical and insensitive.

Here then is how a genuine effulgence of faith might illumine the road of the law. From ancient times, religion has exalted the value of individual personality and has summoned men to understand their neighbors as nearly as possible after the manner of God's understanding, for — we are told — in his eyes all men, created in his image, are equal and alike, yet every man is distinct, unique, and filled with the splendor of human dignity. This is religion's own insight. Applied wholeheartedly in the law, it could help us shape decisions of individualized and creative justice. Applied throughout our national life, it could hallow the pursuit of a free, righteous, and compassionate society.

From Theology Today, *1958.*

The Pathology of Organized Religion

WHILE some people think it is only entertaining to look back at the remote period of the 1960's, others contend that it can also be instructive. There is no denying that the behavior of that period was so unlike what we in our day would consider sensible that we feel on occasion that it is not worth our attention.

Charity requires that we at least endeavor to see what was so strangely wrong with the 1960's before we turn away from them. What looks in retrospect like sheer perversity and folly in their conduct may have been nothing worse than a temporary pathological condition from which, with a few notable exceptions, the whole society was suffering in those days.

Particularly in the field of organized religion, the history of their illness is not hard to reconstruct because both clergymen and laymen were almost embarrassingly frank in reporting the symptoms. A deep and alarming disturbance it surely was, and for quite a while it must have looked as if organized religion in America might be losing its mind. If we examine the huge recorded mass of symptoms, deficiencies, and disorders, we find them falling under three main diagnostic headings: (1) amnesia, (2) escape fantasies, and (3) suicidal impulses.

AMNESIA

Back in the 1960's, the manifestations of amnesia were truly touching. The overwhelming majority of the American people lived in a condition of almost total religious darkness. They knew how to write a check to the order of the church, and not much more. Whereas, during the nineteenth century, the Bible had furnished such a common core of popular reading and culture that an author or orator could safely mention names, places, episodes, and sayings from its pages and assume that his audience gathered what he meant, we find that when the name of "Moses" was put to young college students in 1964, they could only associate it with a man who managed the New York World's Fair of that year, and when the name of "St. Paul" was put, they could only associate it with a city in Minnesota.

Ignorance was not limited to names, it also embraced the theological principles of the past. For about nineteen hundred years, for example, Christians had been taught that the Deity was both omnipotent and omnipresent. Yet when the United States Supreme Court decided in the 1960's that public schools must respect the constitutional separation of church and state, a prominent prelate in New York declared that the Court had "expelled God" from the schools, a governor in Alabama repeated the charge, and virtually no one — except, of course, the justices of the Supreme Court — seemed to find it incongruous that expulsion from school could happen to Omnipotence and Omnipresence. Apparently in that time no one expected the churches to remember their own teachings.

For centuries — ever since, say, the bloody devastations of the Thirty Years' War — sensible men had tolerated the bickerings of the churches and the clergy, and supported their endeavors for one main reason: because the churches provided the means to carry over from one generation to the next an accumulated fund of virtue, wisdom, and comfort. The church or synagogue was worthwhile, despite all its notorious defects, because it transmitted a moral heritage that was deemed too great and rich for any man, however wise and good, to build for himself in his own experience and lifetime. Of course, in every age there were many good men who concluded that, even with this advantage, the faults of the churches and synagogues outweighed their usefulness. But in the 1960's this advantage disappeared, the churches and synagogues — with a few exceptions — failed to transmit, and amnesia set in.

Since nature abhors a vacuum and someone simply had to confer a meaning on solemn occasions like Christmas and Easter, the commercial world assumed the function. The department stores, toy manufacturers, and confectioners explained why people celebrated Christmas, the milliners why they celebrated Easter, the turkey farmers and football coaches took responsibility for Thanksgiving Day, the resort hotels in the mountains and at the shore showed the Jews how to repent on the Day of Atonement, and the greeting card industry did what it could to lift the entire religious calendar to the level of teenage birthdays, graduations from high school, bad colds, and anniversaries of one's first visit to the analyst.

It was in those days that the chaplain of Yale University said, "We churchmen are gifted at changing wine into water — watering down religion. The problem of the church today is ineffectiveness. We've never had attendance so high and influence so low, and maybe the two are not unrelated." The president of the National Council of Churches commented, "What is fair, what is right? You take this problem to your preacher, and he takes to the hills." Whatever Christians had learned in two thousand years of religious experience, whatever Jews had learned in over three thousand, amnesia was rapidly erasing.

Of course, this helps to explain why the sermons of the period were generally so shallow and dull. They also had a tragic side, which was the theme of last year's smashing success on the Broadway stage, the melodrama called *The Pulpit*. The story of *The Pulpit*, which was set in Central China in the 1960's, concerned a group of Chinese natives who kidnaped a Christian missionary and drove him mad by the simple expedient of forcing him to listen to tape recordings of his own oratory. What a tragic denouement that was when, reclining at ease and believing himself safe, he suddenly recognized the opening words of his longest sermon and discovered that the door and windows were locked tight! Unforgettable! (And wasn't it rather a pity that the play had to be withdrawn recently at the height of its run because the Chinese people unexpectedly replaced the Russians as our closest and most gallant allies?) Be that as it may, I wish to go on record as a defender of the sermons of the 1960's. Whatever the historians may say, I shall always contend that most of them were no worse than those of previous eras.

Considering the general state of religious amnesia, the ministers, priests, and rabbis had a difficult task and deserve a measure of sympathy. Things were approaching the point where a sentence in a typical sermon might read like this: "Adam (who, as we all know, was the first man according to the Book of Genesis, which, as we all know, is the first book in the Bible, which, as we all know, contains the sacred scriptures of our faith) said to Eve (who, as we all know, was the first woman and the wife of Adam, whom I have just mentioned as the first man, as you may recall), 'God (who, as we all know, is our Heavenly Father and whom we have come here to worship, as you may remember) told us (that is, you, Eve, and me, Adam, who are the first couple on earth according to the Book of Genesis, which will be the first book in the Bible when it comes to be written, as we know) not to eat the fruit of that tree.' "

In those days no one needed to know anything worthy of an adult intelligence to belong to a church. Just as no one questioned a medieval baron when he deigned to attend a Mass, so no one asked a congregant or parishioner of the 1960's whether he had even the most elementary information about his faith or his church. If he seemed rich, people might try to investigate his income and the amount of his contributions, but no one cared whether he had ever read a book of religious history or ethics. Though at a baseball game ignorance of the fundamentals could subject an American to deep embarrassment, he had nothing similar to fear when he went to church. As long as he said he believed, no one expected him to know what he believed. At that, religion in America was a bit livelier than in England. A report on the condition of English theology published in 1963 concluded as follows: "The creed of the English is that there is no God and that it is wise to pray to him from time to time."

By the 1960's, with the vast spread of educational opportunity, an American boy or girl of reasonable promise would probably pursue formal secular education until age twenty-one and in myriads of instances from three to seven years longer. Yet the majority of these young people would terminate their formal religious education between the ages of thirteen and sixteen, whereupon the churches' ceremonies impliedly assured them that they knew whatever they needed to know.

Religion alone suffered this handicap. It is interesting to imagine what would have occurred if anyone had proposed stopping the study of mathematics or history at the age of sixteen, or law or physics or philosophy or, for that matter, the technique of assembling a television set or piloting a plane. In this period of extreme novelty and instability, when every customary value was challenged and every principle denied, when men needed the resources of religion with utmost urgency, they somehow let their religious memories fade. To say one was a good lawyer or physician or engineer, one had to keep studying diligently all through life. But to say one was a good member of organized religion in those singular times one needed only keep out of prison and send a check with a smile; on occasion, the check would suffice by itself. "To believe" was becoming a strictly intransitive verb.

ESCAPE FANTASIES

In retrospect we have to grant that the realities of the 1960's were somewhat perplexing, what with so many rapid transitions and extreme dangers. Under the circumstances it was not strange that theologians would sometimes err in telling the religious public how to cope with the current reality. It *was* strange — very strange — that quite a few of them abandoned the whole effort, turned their backs on reality, and indulged themselves in escape fantasies.

Since the most popular theological fantasies of the time were only variations on a single theme, we need not go into details about specific theologians or denominations. One general theme ran through all their eloquence — an age-old theme of flight and escape concocted from the fantasy that religion could evade the hard and costly task of improving men's relations with their neighbors and restrict itself to elaborating their beliefs about God. Of course, even in the 1960's most people must have suspected that professed belief without practical action, if it was not sheer hypocrisy, was at best too facile and cheap.

It was in this setting of self-absorption that Albert Camus, one of the foremost moralists of the age, published a brilliant satire called *The Fall (La Chute)*, travestying the fantasies of the theologians and exposing them as futile attempts to escape from oral realities. *The Fall* was a classic work of demolition. What Voltaire had done to one species of escape-fantasy in *Candide*, Camus did to another, perhaps more dangerous, species in *The Fall*, but since Camus satirized more subtly than his great precursor and trusted more to his readers' discernment, we cannot feel sure that everyone who needed the message in that age really grasped it.

What is the story of *The Fall?* It is the tale of a Paris lawyer, told by himself in two main stages. In the first stage, he is a luminary of the bar, defending all sorts of wretched people who, in the excess of wretchedness and passion, have committed homicides. He is highly ethical in his methods, never giving or accepting bribes, never flattering the reporters to get publicity, never bowing and scraping to judges. He refuses the Legion of Honor two or three times. He not only serves poor people without a fee, he actually abstains from bragging about it. In short, he is a paragon of advocates.

But he is more. He goes through every day spraying his surroundings with acts of kindness. He guides the blind man across the street, buys from the poor old peddler, gives cheerfully to the beggar. He enjoys surrendering his seat in the bus to a tired old lady or shifting from one place to another in the theater so a couple can sit together. He donates large sums to charity, and does it with pleasure. He comforts the sick and dying and helps to provide funerals for the needy. When people offend him in some way or other, he always forgets the offense.

Perhaps in order to save the story from becoming totally incredible, he also tells us that he leads a very busy and sensual sex life, changing continually from one woman to another. But since he is unmarried and since the women, at least by his account, derive immense joy from his attentions, we need not take his dallyings too seriously. After all, the city he practices in is Paris.

Well, here we have him in his first stage, and I must say that if we overlook the amours, which are really none of our concern and which we learn about from one side only, the man is an ornament to his profession and a living fountain of good deeds.

Then an incident occurs that agitates him deeply. Walking home one night very tired (his reason for feeling so tired is the usual one), our protagonist hears a young girl who has jumped into the Seine to drown herself call for help. The current is sweeping her rapidly downstream. Whether anyone can possibly rescue her is doubtful. As it is, he yields to weariness, weakness, and paralyzing shock, and stands there motionless for a bit, then continues on his way.

Two or three years later, the memory of this default — if under such equivocal circumstances it really was a default — returns to haunt him and erode his self-confidence. He probes his life in every aspect and decides that the principal motive behind all his noble behavior was only the basest vanity, that he acted modestly because he wanted to shine and charitably because he yearned to squeeze admiration from an audience. In his heart he has really cared for no one except himself and served nothing except his own conceit.

We can pause for a moment to consider the parable. Suppose a man on examining his inner life should discover that though he has been doing many good deeds, his motives for doing them have been dubious or ugly, what ought religion recommend to him for a cure? What would be the right, decent, socially responsible remedy?

In the twenty-first century the answer seems as simple as it must have seemed to Camus. For one thing, since our lawyer was doing so very much good in his day-to-day life, a cure for his moral illness must at least enable him to continue his career and personal beneficences. For another, since he had chosen good and generous deeds to feed his vanity instead of evil and avaricious ones, his character must have been attuned in advance to the possibility of improvement. A truly callous man would not ask whether he ought to have risked his life for a drowning girl, or condemn himself for egotism. Consequently, religion can offer the sensible answer that a man in straits like these should persevere in his good deeds, try hard to overcome his conceit, and, above all, learn to send something of his heart along with his purse and advocate's voice. Incidentally, he should also recognize that on occasion a man must know how to forgive himself and begin anew if he is to help others.

This, more or less, would be the general purport of religion's answer in our century. But it is not the answer in Camus's brilliant parable.

Nothing like it. What does our disconcerted lawyer do, according to Camus?

He proceeds as follows: He destroys his practice and professional reputation, becomes a drunkard, evades his friends, tortures and abuses the women who are unlucky enough to care for him, stops doing favors for the poor, abandons his law practice, flees from Paris, moves secretly to a hovel in Amsterdam (a city whose climate and topography he detests), and frequents one of the worst dives on the Amsterdam waterfront where he supports a sordid existence by counseling burglars, thieves, and pimps. Yet even this is not degradation enough.

There is more. In this new existence, he takes his greatest pleasure in feeling emotions of irredeemable guilt and trying to inflict the same emotions on anyone whom he can buttonhole in the Amsterdam bar. He enjoys guilt; he tastes and savors and relishes it; he wallows in it and pours it like wet mud over his head and down his neck and into his undershirt. He butters his bread with guilt and mixes guilt with his absinthe. Everyone is guilty and everyone is a murderer, he keeps chanting, and there is no plea or excuse for anyone. He begs his interlocutors — as long as he can find any — to join him in a riotous orgy of indiscriminate guilt. And when advancing disease finally silences him, his last words are, "It's too late now. It will always be too late. Fortunately!"

Even in Camus's time perceptive readers probably saw the point of the parable. By entitling it *The Fall,* the author clearly hinted that it was intended for the churches and clergy, which some of them may have understood. At any rate, within five years of the book's appearance a few of the younger clergy in each of the main denominations found that they could no longer tolerate a concept of religion based on mere subjective guilt and social passivity. Proudly they entered the ranks of mass demonstrations on behalf of racial equality — a step that required courage in those days, for the one thing that made the average American angrier than hearing his religion challenged was seeing someone actually practice it.

True, the Negro clergymen's inspiring leadership and the white clergymen's brave participation in racial processions and demonstrations made only a beginning. Some may demur that in the 1960's as at any other time it was easier to find devotion for an hour's dramatic display than for the undramatic demands of the daily round. Perhaps so; yet a beginning it was and a genuine one.

SUICIDAL IMPULSES

Our account will be incomplete unless we mention the occasional outbreaks of suicidal impulse that afflicted some of the important denominations in those days. In all likelihood they symptomized a secret awareness that the deficiencies and contradictions in America's religious life were becoming too gross to be tolerated. Unable to combat the spreading amnesia and despairing of religion's capacity to recover and restore itself, some of the clerical and lay leaders reached out, as defeated men occasionally will, for a dangerous stimulant. The stimulant they demanded was government support for religious practices and public grants of money to parochial schools.

Many of these pessimists were Roman Catholics but they also included a certain number of Protestants and a few Jews, mainly Orthodox. Since they doubtless knew that whenever in history any church had linked itself with the political state it had forthwith mortgaged its independence and compromised its religious mission; since they knew that politicalized religion had written countless discreditable chapters of persecution and torture, distrust and conspiracy, murder and genocide; since they knew that in providing for strict separation of church and state our Founding Fathers had intended to save religion and the churches in America from similar evils: considering all these factors, there does not seem to be room for more than one diagnosis.

For example, when during the 1960's the Supreme Court prohibited a religious ritual of Bible-reading in the public schools, Justice William J. Brennan, Jr. (the only Roman Catholic on the Court in those days; now we have four, all of whom are considered extremely strict in maintaining the separation of church and state) showed in a concurring opinion that Americans needed the wall of separation not less but much more in the twentieth century than in the eighteenth. He said:

> Our religious composition makes us a vastly more diverse people than were our forefathers. They knew differences chiefly among Protestant sects. Today the Nation is far more heterogeneous religiously, including as it does substantial minorities not only of Catholics and Jews but as well of those who worship according to no version of the Bible and those who worship no God at all. In the face of such profound changes, practices which may have been objectionable to no one in the time of Jefferson and Madison may today be highly offensive to many persons, the deeply devout and the nonbelievers alike.

For that matter, Americans of the Catholic faith had only to look at the supposedly Catholic Spain of their day to see what prices might be exacted for state support. Franco's Spain was a land of persecution not only for Protestants; Catholics too were restricted in various aspects of religious freedom. The church could not even appoint its own bishops. When a vacancy occurred, Franco would submit six names of his to the Vatican, the Pope could veto no more than three of them, and

Franco would then fill the vacancy from the remaining three. No wonder that a prominent American cardinal declared in the 1960's, "I cannot see how any government or state would build schools without expecting to control them, in whole or in part. . . . There is no alternative to the voluntary method of financing Catholic school building."

There were wavering elements too among Protestant sects. While the Baptists and Presbyterians, who had striven so hard toward building the original wall of separation, continued as a whole to defend it stoutly, certain other Protestant denominations seemed confused and timorous. And this was strange for they too had merely to look across the Atlantic for warnings.

If they did, they would see the Church of England spending fourteen years of the twentieth century in the preparation of a revised prayer book, only to be told by two successive Houses of Commons (many of whose members did not belong to the established church but were Protestant dissenters, Catholics, Jews, or atheists) that the proposed revisions were not approved and, under English law, could not be made.

If England was not considered Protestant enough to illustrate the point, one could read items like the following about the established church of Sweden:

> The Swedish State Church, which is Lutheran, has long been torn by theological strife. Most of it is of a hair-splitting and almost medieval nature, and has laid churchmen open to the frequently expressed charge of being more interested in debating points than in restoring contact with fast-melting congregations. Last Easter one Stockholm church service had to be canceled because there was not a single person in the pews.

What then of the Jews in America? The Jews at least could be expected to understand the point, for Nazi Germany had just given them the most savage reminder of all time. And it is true that almost all did defend the wall of separation. Nevertheless, as history shows, the one thing Jews could never achieve was unanimity, and even after the example of Nazi Germany, there were some few who did not appreciate the American principle of separation. For instance, in the 1960's we find the president of the largest Orthodox rabbinical group demanding that Jewish foundations and charitable funds give more money to Jewish all-day schools and warning that otherwise they might "against their will be forced to seek relief from the Government." As if the statement were not curious enough, the speaker added that "this indeed would be disastrous." What diagnosis was appropriate for people who talked about taking a course of action that they themselves said "would be disastrous"?

So things went in the 1960's, a peculiar and irrational period if ever organized religion saw one. It began to look as though the argument about government aid to parochial schools might continue indefinitely with increasing divisiveness — until, quite suddenly in the early 1970's, an abrupt change took place and everyone dropped the entire proposal.

We all know who precipitated this unexpected burst of harmony. It was, of course, the sect of Black Muslims who, by then, had established a considerable network of parochial schools for the education of their children. When the Black Muslims first recommended opening the day in every public school with a reading of the Koran, they only complicated the debate; when they insisted on being represented on the list of army and navy chaplains they only intensified it; but when they demanded that the federal government aid their schools to teach what they alleged was a purely objective, empirically tested, and scientifically demonstrable fact — to wit, the the racial superiority of the black man — a sudden silence fell over the halls of Congress and no one heard another word about federal aid to church-connected schools. There was still plenty of argument and dissension in the United States, but not about this issue.

THE I.Q. MOVEMENT

So much for the mental disturbances that afflicted organized religion in those years. To round out the account, we need only mention the small beginnings of a vital recuperative force which soon became known in this country as the "I.Q. Movement." Nowadays, the I.Q. Movement and its auxiliary enterprises are so active and ubiquitous that we can scarcely realize how young it is. Though the exact date and place of its birth cannot be identified, our abler historians say that the movement began during the 1960's in the dormitory of a non-denominational college, possibly in New England. We really do not know.

What we do know is that, at the very start, the I.Q. Movement announced the doctrine to which its multitude of followers still adhere. They proclaimed that while studying religion and digesting its moral insights do not necessarily make a person religious, no one in modern society can perform his full religious duty without them. We have records of some of their early slogans: "Bring your mind to church," "Give religion a thinking chance," "The hire is worthy of more labor," and "Give us one sermon a month that gets down to cases." Eventually the various chapters of the movement adopted a phrase from the Book of Genesis as their permanent motto: "By the sweat of your brow."

There is a tradition — which seems plausible enough though we have no way of verifying it — that the Supreme Court's decision against ceremonial Bible-reading in the public schools was what actually inspired the movement's first meeting. It seems that a group of college students, none of whom had previously given the Bible a thought, completely misunderstood the tenor of the Court's decision. Believing mistakenly that the Court had decided to "ban" the Sacred Scriptures, they inferred that the book, if not quite offensive by contemporary standards, must at least deserve a close and serious inspection. We are told that one of their number, more daring than the rest, smuggled a copy into the dormitory. That night, in a mood of indignant surprise and intense excitement, the I.Q. Movement was launched.

The movement's first decade is all that need concern us here; it saw three important changes made in the law of the land in response to the movement's propaganda, which consisted of parades, demonstrations, sit-ins, lie-ins, and the particularly efficacious "twist-ins."

In the first place, like anyone else who reads the Bible, the members of the I.Q. Movement noticed how very often it demanded that there be only one and the same law for citizens and for resident aliens. They reasoned that repetition meant emphasis, that the Bible would not have reiterated the principle again and again if it were not of the very first importance to a righteous commonwealth. Hammering away at this theme, they persuaded the Congress in 1970 to repeal all laws which provided for the deportation of resident aliens. Since then, Americans have taken for granted that an alien can dwell securely in our midst; if he should violate our laws, he must bear the same punishment as a citizen and no more. Though this may seem rather elementary to us, our grandfathers had to learn it from the Bible and the I.Q. Movement.

Their second reform had unexpected consequences. They read in the Book of Leviticus that in harvest-time the farmers were commanded not to reap the corners of their fields but to leave whatever grew there for the poor. By 1972, yielding to the pressure of the I.Q.'s and acting under the constitutional aegis of the Commerce Clause, Congress had enacted the notorious Corners-of-the-Fields Act, which authorized the Secretary of Agriculture to specify the respective areas to be deemed a "field" and a "corner," the field to be not more than one hundred acres in area and the corner to be not less than one-half acre (unless the field had more than five corners in which case a corner might be as small as one-quarter acre). As we know, the farmers' immediate response to the new legislation was quite discreditable; in defense of their behavior, we can only say that we too might have resented the swarms of indigents and unattractive vagrants who clustered around the edges of every prosperous farm and construed their new rights rather too liberally. At any rate, a compromise was soon effected. In exchange for repeal of the act, the agricultural interests threw their zealous support behind an all-out program of social assistance and welfare. As a result, the United States forthwith became the world's leader in the completeness and generosity of its social security and welfare legislation. This distinction we owe, though I grant somewhat obliquely, to the I.Q. Movement.

The consequences of their third reform may also have occasioned surprise. The movement found in the Book of Numbers and again in Leviticus that, for any very heinous crime, the Bible commanded the entire community to participate in executing the convicted culprit by stoning him to death. They demanded legislation to this effect in all American jurisdictions that still imposed capital punishment and, when it was objected that their plan might disrupt the people's working schedules and leisure pursuits, they adjusted it to provide that the judge and jury who represented the community in condemning the man to death could also represent it in stoning him. Oddly enough, since the reform was enacted two generations ago, not a single person has been convicted of a capital offense in any of these jurisdictions. Apparently, the Bible exerted a greater educational influence than anyone expected.

All in all, did organized religion really lose its mind during the 1960's? At this distance, we can answer, "No, it did not but for a while appearances were ominous." Though the monumental funded experience of Judaism and Christianity had much to say to modern men, few in those days were willing to study and exert themselves for access to it. As the majority had yet to discover, religious belief is neither relevant nor irrelevant to social and moral problems. Men make it relevant in their own time and place through study and experience, empathy and intelligence, responsible thought and costly risk. Like a diploma in the university or a livelihood in the community, the light of religion has to be earned. Only with the sweat of our brow can we reach the paths that lead to justice and peace.

Address delivered at Bates College, March 6, 1964.

The Binding of Isaac: A Case Study

I N *The Moral Decision* it proved enlightening to examine moral values as they were revealed factually and concretely in the circumstances of a specific case. The case method not only brings abstract notions down to earth, it also serves to disclose an entire spectrum of operative moral forces — hopes and fears, lusts, sufferings, and ideals. In this manner even the remotest abstract concept can become fit for our appreciation and comprehension. Consequently, I propose to use the same method here and apply it to the old, familiar case of the Binding of Isaac.

If one can earn the right to discuss his own experience with a passage in the Bible, then I am surely entitled to talk about the Binding of Isaac. More then forty years ago I heard on Rosh Hashanah how God tested Abraham, how He told him to take his son Isaac to the land of Moriah and offer him there for a burnt offering, how Abraham took Isaac up the mountain, how he bound Isaac and raised the knife to slay him, how the angel called out to stop Abraham, how the unfortunate ram was substituted for Isaac, and how God heartily acclaimed the entire episode. Now, more than forty Rosh Hashanahs and forty Bindings of Isaac later, everything in me still utters a vehement "No!"

As a child I found it unintelligible that God could have commanded Abraham to kill Isaac, his son; when I became an adult I found it incredible; when I became a father I found it impossible. Sometimes I would listen in the synagogue with a mood of inarticulate protest and sometimes with an emotion of sheer horror. In these reactions, I probably reproduced the feelings of an overwhelming majority of intelligent Jews throughout the long course of our generations. The only difference is that while the majority seem to have got used to the story, I was more tenacious; I could not get used to it.

Provoked by the annual reminders on Rosh Hashanah and by other references that cropped up in my reading, I would periodically consult the literature of the subject to find some sort of explanation. I observed that the story had challenged many others before me and that it had accumulated a varied treasury of myth, legend, and illustration. Incidentally, I learned that some authorities attributed the passage to a much later period than Abraham's, the period of the Jewish kingdom. But in my state of discontent the historical researches provided no comfort; for what difference did the date of composition make? My problem was not philological but religious. In fact, the later the date at which the scholars set the episode, the more it would shock my sensibility; they were canceling the possible excuse that it was merely a vestige of a very primitive era.

The legends that have encrusted the case of the Binding of Isaac are charming and beautiful in themselves, and particularly poignant when they describe the psychic ordeal and tremor of horror that Abraham is said to have undergone. But descriptions like these only made the divine command appear more atrocious.

In their Rosh Hashanah sermons, the rabbis whom I heard tended to concentrate on two themes by way of palliating the episode. Some, disregarding the remainder of the text, would extract a single phrase to the effect that they (Abraham and Isaac) "went both of them together." The rabbis would expatiate on the phrase with gusto. While admiring its charms as they did, I reflected with a wry smile that the going-together might make a beautiful picture if the father had not been on his way to slaughter the son. Alternatively, the rabbis would tell us that the episode was designed as an admonition against human sacrifice, which they explained was quite prevalent among the neighboring peoples of the time. I would listen with undiminished deference; nevertheless I could not help thinking that the Lord might have found a much less oblique and less confusing way to command the end of human sacrifice — if that was what the story really intended. The Bible is not usually subtle when it comes to utter prohibitions.

According to the literature, there have always been a number of Jews who believe that God is to be reminded of Abraham's and Isaac's meritorious behavior, that He is to be reminded particularly on Rosh Hashanah so that He will be disposed by way of reciprocal courtesy to pardon the sins that Abraham's and Isaac's descendants may have committed. Even the ram's horn that is blown on Rosh Hashanah is to be taken as a reminder of the prototypical ram on Mount Moriah! What can I say about notions like these without giving offense to someone's sensibilities? Do they not violate the Third Commandment, which forbids us to take the name of the Lord in vain? What kind of a conception is it of a divine Judge that He should be considered susceptible to inherited "influence" and ancient connections, that He should be approached as a respecter of persons? Can we worship God and simultaneously think of Him as a respecter of farfetched Jewish genealogies? Let us put the thought away from us.

In my reading, I came upon an astute comment that Rabbi Manahem Mendel of Kosov, one of the late Hasidic masters, had made in relation to the case of the Binding. He said it showed that only God had the right to command us to destroy a man and that if even the smallest angel came forward to countermand such an order, we must obey him. Yet, why God should give this kind of order to a father concerning his son, Rabbi Mendel did not attempt to explain.

Then it occurred to me that perhaps there might be some light in the writings of the more perceptive non-Jews. I turned to what Thomas Mann had said about the Binding of Isaac in his magnificent Joseph Saga. Drawing on comments in rabbinical literature, Dr. Mann suggested that we ought to look at the story from God's point of view and that God surely knew from the beginning that he would never allow Abraham to execute the command; in point of fact, He knew that at the final moment Abraham would be incapable of going through with it. Dr. Mann's analysis seemed ingenious enough, but in my estimate it only made the original command harsher and more unnecessary.

Among the non-Jewish commentators, Kierkegaard at least has tried to confront the story squarely. He had considered what Abraham had done under God's command and had found it indefensible by any ethical standard. Consequently, he had taken the episode as a sort of premise from which to argue for a temporary disregard, or what he called a "suspension," of the ethical. He contended that the ethical could be suspended through personal revelation in an extreme crisis (crisis being a not infrequent condition for a man as brilliantly pathological as Kierkegaard). To this, Martin Buber and Milton Steinberg responded that, under the teachings of Jewish tradition, the sovereignty of the ethical was never suspended. I concluded that they were right and that, one way or the other, Kierkegaard's solution was too irrational to be of use to me. Thus, search and inquire as I might, it was all to no avail and I remained subject to an annual dismay when the Torah was read on Rosh Hashanah.

II

Last Rosh Hashanah was no exception. Again I heard about the Binding of Isaac and again I heard an eloquent sermon explaining that it was admirable for a father and son to go "both of them together." And again I heard a voice inside saying "No!"

Thereupon I decided that if the theologians with their impressive apparatus and the novelists and philosophers with theirs were unable to help me in my dilemma, I must resort to my own professional tools as a lawyer and find some way to help myself. At any rate, it could do no harm to try the lawyer's skills. How then would a lawyer approach the case of the Binding of Isaac?

His first question would be: What is the source of our evidence — that is, who was it that testified to the basic facts of the case? This is the way a lawyer is habituated to begin. Who, he would ask, could have provided the account we have of the Binding of Isaac? Who could have handed it down as part of the oral inheritance which became the Bible? There were only two available sources. Since I believe no one will suggest that we received our report either from the angel or from the ram, the only two possible witnesses to what took place on Mount Moriah were Abraham and Isaac.

If one considers that Isaac was a generation younger than Abraham and survived him by many years, it seems plausible to infer that the version we have received comes from Isaac rather than from Abraham. Nevertheless, if the story, on examination, were reconcilable with everything else we know about Abraham, it would be proper to conclude that Abraham had reported the episode and Isaac had merely transmitted the report.

The truth of the matter is just the opposite. Everything we know about Abraham's behavior, mentality, and character flatly contradicts the story of the Binding of Isaac. It is unthinkable that the Abraham we know as a man of superb dignity and valor would have silently accepted the command to sacrifice his only son. The Abraham we know is a man who left his country, his kindred, and his father's house to migrate to a strange land because he had a mission to perform there. He is the man who, in his old age, laughed when he was told God was going to see that he had a son. He is the man who inaugurated the greatest of all Jewish traditions — not, of course, when he instituted the rite of circumcision, but when he stood outside the wicked city of Sodom and urged God to His very Face that He deal justly and compassionately with its inhabitants. It was the first great mountain peak in Jewish history when Abraham confronted God and said, "Shall not the Judge of all the earth do justly?"

I said that this colloquy at Sodom inaugurated our loftiest tradition. Let me illustrate the tradition's continuity by mentioning some subsequent peaks in the same range. The second instance was when Moses and Aaron, at the time of the rebellion of Korah, told God it would not be right to destroy the entire congregation. Though they fell on their faces in reverence, yet they said, "Oh God, the God of the spirits of all flesh, shall one man sin and wilt Thou be wroth with all the congregation?" The third summit was reached when Jeremiah and Ezekiel repudiated the passages in the Torah which declared that God would hold human beings guilty by association or by inheritance to the third or fourth generation. For the fourth example, there is Job's radiant declaration, "Though He slay me, yet will I trust in Him, but

I will argue my ways before Him." The fifth instance took place when Rabbi Eleazar ben Azariah announced that the efficacy of atonement on Yom Kippur extended only to sins against God and that sins against a fellow-man would not be forgiven unless one had first done his best to reconcile the victim of the wrong. . . .

How could one possibly imagine that Abraham, the indomitable discoverer of the range, had told such a tale as the Binding of Isaac? We may be certain that he did not. It was out of the question. Suppose we consider the other possible — Isaac. Beyond the fact that, having survived Abraham, he had plenty of time to develop the story, is there anything further about it that seems to accord with his personality? What kind of man was Isaac? I think it safe to say that, although the Isaac we know was a tolerably good man, nevertheless if it were not for Abraham, his father, and Jacob, his son, no one would have heard much of him. His enjoyment of venison was manifestly in keeping with Jewish tradition, but scarcely extraordinary. His special affection for Esau indicated rather poor judgment on his part, and his actually preferring Esau to the magnificent and poetic Jacob proved that he did not appreciate the subtler and more civilized qualities of the younger twin. Isaac impresses us as rather soft, submissive, credulous, and ineffectual. Perhaps the most embarrassing bit of evidence is what Rebecca thought of him. It may be unfair to judge a man by his wife's estimate of him, but here we cannot help being influenced — particularly since the later developments showed how much wiser Rebecca's appraisal really was. Everything seems to confirm that the story of the Binding came to us from Isaac.

If Isaac was our original narrator and source (at least in the sense that whatever happened on Mount Moriah is forever unknown to us and that all we know is Isaac's version of it), how do I suggest that he came to tell the story? Often the principal meaning of an episode depends on its context, on identifying the setting in which it arose.

Picture, please, a scene of family dinner during Isaac's old age. The wild and explosive Esau has been quarreling again with his twin brother Jacob, the dreamer. The boys have grown too large for Rebecca to control and she demands that Isaac intervene. Perhaps she nags a bit until he does intervene. He looks at the faces of his two sons and knows in his heart that each of them is stronger than he is and that neither feels any deep obligation to obey him. And so, in a voice that attempts vainly to simulate the tones of his father, he relates the story which we call the Binding of Isaac. He relates it to prove that, when he was young, his feeling of respect and obedience toward his father was as absolute as his father's toward God in heaven. He tells the story to show that sons must obey without questioning, without challenging, without the necessity of first being convinced. He tells it because when his father was alive he did not quite understand him, and now in his old age he does not quite understand these strangely powerful young personalities whom he calls his sons. "Listen to me," he seems to cry, "as my father Abraham listened to God Himself and as I listened to my father."

For once, Rebecca sits there silent; weary though she is of her husband's anecdotes and reminiscences, how can she interrupt and correct him when the episode he is telling took place before she ever met him? And as for the two young men, they simply look down and glower at their laps in an aimless sulk. But Jacob will faithfully remember every word of the tale; and this, I think, is how we eventually came to hear about the Binding of Isaac. If so, one may say that Isaac was indeed bound — not in a rope but in a reverie, in a wish-fulfillment, in the fetters of an ineffectual dream.

III

If the explanation I have offered is tenable, it liberates us from believing that God commanded Abraham to kill his son as a sacrifice. And it has the further advantage of indicating certain characteristic and permanent human attitudes toward religion and the law. It indicates a definite typology which we can use to sharpen our comprehension of both institutions. The typology provides a simple line of contrast between Isaac's type and Abraham's type, and, as we all know, in actual experience very few people will be found to belong completely and invariably on either side of any such line. Nevertheless, it is the extraordinary fidelity to life in the personalities of the Bible that explains why they still appeal to every new generation. The truth is that we do continually meet Isaac's type and Abraham's type in many different fields of human activity, and specifically in the fields of religion and law. One type we associate with submission; the other we associate with consent. By Isaac's type I mean the kind of personality and attitude that is characteristically *submissive*: by Abraham's type I mean the kind that is characteristically *consensual*.

Let me begin by contrasting the two attitudes toward the nature of the religious experience. To a submissive person the religious experience offers a flight from the insecure and the problematical into the realm of the absolute. Under pressure of anxiety, such a person may become morbidly weary of restraint, moderation, and reasonableness. He may see no way to satisfy his emotional needs except in a God whose demands on him are extreme to the point of extravagance. Relishing ordeals of fasting and self-deprivation, he is prepared — in actuality or in imagination — to flagellate himself, castrate himself, slay himself, or slay his only son. He conceives of God as one who will be pleased if he renounces the pleasures and gratifications of the world and seals himself in a monastery. The submissive type finds it easier to believe and obey when his mind tells him that the command is absurd.

Turning to the man of the consensual type, I do not wish to suggest that he lacks occasions for the exercise of humility. He too appreciates discipline and humility, but he finds them not inconsistent with personal dignity and the free play of intelligence. Abraham does not withhold the most reverential rites of worship; he only insists that the value of the rites resides in the motives that prompt them, that the motives are determined by intelligent consent, and that the worthiest of all religious rituals is the rational effort to understand. Obviously, he does not understand the entire pattern of divine legislation and adjudication, if only because God supports the universal interests of the cosmos along with and in addition to the special interests of its human inhabitants. Nevertheless, with due allowance made for this limitation, the consensual type of man does expect that more and more portions of the overall pattern will become intelligible as he and his fellows employ the equipment of reason, science, and critical judgment. Moreover, he acknowledges that even these are poor guides unless they are illuminated by candles of social concern and generosity.

There is the same contrast between the submissive and the consensual type in regard to law and grace. People of the submissive type may actually prefer, though they will scarcely admit it, a legal order so fixed, absolute, exigent, inflexible, and extreme that it is unfit and cruel when applied to human affairs. Such a law gives them an opportunity to enjoy its being annulled or suspended by some fiat of arbitrary grace. Subconsciously they desire the law to be mechanical, hypertechnical and fatuously wooden; they want it to expel compassion and equity so that they can go outside the precincts of reason to intoxicate themselves with a long, undiluted draught of grace.

Consequently the man of the submissive type oscillates between an incredibly mechanical legalism on the one hand and, on the other hand, an escape into antinomianism or the rejection of all principles and rules. He oscillates between a law without compassion and a compassion without law. His own personal brand of compassion, unaffected by practical or rational considerations, reminds one somewhat of pure saccharine: it is not only cloyingly sweet but also devoid of nutritive value.

People of the submissive type have left their mark on various aspects of American law. For example, defining law as the exertion of ruthless power and defining compassion as merely arbitrary grace, they are satisfied to have the state continue to inflict capital punishment provided, once in a while, the penalty is tempered by an unpredictable and impulsive act of executive clemency. They find a certain whimsical charm in the alternation between extreme severity and capricious grace. For the submissive type, there seems to be some sort of hypnotic attraction in the idea of suspending the rule of the ethical; they do not pause to consider that if the ethical can be suspended for the doing of good it can and will be suspended for the doing of evil.

The purpose and operation of law look entirely different when we see them from the view of the consensual type. In this view, equity and compassion do not constitute a remedy of despair beyond the margin of law and ethics; on the contrary, they are working emollients within law and ethics, designed to keep the rules and decisions elastic, flexible, and humane. A concern with justice and compassion is what converts mere legalism into living law. Even in reference to the inhumane laws of capital punishment, executive elemency does not represent a device outside the boundaries of law; it is, on the contrary, an arrangement established by law for the purpose of reducing the fatal toll of error, miscarriage, and oppression. The state executive who commutes a death sentence to a life imprisonment is not authorized to follow his whim or caprice but the disciplined, informed, and rational discretion which is reposed by law in his office.

The consensual type of personality seeks to have all law — political and social, public and private, official and religious — embody the plasticity and reasonableness that Aristotle praised in his famous description of equity. He said:

> Equity bids us be merciful to the weakness of human nature; to think less about the laws than about the man who framed them, and less about what he said than about what he meant; not to consider the actions of the accused so much as his intentions, nor this or that detail so much as the whole story; to ask not what a man is now but what he has always or usually been. It bids us remember benefits rather than injuries, and benefits received rather than benefits conferred; to be patient when we are wronged; to settle a dispute by negotiation and not by force. . . .

Immediately before our eyes, we have excellent working models of this prescription in the numerous state and municipal commissions against discrimination in employment. We have further models in the manifold programs of the United States judiciary for achieving desegregation in our public schools. The models are less than perfect, of course, as all human endeavors must be; but surely they display inventiveness, individualization, and adaptability. What further evidence do we need that law, armed with the support of political power, can proceed patiently and understandingly, through negotiation and conciliation, toward substituting the reign of persuasion for the reign of force?

I should like to suggest that clemency and mercy in the framework of religious experience are no more devoid of sense than they are in the framework of state law. What we have inherited is an intelligible religious constitution, not a mere collection of willful decrees. When we seek forgiveness and atonement on Yom Kippur, the prerequisites have been defined in advance so that all may understand them and qualify for moral purgation. It was on this assumption that Rabbi Eleazar ben Azariah expounded the prerequisite of reconciling oneself with those whom one has wronged before attempting to reconcile oneself with God. The postulate of a consensual religion is that ethics need never be suspended to make room for mercy because it already contains mercy; mercy has already infiltrated and permeated it. As law without mercy is cruel, mercy without law is blind. Being of this view, Rabbi Eleazer stated his abhorrence of the death penalty and Rabbis Akiba and Tarfon, going beyond him, declared they would never inflict it. They understood that the very first place for grace to shine is within the practical workings of the law.

I suggest that it is only this consensual faith, characteristic of Abraham's life, that can effectively unbind Isaac and his fellows from their submissive fears. It is time to recognize that the foremost existential question of our era is not whether one believes in God but whether what one believes about Him is sufficiently worthy. Do we really think well enough of His legislation and adjudication to warrant Him in believing in us? The highest aim of the religious enterprise is to persuade a just, righteous, and compassionate God that He can believe in us.

Address delivered to the Central Conference of American Rabbis, 1960, and published in the Yearbook of the Central Conference of American Rabbis, *1960.*

6

ON THE LEGAL PROFESSION

*E*DMOND CAHN was a full-time practicing lawyer for twenty years before he emerged on the scene as a legal philosopher. This experience accounts in large part for the emphasis throughout his writings on a concrete case, or some situation familiar to the practicing lawyer, in order to develop a philosophic idea. It also made him a remarkable teacher of jurisprudence because his class discussions were studded with references to such private law subjects as trusts, wills, torts and divorce. In his hands jurisprudence had the authentic ring of a "lawyer's" subject, and he undoubtedly preferred the realistic discussion of a law school contracts class to the abstract analysis which frequently dominates the philosophy seminar.

Because he always thought of jurisprudential concepts in terms of concrete cases, he viewed the practicing lawyer as an important instrument of justice. He would heap the most lavish and sincere praise on a lawyer who voluntarily undertook to correct some injustice or who placed his ethical standards above pecuniary gain. When he prodded lawyers to write, to resume post-law school legal education, or to join a committee or sign a statement, he was paying that lawyer the high compliment of assuming that he was capable of performing a professional responsibility in the highest and fullest sense. In the final analysis he knew that the law could never develop into a more humane instrument of social justice without a legal profession which was willing and able to take on "the yoke of a magnificent faith."

N. R.

Some Reflections on the Aims
of Legal Education

Most people would agree that one of the principal aims of education — in whatever faculty or discipline — is the communication
and transmission of the truth. In so far as legal education is a species
of education, it ought to be concerned with truth. In so far as its
specific subject matter is law, it ought to be concerned with justice.
And in so far as it prepares young citizens to practice a profession of
vast individual and social consequence, it ought to be concerned with
their developing a sense of responsibility. Now, unless my observations
are mistaken, there are three significant ways in which contemporary
legal education in every country I have visited appears to neglect or
distort the ideal of truth, justice, and responsibility. I believe I can
best discuss the aims of legal education by calling attention to these
distortions.

THE ACADEMIC DISTORTION

For a generation or more, reflective judges and lawyers in increasing
numbers have recognized that legal rules are not mere machines where
one inserts a controversy and, after turning some sort of crank, extracts
a categorical decision. The practical function of legal rules is to serve
as instruments of analysis, evaluation, and responsible deliberation.
The rules are instruments in the control of decision-makers, themselves controlled by other decision-makers who use other, appropriate
instruments. Rules are not automata; they do not and cannot work of
themselves; they are manipulated and worked with. As we know, the
overwhelming majority of civil lawsuits and criminal prosecutions do
not turn on contested rules of law. They turn on contested issues of
fact, perplexing problems of credibility as among witnesses who relate
entirely different accounts of the same transaction. Often they turn on
inarticulate policies, peculiar local ways of doing things, and base
hidden prejudices or noble flashes of the sense of injustice. Little of

this can be found in the legislative text and perhaps even less in the law schools.

It seems to me that we continue to present rules of law much the way the uninspired professors of philosophy teach the formulas of the respective metaphysical systems, omitting almost everything that could possibly link philosophy with the exercise of judgment or good sense. In the standard philosophy course, one may learn lists of information about, say, Aristotle's causes or categories, but oné does not learn that his pages are spangled with brilliant empirical insights. I mean gems of wisdom like "Wit is well-bred insolence" or "Long introductions are popular with people who have weak cases" or "To praise a man is akin to urging a course of action" or "It is probable that many things will happen contrary to probability." The rules are, at most, the dry, articulated bones of our subject. There is also the living flesh — that is, everything contingent, casual, perverse, unpredictable, vital, and particular; and is not the flesh as real as the bones?

To what do I attribute this distortion? Though, of course, there are probably a number of factors, I believe the academic system itself provides the main cause. The ultimate goal of the system is an examination, written or viva voce, which can be graded and evaluated with a high — perhaps a maximum — show of objectivity. For this purpose, propositions that sound sharp and definite and absolute and precise (however inaccurate they may prove when placed in the market of practical affairs) are always preferred to those that, though relative and imprecise, happen to be genuinely consequential.

But there is much more to the academic distortion, for grading is only the terminus of the process. Before reaching this stage, we find preciseness already emphasized for its mnemonic advantage to any student preparing for the examination. Earlier still, the notes in his notebook will be thought unavailing if they are not precise. And on all these assumptions, preciseness will be the summum bonum of the professor's lectures — has not lecturing been defined as "the process by which the professor's notes become the student's notes without passing through the mind of either"? The professor who pours out torrents of rules and decisions will usually gain general esteem; students cannot praise him enough. It does not seem to matter very much if most of the rules he announces so confidently are modified, circumvented, or simply violated in everyday practice. So much for the academic distortion. Is it remediable; and, if so, at what cost?

Commentary:

Once there were three foxes who, while crossing a river together, were swept into a hole in the rocks and could not get out. For a long time as they lay there, they suffered miserably from swarms of fleas that fastened on them. A friendly hedgehog came along and offered to brush off the fleas. "No, thank you," replied the first fox. "By this time, these fleas are full and are not sucking much blood. If you remove them, others with fresh appetites will come along and drink up all the blood I have left." The second fox gave a different answer. "Thank you, Hedgehog," he said. "Please go right ahead. I am suffering too much to keep these fleas a moment longer. I'll take my chances on new ones that may or may not come along." And the third fox stayed silent for a long while, thinking and deliberating. Finally, he spoke, "Mr. Hedgehog, you are very kind. Both of my brothers are right and both of them are wrong. As for me, I prefer you remove only the fleas on my back where I cannot reach to scratch them. The rest I will either remove myself or learn to live with." Some days later, when the foxes succeeded in freeing themselves, the third fox was acclaimed as the greatest sage in all their tribe, and even his casual sayings are quoted as proverbs of wisdom to this day.

THE STATISTICAL DISTORTION

This distortion results from the fact that laws are proposed, enacted, and taught in wholesale terms, though they are enforced, felt, and experienced by human beings at retail. If we respect the principle of supremacy of law, we teach that the laws are the same for all persons, the rich and the poor, the powerful and the weak; and we state the rules in terms of abstract "reasonable men" or "average men" whom in Anglo-American law we may call John Doe and Richard Roe and in Roman law Aulus Agerius and Numerius Negidius. But like other useful instruments, these abstracts or averages which we use may prove quite dangerous. If, for example, an innocent man is convicted of a crime and confined in prison or sentenced to death, it will scarcely solace him to be told that many guilty men escape punishment and, therefore, the average is exactly as it should be. If the foreign office of a government is too aggressive and bellicose in certain affairs, can it acquire public support by being too backward and diffident in others? If one-half of the appropriations made at a legislative session are too extravagant with the people's money and the other half too scant and niggardly, it is not probable that a sensible electorate will be satisfied just because the averages of the session come out well. In point of fact, none of us has ever met a wholly "average" or wholly "reasonable" man, and I submit no one ever will. Consequently, we do not prepare students to serve suitably as professional trustees of justice unless we make them continually aware that law is consumed at retail and unless we accustom them to prize and defend human diversity and individuality.

THE ADVERSARY DISTORTION

I have suggested that the academic distortion may inhibit us in communicating the truth about law and that the statistical distortion may dull our response to the claims of humane justice. The third kind of distortion, which I call the adversary distortion, inflicts even more serious harm, for it affects our students' sense of responsibility to their community and their nation. There are four factors at work to cause the adversary distortion — two of them old, two new — and it is fair to say that legal education has not been coping adequately with any of them.

The first factor is the regrettable truth that whenever we deal with human affairs and relations, a more or less plausible or specious case can be made for either side of any given proposition. Bright youngsters discover this for themselves about the age of fifteen. They discover that with sufficient dialectical skill the worse cause can be made to appear the better and, in fact, that there is more fun, more occasion for pride, and greater display of virtuosity in choosing to defend what others might consider unjust or vicious than in defending what others consider just and good. This the Greeks demonstrated at least as early as the fifth century B.C. The speeches in Thucydides's history prove that there are simply no *a priori* limits to what an advocate can assert and defend without blushing for shame. In this sense, Thucydides has provided not only one of the greatest of historical works, but also a remarkably suggestive handbook for the young advocate.

The second operative factor is the lust for victory which infects every one of us (not only the young, but likewise the middle-aged and the old) when once we find ourselves engaged in any sort of contest. We lust to win as a fighter or a huntsman lusts to kill. When the fever infects a man, it is not always easy for him to remain scrupulous about the means and methods he employs. For one thing, the ultimate victory can itself appear to legitimatize the methods used to achieve it. For another, in many instances, the public compensates and rewards unscrupulous lawyers extravagantly with wealth, fame, and office, and thereby provides examples of the values it really appreciates. All these influences converge to stimulate the young advocate's natural passion for victory at any price.

Such are the ancient and familiar factors in the adversary distortion.

In addition, there are two modern factors, which augment and inten-
sify the problem for legal educators. Of these, the more obvious
consists in the availability and irresponsible use of new inventions and
gadgets. By "gadgets," I mean not only the mechanisms for wiretapping, the hidden electronic devices for recording and reproducing
private conversations, the forcibly imposed blood tests, the so-called
"truth" serums and drugs, the "lie detectors," and other spurious and
brutal applications of physical science. There are other, equally dangerous gadgets at hand in the guise of public-opinion polls and
psychological tests, many of which are impressive in judicial, legislative, or administrative hearings only because legal educators have
generally failed to prepare their students to analyze the polls or tests
critically, to disclose and welcome whatever truth and light they may
bring, and to expose effectually any inherent limitations, hidden
assumptions, and out-and-out fallacies. Whenever a lawyer evinces
lack of judgment or scruple in using the various gadgets, we cannot
avoid asking whether legal education should bear some portion of the
onus.

Finally, the adversary distortion has gained new significance in
modern times for those of us who live in representative democracies.
Before the emergence of representative government (a political concept which was unknown to the ancients and is still incomplete in
many modern republics), the use of cruel and ruthless procedure might
disgrace the prosecutor and his king, but it did not implicate the mass
of the subject people. The people were not responsible for government; they felt that they, too, were its victims. Now, all this has been
changed, for under a system of representative government, the prosecutor acts in the people's name and by force of their authority. When
he engages in what Justice Holmes called "dirty business" or when he
resorts to torture or forcible somatic tests, he implicates and sullies the
entire electorate and shows them that the law, which belongs to them
and which they have entrusted to him, brings them only discredit and
vicarious guilt. And if a lawyer misuses the other type of gadget (that
is, the opinion-poll or psychological test), he may prevail in his case at
the cost of gulling and deceiving honorable judges, who — not having
been equipped to evaluate evidence of this kind — accept and rely on
it with naive credulity.

Here, then, are the academic, the statistical, and the adversary
distortions. Clearly, they do reduce a preceptor's efficacy as exponent of
truth, justice, and social responsibility in relation to law. By confronting the distortions and grappling with them, we can demonstrate the
earnestness of our respect for education, our attachment to law, and

our aspiration for a better society. It was Aristotle, the greatest of educators, who reminded us that though government and law come into existence to make life possible, they continue in existence to make life good.

*Address delivered at the International Conference
on Legal Education, Ankara, Turkey, 1958, and
published in the* Journal of Legal Education, *1958.*

The Inherent Radicalism
of the Legal Profession

IT seems exceedingly strange that my topic should look so new and fresh. Perhaps it has been passed over and neglected because the radicalism of our profession is such an obvious theme, the kind of theme that practicing lawyers leave to the teachers, the teachers to the doctoral candidates, the doctoral candidates to the undergraduates, and the undergraduates to the practicing lawyers. If that is the case, who can be expected to break the circle and elucidate the obvious if not a legal philosopher? Such indeed I conceive to be my duty here — not to astonish you with bold novelties, or encumber you with additional ideas, but to soothe your spirits and salve your egos by recapitulating that which everyone knows from his own familiar observation. Assuming that "radicalism" means what the dictionary says it means, i.e., the demand for drastic and sweeping changes, then our profession is unmistakably radical. It is radical because it insists on sweeping transformations in the man who becomes a member of the bar; the changes it imposes on him are nothing short of drastic.

Like other systematic demands for the transformation of men, our profession does not always succeed; some of its members, as you know, act remarkably like laymen, and at times like the less desirable species of laymen. But here at the beginning of our portrait, whether the professional ideal succeeds or fails need not concern us; we may reserve the question for later, provided we remember that the ideal we are about to depict may not find complete realization anywhere in actual experience. For the present, it is enough to ask: How is the pattern of the lawyer such a radical one? What are the transformations to be expected in learning and practicing our profession?

They can be summarized briefly under the headings of mental qualities and moral qualities. A lawyer is a man whose mental processes have been trained to accord with the progress of a litigated case. Whatever the problem or policy may be that confronts him, his thinking follows the successive stages of the judicial process. In court, they are (1st) the pleadings, (2nd) the reception of evidence, (3rd) the deliberation, (4th) the attainment of decision, (5th) the drafting and issuance of the opinion, and (6th) the execution of judgment. In the steps of his intellectual experience, these correspond to: (1st) isolating the question to be answered, (2nd) investigation of available data, specifically including contradictory or negative instances, (3rd) weighing and evaluation of the data, (4th) commitment to a resolution of the problem, (5th) logical justification of the course decided upon, and (6th) application of the decision to a concrete set of circumstances. Thus, wherever the problem may arise and in whatever context, his mind is supposed to handle it with "due process of law." His thinking becomes literally "judicious."

Now contrast this quality, if you will, with the practices of his lay neighbors. Notice the two types together, in any kind of conference or friendly conversation. Observe, as indulgently as you can, how the layman generally avoids even beginning the process: likely enough, he is gifted with the ineffable certitude of opinion that Providence dispenses only to those who find thinking very painful. "The human mind," said Alfred North Whitehead, "was not evolved in bygone ages for the sake of reasoning, but merely to enable mankind with more art to hunt between meals for fresh food supplies." If the process of analysis does begin, even the layman will discern the lawyer's persistent sense of relevance, which — like the needle of a compass — veers back again and again to the one true crux of the matter. Annoyingly, the trained professional insists on hearing both sides; he refuses to accept mere assertions without substantiating evidence; and while the others clamor for some sort of immediate action his comments turn to what seems really feasible, what steps would satisfy the various interests in the situation, and how a particular solution might be later justified. The laymen do not enjoy all these hindrances; in point of fact, they quite understandably resent the exhibition of a transformed mentality. But experience teaches them that in every kind of affair it is costlier to stay away from the lawyer than to consult him; so they come, and they balance the account by deriding the profession with gibes and jokes that were stale in the days of Hammurabi.

On the moral side, the metamorphosis demanded of the lawyer may be even more radical. I shall not talk primarily about honor and integrity in large things, because the average life in our society is almost wholly preoccupied with the small things — small things such as opportunities to make pecuniary gains. It was our profession (including of course some ecclesiastical lawyers) that conceived and developed the moral pattern of the trustee, the man who acts devotedly on behalf of another and who is so exempt from the esurient ways of his society that he avoids even the possibility of conflict between his trust duties and his selfish interests. So the lawyer must act in all his relations with clients: he is the perennial trustee, regardless of the existence of a trust fund or the possibility of compensation, and — it is fair to add — regardless of the client's gratitude or reciprocal loyalty. Moreover, since the lawyer must conduct himself worthily as an officer of the court, he has another and more imposing fiduciary obligation: the profession holds justice itself in trust. Rightly then the humblest lawyer may preen himself whenever a court does honor to its function; and by the same token, all instances of corruption are at his cost and to his shame. What a radical standard to erect in this our acquisitive and Philistine society!

II

The problem now is: How does one go about putting such a radical pattern into effect? How can it be made real? Perhaps if we were to consider some other versions of radicalism, the answer might emerge. The legal profession has not been alone in demanding that familiar human attributes be transformed to a drastic extent. Let us, then, observe the methods by which other radicalisms have attempted to bring about the changes they propose in men.

If we do, we are sure to notice that however greatly the classic forms of radicalism may vary as to the kind of human product they consider desirable, they agree with one another in a single basic respect: each of them passes a judgment of final and irrevocable condemnation on the existing social structure and on the way the social structure has influenced men's characters. Each of them finds that the only way to convert men into something markedly better is to take drastic action concerning the evil influence of the social environment. As long as men continue to have their beings in the sort of societies they do live in, so long, according to these various radicalisms, will it remain hopeless to transform the individual's qualities.

Thus, the form of radicalism which is most familiar in our time advocates smashing the established order and building a new one on its ruins so that a better breed of men may rise under the influences of a reconstructed environment. But smashing is not the only remedy that has been preached: to anarchistic prophets on the politico-economic side and to messianic prophets on the ethico-religious side, the cure for society is to bring it to an end by dissolving it. According to them, the transformed man emerges — not when he exchanges the set of coercive bonds that rule his life but when he cuts them through and throws them away. Both of these species of radicalism — those that would smash society and those that would dissolve it — tend to despair of the present they see about them and to idealize the future they can dream of. Sometimes the despair is unfounded; the idealization always is. For after they have had their political smashings and their social severings, they find that the human element remains — well, what does it remain? Let me give the answer in Goethe's words: "An organ on which God plays the keys and the devil works the bellows."

But suppose instead of the kind of radicalism that would destroy society, we consider the kind that would abandon it. Physical abandonment or migration is the radical course our own ancestors adopted, and, viewing the results, we may be inclined to wish they had left the fellow who pumps the bellows on the other side of the Atlantic. In their more boastful hours — of which they had an adequate allotment — they used to flatter themselves that they had left him there. We of course know better. We see now that he was one of the most distinguished migrants to the Western world, where in fact he has been duly naturalized in every country and province. On the other hand, those Europeans who assert that his bellows supplied the breezes for our ancestors' westbound sails are probably exaggerating.

Then we must not overlook the species of radicalism that has found expression in monasteries, hermitages, and such like arrangements of a cloistered nature. They show that a man can abandon his society by simply stepping from the noises and conflicts of the street into some haven of seclusion and isolation. And if the conditions of a particular society are considered utterly beyond redemption, then — whether or not a monastery or a philosopher's chamber happens to be available — the men who have found the ways will emigrate in the intellectual sense and enter into the contemplative realm of pure essence. Mental migration, we are told, can reach whole finality; a spirit which has earnestly ferried itself over to the other shore will soon forget the very existence of this one, much less drift back again within the spell of its illusions. To such departures the rest of us can only be resigned; we have work to do on our shore.

These then are the chief formulas of classic radicalism. Each of them, having denounced the social order, proposes a way to transform human qualities — by smashing the order or dissolving it, by physical migration or withdrawal of the spirit. Not one of these radicalisms admits of the possibility that men may be transformed without either destroying or leaving their society. This possibility — the possibility that a man may continue to participate in his social order and nevertheless become transformed — all of them exclude. And it is this possibility on which we lawyers stake our professional lives! For such is the postulate we have asked the world to accept, the postulate of a mental and moral conversion unaided by revolution, renunciation, or dramatic withdrawal, but intimately coupled, on the contrary, with the ongoing humdrum life of the community.

Let me illustrate this temerarious claim of ours, taking as my example a subject that everlastingly fascinates the members of our profession, that is, the matter of fees. Lawyers have always regarded fees with a tender and solicitous attachment that does credit to our sensibility. We feel keenly in this respect. For instance, when the Emperor Nero issued a decree prohibiting the payment of advocates' fees, he made the burning of Rome appear by comparison like a mere boyish prank, and despite the lapse of these many centuries, lawyers are still disposed to doubt that he was a virtuous ruler. As we all know, even today certain clients seem to entertain the droll idea that in some mysterious way a lawyer can obtain the necessities of life free of charge and that he should be quite indifferent to money — except of course in his representative capacity.

Other clients whom we know insist that lawyers in general are grossly overpaid for their services. These clients happen to be right. The profession as a whole is far too well compensated in terms of dollars, but I think we can rely on progressively higher income tax rates to take care of that problem by directing the attorney's attention to the beauty of nontaxable compensations, such as the luster of legal scholarship, or of services to the underprivileged, or of achievements in law reform. I for one submit that a client who asserts that lawyers are overpaid should be heeded with courtesy and tolerance at least as long as his conduct continues to demonstrate the validity of his assertion.

Now you see how our setting has shifted: we find ourselves in the very center of life's marketplace, where the lawyer — unlike the cloistered philosopher or the secluded anchorite — is required to make himself an active and leading citizen of Philistia. He must know what the businessmen read (if they ever do read), or at least what newspaper slogans and magazine digests supply them with pabulum for what they are pleased to call their thinking. He must know (of course, nobody does know, but then ignorance is a great equalizer) why stocks and securities have just gone up, and why, as soon as one buys them, they will inevitably go down. He must have acquaintance with the world of popular sports, and with some technical details of his clients' businesses. Above all, the lawyer must understand that what he calls a "case," most laymen think of as a "trouble," and understanding this he must instill hope (without boasting) and solace (without condescending). All in all, the profession requires of us: to walk in the mire of mercantile affairs without becoming sullied, to mix with the vulgar without becoming coarse, and though conducting an active business with wily old Mammon, to stand straight as independent contractors, never to bow as servants.

We are not even permitted the luxury of avoiding temptation; on the contrary, our duties bring us to the very center of the avaricious web and keep us there while gains and promotions are dangled before us. No wonder that in such a web judges and lawyers will sometimes fall and be caught; the wonder is that any should have — and many do have — the mental and moral force to hold themselves free in the midst of the general servitude to dollar materialism. And so we continue to assert that the transformed mind and morality are attainable without shattering or abandoning the social order.

Quietly we lawyers have taken on ourselves the yoke of a magnificent faith. We of the law do not join with those radicalisms that relieve an individual of his obligations by attributing all of the blame to his surroundings. We do not concede that men are necessarily tainted even in a vulgar and corrupt society. Ours is the more responsible hope, for it gains or loses its vindication in the example of our own conduct. Ours is also the bolder hope; it dares to insist that our minds, wills, and consciences can rise superior to circumstance. A profession with such a faith deserves the community's gratitude and our chivalrous dedication.

Address delivered at the Toronto University School of Law, 1952, and published in the New York University Law Review, *1952.*

Ethical Problems of Tax Practitioners

WE come now to the main business of this evening, and we were cautioned last year by Dean Niles not to allow the subject to be treated lightly or facetiously. It is one that I think no one present is disposed to treat that way. I think that we all feel deeply concerned and, to some extent, unhappy over the subject which we are met to discuss.

The problem of a departure from ethical standards has always been with us. It is not new in our generation.

A current example of it (outside the field of taxation) which makes excellent reading is Chief Justice Arthur Vanderbilt's opinion in

Driscoll v. Burlington-Bristol Bridge Co.[1] It is interesting to compare that case, which reads like a detective story in which the miscreants are brought to justice in the final chapter, with something that I am going to read to you from a decision some seventy-five years old, a unanimous opinion of the United States Supreme Court, *Trist v. Child,*[2] delivered in the October Term 1874 by Mr. Justice Swayne. He says:

> The foundation of a republic is the virtue of its citizens. They are at once sovereigns and subjects. As the foundation is undermined, the structure is weakened. When it is destroyed, the fabric must fall. Such is the voice of universal history. The theory of our government is, that all public stations are trusts, and that those clothed with them are to be animated in the discharge of their duties solely by considerations of right, justice, and the public good. They are never to descend to a lower plane. But there is a correlative duty resting upon the citizen. In his intercourse with those in authority, whether executive or legislative, touching the performance of their functions, he is bound to exhibit truth, frankness, and integrity. Any departure from the line of rectitude in such cases, is not only bad in morals, but involves a public wrong. No people can have any higher public interest, except the preservation of their liberties, than integrity in the administration of their government in all its departments.

That part read as though it were written yesterday.

But, in order to show this picture in full contrast and to underline the virulence of the present situation, let me read this further statement:

> If any of the great corporations of the country were to hire adventurers who make market of themselves in this way, to procure the passage of a general law with a view to the promotion of their private interests, the moral sense of every right-minded man would instinctively denounce the employer and employed as steeped in corruption, and the employment as infamous.
>
> If the instances were numerous, open and tolerated, they would be regarded as measuring the decay of the public morals and the degeneracy of the times. No prophetic spirit would be needed to foretell the consequences near at hand.

As you know, this subject matter is one of peculiar interest to me, because I approach it in two capacities: as a student of the philosophy of law and as editor of the *Tax Law Review.* I have tried to understand what the causes are in our times that have worked for this degeneracy of morals in government and on the part of citizens dealing with government.

As a philosopher it was my first reaction that possibly the skepticism of the past two generations had undermined moral fabric; but then I remembered that it was the greatest skeptic of them all who had said these famous words: "Men must turn square corners when they deal with the Government."[3]

I think, rather, that the basic cause of this pestilence is the conformism that characterizes our society: the obsessive need to be like everyone else, to have the same possessions as everyone else, to follow the same pattern in the pursuit of material goods. I believe we have lost much of the individuality in action and in expression in our society, and also the sense of moral responsibility that came from that individuality in the past.

One of the things that is conspicuously changed in our society is the absence of cranks. We don't have enough cranks. This conformism involves keeping up with the Joneses in terms of possessions and keeping down with the Joneses in terms of morals. From the standpoint of the bar, it involves those things particularly with relation to the mercantile community. In respect of morals there are lawyers who have become what the Communists have always said the lawyers were in a capitalist society: with characteristic politeness, they have called us "jackals of the bourgeoisie." Lawyers may become worthy of the compliment if all they desire is to participate in the same standards as their mercantile neighbors, live the same lives, obtain for their wives the same type of coats, and ride around in the same automobiles.

In short, with respect to a capacity to distinguish in ethical matters, we may be fast losing our status as a profession and becoming nothing more than skilled merchant-clerks.

There are heavy guilts on both the law schools and the bar in this connection. I believe that within limits, even in a society as corrupt, as avaricious, as unscrupulous as our society seems to have become, there are real things that can be accomplished to overcome this trend and to bring about a bar which will have a sense of moral responsibility and will hold itself up as a sort of civic nobility, which is, as I see it, our duty and our role.

From the standpoint of the law schools, I think everything that we can do must be done during the impressionable period of the beginning of the study of law. I believe further that that must not be done merely by precept or by preaching "thou shalt nots" to young men.

I think the same thing applies with respect to the bar. The second impressionable period in a young lawyer's life is when he gets out of law school and first enters a law office and has association with an older man. The opportunity arises then to teach him things that are rather more important in the long run than the latest provision of the

Civil Practice Act or the Federal Rules or the Internal Revenue Code, things in a code which is considerably older and which he will ultimately need more.

Nothing is more impressive to him than the example of the man who is where he expects to be a few years hence, or at least hopes to be. Here again, I think, it is not a matter of precept but of the living example of the older man.

Let me give an illustration of that.

About thirty years ago my father came home one night and was in an obviously happy mood. When he was happy, he showed it in a stereotyped fashion: He had a rich, resonant voice and he knew only one song, and it was to the effect that he "stood on the bridge at midnight when the clock was striking the hour." He could accompany himself on the Steinway to this song, but only in chords, and he would sit there and throw his head back, the way you feel when you are in the shower, and let out his exuberance, and then, after he had sung this song, he would go mix himself the very best of Sazerac cocktails.

Observing this, I asked him whether he had won a particularly good case that day. He rubbed his hands together and said, "I won the biggest case a lawyer can win. I threw a rich client out of my office for asking me to do something wrong."

You can imagine what that meant to a sixteen-year-old boy who hoped to become a lawyer, and I looked forward to the day when I could have that same thrill. Unfortunately, for years after I began to practice law, no rich client ever asked me to do anything wrong. Then, after the lapse of some time, they started, once in a while, asking me to do something wrong, but the first nine or so of them conformed obediently when I told them they couldn't do that and indicated the proper thing to do. I had to wait for the tenth rich man who wanted to do something wrong before I succeeded in throwing him out of the office and having the belated celebration.

But I want to say that in the meantime there must have been half a dozen not-so-rich men who had to be thrown out for the same reason.

It is interesting when you read the great figures in the literature of our profession that they virtually never mention the subject of professional dishonesty. You don't find that sort of thing in their writings, and the reason for it is not so much that they are trying to hide it from their public, nor is it so much that no one ever attempted improperly to influence, say, Learned Hand's opinions; it is rather that the profession has held for them so many nonpecuniary satisfactions, satisfactions having to do with public service, culture, the advancement of justice, scholarship, and law reform and bar-association activities, that they have kept their eyes on those concerns, and so the pecuniary side has become secondary and has been pretty much taken for granted in their thinking as legitimate but not central.

I believe that that is a way and the only way that we in the schools and the law offices can guide young men as their mentors into becoming the kind of lawyers we have had in the past: Not by telling them, "You must not do this." "Why must I not?" If you have nothing else to offer but the type of picture that prevails in a merchant's establishment, your only answer will be, "Because you will be caught." That then becomes not a matter of honesty but of prudence and self-preservation. But if you have the kind of vision of the profession in which it is possible for a man to obtain these other satisfactions I have talked about, I believe it is very easy to make him see that what you ask him not to do is something that is incompatible with these other ends — not incompatible with his safety, but incompatible with his act of self-dedication in becoming a lawyer, and the causes he is supposed to serve.

In short I submit that these days the very possibility of the honest lawyer is directly dependent on the possibility of a lawyer who is making more than a living out of the profession, but is building in it a life.

Remarks at the Tax Law Review's *1952*
Banquet, published in the Tax Law Review, *1952.*

Eavesdropping on Justice

HARLAN FISKE STONE, Associate Justice of the Supreme Court 1925–1941 and Chief Justice 1941–1946, had a venial defect. He was an excellent legal scholar, a stanch defender of civil liberties, a sound political conservative and a jurist of outstanding integrity. But as his wife and secretary continually warned him, he talked too freely.

Though always eager to observe the proprieties of judicial office, Stone felt a compulsive need to express personal opinions on various delicate subjects. The worst incident occurred in 1938 when, in a series of uninhibited talks with newspaper columnist Marquis Childs, he spilled his raw impressions of a new colleague, Justice Hugo L. Black. Childs forthwith published this "inside view," which brought humiliation and remorse not to Black but to Stone. The scandal inflicted harm on the very institution that Stone strove so earnestly to protect, i.e., the Supreme Court. In a splendid new biography entitled *Harlan*

Fiske Stone: Pillar of the Law, Professor Alpheus T. Mason of Princeton comments:

> Whatever the message Stone tried to convey, it evaporated completely in the shocked reaction to his alleged breach of judicial etiquette. "Honor among judges dictates that they must not talk about one another to outsiders," the *Nation* declared gravely, adding that Childs's accusation, true or not, had "not made matters any easier for the Justices themselves." "It should have been fairly clear," another commentator for the same journal wrote, "that an article purporting to reveal the inner workings of the Court, and purporting to represent Justices as lamenting professional unfitness on the part of another Justice, would be calculated to recoil."

On April 22, 1946, Chief Justice Stone collapsed while presiding over the Court. He died the same day without recovering consciousness. Under the circumstances, others took charge to dispose of the papers in his files, which contained voluminous correspondence, memoranda, private and confidential communications, notes exchanged with his colleagues and preliminary drafts of Court opinions. Among these drafts were not only his own opinions, but also those prepared by other justices, living and dead.

Apparently, Stone's family and executors turned all the papers over to Professor Mason. Exploiting the opportunity to the fullest, Mason has produced a fine and intensely interesting biography, replete with disclosed intimacies and revealed confidences. On the book's jacket, the publisher takes occasion to claim, "A notable feature of this work is the unprecedented use of personal comments which the justices scribbled on the draft opinions that were circulated among them and later preserved in Stone's files."

This is true; the liberality with which Stone's biographer has published confidential notes and communications is genuinely "unprecedented." At least, I know of nothing quite comparable to it. It makes me think the time has arrived to raise the question: Is it socially desirable to expose confidential communications between a deceased judge and his surviving colleagues?

The problem is peculiarly American; it would be regarded as chimerical on the continent of Europe. There, observers long accustomed to a completely different system are baffled by our national cult of judicial personality. On the continent, they believe that justice will be impartial, objective and dispassionate only if every effort is made to repress the judge's personal traits and distinctive mannerisms. Consequently, a decision — even in a momentous case — will generally consist of a few dry sentences, issued anonymously by authority of the court. The view is that it takes an impersonal institution to produce impersonal justice.

We, on the contrary, never stop probing and delving into the motives and personalities of individual judges. Though, like our friends on the continent, we desire justice to be administered as impersonally as possible, we insist that anonymous hands may become irresponsible hands and that no man is fit to judge unless the people can ultimately pass judgment on him. In this perspective, biographical studies of important judges are not mere pabulum to satisfy our idle curiosity; they furnish useful and often valuable aids in understanding the judicial function within the republic. While something can be said on behalf of the European way (for example, timorous judges may exhibit more courage when they act as an anonymous body), the American way has the supreme advantage of linking responsibility directly to the exercise of power.

Nevertheless, our interest in judicial personalities, like all other interests, can be carried too far. When that occurs, we may become so absorbed in incident and anecdote that we lose sight of principle and rational doctrine. This generates a sort of "peephole jurisprudence," an appraisal that disregards everything except the peculiarities of the individual judge. Concededly, personalities and their clashes do possess a special attraction; yet a judge, even a mediocre one, is much more than his personality. To appreciate what he does in government, we must heed Holmes's statement that "The law is the calling of thinkers."

There are nine of them on the United States Supreme Court, nine thinkers of varying capacity. If one of the number sends a private note to another in the course of judicial business, is there a paramount social advantage in withholding the document from the gaze of the outside world? Individual advantages — protections for individual sensibilities — do not concern us here. Whenever the law respects a communication made in confidence, the main reason is public or social, i.e., the law has discovered a greater social benefit in protecting the confidential relation than in extracting the desired information. This is why a witness has the privilege of refusing to reveal confidences imparted to his lawyer, doctor, spouse or priest. In other words, there are prices which our society is not willing to pay, even for as precious a commodity as factual truth. This being so, what prices may we have to pay in order to obtain access to confidential papers like those in Chief Justice Stone's files?

The predictable prices of unlimited publication will be (1) unfairness, and (2) divisiveness — each severe enough to give us pause.

The unfairness is already conspicuous. In some recent biographies of

Supreme Court justices, a reader finds far too many self-serving accounts and self-justifying explanations. Which side will reach the public first depends, rather capriciously, on who happens to die first. The surviving members of the bench feel constrained not to respond or defend themselves. Silence is the sole dignified course, but in a country accustomed to strident voices, few appreciate the rhetoric of silence.

Some of the revelations in Professor Mason's biography of Chief Justice Stone will surely cause unnecessary embarrassment. For instance, there is the incident of choosing a justice to write the Court's opinion in the famous case of *Smith v. Allwright*. The case involved the constitutionality of applying racial discrimination in a party primary held in Texas to choose the Democratic candidate for Congress. After Stone had selected Justice Frankfurter as the Court's spokesman, Justice Jackson induced him to reassign the case to Justice Reed. Jackson's confidential memorandum, which Professor Mason prints in full, argues that the opinion would be "greatly weakened" if written by Justice Frankfurter because among other objections, he is a Jew, a circumstance which "may grate on Southern sensibilities." I think the publication of this memorandum is as unfair to Jackson and Stone as to Frankfurter.

If these revelations are embarrassing and unseemly, they are even more harmfully divisive. Will they not create an atmosphere of suspicion and distrust within the intimate councils and conferences of the Court? From now on, how can a justice feel free to write confidential notes or private memoranda? Every individual judge may decide to establish his own secret hoard of notations, diary entries, and compromising data, so that, in due time, he or his biographer can win the race to the public. If the present trend continues, our lecherous curiosity may produce nine bitter adversaries instead of a Supreme Court. No judge will trust any other judge, for though a particular colleague seems to deserve confidence, who knows about his executor? In fine, a high judicial body cannot function effectually in an atmosphere of internal mistrust.

As far as I can see, the problem is not primarily for biographers or historians. I believe it is a problem of ethics for the individual judge and a problem of policy for the corporate court. If the practice of exposing confidential communications is either unfair or divisive, every judge ought to assume the duty of preventing it. If a judge finds no way to establish his fame without exploiting breaches of confidence, then he should do without fame and put honor before honors. Surely, when a man has devoted his life to serving the cause of justice, he will not wish his biography to inflict injustice on his surviving colleagues, for he knows in advance that they will be muted by the proprieties of their office.

Ultimately, the problem is a corporate one, since it concerns the day-to-day efficacy of the Court itself. If the Court needs a right of privacy, it can secure the right by establishing explicit understandings among the justices. The Court can also adopt appropriate rules to govern the disposition of memoranda, confidential notes, and preliminary drafts. In other words it can safeguard the public interest in free and uninhibited communication among its members.

One proposition is clear. In contemporary America, the right of privacy cannot be obtained by depending entirely on others' good taste and considerateness. It requires vigilance, fairness, and a proud sense of solidarity.

From the Nation, *January 5, 1957.*

7

FACT-SKEPTICISM

*F*ACT-SKEPTICISM — the continuous questioning of factual assumptions — was developed as a philosophical approach by
*Jerome Frank to expose the realities of the judicial process. Frank
demonstrated that legal philosophers who think only in terms of rules
of law ignore something which every litigant knows — that the process
by which the facts are found and judged is the single most important
factor in determining whether, in any given case, justice is done.
Edmond Cahn built on his good friend's foundation and raised fact-
skepticism to its proper place as an essential element in a democratic
legal order. A legal system striving to reach a higher plane of human
values must be prepared to challenge the prejudices of past and
present, to scoff at predictions of an inevitable future, and to pierce
the intellectual fog of biased opinion which frequently cloaks itself in
the safe disguise of pretended fact.*

*The use which Edmond Cahn made of fact-skepticism is shown by
his essay on capital punishment which was prepared as a preface io the
American edition of Arthur Koestler's book* Reflections on Hanging.
*It might well have been entitled "A fact-skeptic looks at capital
punishment." It emerges as one of the most powerful moral indict-
ments of capital punishment ever written in this country because it
poses a fundamental moral question — how can a legal system capable
of making so many mistakes in so many different ways impose a
penalty which assumes a system of absolute perfection?*

*This essay, and the others in this chapter, articulate Edmond Cahn's
view of fact-skepticism as an "unremitting intellectual and moral
search" which, by freeing the human mind from the fetters of falsity,
opens the way for the full development of democratic man.*

N. R.

Skepticism in American Jurisprudence

W E should be neither astonished nor disappointed when we see modern jurisprudence occupying itself with questions which were common in philosophy when Aristotle tutored Alexander. For if there is any secure inference we can draw from the history of our subject, it is that the primordial questions tend to remain the truly fruitful ones. Among general philosophers, the questions have gained sophistication with each succeeding advance in reflective thought and scientific insight; among legal philosophers, they have derived a special concreteness from our growing knowledge of law's purposes and processes. Nevertheless, we are still busy with the elements. So often theories that at first seem radically novel turn out to be only current stages or points in the grand cultural continuum. When we consider them against the past, they take on a sort of familiar genealogy; they become domesticated to the tradition. For these reasons, it might be interesting to place the contemporary doctrines of "juristic skepticism" in a perspective of history, and observe the outcome.

SKEPTICAL TRADITIONS

Probably men started doubting as soon as they started thinking. At any rate, in fifth- and fourth-century Hellas the Sophists disseminated the doctrine that sense perception is chronically uncertain and untrustworthy. Then the Skeptics — Pyrrho, who had accompanied Alexander as far as India, was probably the most influential of them — extended the Sophists' subjectivism to the fields of morals and logic, and insisted that nothing certain could be asserted on any subject. As they would travel about from place to place, the Skeptics would obey the various local laws and customs, not because they approved of them but because the only wise policy for a Skeptic was suspense of judgment (*epoche*), leading to imperturbability (*ataraxia*) and complete indifference (*apatheia*). This initial current of Skepticism, which we may call "Greek" by way of including both Hellenic and Hellenistic thinkers, can be traced for about five hundred years, at least as far as Sextus Empiricus. There are no tenable criteria of truth, Sextus said in effect, no sufficient reasons for the sage to end his suspense of judgment. As one might expect, the Skeptics' opponents were wont to deride them by concocting tales about Pyrrho's helpless indifference when he went for a stroll and approached a precipice, and other equally obvious gibes; but considering that Pyrrho showed great courage during a storm at sea and that he lived to the age of ninety, we may score a point or two in favor of practiced imperturbability.

The Romans, on the other hand, appear to have been skeptical without being Skeptics. The interests of their empire made them philosophic syncretists; the same interests forbade any such thorough-going skepticism as might interfere with practical political decisions. Hence it has been well said that to the Romans skepticism served as a sort of "cement" for all the disparate and frequently contradictory elements they had gathered from foreign systems. But to capitalize skepticism until it might effect a permanent suspension of judgment would have been unthinkable to the Roman temperament of the time: there was a supreme empire to be administered and, if possible, augmented. This worldly, interested variety of skepticism we may call "Roman." Roman skeptics would concede that men need to exercise their judgment, because even the loosest syncretism requires selective acts of acceptance and rejection.

Now, in the household of the human spirit, skepticism is highly expert at throwing out the refuse but quite useless at providing the table with food. Given the conditions of the Roman Empire, scientific technology not being at hand to compete with the satisfactions of religion, skepticism eventually prepared men's minds to welcome a seemingly endless medieval night of dogmatism. Despite some incidental aporetic manifestations during the Middle Ages (doomed, as in Abelard's case, to end in tragedy) philosophic skepticism seems to have remained dormant or at least inconspicuous until the dawn of the magnificent sixteenth century. Then throughout Western Europe we find it bursting the confines of dogmatism. Men like Erasmus, Montaigne, and Sanchez (who wrote *Quod Nihil Scitur*) broke out of the old gate, fairly romped in the forbidden meadows of nescience, and returned only long enough to find a weak spot in the fence and give it a kick. And this time the impact of skepticism was destined to endure, because the negations of the sixteenth century cleared the ground for Francis Bacon's manifesto and for the (much more decisive) technical and theoretical achievements of modern science. Skepticism in the modern version has been employed on every hand as an implement of experiment and challenge, of innovation and reform. It is a conscious doubting-in-order-to-learn. For the sake of convenience, we may call it "Baconian."

Finally, there is a fourth vein to be noted — that is, the vein of "romantic skepticism." After the Age of Reason with its diverse but characteristically urbane "Greek," "Roman," and "Baconian" skeptics, the nineteenth century begins with a tableau by Shelley showing Prometheus shaking his proud and unconquerable fist in the face of a factitious and rather diffident Jove. Two generations later we find that although Jove has not unwisely withdrawn from the scene, Prometheus still continues to beat his breast and bellow defiance. The "romantic" skeptic, having dug the conventional ground away on every side, suddenly discovers himself standing on the very edge of an infinite void, and desires the world to know how valorous he is to hold his position there at the brink of the abyss. Since Jove is no longer available to serve as the audience, there is something rather archaic, if not faintly ludicrous, about maintaining this histrionic posture.[1]

"Romantic skepticism" has inspired some very effective rhetorical flights, not only by such ardent writers as Carlyle and Leslie Stephen but also by their continuators on this side of the Atlantic. The literature of American jurisprudence includes several eloquent examples, which the astute reader may identify for himself. But the exaltations of rhetoric, gratifying as they may be, do not fulfill the purposes of inquiring intelligence or pragmatic experimentation. Nor does the bravest description of the "universal void" assist a judge when he is required to determine a controversy which seems neither universal nor void but exceedingly concrete and existential. In the end, we may find that, through their dread of being beguiled, the "romantic skeptics" have at least partially beguiled themselves. At any rate, we should not lightly dismiss the implications of William James's remark: "Dupery for dupery, what proof is there that dupery through hope is so much worse than dupery through fear?"

THE USES OF SKEPTICISM

Confronted as jurists have been everywhere with the inescapable tension between existence and essence, the Anglo-Americans have almost uniformly found the center of gravity of their interest in existence. Thus while Teutonic thinkers have concentrated on essence at the cost of frequent irrelevance, the Anglo-Americans have tended to emphasize the existential at the cost of frequent hypocrisy. Because of this difference in approach, German skepticism generally serves a dialectic and dogmatic purpose while Anglo-American skepticism has remained relative in most instances and has been employed, as by Jeremy Bentham, for remedial uses. The Anglo-Americans have always suspected that anyone who believes dogmatically that "Vanity of vanities, all is vanity" does not take the trouble of saying so.

There is a hoary anecdote about the skeptical philosopher who conducted himself with utter indifference to all things. He was told in a reproachful manner that for a philosopher he seemed to set no great store on philosophy. "It is that very thing," he replied, "which I call to be a philosopher." Thus while skepticism has long been important in Anglo-American juristic thinking, the theorists have been rather consistently skeptical about dogmatic skepticism. Perhaps they have been motivated by the governmental interests and purposes that brought about the Roman variety of skepticism.

Be that as it may, twenty years before the publication of Locke's *Essay* a relative skepticism became more or less official in English law. It will be recalled that in *Bushell's* case a jury that had tried William Penn and others for unlawful assembly were directed to be incarcerated because they stubbornly refused to obey the court's direction to bring in a verdict of guilty. Mr. Chief Justice Vaughan in a historic opinion ordered them discharged pursuant to a writ of habeas corpus, saying:

> I would know whether any thing be more common, than for two men students, barristers, or judges, to deduce contrary and opposite conclusions out of the same case in law? And is there any difference that two men should infer distinct conclusions from the same testimony? Is any thing more known than that the same author, and place in that author, is forcibly urged to maintain contrary conclusions, and the decision hard, which is in the right? Is any thing more frequent in the controversies of religion, than to press the same text for opposite tenets? How then comes it to pass that two persons may not apprehend with reason and honesty, what a witness, or many, say, to prove in the understanding of one plainly one thing, but in the apprehension of the other, clearly the contrary thing? Must therefore one of these merit fine and imprisonment, because he doth that which he cannot otherwise do, preserving his oath and integrity? And this often is the case of the judge and jury. . . .
>
> A man cannot see by another's eye, nor hear by another's ear, no more can a man conclude or infer the thing to be resolved by another's understanding or reasoning. . . .

With growing sophistication this authoritative recognition of skepticism has characterized the Anglo-American judicial process from Vaughan's time to the present day. In point of fact, despite the surface conflicts in the current literature of Anglo-American jurisprudence, one may suggest that an implicit consensus has been reached concerning the degree of truth ascertainable by the judicial process.

Most writers in the Anglo-American tradition would now agree that the judicial process is, at least in part, legislative, and that the criteria of validity developed by William James and John Dewey epitomize what is meant by "truth" in the judge's performance of his legislative function.

Since, however, the judge's operation is not exclusively legislative there is something more to be looked for in the "truth" of the judicial process. While the judge legislates, it is indubitable that he also resolves, reconstructs, and adjudicates the specific controversy. In this aspect of his function I think there would be very wide agreement on the following conception of "truth," presented by George Santayana:

> The experience which perhaps makes even the empiricist awake to the being of truth, and brings it home to any energetic man, is the experience of other people lying. When I am falsely accused, or when I am represented as thinking what I do not think, I rebel against that contradiction to my evident self-knowledge; and as the other man asserts that the liar is myself, and a third person might very well entertain that hypothesis and decide against me, I learn that a report may fly in the face of the facts. There is, I then see clearly, a comprehensive standard description for every fact, which those who report it as it happened repeat in part, whereas on the contrary liars contradict it in some particular. And a little further reflection may convince me that even the liar must recognize the fact to some extent, else it would not be *that* fact that he was misrepresenting; and also that honest memory and belief, even when most unimpeachable, are not exhaustive and not themselves the standard for belief or for memory, since they are now clearer and now vaguer, and subject to error and correction. That standard comprehensive description of any fact which neither I nor any man can ever wholly repeat, is the truth about it.

It should be noted that the judge's *Gestalt* is expected to synthesize the James-Dewey instrumental objectivism with Santayana's reportorial objectivism. In the two approaches we find common elements of (1) objective relativism, (2) theoretically complete but practically limited verifiability, and (3) a focus on felt involvement and meaningful human consequences in the search for truth.

This relativistic understanding of "truth" has left imprints on virtually every aspect of Anglo-American law and jurisprudence. One example taken from the law and another taken from legal philosophy will be enough to illustrate the importance of the influence. In each example we can see the consequences of a continuous tradition of seasoned skepticism.

First take the law. In the Anglo-American trial process, one of the most obvious and cogent shaping factors has consisted in skepticism concerning the veracity of witnesses, the discriminatory powers of juries, the wisdom of judges, the validity of legal categories, and the efficacy of law as a means of social control. These manifestations of skepticism are critical indeed. Yet even more fundamental has been the skepticism which serves as the enduring gravamen of our civil liberties. The Anglo-American societies have been so thoroughly convinced that dogmatically absolute truth is something unattainable that they have set an official ceiling-price both on truth in the marketplace and on truth in the judicial process. The thought is that such truth as men can attain is too limited to warrant paying an unrestricted price for it in other values. When the price becomes too high in terms of competing individual and social interests, the search for truth is required by law to be frustrated. Sometimes this is done by insisting on freedom for voices that seem utterly erroneous and perverse; sometimes it is done by refusing to permit officials to elicit the truth through means which, though presumedly efficacious, the society considers cruel or repulsive.

To show the impact of skepticism on Anglo-American legal philosophy, it might be interesting to illustrate our point by an inverse or contrasting procedure. Suppose we glance at a fairly representative composition[2] written by an eminent author who has been steeped in the Teutonic tradition of jurisprudence. What will we find? In the first place, the author's logical dialectic is uniformly in binary terms: at each stage of his thinking only two alternatives are accepted and these are cleft with a sharpness to be found only in the realm of pure abstractions. No matter what experience may have taught the reader about anarchic instances and subtle gradations in practical human affairs, he finds here a relentless series of dialectic either-or's. In the second place, the author's vocabulary emphasizes without embarrassment or apology such locutions as "dogmatic," "must," "unique," "simply," "it suffices *ipso facto*," "no possibility of escape," "cannot," "always," "demonstrated," "impossible," "annihilate," "utterly untenable," and again "must." While deprecating "that polemical style peculiar to the cultural sciences" the author nevertheless claims his theory "has drawn the blood" of other men's views, and he refers to certain rival schools as "excrescences which have been discarded." In the third place, consistently with his denominating his own system "dogmatic jurisprudence," he claims for it novelty as well as originality and monopoly as well as authority. By way of epitome, I may say that wherever an Anglo-American would be disposed to use "a," this distinguished author says "the."

When the Anglo-American comes upon this style of analysis and composition he is likely to be reminded of the exchange between Owen Glendower and Hotspur in *King Henry IV:*

> GLENDOWER: I can call spirits from the vasty deep.
> HOTSPUR: Why, so can I, or so can any man;
> But will they come when you do call for them?

SOME CURRENT JURISTIC SKEPTICISMS

As we have seen, the skepticism characteristic of the Anglo-American tradition is both relative and useful. In all probability it is useful just because it is relative. At any rate, until recently one might illustrate the difference between Anglo-American and Teutonic theories of law by pointing out that while Austin considered such values as "justice" to be outside the proper province of jurisprudence, Kelsen dogmatically banished these values for *all* purposes by labeling them as "not subject to cognition." Thus skepticism, which the Anglo-Americans have used as an effectual means, can be converted into a dogmatic and preclusive end. It seems a bit strange that intelligent men who would smile at believing for the sake of believing induce themselves to disbelieve for the sake of disbelieving.

Yet nature is not only wiser than the dogmatic believer, it is also wiser than the dogmatic skeptic. As Santayana says, "the hungry dog *must* believe that the bone before him is a substance, not an essence; and when he is snapping at it or gnawing it, that belief rises into conviction, and he would be a very dishonest dog if, at that moment, he denied it." Dr. Kelsen's attachment to the advancement of justice is one of the prominent facts in his biography. And Pyrrho's most caustic successors in American jurisprudence are judges and lawyers who have rendered outstanding service in a wide variety of righteous causes. Pyrrho himself said, when he was teased for having run away from a threatening dog, "It is a difficult thing to put off the man." Certain it is that the leading American skeptics have not entirely succeeded in "putting off the man."

The interesting phenomenon is that American skeptics have felt somehow obliged to preach dogmatic skepticism in order to justify practicing relative skepticism. In the case of such men as Holmes and Learned Hand, it is rather easy to see how the dogmatic in their essays and speeches is qualified by the relative and pragmatic in their judicial decisions. I see no sign that Holmes took his own sweeping negations so seriously as to be embarrassed by them: perhaps he was shielded by the thickness of his self-assurance, perhaps the hypocrisies and dogmatic certitudes of his contemporaries furnished a target so broad that there was no danger of an arrow hitting the marksman. But Judge Hand's posture appears to be less happy.[3]

The arrows may find strange targets and cause disturbing infections. For example, readers of Judge Hand's collected addresses,[4] while enthralled by the beauty of his thinking and style, have expressed chagrin at coming upon the transcript of his appearance before a congressional subcommittee which was concerned with the low state of public morals and had turned to him for guidance; they were not prepared for the Pyrrhonic unconcern in his testimony. By the same token, when Charles P. Curtis, a distinguished member of the Massachusetts bar, recently announced that a lawyer is sometimes required to be disingenuous in his client's behalf, is then absolved from veracity, and is bound to "treat outsiders as if they were barbarians and enemies," he made many members of the bar wonder whether he was acting the devil's advocate in the traditional sense or in earnest. No one worries about Judge Hand's or Mr. Curtis's moral safety when they play with cynical acid: the anxiety should be and is reserved for the bystanders.

Such questions apart, the central preoccupation of American juristic skepticism has, properly enough, coincided with the central interest of American jurisprudence. Like Jeremy Bentham, Gray and Holmes made use of skepticism in order to ascertain what a judge really does when he decides a case, as distinguished from what he professes to be doing. They refused to blink the truth that the judge exercises a creative and legislative function. When the Supreme Court majority of their day interpolated economic and social predilections in the due process clause of the Constitution, they refused to be deceived by the disguise. For, then as now, the fundamental inquiry is not whether the predilections are right or wrong, not even whether the justices are warranted in considering their predilections. Beneath these questions lies a deeper one. It is: What are the justices actually doing? Until the various conventional disguises are removed so that this question can be answered, no effectual valuation seems possible.

For the most part, Jerome Frank has employed his skeptical virtuosity in order to liberalize and reform the trial process, to discover means by which a closer conformity may be achieved between findings of fact and relevant objective events, and to individualize the administration of justice sympathetically, rationally, and purposively. I think this propaedeutic use of skepticism can be properly termed "Baconian."

To recapitulate here: the general trend of American skepticism in jurisprudence has been of the Roman variety. The philosophic assumptions involved in the jurisprudence have been so many and diverse that an American jurist is almost bound to emulate the eclecticism he finds in Cicero and to use skepticism similarly as a "cement." The reformers among our theoreticians (Jerome Frank, Thurman Arnold, Karl Llewellyn and others) address their skepticism to the several aspects of the legal apparatus which they desire to improve. Their doubts are of the sort that Bacon would have recommended, that is to say, they consist in putting searching questions to the received subject matter.

If we set aside various manifestations of "romantic skepticism" which serve merely to put a more attractive face on expressions of dogmatic disbelief, there remains for consideration only the Pyrrhonic or Greek version of skepticism. As to this version, some further comments are needed in order to challenge the inference that, because a modicum of salt is indispensable to a healthful diet, the more salt the better the diet.

THE CREDULITY OF THE SKEPTICS

By way of retort to the dogmatic skeptics, philosophers have advanced the rather cogent propositions that the way we recognize that certain sense perceptions are untrustworthy is by means of other sense perceptions which we deem trustworthy, that mistaken sense perceptions are remediable by further sense perceptions, that the only way we can arrive at the expression of generalized doubts is to give credence to our powers of reason and inference, that the cure for faulty inferences consists in less faulty ones, and that our natural existence and activity constitute of themselves expressions of belief which refuse to be contradicted by any dogmatically skeptical posture. In so far as philosophy is availed of as a guide to life, skepticism remains relative; even if philosophy should be conceived as the end and goal of all pursuits, the philosopher while he lives never entirely "puts off the man."

There seem to be psychological satisfactions in dogmatic skepticism that prompt men to espouse it even at the cost of a rather embarrassing credulity. Just as the dogmatic skeptic must believe those sense perceptions that tell him that other sense perceptions are untrustworthy, so Holmes felt himself compelled to take a credulous position with regard to his so-called "can't helps." He was content to stop his inquiry with them. But if skepticism leads us to a series of "can't helps," there is no conclusive reason why the inquiry should not proceed further for the purpose of explaining the genesis and configuration of the "can't helps." If on the other hand they are required to be taken as ultimate and irreducible data, then they provide something very concrete on the basis of which to build other knowledge. They can scarcely be said to partake of existence yet be entirely void of essence.

Learned Hand appears to have been led by skepticism into an even more chimerical position. In his case, skepticism seems quite dogmatic when it turns inward but relaxed to the point of credulity when it faces what he calls "the community" or "the public." Fleeing from the old heresy (that the judge should act like a despot over the community's legal mandates), he has sought refuge in what looks like a new heresy (that the judge should act like an automaton recording and enforcing community opinions). But with characteristic dignity and candor Judge Hand has confessed his bewilderment at learning that the fancied refuge is not to be located.

Kierkegaard said over a century ago:

> Years might be spent gathering the public together, and still it would not be there. This abstraction, which the individuals so illogically form, quite rightly repulses the individual instead of coming to his help. The man who has no opinion of an event at the actual moment accepts the opinion of the majority, or if he is quarrelsome, of the minority. But it must be remembered that both majority and minority are real people, and that is why the individual is assisted by adhering to them. A public, on the contrary, is an abstraction. *To adopt the opinion of this or that man means that one knows that they will be subjected to the same dangers as oneself, that they will go astray with one if the opinion goes astray.* But to adopt the same opinion as the public is a deceptive consolation because the public is only there *in abstracto.* . . .
>
> A public is neither a nation, nor a generation, nor a community, nor a society, nor these particular men, for all these are only what they are through the concrete; *no single person who belongs to the public makes a real commitment;* for some hours of the day, perhaps, he belongs to the public — at moments when he is nothing else, since when he really is what he is, he does not form part of the public. Made up of such individuals, of individuals at the moments when they are nothing, a public is a kind of gigantic something, an abstract and deserted void which is everything and nothing. . . .

No one would expect Judge Hand to believe that Jones, Smith, and Brown possess ready and considered opinions on the various issues he seeks to refer to community judgment. No one would expect him to entertain much respect for the offhand, irresponsible answers most of his neighbors would proffer if they were questioned. In fact, Judge Hand would be among the first to insist that many individual opinions are given voice without comprehension of the question to be answered. Nevertheless, if, under the magical rubric of "community," all these minus quantities and zeros are aggregated they somehow produce a decisively imposing total in Judge Hand's arithmetic.

A very recent formulation would appear to go even further.[5] It states that we have *no* means of "vicarious choice" between the desires and values of conflicting social groups "except in so far as we can imaginatively project ourselves into the position of the groups between which we must choose." I do not think that Judge Hand meant by this to adopt a syndicalist view of society or to advocate disregard of the general welfare. What he does seem to assume here is that each social group is sufficiently compartmentalized to have a "general will" or diminutive *Volksgeist* of its own, and that somewhere in the *Volksgeist* there is a discernible line of self-discipline, compromise, and renunciation. He appears further to assume that the compromise-values for one group will somehow match those for the group with which it conflicts. Putting aside the possibility that one of the groups may be entirely wrong in the presented controversy or that both groups may be quite intransigent, it nevertheless seems that Judge Hand has constructed some exceedingly implausible fictions and, doing so, has rendered his own function more difficult.

It is no easy task to ascertain the applicable standard even when the mandate to the judge has been conveyed in specific statutory language. If the legislature should try to do something more than provide the judge with a standard, that is if it should try to take to itself his function of deliberation and appreciation, he would call the attempt a bill of attainder, or a legislative exercise of judicial power, or an invasion of the independence of the judiciary. He would hold the enactment void — rightly of course, because the legislative representatives of the community are authorized to furnish him with *standards* of judgment but not to execute for him his *act of judgment*. It would then be strange indeed if the murky sentiment of the community (assuming the sentiment could be identified) were empowered to exert an authority over the judge which is denied to the legislature.

In former days the judge's creative function was cloaked under a fictional doctrine which we have learned to call "mechanical jurisprudence." Flimsy though the masquerade was, the judge could at least point to official precedents or an official text. Now this new version of mechanical jurisprudence lacks even that safeguard. It produces scarcely anything identifiable on which to predicate judicial responsibility.[6]

Like ancient Greek skepticism, the American variety has produced some strikingly noble personalities. Perhaps like their precursors in classical times, the American skeptics presage an era of decadence, corruption, and decline. There are strong indications to that effect.

On the other hand, a disciplined, instrumental skepticism appears indispensable to the evolving life of the law and to the growth of a humanistic jurisprudence. Dogmatic skepticism cannot plunge men into despair unless they first rest their weight on an arrogant and contrived certitude. It remains to be seen whether the American mind has become mature enough to accept such relative certainties as nature and scientific progress provide, to discern opportunities in them and in our uncertainties as well, and to put intelligence to work on the materials at hand. If it has, hope may be vindicated for "my brother general, the commonwealth."[7]

From the 1952 Annual Survey of American Law.

"Courts on Trial": An Analysis

I N one of the dream-sequences of *Through the Looking Glass*, Alice found herself in a little dark shop where an old sheep sat knitting behind the counter. She looked around her to see just what was on the shelves. "The shop seemed to be full of all manner of curious things — but the oddest part of it all was that whenever she looked hard at any shelf, to make out exactly what it had on it, that particular shelf was always quite empty; though the others round it were crowded as full as they could hold."

This is the kind of nightmare sensation that is likely to come when for the first time one examines critically some shelf or other in the shop he is used to call his cosmos. Philosophic inquiry at its outset is an agitating experience, charged with vertigo and sudden discomforts. Whoever engages in it in the skeptical manner that intellectual honesty compels will appear to be snatching away his neighbors' familiar supports. Hence for some twenty years (since *Law and the Modern Mind*) Jerome Frank's writings have met with two classes of readers: one, those whose disturbance led only to resentment; the other, those whose disturbance prompted them to reassess old assumptions, to grapple with new challenges, and to feel grateful for the light he had let into the dark shop. For the latter group and for anyone hardy enough to join them, the publication of *Courts on Trial** is an important event, because this is his most illuminating work.

Addressed as it is to the general public, the book is written in an easy, pungent, and relatively simple style. Thus it invites reading on more than one level; in fact, sophisticated students are likely to find more beneath than above the apparently smooth surface of the text.

* *Courts on Trial: Myth and Reality in American Justice* by Jerome Frank (1949).

And to those who, like this reporter, receive a very modest income of insights and ideas, Judge Frank seems, as in his earlier works, to be flinging his revenue about in an almost prodigal fashion. But then, considering the intellectual expenditure he has been able to maintain these many years, who will venture to call him a spendthrift? Fortunately, certain of the book's ideas can be recognized as variations of what Judge Frank has said before, and it is enlightening to see how these familiar thoughts draw new cogence and direction from the general thesis to which they contribute.

The thesis is entitled "fact-skepticism." It is developed with such a variety of illustration, analogical digression, and exposition of corollary applications (e.g., to the problems of legal education) that this review will become hopelessly lost unless we resolve to stay on the highway. The highway is directed toward a fundamental reformation of popular understanding of the nature of the judicial process. En route, certain significant procedural reforms are recommended, but Judge Frank would probably agree that they are not inextricably attached to "fact-skepticism" and that his principal theme may be considered independently, on its own merits.

Stated as bluntly as possible, this theme is: a court generally decides a case without knowledge of the relevant circumstances that actually occurred and in reliance on a mistaken belief in other circumstances that actually did not occur, i.e., on "the wrong facts." Judge Frank buttresses this conclusion with copious reasons and illustrations, neglecting no argument in vindication of his "fact-skepticism." Some of the reasons (those that result from defects in judicial method) are curable or at least mitigable, but others, arising out of the faulty human capacity to observe, to remember, to articulate, etc., are bound to remain with us permanently. Modern litigation, heir of the magical ordeal and of the resort to brute force, is miles removed from a scientific investigation into the truth of "what actually happened." Amid the conflicts of testimony, the stratagems of counsel, the prejudices and perjuries, amid the blind of eye, the lame of memory, and the halt of articulation — the judges and the juries, themselves myopic and inept, sit and render judgment; and no one ever discerns the "true" facts of the case.

On the way to this conclusion, the lay reader (and many of us at the bar) will learn much concerning the operations of the courts and the views of contemporary theorists. These by-products are very valuable regardless of one's attitude toward the author's incidental positions. Some of us would be inclined to except to (1) the sharpness of the dichotomy between rule of law and finding of fact, which is maintained through most of the book and appears inadequately relieved by the brief treatment of *Gestalt*,[1] (2) the supposed relative clarity of the law-rules, and (3) the treatment of "natural law" as an influence on the law side only of the dichotomy. But as to Judge Frank's principal thesis — the inaccessibility of the "true" facts — most readers will be convinced and will freely assent.

Once having assented, however, they may suggest that the thesis gives rise to certain further questions that Judge Frank may see fit to consider fully in the future. (That the questions are phrased here tendentiously does not mean that they are intended as answers.)

In an ordinary civil litigation, are we or the parties really interested in ascertaining the "true," transcendental, mind-of-God facts? Is it not enough to conduct a rigorous examination of recollections to make them as sincere and careful as possible in the *present* (which is all we ever have)? Is not the controversy causing its individual and social disturbances *now*? Should we not focus on a *decision* (a value judgment), i.e., some concededly imperfect and approximate resolution that will send the litigants back to their respective pursuits and to the use of their nonlitigated rights?

Does not the adversary method of litigation at least promote relative impartiality of the tribunal? If our objective is a *decision* rather than a *finding* of scientific accuracy (verification by controlled experiment being generally impossible), is not the partisan political debate a relevant analogy to the same limited extent as scientific method?

The answers to these questions would probably indicate that the shelf of adjudication is not nearly so bare as it first appears in the light of Judge Frank's thesis. If the answers are in the affirmative, then the litigative process is not a mere juggling with myths and its decisions are not congenitally based on the "wrong facts." In general, such data as a liberalized procedure would disclose do seem to be all the data that make up the controversy at the time of trial. They are the "right facts" to be evaluated in deciding it, whether or not they have noumenal counterparts in the past.

On the other hand, future fact-findings appear quite as unpredictable as Judge Frank insists they are. And that unpredictability (both *lex* and *justitia* being feminine) is almost completely irreducible. Such being the case, how much utilitarian value remains in Holmes's treatment of a legal right as "the hypostasis of a prophecy"? Viewed in the light of this radical unpredictability, Holmes's analysis might seem to deny the existence of any rights except those already adjudicated in specific litigations between the same parties: the outcome of future litigation concerning other rights or other parties would be mere guesswork. "Hypostasis of a prophecy" may somehow be made to include a reservation (or an auxiliary prophecy) that, in all probability, the instant right will not be contested before a court or administrative agency. Perhaps the moral is that Holmes's highly useful insight has been extended beyond its legitimate province. Perhaps societal practice, which pays aright its wages on the assumption of good health and regards the advent of litigation the way we regard cancer (as something terrible that may happen to someone else) is an equally suggestive criterion. These are indeed profound questions, but it will not do to withhold praise of a preeminent book until they can be thought through to a firm position.

Those of us who were introduced to the law in the conceptualistic murk of the 1920's are bound to remember with gratitude the brave company of so-called "realists" who forced the windows open and gave us light and air. Foremost of that band, Jerome Frank continues — with zest and sparkle — to disturb the complacent, to shock the intellectual prudes, and to lay a youthfully tempestuous siege to the heart of justice. Of all men, he may be least concerned by the gap between the excitements of the present and the past's pathetic illusion.

From the 1950 Annual Survey of American Law,
adapted from a review in the Yale Law Journal, *1950.*

Jerome Frank's Fact-Skepticism and Our Future

WHEN Dean Rostow asked me to describe the main features of Jerome Frank's legal philosophy, I resolved that — no matter how tentative my summary might be — I must speak in the perspective of the future. For one thing, this is the way he habitually faced and spoke and wrote; it is the way to be faithful to his thought. For another, his philosophy — which he called "fact-skepticism" — is nothing more or less than a bold confrontation of the future and a flinging of gages at its feet. I believe that Jerome Frank's fact-skepticism represents an epoch-making contribution not only to legal theory and procedural reform, but also to the understanding of the entire human condition. The history of our time will record whether we profited by the challenges he bequeathed to us.

For about twenty-five years Jerome Frank's coruscating and marvelously restless mind planned and built and developed the meaning of fact-skepticism. Fully aware that his approach was novel, he deliberately repeated and reiterated his doctrines, phrased them first this way then that, and summoned analogies from every corner of the cultural world to make his ideas clearer. To justify the repetitions, he used the following story:

> Mr. Smith of Denver was introduced to Mr. Jones at a dinner party in Chicago. "Oh," said Jones, "do you know my friend Mr. Schnicklefritz, who lives in Denver?" "No," answered Smith. Later in the evening, when Smith referred to Denver, Jones again asked whether Smith was acquainted with Schnicklefritz, and again received a negative reply. As the dinner party broke up, Smith remarked that he was leaving that night for Denver, and Jones once more inquired whether Smith knew Schnicklefritz. "Really," came the answer, "his name sounds quite familiar."

Gradually, beneath the surface of the repetitions, the essential doctrine cumulated and moved forward. In 1930 when he wrote *Law and the Modern Mind,* the final chapter, filled with uncritical enthusiasm, was entitled "Mr. Justice Oliver Wendell Holmes, the Completely Adult Jurist." Holmes had originated the so-called "prediction theory" of law. He had declared that "the prophesies of what courts will do in fact, and nothing more pretentious are what I mean by the law. . . . The primary rights and duties with which jurisprudence busies itself . . . are nothing but prophesies." Such was the basis of Holmes's approach, which Jerome Frank accepted as unimpeachable in 1930. By 1949 when *Courts on Trial* was published, it began to be apparent that fact-skepticism either canceled the value of Holmes's theory or at least required a drastic reformulation.

Finally, in 1954 Jerome Frank acknowledged openly that he had traveled far from his initial discipleship. Here in a single passage we have an epitome of fact-skepticism and of its relation to Holmes's doctrine:

> More than twenty years ago, I tried pragmatically to apply Holmes' prediction theory to future specific decisions of trial courts. If such decisions could not be prophesied, then usually lawyers' prophesies would be of comparatively little worth, since very few trial court decisions are appealed and the upper courts affirm most of those that are appealed. So I enquired whether, before suits commenced, lawyers usually could, with some high degree of accuracy, foretell the specific decisions of the trial courts in particular cases. . . .
>
> I discovered that this sort of prophesying was markedly uncertain. Why? Briefly stated, these are the reasons: Most law suits are, in part at least, "fact suits." The facts are past events. . . . The trial judge or jury, endeavoring (as an historian) to learn those past events, must rely, usually, on the oral testimony of witnesses who say they observed those

events. The several witnesses usually tell conflicting stories. This must mean that at least some of the witnesses are either lying or (a) were honestly mistaken in observing the past facts or (b) are honestly mistaken in recollecting their observations or (c) are honestly mistaken in narrating their recollections at the trial. . . . The trial court (judge or jury) must select some part of the conflicting testimony to be treated as reliably reporting the past facts. In each law suit, that choice of what is deemed reliable testimony depends upon the unique reactions of a particular trial judge or a particular jury to the particular witnesses who testify in that particular suit. This choice is, consequently, discretionary: The trial court exercises "fact-discretion." . . . No one has ever contrived any rules (generalized statements) for making that choice, for exercising that fact-discretion. It therefore lies beyond — is uncapturable by — rules, and it is "unruly." Being unruly, it is usually unpredictable before the law suit commences.

. . . The upper courts in most cases accept the trial courts' "unruly" fact-findings, i.e., the trial court's exercise of its fact-discretion remains, ordinarily, unreviewable, final, undisturbed. . . . Lawyers can often (not always) make fairly accurate guesses as to what rules the courts will apply in uncommenced law suits. The difficulty lies in guessing to what facts the courts will apply those rules. Only in a modest minority of cases is that element of the decisions foreseeable. Therefore, seldom can a "bad" man or a "good" man obtain from his lawyer the sort of prophecy Holmes' theory envisioned. . . .

The foregoing represents but a sketch of a complex subject. However, it will suffice to show the shakiness of Holmes' prediction theory. For the most part, that theory succumbs to what I call "fact-skepticism."

II

As we know, Jerome Frank had not set out to answer or criticize Holmes; in point of fact the outcome proved a surprise to him, a rather curious by-product of his enterprise. His chosen goal was quite different. He wished to dispel various popular myths about courts and trials so that truth might light the path to a more rational and humane judicial process. Fact-skepticism led him to advocate a number of procedural and administrative changes, which he hoped would be informed by special studies in comparative law. Though even fact-skeptics may dispute the desirability of this or that detailed proposal, no one can doubt that Jerome Frank's disclosures have helped make American judges and lawyers increasingly impatient — as they should be — with the wooden technicalities in traditional procedure. If you apply the goad often enough, even an ox may eventually move.

Nevertheless, the philosophy of fact-skepticism far transcends any question or program of procedural reform. It cannot be understood if one regards Jerome Frank merely as a penetrating, critical and imaginative jurist. "Merely," forsooth; there is an entire image of him implicit in that "merely." To know him at all was to be overwhelmed by the extraordinary scope, the opulent universality of his reading and thinking. Fortunately for fact-skepticism, it grew and developed in that phenomenally gifted mind of his. There it acquired depth and spaciousness, and became coordinate with the other main currents of his philosophy.

The first neighboring current was Jerome Frank's historiography. From the 1920's until the very end of his days, he consistently defended the attitude called "historical relativism." Among the various relativists, he found particular clarity and candor in Carl Becker. It was Becker who told the American Historical Association in 1926:

> The historian has to judge the significance of the series of events from the one single performance, never to be repeated, and never, since the records are incomplete and imperfect, capable of being fully known or fully affirmed. Thus into the imagined facts and their meaning there enters the personal equation. The history of any event is never precisely the same thing to two different persons; and it is well known that every generation writes the same history in a new way, and puts upon it a new construction. . . .
>
> In this way the present influences our idea of the past, and our idea of the past influences the present. We are accustomed to say that "the present is the product of all the past"; and this is what is ordinarily meant by the historian's doctrine of "historical continuity." But it is only a half truth. It is equally true, and no mere paradox, to say that the past (our imagined picture of it) is the product of all the present. . . .

This was the first of the persistent currents that fact-skepticism met and blended with in Jerome Frank's philosophy. The second was typified by William James and Horace Kallen. As Becker vitalized the dry records of the past, these philosophers humanized the dry notions of conceptual thinking. Concepts, though necessary and valuable, must be treated as implements and ministers, not as monarchs. Every human being is more than a member of the genus, he is also a unique individual. In fact, a human being's most generic characteristic is his very uniqueness. Many of the relations and transactions that make human experience are fortuitous, exuberant, filled with uncaptured residues, at best pluralistic, not to be domesticated completely by any of our abstract terms. To Jerome Frank's delight, William James used to refer to "wild facts," that is, those which furnish so much of the spirited element in our existence and which our logical propositions and scientific laws simply fail to net. It takes a more alert and compassionate nature than most men possess to sense the presence of "wild facts" and respect their worth and influence.

But it was in the juristic thought of Aristotle that fact-skepticism found its closest affinity. I mean, in Aristotle as Jerome Frank read and understood Aristotle. Not that I disagree with his interpretation of Aristotle; I find it completely valid. Nevertheless, since there are various and conflicting interpretations, and since I have just referred admiringly to William James's pluralism, I can hardly insist here that Jerome Frank was alone equipped to understand Aristotle.

What did he find in Aristotle? He found: that the general rules of any legal order, if applied automatically and impersonally, are often unfit to handle the "wild facts," the subtle, unexpected particulars and the infinite diversity of human affairs; that general rules must be continually adjusted, individualized and alloyed with considerations of equity to make them more malleable; and that the excellence of equity consists not in its following but in its refusing to follow established propositions of law. Apparently Aristotle realized that if the rigid, abstract, impersonal norm is made our king and hero, our tale is liable to become a tragedy, for the hero suffers from a fatal flaw. In this view of things, what Carl Becker did to the inflexible past, what William James did to the abstract concept, Aristotle in his wisdom had done to the mechanical and impersonal rule of law.

These were the three currents of thought with which fact-skepticism merged, and among them Aristotle was foremost. On the only occasion I recall when Jerome Frank wrote as though he were speaking through the mouth of another, it was Aristotle whom he chose for his alter ego. This is what he suggested Aristotle would say if he were to return after 2300 years:

> It is shocking, of course, to see how this personal element in justice has been shamefully exploited by totalitarian governments. They have put the best of things to the most evil uses. But that personal element, whether one likes it or not, is an inherent part of the decisional process, under any form of government. It is therefore folly to conceal its presence in the working of courts in a democracy. To conceal it, indeed, is to ensure that it operates at its worst, surreptitiously, without such intelligent ethical restraints as experience and wisdom show us both can be and should be imposed. Here, as elsewhere, we must distinguish the desirable and the possible. The wise course is openly to acknowledge the personal element, and then to do whatever can practically be done to get rid of its evils and to bring about its constructive uses. For the rest, we shall have to put up with it, however bad, as we do with ineradicable sickness and death.

These, I believe, are the main attributes of Jerome Frank's skeptical philosophy — it is vitalistic, pluralistic, and above all, personalistic.

Suppose now a lawyer is willing to say that everything in this exposition is true: will that make him an authentic fact-skeptic? No, it will not, for acquiescence is not enough. Even the naive lawyers who still live in the conceptualistic murk of the 1920's will acknowledge that past incidents may not always be reconstructed accurately in court. They will concede quite cheerfully that predictions are very uncertain before a controversy has developed — provided, of course, no one objects to their being paid, as all of us are, for making the predictions.

Acquiescence does not suffice. Too many who aver they have acquiesced are ready to rejoin their colleagues in the same old idolatry of concepts, where they chant the same old platitudes in praise of a wholly impersonal "government under law," "a government of laws and not of men." No wonder this sort of self-delusion provoked John Dewey to remark, "A government of lawyers and not of men!"

Who then is a genuine fact-skeptic? I should say, only those who employ fact-skepticism among the constant postulates of their thinking, who use it as lenses to read the daily newspaper, and who endeavor to respond to its profound and manifold challenges. What are these challenges?

III

Before listing them (quite incompletely, of course), let me recall that fact-skepticism is a single doctrine with three associated prongs. It criticizes our capacity to ascertain the transactions of the past; it distrusts our capacity to predict the concrete fact-findings and value judgments of the future; and finally, it discloses the importance of the personal element in all processes of choice and decision. Now we can begin with:

The Challenge to the Law. Wherever we look at the law, fact-skepticism has a leading role to perform. Consider, for example, the application of the Fourteenth Amendment. It would seem very curious if the fundamental human fabric of the world's most powerful nation were to be determined by what a few senators of varying intellectual caliber may have intended — or hinted they intended — during the remote and unattractive year of 1868. Curious it would be; curious enough to be insupportable, I should think. We were rescued from any such tyranny of the dead, at least in respect of desegregation, by the way the Supreme Court treated the strictly historical arguments in *Brown v. Board of Education.* It was fact-skepticism that emancipated us. The Supreme Court declared that if 1868 aspired to rule the 1950's, 1868 ought to have been less ambiguous. With this profitable example to work with, the legal profession's next question may be: how many other despotisms of past over present can we undertake to subvert by the same technique; how many more historical bonds can fact-skepticism loosen, then dissolve?

Yet it is wise to remember that the shackles of the anticipated future can be tighter than those of the conceived past. Our entire juristic order — civil, criminal and administrative — is permeated with uncritical assumptions about future deterrence. The law takes property, liberty and even life under the supposed warrant of deterrence. What the judges call "public policy" they deduce in large part from inarticulate premises of deterrence. Deterrence shapes the rules of tort liability; deterrence attempts to vouch for censorship and sedition laws. In short, cool, self-possessed deterrence has its roster of victims no less than hot vindictiveness.

Fact-skepticism challenges us to make a detailed and radical re-examination of the entire rationale of deterrence. Does this or that assumed deterrent really deter? What other, uncalculated effects does it have? If in many instances it does deter, then how far dare the community go in penalizing one person to influence the behavior of others?

Let me mention a single practical application among many. Fact-skepticism, in and of itself, would provide two severally sufficient reasons for ending that national infamy of ours, capital punishment: first, because capital punishment is not demonstrated to deter in fact; second, because under our system there is substantial danger of convicting and executing the wrong person. Jerome Frank concurred that each of these reasons is more than sufficient for abolishing the death penalty.

The Challenge to Political Theory and Cultural Anthropology. Here I suggest that fact-skepticism calls for a thoroughly candid review of what is taken for granted in phrases like "the rule of law," "representative government," "popular mandate," and "the consent of the governed." Let the timorous have no misgivings: our fabric of government is so superior to Russia's that we can easily afford to turn the full force of fact-skepticism on it. For example, Cold War or no Cold War, no American needs to deny or disparage the important human and personal factors that animate every variety of so-called "constitutionalism," including our own. One of the best features of fact-skepticism is that it warns men away from false supports and treacherous comforts. In this way, it impels them toward truth, which remains their faithful ally.

The Challenge to Philosophy in General and Pragmatism and Analytic Empiricism in Particular. A few years before the publication of *Courts on Trial,* a professor of philosophy and historian of American pragmatism declared that Holmes's analysis was "the only systematic application of pragmatism that has yet been made." If then fact-skepticism should edify the legal profession, how much more should it excite philosophers, ethicists and all who are concerned with the meaning of language and the foundations of moral responsibility! Surely they will wish to consider how deeply and how far fact-skepticism may affect Peirce's doctrine that the meaning of a concept is to be found in its conceived consequences and James's doctrine that "the true" is the long-run expedient in our way of thinking. In basic respects, are not these also prediction-theories? In so far as they are, it seems fair to analogize them to Holmes's. Since their subject matter is so very general, they may prove even more vulnerable to the prongs of fact-skepticism. Pragmatists and instrumentalists in every profession will appreciate the force and imminence of the challenge.

Now we approach fact-skepticism's ultimate contribution. Let us suppose along with Jerome Frank and Carl Becker that accurate knowledge of the past is generally elusive. Let us suppose along with Jerome Frank and William James that our abstract concept is often like the iron claw of a toy crane in an amusement arcade: while it may succeed in grasping the ordinary, humdrum objects in the cage, it will continually miss the things that are interesting, deviant or eccentric. Further, let us grant — for grant we must — that though occasionally we may be able to foretell certain direct and immediate consequences of a proposed statute or decision, we cannot pretend to prophesy the spreading network of eventual, indirect, mediate, oblique consequences. As Judge Learned Hand has said, "Such prophecies infest law of every sort, the more deeply as it is far reaching; and it is an illusion to suppose that there are formulas or statistics that will help in making them." No substitutes for critical judgment, no escapes from personal responsibility, no formulas? Yet prophecies and the making of prophecies "infest" not only the law but the totality of human experience. Surely then our account has reached its climax, which is:

The Challenge to American Society. If fact-skepticism can accomplish its full work of emancipation, perhaps we shall at last be free to realize the pristine American dream. In the years when our nation began, there was a sort of axiomatic expectation that this "new order of the ages," this unprecedented experiment in republican government would develop a wholly superior breed of human beings. On American shores men would flourish as never before, and gain new personal stature. Here nature and society would invite them to unfold their individual talents, to discover themselves — as it were, to reach out and push back the cultural frontiers. Eventually this democratic republic of ours would exhibit a new kind of political community composed in large part of moral aristocrats.

Today most of us would acknowledge that what was then a charming vision has become a matter of arresting urgency. It is no longer merely desirable, it is virtually indispensable that American society produce a multitude of superior human beings, men and women of understanding judgment and moral rectitude, of expansive horizons and humane sensibilities, who can feel the full pathos of individual misfortunes and predicaments, yet venture to act on occasion as though the world were plastic.

By insisting on the personal element in all processes of decision, fact-skepticism underscores our state of need. It admonishes that the best and wisest propositions of social ethics, politics and law will not preserve us if the men who apply them to concrete transactions are themselves Philistines and mediocrities, even affable mediocrities. Nothing earthly can preserve us without sharply improved human qualities of leadership and citizenship.

Here, at this critical juncture, the fact-skeptic may be heard speaking a message of (perhaps) unexpected but entirely reasonable optimism. Once he has shown that the grip of the past is loose and the grip of the future even looser, he may fairly contend that we enjoy considerable new elbowroom in the realm of the present. He relishes the present with a special confidence. His very questionings and doubtings have earned him the right to declare that men possess an enormously wider and more diverse register of individual and social choices than they have ever exercised. He may go on to explain that fact-skepticism is as suspicious of alleged impossibilities as it is of pseudoscientific nostrums. He may add — rather firmly — that one approved way to lift the heart is to exert the intellect. Who knows? — he will ask — while his congeners sit and fret in the darkness, some powerful source of enlightenment may be dangling there, within easy reach. This was the vital pattern of Jerome Frank's faith. He incessantly prodded and encouraged all our social institutions to produce *qualitative* men, and thus he paid a supreme tribute to the ideal of human dignity.

There — in the dignity of individual human beings — was the very core of Jerome Frank's religion. Though he counted himself as one of the "unchurched," he served and worshiped the divine through countless deeds of righteousness, charity and loving-kindness. Orthodox religions of every sort repelled him; by claiming despotic authority, they always prompted him to deny when he yearned to affirm. Then, not many years ago, in a novel by St. John Ervine, he happened upon something quite close to the belief he had been searching for. Here is the quotation:

It seemed to him that God was not a Being who miraculously made the world, but a Being who labored at it, suffered and failed, and rose again and achieved. He could hear God, stumbling through the Universe, full of the agony of desire, calling continually, "Let there be light! Let there be light!"

So it was with you, beloved friend, and so it must be with us. There will be many times when the vision grows dim, the judgment stumbles and the courage falters. Yet we will never give ourselves to despair. Guided and sustained by your example, we will never leave off calling, "Let there be light, let there be justice, and above all else let there be compassion!"

*Address delivered at services conducted by the
Yale Law School in memory of Jerome Frank, and
published in the Yale Law Journal, 1957.*

Fact-Skepticism and Fundamental Law

WHEN Jerome Frank died on January 13, 1957, many American judges and lawyers began to realize how much they had gained by viewing the law over his shoulder. Among his scintillating contributions to enlightenment and justice, he rightly considered that fact-skepticism was most needed, most basic, and most representative of his juristic thought. He had developed and elaborated the theme with increasing emphasis from *Law and the Modern Mind* in 1930, through *Courts on Trial* in 1949, and in subsequent law review articles until the end of his life. In expounding it, Judge Frank was sustained by a strong sense of moral impulsion. Since his doubtings and questionings were on a plane of high seriousness, far removed from the flippant, corrosive, or cynical, he could agree unreservedly when John Dewey said, "Skepticism that is not . . . a search is as much a personal emotional indulgence as is dogmatism." In short, to appreciate the full value of fact-skepticism, one should regard it as an unremitting intellectual and moral search. . . .

THE VARIETY OF INSIGHTS: A HISTORICAL EXAMPLE

An Invitation to Thinking. Fact-skepticism, as Jerome Frank developed it, is a rational inquiry or critique, not a philosophic system in competition with other systems. When it challenges old myths, upsets old certitudes, and exposes old delusions, it does not do so in order to hawk a set of substitutes or a new brand of orthodoxy. It admits complete freedom of individual elaboration and interpretation. For example, fact-skepticism led Judge Frank to infer that the civil jury was such an inept institution that it ought to be abolished. Emphasizing the "irresponsibility" and "lawlessness" of the civil jury's general verdict, his criticisms were characteristically powerful. Yet, as he fully realized, these criticisms, which seemed so effective to some, failed to convince other leading jurists whom he was proud to denominate authentic fact-skeptics (e.g., Justice William O. Douglas).

Welcoming diversities and disagreements of the kind, he neither sought nor desired an attitude of unanimity among fact-skeptics. Habitually he reacted with distrust to suggestions of "unity" or "integration." For, as Holmes once put it when writing to William James about pragmatism, "If we all agreed, we should only have formulated our limitations." Conceived in the classic empirical tradition, fact-skepticism was intended to embrace a wide variety of personal insights and practical remedies, which might occasionally be seen to progress in worth and cumulate in social wisdom.

To illustrate the possibilities of the process, we are about to sketch three historical stages in the development of a single, very precise insight which can be attributed, in both ancient and modern times, to the creative influence of fact-skepticism. Our insight is one that deals with the subject of capital punishment. It can be stated as follows: That the death penalty belongs in a class of its own and ought not to be categorized with other customary modes of punishment, because *it alone is irreversible.* It is this "insight of irreversibility" that we propose to trace.

The Insight of Irreversibility in the Talmud. During the early centuries of the Christian era, the opposition to capital punishment seems to have been more earnest and conscientious than at almost any subsequent period, including our own. The attitude of eminent Christian leaders stemmed partly from a general religious aversion to the taking of human life and partly from their interpretation of particular New Testament passages where Jesus preached an ethic of nonresistance. As late as the fourth and fifth centuries, Ambrose and his great disciple, Augustine, insisted that, although a soldier might be justified in killing an enemy in combat, a private individual had no right to kill even in defense of his life.

During the same centuries the Jewish opposition to capital punishment was equally pronounced. Since, however, the ancient Mosaic Code had specified the death penalty for many offenses, ethical leaders among the Jews were faced with a more difficult intellectual problem.

No matter how the rabbis might dislike a provision for capital punishment, they felt bound by it (as, say, modern humanitarian judges like Benjamin N. Cardozo and Jerome Frank felt bound by the provisions for capital punishment in the secular law which they had sworn to administer). Not being able to ignore or annul the death penalty, the rabbis did their utmost to see that it was not inflicted. Among the ingenious devices they developed were: (1) requirement of almost impossible proof that the accused had received warning just before committing the act to establish that he had a consciously guilty purpose, (2) heavy emphasis on the presumption of innocence and severe inquisition of accusing witnesses, (3) elaboration of the liabilities and punishments of false witnesses, and (4) convicting the accused of a lesser offense which did not involve capital punishment. Two of the most revered rabbis (Tarfon and Akiba) said that if they were members of the court, no person would ever be put to death.

So much for the general background as distinguished from the very specific idea which we have called "the insight of irreversibility." This insight, which seems so evident to us — now that others have made it evident for us — was scarcely reached during ancient times. Apparently there were not enough fact-skeptics in those days to contend that the fallibility of witnesses and judges was itself a sufficient reason for abolishing the death penalty. Nevertheless, some fact-skeptics there were, at least among the early rabbis. Having become aware of "the insight of irreversibility," they employed it to admonish and warn accusing witnesses in capital cases before permitting them to testify:

> How were the witnesses inspired with awe? Witnesses in capital charges were brought in and intimidated thus: perhaps what ye say is based only on conjecture, or hearsay, or is evidence from the mouth of another witness, or even from the mouth of a trustworthy person: perhaps ye are unaware that ultimately we shall scrutinize your evidence by cross-examination and inquiry? Know then that capital cases are not like monetary cases. In civil suits, one can make monetary restitution and thereby effect his atonement; but in capital cases he is held responsible for the accused's blood and the blood of his potential descendants until the end of time.

This solemn and awesome admonition, which might serve to improve the quality of identification testimony in our own courts, constituted an outstanding ancient application of "the insight of irreversibility."

The Insight of Irreversibility in Montaigne. After the passage in the Talmud, I have not come upon any statement of our insight during the entire medieval period. It would be temerarious to insist that there was no such statement. Surely, there were plenty of fine minds to recognize the irremediability of the death penalty and plenty of fine consciences to protest against the possibility of executing innocent people. If, then, no medieval writer has left a mention of "the insight of irreversibility," the reason probably had to do with the nature of trial procedure during the Middle Ages. Medieval criminal procedure was so grossly irrational, on the one hand, and so firmly defended from rational criticism, on the other, that few observers (except those who believed the ordeals were guided supernaturally) could have expected to find any semblance of truth in the fact-finding process. Torture was employed systematically to obtain confessions and then employed again, with careful skill, to prolong the execution of death sentences based on the confessions. In fact, when at the end of the sixteenth century Montaigne dared to say, "All that is over and above simple death appears to me pure cruelty," he incurred the censure of ecclesiastical authority.

Having the advantage of considerable experience as lawyer and magistrate, Montaigne had learned that judicial procedure was quite fallible. In the Second Book of his superb *Essays,* written not long after he withdrew from the practice of law, he declared, "Thousands and thousands have, by means of torture, loaded their heads with false confessions." When, some years later, he added a Third Book, he summarized in it the cruelties, injustices, and inhumanities he had noticed during a lifetime of observation. In this epitome of his experience, Montaigne reached and expressed "the insight of irreversibility":

> How many innocent people we have known to be punished, I mean without the fault of the judges; and how many are there that we have not known of! This happened in my time: Certain men are condemned to death for murder; the sentence, if not pronounced, is at least decided and fixed. At that point the judges are informed, by the officers of an inferior court near by, that they hold several men in custody who openly confess to that murder, and are able to throw a light on the whole business that admits of no doubt. And yet they deliberate whether they shall interrupt and defer the execution of the sentence passed upon the first accused. They consider the novelty of the case, and its consequence for suspending judgements; that the sentence is juridically passed, and the judges have no reason to repent of it. To sum up, those poor devils are sacrificed to the forms of justice.
>
> Philip, or some other, dealt with a like dilemma in this way: He had pronounced judgement on a man and condemned him to pay a heavy fine to another. The true facts of the case having come to light some time

after, it was found that he had condemned him wrongfully. On the one side was the right of the cause, on the other the right of judicial forms. He in some sort satisfied both by allowing the sentence to stand, and making up the loss to the condemned out of his own purse.

But he had to do with a retrievable miscarriage; my men were irretrievably hanged. How many condemnations I have witnessed more criminal than the crime!

Having reached the insight, what inference did Montaigne draw from it? He had advocated abandoning the use of torture as a mode of execution, and even this modest proposal had involved him in difficulties with the church. It was not likely that, in his later years, he would incur further risks by suggesting a reform as unattainable as abolishing the death penalty. Given his extraordinarily kind and sympathetic nature and the brutal, disorganized conditions of his time and country, one might reasonably expect that he would react — as he did — not by way of intervention but by way of recoil. He had read too much about justice and seen too little of it. Overwhelmed by the cruelty and hypocrisy of the courts and the apparent hopelessness of reforming them, he spewed out his disgust:

Now the laws maintain their credit not because they are just but because they are laws. That is the mystic foundation of their authority, and they have no other. And that is, indeed, their advantage. They are often made by fools; more often by men who, in their hatred of equality, are wanting in equity; but always by men, vain and unsteadfast authors. Nothing is so clumsily and widely, nor so ordinarily, faulty as the laws. Whoever obeys them because they are just does not obey them for the reason for which they should rightly be obeyed.

These, too, were inferences drawn from "the insight of irreversibility" and quite plausible ones in the historical setting. Even if we apply them to America and the twentieth century, Montaigne's caustic remarks still contain an important measure of truth.

The Insight of Irreversibility in Beccaria. Despite the clear strain of fact-skepticism in the writings of men like Bayle and Voltaire, the insight we have been tracing remained without notable influence until the last decade of the eighteenth century. In 1764 Cesare Beccaria published his *On Crimes and Punishments,* inaugurating the modern movement for abolition of the death sentence. Though the book had an enormous impact, which continues to be felt even now, it did not expound "the insight of irreversibility" or marshal it as an argument for abolition. In his famous work, Beccaria tended to categorize the death penalty along with various other forms of excessive and dispro portionate punishment. He assailed capital punishment because it violated natural law, because it brutalized officials and citizens, and because it inspired more violent crimes than it prevented.

Some twenty-eight years later, Beccaria seems to have realized that his arguments were incomplete: they had all tacitly assumed that capital punishment, when inflicted, was inflicted on the right person. Experience and observation had meanwhile taught him that this is not uniformly the case, and that judicial procedures for establishing guilt are inherently susceptible to error. He expressed his new wisdom in a report prepared in 1792. After restating the several objections which he had advanced in *On Crimes and Punishments,* he went on to a special passage on "the insight of irreversibility":

> Finally, we submit that since the death penalty is irreparable, it cannot be reconciled with the inevitable imperfection of human proofs. Even if the death penalty were just, if it were the most efficacious of all, to be justly applied to an accused person it would be necessary that he had been proved guilty in a manner that excluded any contrary possibility. This follows manifestly from the irreparability of the death penalty; and if proof of this kind were required before a prisoner could be sentenced, there would never be a case where capital punishment would be inflicted.[1]

Since Beccaria's time, it is fair to say that "the insight of irreversibility" has entered the public domain of Western thought. It has become one of our familiar assumptions. When employed — as Beccaria employed it — to demonstrate the wrongfulness of capital punishment, the insight shows fact-skepticism at the height of its moral power. Jerome Frank heartily approved this way of using it; he insisted that capital punishment necessarily involved an indefensible risk of "convicting the innocent" and committing "judicial homicide."

Modern Uses and Misuses. Although a handful of states have abolished capital punishment, the federal government and the majority of the states still retain it in the latter half of the twentieth century. These jurisdictions have adopted a variety of procedural devices to reduce (though, of course, they cannot eliminate) the risk of executing innocent persons. For example, under the constitution of New York, the Court of Appeals, which in almost every other type of proceeding reviews questions of law only, possesses and exercises jurisdiction to review the facts in capital cases. Thus even where the death penalty has been retained, we find "the insight of irreversibility" serving a mitigating purpose.

Yet there is nothing human that cannot be put to dubious uses. Up to now, we have seen "the insight of irreversibility" and the distinction between death and other forms of punishment employed either to warrant abolishing capital punishment or to establish special procedural safeguards against convicting the innocent. Neither of these applications can be made to justify an attitude of relaxation or indifference toward the noncapital forms of punishment. The fact that capital punishment is uniquely irreversible does not make incarceration at hard labor less disgraceful and severe. To be charged with a major crime is serious business under any circumstances. When, therefore, the authors of the Fifth Amendment used the phrase "a capital, or otherwise infamous crime," they must have intended to provide strict procedural safeguards in the trial of the noncapital infamous crimes as well as the capital ones. They directed that *all* prosecutions which threaten major forms of punishment must be conducted with uniformly respectful solicitude for the rights of the accused.

Unfortunately, in recent years there has been a marked tendency to misuse "the insight of irreversibility" by reducing the procedural status of the noncapital or "otherwise infamous crime." In *Betts v. Brady,* the Supreme Court majority distinguished *Powell v. Alabama* on the ground, among others, that the *Powell* case involved a capital charge while the *Betts* case involved only an eight-year sentence for the crime of robbery. Consequently, the indigent Powell was entitled to have counsel provided by Alabama but the indigent Betts was not entitled to have counsel provided by Maryland. In short, instead of employing "the insight of irreversibility" as a shield for the rights of the accused, the majority used it as an ax to shatter his right to assistance of counsel.[2]

In *Reid v. Covert,* one of the Court's great decisions of 1957, there are clear auguries of an analogous misuse. Justice Black's admirable opinion, in which the Chief Justice and Justices Douglas and Brennan joined, involved no distinction between "capital" and "otherwise infamous" crimes. It held that a serviceman's civilian dependent, abroad in time of peace, cannot constitutionally be tried by a court martial for an offense against the United States (in this instance, murder). Justices Clark and Burton, dissenting, likewise could "find no distinction in the Constitution between capital and other cases." The distinction emerged to play an ominous role in the concurring opinions of Justices Frankfurter and Harlan. Both justices explained at length that their concurrence with the outcome did not imply that they would vote the same way in a noncapital case. After stating his characteristic formula that "We must weigh all the factors," Justice Frankfurter went on to say: "The taking of life is irrevocable. It is in capital cases especially that the balance of conflicting interests must be weighted most heavily in favor of the procedural safeguards of the Bill of Rights." This would be a welcome recognition of "the insight of irreversibility" if it did not hint so openly that the insight will be used to vilipend procedural guarantees as soon as a noncapital case arises. In a noncapital case, Justice Frankfurter's phrases tell us, he would revert to the pattern of *Betts v. Brady*.

Be that as it may, we have seen "the insight of irreversibility" lead to a provocative variety of inferences, most of them beneficial to the quality of justice. This kind of creative pluralism is central to Jerome Frank's philosophy. With John Locke, he submits that "Men may choose different things, and yet all choose right."

AGENDA IN CONSTITUTIONAL LAW

Critique of Social Science Evidence. To many of his friends, Jerome Frank's most impressive attribute consisted in his matchless command of humanistic studies and social sciences. He seemed to have read almost everything in these fields, and remembered all that he had read; what is more important — his brain was so richly provided with active synapses that the thought currents moved like lightning from one area to another, from law to psychology, from economics to ethics, from theory of knowledge to sociology to semantics and back to law. In these attainments, he was unrivaled. As his friend Justice Hugo L. Black has said: "I rate him as one of the great judges. No judge that I know had so great a knowledge of the history and development of human societies. . . ."[3] When, therefore, we find Jerome Frank expressing profound skepticism about the pretensions of social science experts, we may feel confident that it is a judgment formed after the most thorough and intelligent examination of their wares. His familiarity with past and current theories and methods earned him the right to doubt.

Here again we confront an issue of the moral obligations which lawyers, legislators, and judges ought to recognize and assume. Nothing becomes a lawyer worse than credulity; it sits on his head like a dunce cap. To be cozened by academic degrees and specious statistics, gulled by pompous tones and fallacious tests, duped by a display of flatulent nomenclature: What an embarrassment for a profession seasoned with experience and charged with responsibility for the jural development of society's values!

After a lifetime of prodigious study and analysis, Judge Frank summarized his criticisms in a pungent article entitled "The Lawyer's Role in Modern Society." He recommended:

> In the courts' approach to administrative agencies, we have an excellent analogy for the judicial approach to all specialists or experts: Their competence should be carefully scrutinized, their logic examined,

and their findings should be rejected when reached arbitrarily or irrationally. I venture the following tentative suggestions:

(a) Not alone the competence of the specialists but also the limits of their competence needs attention; whatever exceeds those limits should be treated by the courts like any other layman's views.

(b) Where there are — and usually there are — conflicting positions as between the specialists in respect of any particular social study, the courts should beware of adopting any one position without considering the opposing positions.

(c) A court should ascertain whether a specialist's opinion rests on a doctrine that has won the substantial, if not general, acceptance of his fellow-specialists. . . .

I think we should forego the dream of anything remotely like "social science." But to surrender that dream is not to despair of vastly improving our knowledge of mankind and of individual human beings. Such knowledge demands modesty and constructive skepticism, or what may be called the "scientific spirit" which entails the discipline of suspended judgment; the rigorous examination of all the evidence; a consideration of all possible theories; the questioning of the plausible and the seemingly self-evident; a passion for verification and a recognition of the unverifiable; what Fries describes as a willingness to "doing one's damndest to poke holes in one's theoretical assumption," plus a desire not to be deceived.

Most men being gullible by nature, it is necessary to keep prodding and awakening the "desire not to be deceived." For example, in a concurring opinion composed only a few months before his death, Judge Frank felt compelled to say: "I think it is a mistake for my colleagues needlessly to embark — without a pilot, rudder, compass or radar — on an amateur's voyage on the fog-enshrouded sea of psychiatry." The remainder of the opinion showed how conversant he was with "the fog-enshrouded sea"; his warning was based on knowledge. In short, though some of us may be less pessimistic than he was concerning the future potentialities of social science, all ought to emulate his example of vigilance, critical examination, and searching inquiry. These we should count among our permanent professional responsibilities.

Critique of Legislative Action. Turning now to the subject of legislative action, I suggest it would be profitable for fact-skeptics to reexamine many of our most familiar assumptions. For example, we need a much greater ability to detect when items of so-called legislative history have been deliberately "planted." We also need to establish a firmer distinction between instances where the legislature has performed its constitutional duty by deliberating before voting and instances where the legislature has shirked the duty and passed it along to the judiciary. If transactions of the latter type are frequent enough, they will eventually modify our theory of judicial review.

Let me point to the recent instance of the vote in the United States Senate to cite Corliss Lamont for contempt. Of ninety-six members of the Senate, only three (Lehman, Langer, and Chavez) took their responsibility seriously enough to contend that the Senate ought to study and appreciate the constitutional contentions in the case before it cited an honorable citizen for contempt. Only these three argued for understanding before voting. In contrast, Senator Morse, wielding the prestige of his former post as a law school dean, helped lead the drive in favor of McCarthy's contempt resolution. Repeatedly Senator Morse opposed further study or deliberation. If there were legal questions to resolve, he submitted, let Lamont be indicted for contempt of the Senate and he could raise the questions when he appeared in court for a criminal trial. In addition to showing a curious personal insensibility, the incident bears materially on the deference which courts should feel obliged to accord legislative findings.[4]

Behind the "Preferred Position" Controversy. Before beginning the next topic, let us remind ourselves that one of the three associated prongs of the doctrine of fact-skepticism is the prime importance of the personal element in all processes of choice and decision. Consequently, an adequate appraisal of the role of fact-skepticism ought to include some consideration of personal factors and personal philosophies in constitutional review. To illustrate the importance of the personal element, I propose to show what I believe is at least part of the substantial truth behind the "preferred position" controversy.

It is generally understood that Justices Black and Douglas believe in according a preferred position to First Amendment rights and that Justice Frankfurter does not. A critical analysis will disclose, I believe, that the substance of the conflict between the two views is very different from its form.

Twice in the year 1949, Justice Frankfurter stated and accepted a version of the preferred position doctrine.[5] However, in his concurring opinion in the *Dennis* case, he rejected the entire doctrine rather scornfully,[6] his terms indicating a mistaken belief that it had originated as late as Justice Stone's famous *Carolene Products* footnote.[7] During recent years, Justice Frankfurter has held insistently that all provisions of the Bill of Rights are to be treated as equals, without favor or distinction among them. He wrote in *Ullmann v. United States:* "As no constitutional guarantee enjoys preference, so none should suffer subordination or deletion. . . . To view a particular provision of the Bill of Rights with disfavor inevitably results in a constricted application of it. This is to disrespect the Constitution."[8]

These sentiments may seem quite moving and praiseworthy — until one recalls, perhaps with a sense of shock, that Justice Frankfurter is the Supreme Court's leading exponent of the *Palko* doctrine and of the majority view in *Adamson v. California*. Whenever a problem arises of the kind presented in the *Palko* case, it is he who insists that all constitutional guarantees are not on the same plane and that some enjoy a superior or preferred status while others must suffer subordination.[9] This is why one is warranted in saying that the substance of the preferred position controversy must differ somehow from its superficial form.

Let me put the problem again. When the issue in a case involves incorporating the entire Bill of Rights and making all the guarantees applicable against the states via the Fourteenth Amendment, it is Justices Black and Douglas who insist that the guarantees be treated equally and that none suffer subordination or deletion; yet when a First Amendment issue is presented to the Court, these same justices in effect grade the respective guarantees and assign a preferred position to the First Amendment. Justice Frankfurter's perspective is precisely the reverse. When the question is one of applying the Bill of Rights to state action, he grades the rights in terms of preferences and deletions, incorporating some and declining to incorporate others; yet when an issue of free speech, press, religion, or assembly comes before him, he refuses to distinguish among the rights by raising the First Amendment to a preferred position. I think an objective observer would conclude that all three justices do grade the rights in certain circumstances and refuse to grade them in others.

If such is the real posture of affairs, it is no longer a matter of deciding whether the rights should or should not be graded. It is rather a matter of identifying *why* the respective justices grade them in one contingency and decline to grade them in another. Since we are dealing with three very intelligent and self-conscious mentalities, we may fairly assume that they have intended to do whatever in fact they have done, i.e., that purposes and motives can be traced and identified in the practical consequences. In any event, it is the consequences, not the verbal formulas, that shape our constitutional realities from day to day. What are the practical consequences?

Reduced to this level, the question leads directly to an answer. When Justices Black and Douglas grade the guarantees in First Amendment cases, the practical consequence is that they thereby promote the legal efficacy of the immediately contested guarantee.

When the same justices refuse to distinguish or grade the guarantees for purposes of incorporating them by reference and making them applicable to state action, the consequence again is that they promote the efficacy of the pertinent contested guarantee. When, on the contrary, Justice Frankfurter grades the rights in cases of the latter (or *Palko*) type, the consequence is that he thereby subordinates, demotes, or deletes one or more constitutional guarantees. So also when, in cases involving freedom of speech, press, or religion, the same justice declines to grade the rights or grant a preferred position to the First Amendment, the consequence is that he subordinates, demotes, or deletes the pertinent constitutional guarantee.

If, then, we are permitted to judge philosophies by their fruits, the composite doctrines of Justices Black and Douglas are designed consistently to promote the constitutional guarantees, and the composite doctrines of Justice Frankfurter are designed as consistently to subordinate, demote, or delete them. The fruits are rather important, for in final analysis it is from them that the republic draws its sustenance. As we see, whether the fruits are safe or unsafe to consume depends largely on the personal element in the process of decision.

Harmless Error and Human Dignity. For a final and culminative application of fact-skepticism, we can rightly turn to the principle of harmless error and its proper use on appeals from jury verdicts. All of Jerome Frank's studies led him to conclude that the motives which prompt a jury to convict or acquit are manifold, complex, often irrational, and even incommunicable; that no one can tell how the several members of a jury reacted to any single item of evidence in connection with the remainder of the evidence; that no appellate judge, reading the written record, can put himself effectually in the position of those who attended the trial and observed the witnesses; and, therefore, that any error of substance in the conduct of a trial should be presumed prejudicial unless the evidence is so overwhelming "that no sensible jury, had there been no error, would conceivably have acquitted. . . ."

Year after year, Judge Frank's judicial colleagues of the Second Circuit persisted in affirming convictions and denominating errors harmless because they concluded that the same verdict would have been reached if the error had not been committed. Dismayed and outraged by this policy, Judge Frank filed a series of dissents which contained some of his most eloquent utterances. In one of the last of these, vindicated after his death by judgment of reversal in the Supreme Court, he announced valiantly that when an error consists in invading a constitutional right, it can never be deemed harmless.

We come thus to the very bedrock of Jerome Frank's philosophy, that is, his belief in the worth and dignity of individual human beings. All his thinking was somehow linked with and supported by this fundamental belief. Though he cared much about the efficiency of courts and the rationality of procedure, he always cared more about the impact of official force on human beings, their aspirations, and their daily lives. He could not learn to regard a person in trouble with the law as just another case, or an error of substance affecting such a person as inconsequential and harmless. He implored all judges to consider:

> The conventions of judicial opinion-writing — the uncolloquial vocabulary, the use of phrases carrying with them an air of finality, the parade of precedents, the display of seemingly rigorous logic bedecked with "therefores" and "must-be-trues" — give an impression of certainty (which often hypnotizes the opinion-writer) concealing the uncertainties inherent in the judging process. On close examination, our legal concepts often resemble the necks of the flamingos in *Alice in Wonderland* which failed to remain sufficiently rigid to be used effectively as mallets by the croquet-players. In a case like this, all our complicated judicial apparatus yields but a human judgment, not at all sure to be correct, affecting the life of another human being. If we are at all imaginative, we will comprehend what that judgment will mean to him, and what a horror it will be if we wrongly decide against him. To be sure, one can say that it does not pay to take too seriously the possibility that one man, more or less, may be unjustly imprisoned, considering the fact that, in the recent war, millions have died and that the Atomic Age just begun may end any minute in the destruction of all this planet's inhabitants. Yet (perhaps because I am growing old or because, despite my years, I have not yet fully matured) it seems to me that, if America's part in the war was meaningful and if mankind's development has any significance against the background of eternity, then the dignity of each individual man is not an empty phrase. If it is not, then we judges, part of a human arrangement called government, should proceed with great caution when we determine whether a man is to be forcibly deprived of his liberty.

This is the beginning and the end of fact-skepticism when viewed "against the background of eternity." It begins with faith in the exercise of critical intelligence and ends with conviction of "the dignity of each individual man." Between the beginning and the end lies a ceaseless endeavor to "comprehend what that judgment will mean to him."

From the New York University Law Review, *1958.*

Reflections on Hanging:
Preface for Americans

I n my judgment, this* is the ideal book on capital punishment for an American reader. . . . By concentrating on capital punishment as inflicted overseas in England, Mr. Koestler gives us an unprecedented opportunity to see the issue objectively and without passion, rationally and without sentimentality.

Here is the pith of the matter. In 1764, when Cesare Beccaria first assailed the death penalty in his *On Crimes and Punishments,* he appealed to men's intelligence, practical wisdom, and political judgment. He believed that the case against capital punishment was entirely safe in the forum of reason. That, of course, was why his theme succeeded as well as it did with philosophers and even with despots in an Age of Reason. For decades, capital punishment fell back in continual retreat before the Enlightenment. And when, in later times, the process was reversed and the death penalty reinstalled in this or that state, we can readily identify the specific wave of popular passion which flooded and overwhelmed the discipline of reason. If emotion and feeling were the only propelling force in public affairs, there would be no prospect of abolishing capital punishment, for hatred of hangings would be matched by hatred of murders, and sympathy for the plight of the convict by sympathy for the victim and the victim's family.

Reason — indispensable though it be — will not respond to the snap of an author's fingers. It is hard to induce people to examine their own institutions objectively. Various ways have been tried. One way is to present an imaginary republic or utopia; another is to depict one's native country as it might appear in the eyes of fictional visitors from a remote and completely different culture. The principal difficulty with these devices is that readers who appreciate the point may find only entertainment in it. Consequently, utopias are more likely to make good literature and conversation than good law.

I think *Reflections on Hanging* offers a nearly perfect solution, at least for Americans. When Mr. Koestler denounces the social attitudes of English judges, we can read without antecedent bias, however we might smile or scowl if he were discussing American judges. When he commends or criticizes a Home Secretary in connection with granting

---

* *Reflections on Hanging* by Arthur Koestler (1957).

or refusing a reprieve, the chances are we can judge the incident fairly and with detachment. The political parties he mentions are not ours. His murder trials are held at a calm distance from our homes.

Yet on every page, we are engaged in judging ourselves, for whatever is not literally in America is nevertheless about America. Who will forget that our political ancestors brought their main concepts and institutions along with them from England? Who of us can eradicate the pictures of lawyers, judges, courts, and jails which memory lifts from the pages of English novelists and dramatists? Granted that there are some differences between English and American courts as well as resemblances; they are just such differences and resemblances as one would expect to find within a family.

JUDGING THE JUDGES

In this book, you are about to meet some harsh comments on British judges and their support of capital punishment. When you come to passages of the kind, I hope your only question will be whether the criticisms are sincere and reasonable. Though in England and in the United States there are certain judges who would like to be considered immune from criticism, their attitude is neither sound political democracy nor valid public law. On the one hand, judges are entitled to perform their functions absolutely free of pressures, influences, and outside clamor. On the other hand, any action in the name of and by authority of the public is necessarily subject to the public's comment and appraisal. The principle applies to judges. As Lord Atkin said in a judgment of the Privy Council:

> Justice is not a cloistered virtue: she must be allowed to suffer the scrutiny and respectful, even though outspoken, comments of ordinary men.[1]

Speaking for the United States Supreme Court, Justice Hugo L. Black stated the American view:

> The assumption that respect for the judiciary can be won by shielding judges from published criticism wrongly appraises the character of American public opinion. For it is a prized American privilege to speak one's mind, although not always with perfect good taste, on all public institutions. And an enforced silence, however limited, solely in the name of preserving the dignity of the bench, would probably engender resentment, suspicion, and contempt much more than it would enhance respect.[2]

No man who is unwilling to be judged can be fit to judge. In this, the best judges of both countries concur.

ARE WE MORE RIGHTEOUS THAN THE ENGLISH?

There are various ways to create the impression that, in America, capital punishment is not really so obnoxious. For example, you may have heard it argued that, unlike the English, our penal laws generally distinguish "degrees" of murder. First-degree murder involves capital punishment but second-degree murder does not. Though the statutes say that one of the tests of first-degree murder is "premeditation and deliberation," American courts and juries have often made a travesty of the requirement. A few years ago, the United States Supreme Court (5 to 3) affirmed a first-degree murder conviction of a Negro janitor who was subnormal mentally and had a psychopathic personality.[3] This janitor, having been told that a woman librarian had complained of his work, got into a fierce argument with her and, when she called him a "black nigger," struck her. Her screams sent him into a wild panic. To stop them, he hit her with a piece of wood and, when that broke, stabbed her with his pocket knife. On his confession, the verdict was murder in the first degree and the sentence was death. So much for what the judges and juries may accept as adequate proof of "premeditation and deliberation."

This case came to the United States Supreme Court from the federal courts in the District of Columbia. Not long after, the judges in that small yet important jurisdiction apparently decided that their test of criminal responsibility had not kept pace with modern psychiatric progress. They were deeply discontented with the old M'Naghten test, imported by American courts from England. The test, which Mr. Koestler criticizes so keenly . . . is based on the mental capacity of the accused to distinguish right from wrong and to tell that the act he was committing was wrong. In 1954 the District of Columbia court adopted a new test, holding that if the unlawful act was the product of a mental disease or defect, the accused could not be convicted.[4] Some criminologists have hailed the change; others have attacked it severely, because it throws the whole question of criminal responsibility into the lap of the jury without providing standards or guides to decision. One thing is certain: No matter how we amend or restate the legal test of criminal responsibility, we shall never feel sure that we are not sending mentally defective, diseased, or irresponsible persons to the electric chair. A poor legal test of responsibility can aggravate the wrongs of capital punishment, but a satisfactory test cannot remove them.[5]

There is one more purported palliative to mention. Mr. Koestler relates some gruesome incidents of technical incompetence on the part of English hangmen, resulting in devastating cruelties. In a number of

American states, hanging has been replaced by electrocution. Yet blunders still occur. A few years past, the United States Supreme Court (5 to 4) held that it was not "cruel or unusual punishment" for the State of Louisiana to "electrocute" a convicted murderer a second time, the current having been insufficient to extinguish life on the first attempt.[6] In short, the social question is capital punishment itself, not the modernity of the particular gadget that inflicts it. Gibbets and electric chairs and gas chambers are all the same *sub specie humanitatis*.

In one respect, we Americans do have a slim justification for optimism which the English seem to lack. Unlike English judges, American judges have not presented a solid phalanx to defend capital punishment. Justice Benjamin N. Cardozo, our paragon of moral ideals on the bench, said, a generation ago:

> I have faith . . . that a century or less from now, our descendants will look back upon the penal system of today with the same surprise and horror that fill our own minds when we are told that only about a century ago one hundred and sixty crimes were visited under English law with the punishment of death, and that in 1801 a child of thirteen was hanged at Tyburn for the larceny of a spoon. Dark chapters are these in the history of law. We think of them with a shudder, and say to ourselves that we have risen to heights of mercy and of reason far removed from such enormities. The future may judge us less leniently than we choose to judge ourselves. Perhaps the whole business of the retention of the death penalty will seem to the next generation, as it seems to many even now, an anachronism too discordant to be suffered, mocking with grim reproach all our clamorous professions of the sanctity of life.[7]

Recently Judge Jerome Frank, champion of humane justice, insisted that we ought to put an end to the "grim reproach."

AT ANY RATE, ARE WE NO WORSE THAN THE ENGLISH?

A historical comparison would be inconclusive, for we began rather well and continued poorly. During the era when we were forming a nation of our own, the horizons seemed to glow with new hopes. On this side of the Atlantic as in Europe, intellectual leaders responded ardently to the Enlightenment. Beccaria's *On Crimes and Punishments* (1764) became popular with John Adams, Thomas Jefferson, James Madison, Dr. Benjamin Rush (pioneer in medical science and signer of the Declaration of Independence), and William Bradford (Attorney General of Pennsylvania and later of the United States). In point of fact, the American movement to abolish capital punishment began a couple of months before the opening of the Constitutional Convention, for on March 9, 1787, Dr. Benjamin Rush read a paper against the death penalty to a select meeting in Benjamin Franklin's home. Since that date, the movement has marked some fine victories and suffered some disconcerting setbacks. Its history varies from penal code to penal code in forty-eight states, the District of Columbia, and the federal government. A minority of the states — usually between one-fourth and one-third at a given time — have abstained from using the death penalty; among these, Maine can claim temporal priority and Michigan the most continuous and consistent policy. Nevertheless, even after allowance made for differences in population, the executions taking place annually in the United States are many more than the corresponding totals of capital punishment in England.

How, then, may one decide whether we are worse than the English on the score of capital punishment? What can we take for the criterion of comparison? Here again, I think, Cesare Beccaria has furnished us with a guide. It is not to be found in *On Crimes and Punishments*, the book from which Dr. Benjamin Rush and the other early disciples derived their reasoning. In chapter after chapter of his famous book, Beccaria was engaged in attacking one or another form of excessive and disproportionate punishment. Since hanging was a specific instance of excessive punishment, he denounced it. The death penalty should be abandoned, he said, because it infringed natural law and the social compact, because it was unnecessarily severe, because it brutalized the state, because it barbarized the citizenry, and because it was more likely to inspire than prevent crimes of violence. These were Beccaria's contentions then and for the rest of his life.

Twenty-eight years later, Beccaria seems suddenly to have discovered that he had been taking much for granted. He had been assuming (had he not?) that whenever capital punishment was inflicted, it was inflicted on the right person! All his arguments amounted to contending that the right person, the responsible criminal, had received the wrong punishment. But suppose, as he had observed so many times during the twenty-eight years, the person executed was not responsible for the crime. Suppose either he had nothing to do with the crime, as in a case of mistaken identity, or, though he had participated physically in some way, he was not morally or legally "responsible." Then — Beccaria recognized for the first time — capital punishment is not merely another instance of excessive penalty; it belongs in a class entirely of its own because it alone is irrevocable and irreparable.[8]

Here we have a workable criterion of comparison. In his new wisdom of 1792, Beccaria insisted that trials at law never achieve a completely certain outcome, that at very best they reach what we call "moral certainty," and that the chance of error constitutes, of itself, a sufficient reason to abolish capital punishment. Death was irreversible in Beccaria's day; it is still irreversible.

This proposition may strike a reader in his moral solar plexus. For even if he can feel uninvolved and indifferent when the "right" man is executed, how can he live in company with the thought that it may not be the "right" man? If courts are susceptible to error, then the officials in his own state may be putting innocent people to death under the laws. The lot of irreversible mistake may fall on any of us, even on him — the formerly indifferent reader. It is an interesting thought. With it before us, we can attempt a practical comparison — perhaps an uncomfortably practical one — between the American system and the English. We need only ask: By and large, is there a greater chance of convicting and executing the "wrong" person in England or the United States?

The question is inexorable and our opportunities to temporize are over. All informed American lawyers know that, by and large, there can be only one truthful answer. The general inferiority of criminal justice in the United States has been notorious for generations. Despite minor reforms and advances here and there, our penal administration stands indicted as grossly deficient when measured against minimum standards. Let me list some of the main counts.

AN INDICTMENT FILED AGAINST AMERICAN CRIMINAL PROCEDURE

Count I. Race prejudices and hatreds have often vitiated the administration of criminal justice, have influenced and intimidated jurymen and public officials, and have made conviction of the innocent highly possible.

As I am addressing American readers, I need not elaborate this count.

Count II. Even in the absence of racial conflict, criminal proceedings often lead to false results because of our excitability and propensity to haste and violence.

This count, also, can find its own confirmation in the experience of the average American citizen. We are still disconcertingly close to the impetuous methods of frontier justice. Our impulses are often too quick for our discretion; they convince us against our sober sense; they blind us to rational evidence.

Impulse and excitement led American courts and juries to so many wrongful convictions that at length the law's mask of infallibility wore through and had to be discarded. In 1938, Congress enacted that any prisoner who had been unjustly convicted and imprisoned by the

United States might file a claim against the government for damages, not exceeding five thousand dollars.[9] There is similar legislation in several of our states. It constitutes public and official acknowledgment — if any were needed — that at times justice does miscarry and innocent persons are convicted and imprisoned. To make reparation to the imprisoned innocent is splendidly right; but what can we say to conscience if we have put the innocent beyond the possibility of receiving reparation?

Count III. Most American newspapers handle crime news so unfairly and sensationally that they deprive the accused of an impartial jury.

If they lived in England, the majority of American newspaper editors and crime reporters would be sent to jail for interfering with the administration of justice and depriving accused persons of a fair trial. How the members of a panel of jurymen can claim to be unbiased in a typical American murder case is quite a mystery; illiteracy might protect some of them from the pre-judgments of the press, but surely they cannot all pretend to complete illiteracy. Here is the setting in a respresentative example of quite recent date:

> Murder and mystery, society, sex and suspense were combined in this case in such a manner as to intrigue and captivate the public fancy to a degree perhaps unparalleled in recent annals. Throughout the pre-indictment investigation, the subsequent legal skirmishes and the nine-week trial, circulation-conscious editors catered to the insatiable interest of the American public in the bizarre. Special seating facilities for reporters and columnists representing local papers and all major news services were installed in the courtroom. Special rooms in the Criminal Courts Building were equipped for broadcasters and telecasters. In this atmosphere of a "Roman holiday" for the news media, Sam Sheppard stood trial for his life.[10]

You have just read the first paragraph of an opinion of the Supreme Court of Ohio. Are you not disposed to infer that the court was about to set aside the conviction, rebuke the trial judge, and, at very least, reverse the ruling by which he had refused to grant a change of venue? If these are your inferences, I fear you are unfamiliar with the standards obtaining in many American courts.[11] As a matter of fact, the Supreme Court of Ohio affirmed the conviction of Sam Sheppard. True, the evidence against him was entirely circumstantial and partly inconsistent; true, the trial judge had committed several errors of law; true, the jurymen had violated a state statute by communicating with their families during their consideration of the case. Yet after all, the verdict was merely murder in the second degree, and even Sheppard could not deny that someone or other had brutally killed his wife.

As we see, English judges are not the only ones who could profit from the attention of Arthur Koestler's pen.

Count IV. A verdict of guilt may result less from the evidence than from the prosecutor's political ambitions, the "third degree" and other brutal police methods, and the intricate technicalities of local procedure.

The facts in support of this count are humiliatingly familiar. Fired by political ambition, a district attorney may recklessly prosecute the wrong man, whip up popular hatred against the accused, suppress truthful evidence that might lead to acquittal, and even (in rare but terrible instances) proffer testimony that he knows to be false and perjurious. Nor is this all. At least since 1893, when Governor John Peter Altgeld of Illinois ruined his career by freeing three prisoners convicted — as he believed, falsely and unfairly — for participating in the Haymarket Massacre, the majority of executives and parole boards have been excessively sensitive to newspaper clamor. The very passions that induce an erroneous conviction can prevent the exercise of executive clemency.[12] If a President or governor hears a substantial public group baying for blood, he may take precautions to see that the blood they get is not his.

Amid a surfeit of examples, let me mention only the case of James Smith, trapped and enmeshed in the technicalities of Pennsylvania procedure.[13] Smith was a schizophrenic who had been adjudged insane by a New York court and had begged to be committed to a naval hospital because, according to his own statement, he was afraid he might kill someone. From 1941 when he was nineteen until 1948 when he did kill someone, he had not been at large for any period longer than nine months. His years had been spent in various prisons and state hospitals. When he was arraigned in the Pennsylvania court and charged with the killing, Smith was "overreached"[14] into pleading guilty to the capital offense of murder in the first degree. Thus he was never permitted to prove his mental state to a jury. As he was impecunious, his lawyer asked the court to provide a psychiatrist to advise and assist in defending him. The Pennsylvania judge declined this request, and decided that Smith was legally sane. The basis of the judge's decision was the testimony of a court psychiatrist who had gone to the prison and talked with Smith all of an hour. The atrocity became complete a couple of years later when the court psychiatrist was himself committed to an institution because he had "an incurable mental disease which had deprived him of any judgment or insight." The United States Supreme Court (6 to 3) affirmed the conviction.

How can a case like this penetrate so far into a labyrinth of horrors? Surely, at some point or other, the prosecutor can find a way to retrace his steps and take the situation back to the light of social sanity. When, on the contrary, we see the shutting and sealing of door after door that might have led to a civilized outcome, we may appreciate why Justice William O. Douglas commented in a recent public address:

> During that time [of sitting on the Supreme Court] it has seemed to me that the quality of prosecutors has markedly declined. . . . Sometimes they treated the courtroom not as a place of dignity, detached from the community, but as a place to unleash the fury of public passion.[15]

Of course, our state and federal governments do not lack prosecutors and judges of the highest professional caliber and most scrupulous official behavior. Some of them exemplify the very finest and noblest ethical qualities. Owing, I believe, to the statesmanlike capacities that our American system of constitutional review requires of our jurists, the best among them seem, at least during this century, to excel England's best contemporary judges in wisdom and intellectual vigor. But control over trials and the death penalty is not confined to the hands of our best; it resides also with the many officials and judges who are insensitive and mediocre, not to mention the minority who are cynical, ruthless, and corrupt.

These are four principal counts in the indictment of our penal justice, demonstrating how readily it may slip into error and send the "wrong" person to the scaffold. Surely the counts are awesome enough to trouble a man's imagination, afflict his conscience, and make him pay heed when Judge Jerome Frank says:

> Were human judgment about guilt infallible, still a death sentence would be immoral because no man may morally play God. But such a thesis need not be considered, for it assumes the impossible. Experience teaches the fallibility of court decisions. The courts have held many an innocent man guilty. How dare any society take the chance of ordering the judicial homicide of an innocent man?[16]

I would have us take Judge Frank's phrase very seriously. If, instead of presuming to "play God," we should determine to pursue His ways in humility and reverence, then we would never consent that the law destroy our fellows, His creatures, whose breath — as it were — flows to them from Him. All our learning and experience teaches that the most confident of human judgments are inherently fallible; the judgments of courts in every country are quite fallible; and the judgments of many American courts are far more fallible than they need be.

CRITICISM AND PATRIOTISM

As *Reflections on Hanging* demonstrates in every chapter, there are many good reasons — some of them merely persuasive, some ethically peremptory — for abolishing the death penalty. The fact that prosecutors, judges, psychiatrists, juries, and executives are so fallible is not the only reason; perhaps other considerations will appear, and deserve to appear, loftier or more dignified. But at least the inveterate fallibility of penal administration constitutes a *sufficient* reason. If it stood entirely alone, it would be powerful enough to enlist rational and patriotic readers in the struggle against capital punishment.

Rational, yes, but also patriotic, for this book which Arthur Koestler has written is a work of intense patriotism. Of course, Koestler's kind of patriotism may not appeal to citizens who sit at ease in their fancied security and, like carved ivory monkeys, decide to hear no evil, see no evil, speak no evil concerning the inherited laws and hoary customs and unlettered prejudices of their nation. Let them sit there on the shelf. The patriotism I mean is no synonym for looking smug and shutting one's mind. It consists rather in prizing what one's country might become if it would live according to its best aspirations and potentialities.

This is why a genuine patriot will never overlook a cruel practice or condone a social injustice on the ground that it happens to obtain at home. On the contrary, to him an injustice seems the more repulsive for arising at home and marring the image of his land and people. When his own state inflicts a wrong, the burden of responsibility becomes peculiarly his, at least in some part. He bears the guilt, the duty to repair as far as possible, and, above all, the duty to prevent.

We who live as free citizens in a democratic society are responsible for capital punishment imposed by our law. Every day the penal codes draw their validity from our name, the executions are ordered by our authority, and the rope or electric current or lethal gas is bought with our tax money. There is no one else: it is we who arrange, through hired deputies, for pulling the lever or pressing the button.

As the moral responsibility is ours, so too is the political power to object and prevent. If we resolve that capital punishment is not civilized enough for America, we can unite and abolish it. The task requires only dedication and courage. Who, living under these skies, dares not hope? America may yet fulfill its earliest vision and every state become worthy of the just, the understanding, and the compassionate.

From Preface to Arthur Koestler, Reflections on Hanging, *Macmillan Company, New York, 1957.*

Fact-Skepticism: An Unexpected Chapter

So far, fact-skepticism has been lucky in this country. While various distinguished fact-skeptics like William O. Douglas, William J. Brennan, Jr., Roger J. Traynor and Leon Green may reject this or that specific item in Jerome Frank's agenda of reform, they consistently share and sustain his fundamental humanitarian outlook. In recent years, we have become so accustomed to seeing fact-skepticism applied in conjunction with a consumer perspective that we take the union of the two for granted. Yet they are not inseparable in either theory or action. When considered by itself, fact-skepticism is only a very conscious, persistent, and systematic species of doubting, and in human affairs doubting frequently looks more like Janus than like Minerva.

Rulers in every age of history have used their doubts to rationalize inertia as well as moderation, prevarication as well as inquiry, indifference as well as clemency, oppression as well as justice. Skepticism, like everything else, has its times and places and potentialities for good or ill; the value of a human being may be said to depend on what he does with his doubts. For these reasons, among others, it is important to examine an earlier, pre-Frank version of fact-skepticism.[1] The author of this previous version, first published in 1872, was the eminent British jurist, James Fitzjames Stephen.

SOMETHING ABOUT FITZJAMES STEPHEN

Before giving a brief sketch of Stephen's life and personality,[2] which have much to do with his distinctive manner of using fact-skepticism, I believe it only fair to mention the influence he exerted on American legal thought. Even omitting the massive contribution he made to positive criminal law, from which American scholarship still draws benefits, one stands almost in embarrassment before the spectacle of Holmes's immense indebtedness to Stephen's insights, concepts, and general perspectives — an indebtedness never adequately acknowledged until the appearance of Mark Howe's biography. Of course, since he conceived of himself as a thinker in the profession, Holmes quite understandably found it easier to commend wise and experienced practitioners than other juristic thinkers, no matter how able. It is not our debtors we find trouble in forgiving, it is our creditors.

This was not the case with Jerome Frank, who quoted amply from Stephen's passages of fact-skepticism as soon as he came upon them. Unfortunately, he did not discover the material until *Courts On Trial*

(1949) had already been published.[3] Stephen made his initial appearance in Frank's very next article.[4] But all this happened a decade or two too late to contribute to Jerome Frank's development of fact-skepticism; to him, Stephen remained no more than another apt quotation among a cabinetful. Perhaps he did not exploit what he found in Stephen because he sensed the disparity we are about to note between their respective perspectives.

Sir James Fitzjames Stephen (1829–1894) came from a family that had furnished generations of superior public servants and reached its full flower in his day. His younger brother, Leslie Stephen, was long one of England's leading men of letters, and Leslie's daughter was the famous novelist, Virginia Woolf. Though Fitzjames's own career did not lack conventional marks of success, it was Leslie's verdict, which I think unbiased observers may share, that he never won adoption of some of his most valuable projects and never enjoyed the high measure of public regard and acclaim that he deserved. Perhaps Leslie's affectionate biography of Fitzjames suggests the explanation: Fitzjames was not only upright and forthright, he was also a shade too downright.

After education at Cambridge and the Inner Temple Fitzjames became an indefatigable worker in his profession, trying cases whenever he could get them and writing a steady stream of articles on social, moral and educational themes. In a certain sense he remained a journalist or publicist throughout his life. Among his friends and associates were figures as important as John Stuart Mill and Henry S. Maine.

Shortly after 1868 Stephen received an offer to succeed Maine as legal member of council in India and his acceptance, given after considerable hesitation, proved to be a turning point in his life and thought. In India, where he remained over two years and completed work that would normally have taken five, Stephen carried on the program of codification which had been begun by Macaulay and continued by Maine. His crowning personal achievement was the Evidence Act of 1872, and it is from the brilliant introduction to this statute that we have reproduced Stephen's exposition of fact-skepticism.

On returning from India, Stephen attempted similar codifications for the home country, but none was enacted. He took note that his reform philosophy, however successful it might be in the benevolent council of an imperial colony, met continual rebuffs in the partisan mechanisms of a democratic Parliament. The contrast left a deep impression.

Meanwhile, though he handled some few important cases, Stephen's practice as a barrister was, in his biographer's words, "always irregular." After service on various public commissions, he was appointed to the bench in 1879. It was while performing his full judicial duties that he prepared and published his famous *History of the Criminal Law*. The years of relentless overwork impaired his health so gravely that in 1891 he felt constrained to resign from the bench.

As a judge, Stephen displayed a combination of qualities that made some lawyers feel uneasy with him: a massive common sense, a certain want of subtlety, a dislike of technicalities, a downright forcefulness, a love of fair play, and a hatred of brutality that gave him a reputation for severity. ("Brutality" here means the brutality of a criminal act; not being an American judge, Stephen was not prompted to associate brutality with law-enforcement officers.) In his last period, when he could no longer profit from them, Stephen received some of the official and academic honors by which civilized societies mask their failure to encourage talent during its years of youth, insecurity, and financial need.

THE IMPERIAL PERSPECTIVE AT ITS BEST

Reading Stephen's fine introduction to the Indian Evidence Act, we meet a jurist who exemplifies the old pre-democratic perspective — the perspective of the rulers, the governors, the officers, the processors of law — at its very best. His understanding of fact-skepticism is such as befits a responsible lawyer and administrator, a conscientious member of the class whom destiny has charged with the duty of governing. To Stephen the defectiveness of the fact-finding process represents one more regrettable component of the ruling man's burden. He faces it, accepts it, consents to bear it. He would never think of misusing it or treating it as an excuse with which to cloak an injustice.

That men can use their doubts for bad purposes is all too apparent. When those in authority desire to evade a duty of inquiry or review, when executives wish to cover the reputations of guilty subordinates, when judges fear to provoke political criticism, they can always find a convenient pretext in their uncertainty about the true facts of the case. They can wash their hands before the multitude and insist on evincing "proper respect" for other officials and tribunals who have considered the matter at length and have disposed of it. To show how fact-skepticism may be avowed hypocritically and put to unjust use, there are no more classic instances than the behavior of France's military and civilian authorities during the Dreyfus case or the decision of the United States Supreme Court in *Frank v. Mangum*.[5]

But none of this really applies to Stephen. In him we witness the official or imperial perspective at its dedicated best: diligent, competent, attached to the business that life has assigned him though its nature be difficult and its purpose unintelligible, and determined to perform it creditably at all costs. Sometimes when the mood of such men becomes a bit exalted, they may sound rather like a reunion of the Light Brigade on an anniversary of the famous charge, but generally their tone is sober, stoical, appropriately reminiscent of the Roman praetors who somehow kept things going from day to day in the far reaches of the empire while at home Caesar and the populace seemed to be going mad.

One can see the perspective foreshadowed in Stephen's defiant article on "Doing Good," where he caustically ranks the butcher and baker above the doctor, the loom and the plow above the school and the hospital. Performing the functions of one's post, he submits, is worth more than philanthropy, altruism, idealism, or any other species of "doing good." Do your job, he admonishes, stick to your last, and stop talking like a "lubber" about progress. Unquestionably it was this doctrine of Stephen's that gave Holmes the notion, repeated often in his conversation and correspondence, of an imaginary association whose members, accepting their destiny with stoical detachment and executing their assigned duties with notable competence, would call themselves the "Society of Jobbists." Here is Fitzjames Stephen's version of the philosophy, condensed by his biographer:

I dreamt, he says, after Bunyan's fashion, that I was in the cabin of a ship, handsomely furnished and lighted. A number of people were expounding the objects of the voyage and the principles of navigation. They were contradicting each other eagerly, but each maintained that the success of the voyage depended absolutely upon the adoption of his own plan. The charts to which they appealed were in many places confused and contradictory. They said that they were proclaiming the best of news, but the substance of it was that when we reached port most of us would be thrown into a dungeon and put to death by lingering torments. Some, indeed, would receive different treatment; but they could not say why, though all agreed in extolling the wisdom and mercy of the Sovereign of the country. Saddened and confused I escaped to the deck, and found myself somehow enrolled in the crew. The prospect was unlike the accounts given in the cabin. There was no sun; we had but a faint starlight, and there were occasionally glimpses of land and of what might be lights on shore, which yet were pronounced by some of the crew to be mere illusions. They held that the best thing to be done was to let the ship drive as she would, without trying to keep her on what was understood to be her course. For "the strangest thing on that strange ship was the fact that there was such a course." Many theories were offered about this, none quite satisfactory; but it was understood that the ship was to be steered due north. The best and bravest and wisest of the crew would dare the most terrible dangers, even from their comrades, to keep her on her course. Putting these things together, and noting that the ship was obviously framed and equipped for the voyage, I could not help feeling that there was a port somewhere, though I doubted the wisdom of those who professed to know all about it. I resolved to do my duty, in the hope that it would turn out to have been my duty, and I then felt that there was something bracing in the mystery by which we were surrounded, and that, at all events, ignorance honestly admitted and courageously faced, and rough duty vigorously done, was far better than the sham knowledge and the bitter quarrels of the sickly cabin and glaring lamplight from which I had escaped.

I suppose there are few reflective lawyers who do not experience such a mood at one time or another. Let us compare Learned Hand's essentially similar, though somewhat gayer, paraphrase of Holmes's faith:

> Are you a member of the Society of Jobbists, or do you know the guild? If not, let me tell you of it. All may join, though few can qualify. . . . It is an honest craft, which gives good measure for its wages, and undertakes only those jobs which the members can do in proper workmanlike fashion, which of course means no more than that they must like them. Its work is very various and indeed it could scarcely survive in these days, if the better known unions got wind of it, for quarrels over jurisdiction are odious to it. It demands right quality, better than the market will pass, and perhaps it is not quite as insistent as it should be upon standards of living, measured by radios and motorcars and steam-heat. But the working hours are rigorously controlled, because for five days alone will it labor, and the other two are all the members' own. These belong to them to do with what they will, be it respectable or not; they are nobody's business, not even that of the most prying moralists.
>
> I confess that I have often applied for admission and have been always rejected, though I still live in hope. The membership is not large, at least in America, for it is not regarded with favor, or even with confidence, by those who live in chronic moral exaltation, whom the ills of this world make ever restive, who must be always fretting for some cure; who cannot while away an hour in aimless talk, or find distraction for the eye, or feel agitation in the presence of fair women. Its members have no program of regeneration; they are averse to propaganda; they do not organize; they do not agitate; they decline to worship any Sacred Cows, American or Russian. But none the less, you must be careful how you thwart them. They are capable of mischief; for you must not suppose, because they are amiable and gay and pleasure-loving, because they are not always reverent, that they are not aware of the silences, or that they do not suppose themselves to have embarked upon a serious enterprise when they began to breathe. You may go so far with them in amity and

fellowship; you may talk with them till the cocks crow, and differ as you like and as you can, but do not interfere with the job, and do not ask for quarter if you do — you will not get it. For at bottom they have as much faith as you, and more, for it is open-eyed and does not wince. They have looked in most of the accessible closets, and though many are too dark to explore and they know little about what is in them, still they have found a good many skeletons, taken them apart, and put them together. So far as they have got, they are not afraid of them, and they hope that those they have not seen may not be worse than the few they have.[6]

Unfortunately, despite its attractive features, a juristic perspective of this kind may leave little more room for humanitarian impulse and compassionate action than for social hope. It tends to sharpen the aristocratic bias of cultivated minds and sometimes blunts their capacity for projection and empathy. Thus it may lead really superior judges into crude and unbecoming errors, like Holmes's in *Bailey v. Alabama*[7] and *Weems v. United States*.[8]

Yet, under special circumstances, the bias may prove advantageous by alerting judges to the dignity of their position and preparing them to resist external pressures. Judges of the imperial perspective may be most valiant to defend justice when the threat comes not from legitimate authority but from some unruly and impertinent mob.[9] In such a crisis they take their noblest stand, as Holmes did in his *Frank v. Mangum* dissent.[10] Judge Hand was deadly serious when he warned, "Do not interfere with the job, and do not ask for quarter if you do — you will not get it." Mob violence interferes with the job.

Nor will such judges permit one to suggest that there may be good mobs as well as bad ones, mobs for example that aim to overthrow a tyrant as well as mobs that aim only to loot and lynch. In the imperial or official perspective, all mobs are fungible. Motive makes no difference; they are all obnoxious because they embody insubordination, disorder, and the repudiation of established authority. Fitzjames Stephen was only nineteen years of age when the Revolution of 1848 swept over the continent; yet he never forgot the decisive impressions and feelings that it inspired:

They were feelings of fierce, unqualified hatred for the revolution and revolutionists; feelings of the most bitter contempt and indignation against those who feared them, truckled to them, or failed to fight them whensoever they could and as long as they could: feelings of zeal against all popular aspirations and in favour of all established institutions whatever their various defects or harshnesses (which, however, I wished to alter slowly and moderately): in a word, the feelings of a scandalised policeman towards a mob breaking windows in the cause of humanity.

Stephen seems to have taken some of this spirit from the wholesale realm of politics and mass behavior over into the retail realm of criminal law and individual behavior. In his opinion, the criminal law of England assumed that it was right to hate criminals, and he regarded the hatred as a "healthy natural feeling." The "healthy natural feeling" would explain, of course, his reputation for severity as a judge trying criminal cases. It might also account for some conscientious scruples and inner conflicts that he felt during the years when he was serving as counsel for the defense. I am not sure that an accused who really knew his views would have desired his services in that important capacity. For example, one of Stephen's clients was convicted of cutting the throat of a girl who had jilted him and was sentenced to death. Then:

> After the conviction Fitzjames felt that the man deserved to be hanged; but felt also bound to help the father in his attempts to get the sentence commuted. He could not himself petition, but he did his best to advise the unfortunate parents. He used to relate that the murderer had written an account of the crime, which it was proposed to produce as a proof of insanity. To Fitzjames it seemed to be a proof only of cold-blooded malignity which would insure the execution of the sentence. He was tormented by the conflict between his compassion and his sense of justice. Ultimately the murderer was reprieved on the ground that he had gone mad after the sentence. Fitzjames had then, he says, an uncomfortable feeling as if he were partly responsible for the blood of the murdered girl. The criminal soon afterwards committed suicide, and so finished the affair.

Now we are ready to consider fact-skepticism in Stephen's version, which can be assessed more understandingly if we compare it with Jerome Frank's. Frank's regularly involved five more or less distinguishable stages:

(1) a demonstration that the law's fact-finding process is uncertain, seriously fallible, and largely unpredictable;

(2) a set of proposed reforms — affecting judicial procedure, the rules of evidence, and the mode of jury trial — to the end of reducing the incidence of fact-finding errors;

(3) a set of proposed changes in the education of lawyers and the equipment of judges, in order to increase their professional competence and reduce their biases;

(4) an agenda of substantive reforms, such as abolition of capital punishment, in order to mitigate the harms resulting from erroneous fact-finding; and

(5) an all-pervading search for enlightenment (by every available

means but most persistently by refuting false pretensions in the sciences of human behavior) and for humility and compassion (motivated by awareness of how little judges can be sure they know).

It is striking to see how much of what Frank had to say about the fallibility of fact-finding (number 1 above), Stephen had anticipated. That Frank carries the demonstration considerably further can be granted; nonetheless, Stephen's compact exposition proves quite sufficiently that judicial fact-finding is unruly and unpredictable. Stephen sees the inherent sources of error and tags them for the reader in his usual downright manner.

But despite the admirable rationality of the Indian Evidence Act, Stephen keeps us continually aware that his main concern is with the arbiter and prudence, not — as in Jerome Frank's works — with the consumer and justice. He says in effect: If the defects of the evidence make us doubt that the accused is guilty, it may be "imprudent" to hang him. He does not say: If the defects of the fact-finding process have not been cured (and some of them are surely incurable), it may be unjust to hang any man. Stephen's counsel looks only to prudence. He recommends that we rest content with "such a degree of probability as a prudent man would act upon under the circumstances in which he happens to be placed"; but where is the prudent man whose usual course of life prepares him or gives him skill when he comes to stamping people as security risks or deporting or electrocuting them?

Prudence is a splendid quality, esteemed among men; it is the patron of abundance and the guardian of prosperity. It teaches those who practice it how to be as safe as their neighbors will let them be, provided chance, accident, and the unforeseeable do not intervene and disrupt the whole show. Prudence always achieves security — except, that is, when imprudence achieves it or when security is not to be achieved. The prudent man sets aside savings for his later years; it is not his fault when war and inflation make them worthless. He strolls sensibly on the sidewalk; it is not his fault when an auto runs out of control and strikes him there. Thoughts like these comfort him.

In imperial and governmental affairs, prudence is an equally worthy mentor. It counsels the governors to make sure of the people's obedience by resisting their demands, that is, until the demands become irresistible, whereupon to make sure of the people's gratitude by granting some minor and inexpensive item. In the imperial perspective, prudence has never hesitated to sacrifice one righteous man that the entire group may be made safe. It prompts officials to distrust one another only a shade less than they distrust the people. Prudence triumphed for Stephen in India where his legislation promptly became law. It fell short in England where partisan politicians found various other concerns more interesting to themselves and their constituents. Quite naturally, Stephen inferred that England needed a strong government like India, one that would eschew liberal nonsense and sentimental solicitude for the lower classes.

On all such issues, history has cast its vote decisively against Fitzjames Stephen. Yet the majority of lawyers and judges in Britain and America still share his faith and apply the same official or imperial perspective. Few of them could match him for competence, integrity, candor, and unselfish public service. But it appears that the world needs something more. Amid the tornadoes, eruptions, and typhoons of the present age, prudence and doing one's job are as insufficient as they are indispensable. We have all been summoned beyond our jobs.

Our unexpected chapter discloses an important aspect of fact-skepticism that American jurisprudence has heretofore overlooked. It demonstrates that fact-skepticism alone does not assure the advancement of justice, that its capacities for application are morally ambivalent, and that, in order to serve the high purposes to which Jerome Frank was dedicated, it requires the extrinsic governance of a sympathetic intelligence and a humane conscience.

From the 1963 Annual Survey of American Law.

8

SOCIAL PSYCHOLOGY, EXPERIMENTATION AND THE LAW

*E*DMOND CAHN *abhorred any process of decision-making whereby judges exercise the power of decision but dodge the responsibility by pretending that the decision, while admittedly wrong, is imposed upon the court by some external source. Of course, in many instances courts are bound by precedents or legislative acts which preclude independent judicial judgment. But very often, perhaps in the majority of instances, the result is compelled by nothing more than the moral and intellectual insensibilities of the judges themselves.*

In this century the growth of the social sciences and the emergence of legal realism have often caused lawyers and judges to abdicate judicial responsibility in favor of unverified data offered up with all the trimmings of hard scientific fact. In criminal law we have the psychiatrists and sociologists, in antitrust law and taxation we hear from the economists (invariably paid for their testimony) and in the area of civil rights we have been told that the moral outrage of racial segregation was really not a moral problem at all but was primarily a problem of psychology (the scars which segregation leaves on the Negro personality) or sociology (Negro housing and schools were inferior).

Edmond Cahn knew, however, that the social sciences were morally neutral. "Experts" could be found to testify that it was psychologically harmful to desegregate the Negro. Under the guise of scientific experimentation the Nazis perpetrated some of the worst horrors of the World War II murder factories. Although the social sciences have a proper place in the formulation of judicial decisions, they must never be permitted to dominate man's ethical and moral judgments.

Because he believed that law without a moral foundation was synonymous with tyranny, Edmond Cahn found it essential to define the proper relationship between the social sciences and the law.

N. R.

A Dangerous Myth in the
School Segregation Cases

IN legal philosophy it is a very dangerous thing to comment on happenings that one welcomes and approves. By doing so, an unwary observer may expose himself to the occupational disease of jurisprudence, which in its most virulent form consists in finding the law "the true embodiment of everything that's excellent." When the disease takes hold, its victim gradually loses his early vigor of discontent and passion for reform; by slow stages he subsides into a state of complacency; in course of time, sitting at ease among his memories, he grows to resent the process of change as ardently as he used to welcome it. To him the crop of occurrences seems annually to present more and more of the irremediable, though not necessarily less of the evil, in juristic affairs; and so at last he becomes a recognized sage and elder statesman of the profession. The risk is a dire one. Nevertheless, in the teeth of the danger, I shall proceed to comment here on 1954's most important development: the Supreme Court's decisions in the *School Segregation* cases. When the sense of injustice has triumphed on a scale so extensive, comprehension of the meaning of victory may prove useful to it in other conflicts. The decisions have added to the dignity and stature of every American.

THE OPINIONS

Considerations of Style. There is no need to speculate on the Supreme Court's unanimity in *Brown v. Board of Education* and *Bolling v. Sharpe.* Before the opinions were announced, there may have been considerable room for doubt concerning their purport, but, at least in the eyes of sophisticated observers, there was hardly any question that the Court would be unanimous or nearly unanimous. The train of previous decisions dealing with the same subject matter had long since established this institutional policy.

Chief Justice Warren's style in the *Brown* and *Bolling* opinions is most commendably bland. Very wisely he declined the opportunity — one may say, the temptation — to indulge in democratic rhetoric. There is not a word of reproach or provocation in either opinion. To his credit, the Chief Justice was less concerned with getting into the anthologies than with presenting the country with a model of rational calm.

Two Canards. Before going deeper into the cases, it is just as well to clear the air of some historical fictions concerning them. History is a grab bag of such diverse and contradictory contents that a theorist is likely to find there whatever he needs for his immediate purpose. But to say that it will furnish evidence in support of almost any theory does not mean that the evidence it does furnish should be misrepresented or distorted.

On the one hand, therefore, the current practice of turning back to 1896 when *Plessy v. Ferguson*[1] upheld "separate but equal" facilities, and laying the blame for that decision, as some now do, at the door of a conciliatory Negro leader like Booker T. Washington, is anachronistic and unhistorical. Washington's policy may have been wrong; if he erred, his mistake consisted mainly in expecting the majority of Southern whites to become educated in the principles of racial equality faster than in fact they did. Condemning him at this late date seems uncharitable; it is always easier to be right sixty years after the event. Moreover, those who attribute the *Plessy* decision to Booker T. Washington's Atlanta speech of 1895 employ a very strange theory of social causation. To say that the decision was the result of the 1895 speech, one must overlook everything else that had happened in the thirty years since Lincoln was assassinated. At worst, Washington's address may have been a straw in the fierce wind of bigotry.

The other canard is that the *Brown* and *Bolling* cases were decided as they were for the purpose of placating foreign countries whose good will had been jeopardized by racial segregation in the United States. Of course, it is possible that some few white people in the South will reconcile themselves more readily to mixed schools if they believe that their country's international position will be advanced by ending discrimination. But so many white Southerners are already willing to do away with segregated schools that considerations of the international order can hardly be given much weight. The same is true of the Supreme Court: while one trusts that the simplicity and clarity of the two opinions were intended to facilitate reading abroad as well as at home, it would be quite fallacious to suggest that the decisions themselves were motivated by subservience to foreign reactions. From Mr. Justice Harlan's ringing dissent in the *Plessy* case down through the sequence which began in 1938 with the *Gaines* decision, there is demonstrative proof that the Supreme Court is perfectly capable of reading the Fourteenth Amendment through lenses molded and ground in the United States.

Histories and the Constitution. Among the many interesting aspects of these opinions, the Court's mode of interpreting the Fourteenth Amendment deserves very special attention. Never was Thomas Jefferson more clearly vindicated in his insistence that the Constitution belongs to the living generation of Americans. The question has become: What do the phrases mean here and now? The meaning of the Amendment is to be found in the relation of its language to a total haecceity, including everything that has changed and everything we have learned and unlearned since 1868 when it was adopted. There were two lines of history for the Court to evaluate. The first of them — the history of the framing and adopting of the Fourteenth Amendment — proved to be only a casual element in the social and constitutional complex, an element far too ambiguous to be considered very important, much less decisive.

This was demonstrated rather adroitly. In an order for reargument, the justices requested the parties to dredge up whatever they could to show what the men of post-Civil War days had had in view concerning public education; zealously the various parties complied; after heavy labors, they adduced evidence as contradictory, amorphous, and confused as might have been — and, I suspect, was — anticipated; whereupon the Court, with little show of disappointment, turned brusquely away from the mind of the nineteenth century and proceeded to put the mind of the twentieth century to work. The historical data continue to make interesting matter for reading, and not much more. Meanwhile, the order for reargument had hinted the outcome of the cases broadly enough to remove any resentment based on mere surprise.

Turning from history of the Amendment to history of the development of public education, the Court provided itself with much more consistent and objective indicia. One can see rather clearly the progression from what public education had been in 1868, when the Amendment was adopted, to 1896, when *Plessy v. Ferguson* was decided, and on to what it has become in our time. In view of this enormous growth, the Chief Justice rightly emphasized the new and paramount significance of free education in the political and cultural life of mid-twentieth-century America. Surely then, the past cannot be allowed to decide for us what it did not have to decide for itself.

Some Dialectic Legerdemain.   The strategic considerations under-lying the *Brown* and *Bolling* cases are fascinating to spell out. Appar-ently, the justices determined that, in striking down segregated educa-tion, they were accomplishing quite enough for present purposes, and that the chances of obtaining cooperation from the rank and file of white Southerners would be reduced if the decisions should seem to touch even by implication on wider issues. If this is the way they reasoned, one must further commend their sagacity. On this reasoning, *Plessy v. Ferguson* must not be disturbed except as it related to matters of public education.

The 1896 case, it will be remembered, did not bear in any direct sense on issues of segregated education. Holding only that segregated transportation did not violate the Fourteenth Amendment, *Plessy* seemed easy to distinguish. But the problem was not so obligingly simple, for the *Plessy* opinion had not only recounted the early development of segregated public schools, but had reasoned more or less explicitly that segregated transportation was valid just because it followed the same pattern as segregated educational facilities. These passages were embarrassing. Chief Justice Warren had, in effect, to snatch the cloth of reasoning from under the *Plessy* case without spilling the content of its holding. If one examines the *Brown* opinion with these considerations in mind, the Chief Justice will appear to have executed his difficult assignment quite deftly.

The Brandeis-Brief Dilemma.   Professor Paul Freund has indicated more than once that while the Brandeis brief, filled with sociological and economic data for the judges' information, is an excellent device for upholding legislation, it creates an awkward logical predicament when the objective becomes one of overturning legislation. If statistics, expert opinions, graphs, and similar data are sufficient to establish that the legislative or administrative authorities have acted rationally, then is it ever possible to prove that they have acted otherwise? Shrewd, resourceful lawyers can put a Brandeis brief together in support of almost any conceivable exercise of legislative judgment. Moreover, the mere fact that the legislature has acted in the premises ought normally to imply that the action had some rationally explic-able basis.

The *Brown* and *Bolling* records, for example, included considerable evidence to show that school segregation was not unreasonable. In addition to explicit provisions in the respective state constitutions and statutes, there was the testimony of experienced school administrators, supported to some extent by the expert opinions of psychological and psychiatric witnesses (especially in the case from Virginia). Hence, whatever else the Supreme Court's action may accomplish, it does demonstrate satisfactorily that a challenge to constitutionality *can* overcome the kind of defense which is implicit in a Brandeis brief.

It is fair to suspect that the impact of the Brandeis brief is no longer so great as when the device was novel and judges were more readily impressed by the paraphernalia of science or pseudoscience. In the last two decades, many Brandeis briefs have been conspicuously vulnerable in respect of statistical method, rationality of inferences from assembled data, adequacy of sampling, and failure to allow for — or to disclose — negative instances. Perhaps their quality will improve with a more critical attitude on the judges' part.

The Federal "Equal Protection" Clause. In the *Brown* case, the challenged state action was held to violate the equal protection clause of the Fourteenth Amendment. Chief Justice Warren commented, "This disposition makes unnecessary any discussion whether such segregation also violates the Due Process Clause of the Fourteenth Amendment." Resuming the subject in the *Bolling* opinion, he went on:

> The legal problem in the District of Columbia is somewhat different, however. The Fifth Amendment, which is applicable in the District of Columbia, does not contain an equal protection clause as does the Fourteenth Amendment which applies only to the states. But the concepts of equal protection and due process, both stemming from our American ideal of fairness, are not mutually exclusive. The "equal protection of the laws" is a more explicit safeguard of prohibited unfairness than "due process of law," and, therefore, we do not imply that the two are always interchangeable phrases. But, as this Court has recognized, discrimination may be so unjustifiable as to be violative of due process.

Slowly and with painful equivocation, the Court seems to approach the position that the guarantee of "equal protection" should be read into the Fifth Amendment with exactly the same jural force it carries in the Fourteenth. Under this doctrine, the only difference between the federal duty of equal protection and the states' duty is one of incidence resulting from the disparity of their respective governmental functions. When the facts presenting a constitutional issue happen to be similar, as they were in the *Brown* and *Bolling* cases, the duties of the respective governments will coincide. Indeed, in the *Bolling* opinion the Chief Justice exclaims that "it would be unthinkable that the same Constitution would impose a lesser duty on the Federal Government." If it would not be quite unthinkable, it would certainly be erroneous — which ought to suffice.

INDIVIDUAL AND COMMUNITY

Official and Unofficial Segregation. Occasionally everyone meets with an argument which he feels unworthy of the compliment of rational refutation. In defense of racial segregation many such arguments have been advanced, enough in fact to create a danger that judgment and analysis may be entirely suspended and, instead of a reasoned debate, a blind struggle of wills may eventuate. Fortunately, since time is on the side of those who insist on desegregation, they can afford to keep their heads without weakening their cause, which those who stand for the old order cannot.

For example there is the argument that it would be fruitless to end segregation in the schools because "voluntary" segregation will continue in the social community. It is hard to dignify this proposition by discussing it; and I do not propose to vilipend my readers' intelligence by listing the obvious answers. But the thought, once spurned, should not necessarily be forgotten. For if we regard it as an arrow and follow the direction indicated by the feathers instead of by the head, it may prove quite instructive. It points to the fact that a firm functional tie exists between segregation imposed or administered by government officials and segregation practiced unofficially by individuals or by the social community. When imposed by the government, segregation constitutes an official disparagement of the Negro group. The disparagement is the crueler because, the United States being a political democracy, the government's implied judgment that Negroes are inferior is imputable to the entire citizenry. On the other hand, as the recent experience of the armed forces has demonstrated, when desegregation is effected under official auspices, both groups benefit from the lesson in decency and fair dealing.

But there are limits — even to the just claims of a political democracy. It would be ridiculous to contend that every citizen ought to select his or her social companions from a proportionate cross section of the ethnic groups that make up the American people. If there is any area in which personal tastes, affinities, and irrational preferences may healthfully govern our behavior, it is in the process of selecting our social companions. When we resolve to observe the principles of the Constitution in every activity that is sponsored or controlled by government, our ability to do so in a willing and congenial manner may well depend on our being free, spontaneous, and unhampered in the remainder of our relationships. Somehow, sometime, people will consort with whom they choose. For this reason, the distinction between official and unofficial segregation — a distinction to which the Supreme Court has adhered consistently — seems indispensable to furthering harmony among diverse racial groups. Discrimination in regard to corporate advantages (such as transportation, housing, employment, political franchise, or educational opportunity) violates the American promise; but discrimination in the choice of friends and private associates may furnish the very safety valve that many Americans require for psychic health. Friendship draws its sustenance from a fund of common experiences and inclinations, and in the majority of cases, group culture and affiliation will continue to be a primary factor.

Here we see again the falseness of the widespread popular belief that, with regard to moral values, the law imposes only "minimum standards." While there are some fields in which this belief may be warranted, it becomes baseless when we enter the area of the Bill of Rights and the Fourteenth Amendment. Far from being merely "minimum standards," the substantive and procedural requirements of the Bill of Rights are so high that virtually no citizen lives up to them consistently in his personal relations and transactions. In the forum of conscience and private judgment, due process is violated continually by every one of us, including the lawyers and jurists who seek most earnestly to impose it on official action. Thus while the *Brown* and *Bolling* cases make us sensible of improvement in government performance, they do raise some disquieting questions concerning our behavior in the realm of the domestic and unofficial.

The decisions likewise cast a revealing light on the institution of judicial review. Since as a practical matter it would have been impossible to secure adoption of a constitutional amendment to abolish "separate but equal," only the Court possessed effective power to relieve American education of the incubus. It was to be court action or an impasse, and an impasse could not last indefinitely. For decades the public sense of injustice had denounced racial discrimination more and more resentfully. I suggest therefore that the *Brown* and *Bolling* decisions spared the nation a genuine constitutional crisis, and that in this exigency the institution of judicial review rendered an invaluable service.

SCIENCE OR COMMON SENSE?

A Dangerous Myth. In the Virginia case[2] and to a lesser extent in the other litigations, various psychiatrists, psychologists, and social scientists gave expert testimony concerning the harmful effects of segregation on Negro school children. In addition, some of appellants' witnesses prepared an elaborate statement on the subject, which, signed by a total of thirty-two experts, was submitted to the Supreme Court as an appendix to appellants' brief. In the months since the utterance of the *Brown* and *Bolling* opinions, the impression has grown that the outcome, either entirely or in major part, was caused by the testimony and opinions of the scientists, and a genuine danger has arisen that even lawyers and judges may begin to entertain this belief. The word "danger" is used advisedly, because I would not have the constitutional rights of Negroes — or of other Americans — rest on any such flimsy foundation as some of the scientific demonstrations in these records.[3]

The moral factors involved in racial segregation are not new — like the science of social psychology — but exceedingly ancient. What, after all, is the most elementary and conspicuous fact about a primitive community if not the physical proximity of human beings mingling together? When the members of a community decide to exclude one of their number from the group life without killing him outright, what else can they do but force him to remove himself physically (as in the case of Cain), ostracize him for what they consider the general welfare (as the Athenians did), banish him from the cluster of community dwellings (as in outbreaks of leprosy or other plague), assign him a fixed area or ghetto to occupy (as with the Jews in medieval times), or lock him in a penitentiary (as we do with convicted criminals)? Hardly anyone has been hypocritical enough to contend that no stigma or loss of status attaches to these forms of physical separation. Segregation does involve stigma; the community knows it does. It knows full well that if "Stone walls do not a prison make nor iron bars a cage," they certainly do hamper a person's freedom to move about and consort with whom he pleases. Possibly as the poet said, the walls can be understood as a "hermitage" or retreat or monastery, but only for those who choose them without being compelled by the social group.

There are people who argue, sometimes quite sincerely, that racial segregation is not *intended* to humiliate or stigmatize. On first impression, the argument seems to have some slight mitigative value, for surely a deliberate insult is liable to cut deeper than one inflicted out of mere crudeness or insensibility. But the mitigation comes too late. An excuse that one did not intend to injure does not stand much chance of reception when the offender, having been informed of the damage he has done, continues and persists in the same old callous insults. As is observed in the ancient Babylonian Talmud, to shame and degrade a fellow creature is to commit a kind of psychic mayhem upon him. Like an assailant's knife, humiliation slashes his self-respect and human dignity. He grows pale, the blood rushes from his face just as though it had been shed. That is why we are accustomed to say he feels "wounded."

Moreover, if affronts are repeated often enough, they may ultimately injure the victim's backbone. We hear there are American Negroes who protest they do not feel insulted by racially segregated public schools. If there are any such Negroes, then they are the ones who have been injured most grievously of all, because segregation has shattered their spines and deprived them of self-respect.

So one speaks in terms of the most familiar and universally accepted standards of right and wrong when one remarks (1) that racial segregation under government auspices inevitably inflicts humiliation, and (2) that official humiliation of innocent, law-abiding citizens is psychologically injurious and morally evil. Mr. Justice Harlan and many other Americans with responsive consciences recognized these simple, elementary propositions before, during, and after the rise of "separate but equal." For at least twenty years, hardly any cultivated person has questioned that segregation is cruel to Negro school children. The cruelty is obvious and evident. Fortunately, it is so very obvious that the justices of the Supreme Court could see it and act on it even after reading the labored attempts by plaintiffs' experts to demonstrate it "scientifically."

Claims and Facts. When scientists set out to prove a fact that most of mankind already acknowledges, they may provide a rather bizarre spectacle. Fifty years ago, certain biologists who were engaged in just this sort of enterprise, provoked George Bernard Shaw to denounce their "solemnly offering us as epoch-making discoveries their demonstrations that dogs get weaker and die if you give them no food; that intense pain makes mice sweat; and that if you cut off a dog's leg the three-legged dog will have a four-legged puppy." Then Mr. Shaw called the scientists a number of fearful names (beginning with "dolts" and "blackguards"), none of which would be remotely applicable to the psychologists and psychiatrists who testified in the desegregation cases. So far as I can judge, all of these are fine, intelligent, dedicated scholars. Yet one can honor them as they deserve without swallowing their claims.

Professor Kenneth B. Clark of the psychology department of City College acted as general social science consultant to the NAACP legal staff and served as liaison between the lawyers and the scientists. His endeavors having been long and arduous, perhaps it was natural that he should exaggerate whatever the experts contributed to the case. In an article written while the country was waiting for the Supreme

Court's decisions, he asserted, *"Proof* of the arguments that segregation itself is inequality and that state imposed racial segregation inflicts injuries upon the Negro *had to come from the social psychologists and other social scientists."*[4] (Emphasis supplied.)

When Professor Clark wrote thus, he could not know that Chief Justice Warren's opinions would not mention either the testimony of the expert witnesses or the submitted statement of the thirty-two scientists. The Chief Justice cushioned the blow to some extent by citing certain professional publications of the psychological experts in a footnote, alluding to them graciously as "modern authority." In view of their devoted efforts to defeat segregation, this was the kind of gesture a magnanimous judge would feel impelled to make, and we are bound to take satisfaction in the accolade. Yet, once the courtesy had been paid, the Court was not disposed in the least to go further or base its determination on the expert testimony.

As I have said, these developments Professor Clark could not have known when he staked so wide a claim for his profession. But he did know that circumstances in the Virginia litigation — the one he participated in most actively — had reflected very directly on his assertion. The Virginia school board had offered the testimony of three expert witnesses, and all three (psychiatrist Kelly, psychologist Buck, and Professor Clark's own former teacher, Professor Garrett of Columbia) had *admitted,* in one way or another, that racial segregation in the schools does injure Negro children's personalities. They admitted, as we have said, a fact of common experience. On the defendants' behalf, they testified as persuasively as they could against the Court's adopting what they called "disruptive" or "coercive" measures, and they spoke regretfully about the firmness of established regional customs. Buck summarized their attitude in two statements: "I feel that as an abstract idea, segregation is bad," and "I think the whole society is sick."

When we come to explain why the statement signed by the thirty-two social scientists went without mention by Chief Justice Warren, I find myself at a disadvantage. Only the reader's assistance can rescue me. I have examined the text of this statement, which has become easy of access by being reprinted in a law review.[5] My personal, subjective reaction is that the text conveys little or no information beyond what is already known in "literary psychology" (by which I mean such psychological observations and insights as one finds continually in the works of poets, novelists, essayists, journalists, and religious prophets). The statement's vocabulary and style would not be called "literary"; I refer only to its substance. If my readers will inspect the statement for themselves, they will ascertain whether it impresses them as it did me.

At that, my reaction may be due to a lack of technical training in scientific psychology and psychological testing.

The "Generally Accepted" Test. When a scientist is engaged in demonstrating a fact of common knowledge (e.g., that fire burns, that a cold causes snuffles, or that segregation degrades), it is not easy to pass a fair judgment on the validity of his proof. Our minds tend to supply his conclusion before he is ready to deduce it. Subconsciously we reinforce his evidence with the facts and feelings of our own experience, and if his reasoning should contain a flaw, we are too preoccupied with reaching the familiar destination to detect it. Moreover, in the present situation, men who specialize in conducting psychological tests might discover all sorts of weak assumptions and fallacies that mere lawyers would never notice. Under these several disadvantages, the most I can do here is present Professor Clark's evidence concerning the "generally accepted" test,[6] together with the comments that suggest themselves to an untrained but interested observer.

Professor Clark testified as an expert in the South Carolina, Delaware, and Virginia litigations. The clearest description of the test appears in his testimony in the South Carolina case. He said:[7]

A. I made these tests on Thursday and Friday of this past week at your request, and I presented it to children in the Scott's Branch Elementary School, concentrating particularly on the elementary group. I used these methods which I told you about — the Negro and White dolls — which were identical in every respect save skin color. And, I presented them with a sheet of paper on which there were these drawings of dolls, and I asked them to show me the doll — May I read from these notes?

JUDGE WARING: You may refresh your recollection.

THE WITNESS: Thank you. I presented these dolls to them and I asked them the following questions in the following order: "Show me the doll that you like best or that you'd like to play with," "Show me the doll that is the 'nice' doll," "Show me the doll that looks 'bad,' " and then the following questions also: "Give me the doll that looks like a white child," "Give me the doll that looks like a colored child," "Give me the doll that looks like a Negro child," and "Give me the doll that looks like you."

By Mr. Carter:

Q. "Like you?"

A. "Like you." That was the final question, and you can see why. I wanted to get the child's free expression of his opinions and feelings before I had him identified with one of these two dolls. I found that of the children between the ages of six and nine whom I tested, which were a total of sixteen in number, that ten of those children chose the white doll as their preference; the doll which they liked best. Ten of them also considered the white doll a "nice" doll. And, I think you have to keep in mind that these two dolls are absolutely identical in every respect except skin color. Eleven of these sixteen children chose the brown doll as the doll which looked "bad." This is consistent with previous results. which we have obtained testing over three hundred children,[8] and we interpret it to mean that the Negro child accepts as early as six, seven or eight the negative stereotypes about his own group. And, this result was confirmed in Clarendon County where we found eleven out of sixteen children picking the brown doll as looking "bad," when we also must take into account that over half of these children, in spite of their own feelings — negative feelings — about the brown doll, were eventually required on the last question to identify themselves with this doll which they considered as being undesirable or negative. It may also interest you to know that only one of these children, between six and nine, dared to choose the white doll as looking bad. The difference between eleven and sixteen was in terms of children who refused to make any choice at all and the children were always free not to make a choice. They were not forced to make a choice. These choices represent the children's spontaneous and free reactions to this experimental situation. Nine of these sixteen children considered the white doll as having the qualities of a nice doll. To show you that that was not due to some artificial or accidental set of circumstances, the following results are important. Every single child, when asked to pick the doll that looked like the white child, made the correct choice. All sixteen of the sixteen picked that doll. Every single child, when asked to pick the doll that was like the colored child; every one of them picked the brown doll. My opinion is that a fundamental effect of segregation is basic confusion in the individuals and their concepts about themselves conflicting in their self images. That seemed to be supported by the results of these sixteen children, all of them knowing which of those dolls was white and which one was brown. Seven of them, when asked to pick the doll that was like themselves; seven of them picked the white doll. This must be seen as a concrete illustration of the degree to which the pleasures[9] which these children sensed against being brown forced them to evade reality — to escape the reality which seems too overburdening or too threatening to them. This is clearly illustrated by a number of these youngsters who, when asked to color themselves — For example, I had a young girl, a dark brown child of seven, who was so dark brown that she was almost black. When she was asked to color herself, she was one of the few children who picked a flesh color, pink, to color herself. When asked to color a little boy, the color she liked little boys to be, she looked all around the twenty-four crayons and picked up a white crayon and looked up at me with a shy smile and began to color. She said, "Well, this doesn't show." So, she pressed a little harder and began to color in order to get the white crayon to show. These are the kinds of results which I obtained in Clarendon County.

Q. Well, as a result of your tests, what conclusions have you reached, Mr. Clark, with respect to the infant plaintiffs involved in this case?

A. The conclusion which I was forced to reach was that these children in Clarendon County, like other human beings who are subjected to an obviously inferior status in the society in which they live, have been definitely harmed in the development of their personalities; that the signs of instability in their personalities are clear, and I think that every psychologist would accept and interpret these signs as such.

Q. Is that the type of injury which in your opinion would be enduring or lasting?

A. I think it is the kind of injury which would be as enduring or lasting as the situation endured, changing only in its form and in the way it manifests itself.

MR. CARTER: Thank you. Your witness.

General Comments. We are not provided here with any proof of the numerical adequacy of the sampling or of its being a representative cross section. We have no demonstration that abnormal or eccentric backgrounds of the individual children have been investigated. Among these sixteen children (or three hundred, including the other groups mentioned) there would probably be a certain proportion with untypical private experiences. In such a strikingly small sample, the results could easily mislead.

Moreover, if one follows the arithmetic in Professor Clark's testimony — which is not easy for me — some of his interpretations seem to be predetermined. For example, if Negro children say a *brown* doll is like themselves, he infers that segregation has made them conscious of race; yet if they say a *white* doll is like themselves, he infers that segregation has forced them to evade reality.

Perhaps the main point is that this test does not purport to demonstrate the effects of *school* segregation, which is what the court was being asked to enjoin. If it disclosed anything about the effects of segregation on the children, their experiences at school were not differentiated from other causes. Considering the ages of the children, we may conjecture they had not been long at school.

Comment on the Opening Questions. We do not know how the children took these questions. If Professor Clark had offered to give real dolls instead of showing pictures of dolls, the reaction might have been more serious. In any case, I do not think any certain inference follows from ten out of sixteen pointing to the picture of the white doll. Habituation with *dolls* (as distinguished from people) should be allowed for. Manufacturers and commercial fashions practically restrict a child's concept of what a "nice" doll would look like. Many white children of certain generations were taught to prefer "Topsy" or other colored dolls;[10] some children would say that there is no really "nice" doll but a teddy-bear. At this point, the response seems uninformative.

Comment on the "Bad Doll" Question. Here, it seems to me, the children were tricked. Perhaps that is how some of them felt. There had been no previous question about a "good doll," only about a "nice" one, which the children clearly understood meant one "you'd like to play with." What is a "bad doll"? Some children might consider this a term of preference for play purposes: all little "mothers" love to rebuke and punish naughty dolls. Other children, on hearing the question, would be simply bewildered by the sudden, unexpected introduction of moral or disciplinary references. Some may have responded by pointing to the brown doll because the question seemed to imply that a process of elimination was contemplated. But I hope the children asked themselves: Why must there be a "bad" doll at all? Why cannot both dolls be "nice"? We observe that five children declined to answer this question. Probably they felt it unfair or at least very confusing in the circumstances.

Comment on the Remaining Questions. It is noteworthy that seven Negro children picked the white doll "when asked to pick the doll that was like themselves." Professor Clark leaps to infer that they were evading reality. This I doubt. Although his testimony does not make me clear on the point, I gather that these seven children were among the ten who had previously chosen the white doll as "nice." Were they wrong, then, to claim that the white doll was very much "like themselves" because they too were "nice"? No one can state positively what these children were thinking at the time; but if they did have perception enough to insist to themselves that the "niceness" was decisive and not the color, lo and behold! This would be wisdom indeed! "Out of the mouths of babes and sucklings — "? Perhaps, merely perhaps. In any event, I cannot see that the opposite interpretation (Professor Clark's) is so evident that it deserves to rank as scientific proof.

Aid from an Unexpected Quarter. Fortunately, the outcome of the *Brown* and *Bolling* cases did not depend on the psychological experts' facing and answering the objections, queries, and doubts I have presented. It is possible that if the questions had been put to Professor Clark on cross-examination, he would have come forward with convincing answers. But, to all intents and purposes, the questions were not put. The doll test was not analyzed in suitable detail by any of the cross-examiners, probably because they, too, realized that segregation does degrade and injure Negro school children.

In the Virginia trial, the defense appeared particularly inept. Far from caring to concentrate on the doll test and its scientific validity, the lawyer for the defendants was preoccupied with other lines of cross-examination. He had a different set of values to display. Why concern himself with dissecting the experts' logic and the correctness of their inferences? Instead, questions were asked which would convey disparaging insinuations about a professor's parents, his ancestral religion, the source of his surname, the pigmentation of his skin, or the place of his birth. If these items did not discredit him satisfactorily, then one went on to inquire how many years he had spent in the South; if he had lived in the South, how long in Virginia; and so on — implying all the while that science, common sense, and human nature would not dare to cross Virginia county lines. And, of course, there would be continual hints that what the plaintiffs' witnesses really desired to achieve was miscegenation and a mixed race.

As any healthy-minded person reads the Virginia trial record, it is impossible not to contrast the altruism and sober dignity of the scientists with the behavior of defendants' counsel, who, by his manner of espousing the old order, exposed its cruelty and bigotry. Here was a living spectacle of what racial segregation can do to the human spirit. The segregated society, as defendants' own expert had said, was "sick"; and the tactics of cross-examination used by defendants' lawyer showed how very sick it was. I suggest that these pages of the record did not fail of notice in the deliberations of the United States Supreme Court.

Without Salt, No Science. We may as well resign ourselves to letting the troglodytes remain troglodytes, and turn our attention back to our civilized friends, the social psychologists. As the courts' exclusionary rules of evidence tend to relax more and more, the scientists will appear more frequently to testify as expert witnesses. How much respect should the judges extend to their testimony?

The answer depends in large measure on the scientists. If I have been right in suggesting that their evidence in the desegregation cases seemed persuasive because it happened to coincide with facts of common knowledge, they surely cannot rely on having the same advantage in every future litigation. It is predictable that lawyers and scientists retained by adversary parties will endeavor more aggressively to puncture any vulnerable or extravagant claims. Judges may learn to notice where objective science ends and advocacy begins.[11] At present, it is still possible for the social psychologist to "hoodwink a judge who is not over wise" without intending to do so; but successes of this kind are too costly for science to desire them.

For one thing: Merely translating a proposition of "literary" psychology into the terms of technical jargon can scarcely make it a scientific finding. For another: Just because social psychology is in a youthful and somewhat uncertain stage, the utmost rigor should be imposed on its *intermediate* processes.

The point is vital, involving as it does not only social psychology's prestige in the courts but — what is ultimately more valuable — its capacity to evolve and progress as a cumulative body of tested knowledge and approved method. Among the major impediments continually confronting this science are (1) the recurrent lack of agreement on substantive premises, and (2) the recurrent lack of extrinsic, empirical means for checking and verifying inferred results. As long as these disadvantages remain, and they are likely to remain in some measure for a very long time, social psychology will need, above all things, the use of scrupulous logic in its internal, intermediate processes. If the *premises* must be loose, the *reasoning* from them should be so much tighter; and if the final *results* cannot be validated precisely by external tests, then the *methods* of inference should be examined and reexamined all the more critically. It is meticulous standards that bring respect and credence to scientific testimony. When a social psychologist is called to serve as a "friend of the court," he should be able to assume our belief that his best friend, his premier loyalty, is always the objective truth.

Some of the Consequences. Obviously, the *Brown* and *Bolling* opinions are susceptible of more than one interpretation. My views do not agree with those of some very able commentators, who consider that the opinions show important marks of the psychologists' influence. Granting this variety of interpretations, does it really matter whether the Supreme Court relies or does not rely on the psychologists' findings? Does it make any practical difference?

I submit it does. In the first place, since the behavioral sciences are so very young, imprecise, and changeful, their findings have an uncertain expectancy of life. Today's sanguine asseveration may be canceled by tomorrow's new revelation — or new technical fad. It is one thing to use the current scientific findings, however ephemeral they may be, in order to ascertain whether the legislature has acted reasonably in adopting some scheme of social or economic regulation; deference here is shown not so much to the findings as to the legislature. It would be quite another thing to have our fundamental rights rise, fall, or change along with the latest fashions of psychological literature. Today the social psychologists — at least the leaders of the discipline — are liberal and egalitarian in basic approach. Suppose, a generation hence, some of their successors were to revert to the ethnic mysticism of the very recent past; suppose they were to present us with a collection of racist notions and label them "science." What then would be the state of our constitutional rights? Recognizing as we do how sagacious Mr. Justice Holmes was to insist that the Constitution be not tied to the wheels of any economic system whatsoever, we ought to keep it similarly uncommitted in relation to the other social sciences.

There is another potential danger here. It concerns the guarantee of "equal protection of the laws." Heretofore, no government official has contended that he could deny equal protection with impunity unless the complaining parties offered competent proof that they would sustain or had sustained some permanent (psychological or other kind of) damage. The right to equal protection has not been subjected to any such proviso. Under my reading of the *Brown* and *Bolling* opinions, this would remain the law. But if, in future "equal protection" cases, the Court were to hold that it was the expert testimony that determined the outcome of *Brown* and *Bolling*, the scope of the constitutional safeguard might be seriously restricted.[12] Without cataloguing the various possibilities, one can discern at least that some of them would be ominous. It is not too soon to say so, for basic rights need early alarms.

WHOSE VICTORY, THEN?

When the American people suffered a moral defeat in *Plessy v. Ferguson*, Mr. Justice Harlan's dissent survived on the record. It reminded the people of the solemn promises and mutual pledges that had inspired their beginnings as a nation, and appealed from what was narrow and mean in their traditions to what was broad and fraternal. As years went by, Harlan's prophetic phrases were taken up, repeated, and reiterated — until they passed gradually into the popular vocabulary. Clergymen, social scientists, publicists, and jurists imagined they were coining novel phrases as they unwittingly borrowed his, which he would have been glad to lend them. By the end of the 1930's, when the Supreme Court began to utter its series of lessons to the states on fair treatment in education, the American people were fully prepared to support their judicial pedagogue. Now the advance has reached its climax, with the principle of equality firmly established. In this struggle, there can be no one to hail as victor except the whole American people, who alone have the power to ensure that the principle becomes a living reality in their public schools. The achievement is theirs. With this, I believe, the lone dissenter of 1896 would agree. Even as the shame of his time belonged to all, so should the vindication of our time; and so too the hope of a more benevolent American community.

From the 1954 Annual Survey of American Law.

The Lawyer, the Social Psychologist and the Truth

WE may be moving into a new phase of the relations between law and the social sciences. If recent experience with the testimony of social psychologists is typical, the several elements of the American bar are facing unaccustomed challenges. For a generation or more, liberal lawyers had regarded the claims of social scientists with cordiality and encouragement. Then in 1954, when the Supreme Court decided the *School Segregation* cases, Chief Justice Warren devoted a footnote to citing certain works written by social psychologists. Thereupon the impression rose, and was ardently fostered, that it was their testimony and scientific findings that had won the victory. Seconding this impression, Senators Strom Thurmond of South Carolina and James O. Eastland of Mississippi publicly charged the Court with following the social psychologists instead of the law.

THE CONFUSION AND ITS SOURCES

Some Previous Developments. Last year, in an article[1] analyzing the most conspicuous "proof" offered by the social psychologists in the *School Segregation* cases, I submitted that: (1) neither the testimony nor the cited publications of the social psychologists determined the outcome of the *School Segregation* cases; (2) their testimony and cited publications had only reiterated facts of common knowledge; (3) the purported demonstration in Professor Kenneth Clark's highly publicized "doll test" did not approach the level of scientific proof; and (4) it would be dangerous for constitutional law to drift away from the established doctrine that discrimination is itself an injury (*injuria*) regardless of psychological or other kinds of damage (*damnum*). While uttering these warnings, the article endeavored to make clear that the outcome of the cases was entirely right, that the attorneys who offered the social psychologists' testimony were tactically justified in doing so, and that the trial courts had acted properly in admitting the testimony for whatever it might be worth. All in all, the attitude I favored toward social psychology would express receptivity seasoned with critical judgment.

Shortly thereafter in a lively symposium on law and the social sciences, Judge Frank demonstrated his encyclopedic command of the pertinent literature and reached conclusions which were more skeptical and pessimistic than mine.[2] In *Courts on Trial* he had described various unreliable features of the so-called "Brandeis brief." Indulgence in statistical fallacies was encouraged by the traditional use of the Brandeis brief, which looked merely to *vindicate* the reasonableness of legislative action. For this limited use, it did not matter whether the alleged scientific data were strictly accurate and sound; even if inaccurate or unsound, they could support a claim of reasonableness when relied on by the legislature. Now, however, that scientific demonstrations were being offered for the purpose of *overturning* legislative action, lawyers were bound to scrutinize the sampling methods, statistical adequacy, and logical validity of every expert assertion. The old lax ways would no longer serve.

Are They Like Other Experts? Commenting on the subject, a few lawyers have been disposed to take a completely indifferent, if not cynical, stand. In effect, they ask, "When is a scientist not a scientist?" and reply, "When he's a witness." They insist that the victory in the *School Segregation* cases provides a sufficient answer to all objections. They contend that everyone knows that expert witnesses are partisan and biased, that everyone discounts expert testimony to a great extent (even to the extent of not crediting it at all), and that the courts' daily experience with, say, medical experts shows that the process does not cause any extraneous social harm. We do not worry, they say, about lawyers' corrupting the medical profession or the doctors' corrupting the lawyers with regard to objectivity and scientific truth. Why then feel concern about the reciprocal influence of social psychologists and lawyers?

There are several answers. The dangers to both law and social psychology seem quite different in degree when compared with the possible influence of medical testimony. For one thing, the court testimony of social psychologists is concerned not so much with individual as with public issues. Hence, if accepted uncritically, it can cause immense public harm. Moreover, the dangers to the progress of psychological science are more serious. The medical profession does not owe its prestige and social importance to appearances in court but to theoretical and practical achievements in laboratories and hospitals. There is no significant hazard that, however physicians might testify in court, they could impair the general objectivity or impede the beneficent advance of medical science. By way of contrast, social psychology, a young profession, has not enjoyed the prestige which the American public accords to medicine, engineering, and even to economics. To some social psychologists, the new wine of public attention and influence seems quite heady. The temptations are not trivial. If a social psychologist finds it hard to prove his assertions, will not anyone else find it still harder to disprove them? With the most idealistic motives he may come to acquiesce in compromises that physicians or engineers would not dare consider.

Some Misunderstandings of Court Procedure. Among the social psychologists who testified in the *School Segregation* cases was Professor Isidor Chein, two of whose articles were cited by Chief Justice Warren in footnote 11 of *Brown v. Board of Educ.* Professor Chein read the manuscript of my article analyzing Professor Kenneth Clark's doll-test evidence. One of his comments was:

> Let us suppose that what we had to offer was nothing more than common knowledge. Does Professor Cahn know of any legal device for getting common knowledge into the record except through the device of expert testimony? If he does he ought to devote some attention to this in his paper.[8]

This comment helps to explain how the social psychologists were led to claim their testimony won the *School Segregation* cases. Seemingly they have not understood that every legal system operates within the matrix of the facts, circumstances, and value patterns obtaining in the social order. A legal system simply has to take "the given" of its society for granted; otherwise, the trial of any issue would involve an infinite regress of testimony. There are many cases to show how the Supreme Court recognizes the changing normative force of "the given" without benefit of expert testimony regarding social values. If examples are necessary, they are furnished by the interesting reversals in the respective *Flag Salute* cases and the respective *Pacifist Naturalization* cases.

Of course, the social psychologists ought also to become acquainted with the device of "judicial notice." Some propositions of social valuation emerge only when the judge writes his opinion deciding the case. Other propositions are articulated and fixed in the course of the trial by means of "judicial notice." A matter of common knowledge in the specific society, though never articulated in the record, may — and frequently does — decide the outcome. Sometimes, counsel believes that the matter of common knowledge belongs explicitly in the record, and requests the taking of judicial notice.

Professor Chein comments further:

> More fundamentally, I think that Professor Cahn does not understand the use of expert testimony in juridical processes.
> He complains that the social scientists did not prove their case. In point of fact, I believe that expert witnesses never state the scientific basis of their opinions in their direct testimony and rarely even under

cross-examination. When expert testimony becomes detailed and technical it is generally to specify that about which the expert is delivering an opinion rather than to indicate the basis on which he reached that opinion. . . .

I would defy an ordinary judge and jury to be able to follow the cogency of the technicalities of scientific evidence and hence I would assume that the above described state of affairs is justified. The law provides an entirely different device to prevent a scientific expert's abuse of his status and prestige as a scientist — namely by permitting the appearance of opposing experts if such can be found. In the segregation cases, apparently, no such opposing experts could be found with respect to our testimony.

Here again, extended discussion of the comment is unnecessary. While Professor Chein's notion of the way to test expert testimony may be appropriate for certain countries on the European continent, the Anglo-American system places considerable faith in the efficacy of cross-examination. No one should reproach Professor Chein for not endorsing the faith. As I pointed out in my previous article, the cross-examination of Professor Clark on his doll test was most unimpressive. Thus, the professional ineptitude of the lawyers can contribute to the impairment of scientific testimony. When objectivity and accuracy decline, we share in the blame.

A NEW AND EXTREMELY CONVENIENT VERSION OF SCIENTIFIC METHOD

From Scientist to Expert. Is it possible that we have started from the wrong premises and have erred in our expectations of scientific method? I must admit having approached the testimony with what now appears a rather old-fashioned idea of the scientific attitude. I picture the scientist as a dedicated man who follows the inquiry wherever it may lead, considers nothing exempt from examination, loves to have his conclusions challenged, welcomes searching questions, refuses to accept even the loftiest wishes in lieu of proof, and worships singlemindedly at the altar of truth. "The scientific attitude," John Dewey said, "may almost be defined as that which is capable of enjoying the doubtful; scientific method is, in one aspect, a technique for making a productive use of doubt by converting it into operations of definite inquiry."

But against my view, Professor Chein seems to speak for a different understanding of the scientific attitude. He says:

In any event, I can here testify on behalf of the expert witnesses in the segregation cases that nobody asked us for the bases on which we reached our conclusions. I might add that, in another case, I pointed out to counsel in the course of our preliminary discussion that whereas I had an opinion on a certain matter I did not know whether I could marshal sufficient scientific evidence to support that opinion. I was told in reply that this was all that the court was interested in, my opinion — that the presumption is that, if I qualify as an expert, my *opinion* carries weight that is not carried by ordinary opinion. I suppose that the issue should concern, who will be permitted to qualify as an expert?

If I read this statement correctly, it means that once a scientist has employed his scientific education and training to qualify as an expert witness, he may cease feeling all the old bothersome inhibitions of adherence to empirically established facts and insistence on verification. In short, this seems to mean that scientific method imposes on him no duty to volunteer a statement, "Now I am no longer talking as a scientist but only as a person with a plentiful supply of experience and opinions." It is scarcely my function to evaluate the ethical problems here, but no one can say that Professor Chein has not served notice on judges, lawyers, and others who receive his future testimony.

It is interesting to consider the ways Professor Chein's policy can influence the future of scientific method. In the *School Segregation* cases, Professor Kenneth Clark's doll test at least purported to offer empirical proof of the effects of segregation. Of course, a competent cross-examination might have neutralized the testimony by revealing the fallacies in the test. Professor Chein has apparently noted this danger and has devised a new and convenient technique to avoid it. In order to illustrate the new technique, we will look at some of Professor Chein's testimony in the *Girard College* case,[4] which was tried and decided in 1955 in the Orphans' Court of Philadelphia County, Pennsylvania.

A condensed statement of the issues will suffice. Stephen Girard, who died in 1831, left property to the City of Philadelphia to establish an institute for the education and maintenance of "poor male white orphans." Certain Negro orphans, having applied for admission to the institute, were rejected by the trustees because of their race. The Orphans' Court was asked to determine that they were eligible for admission on the following grounds: (1) Girard's directions should be conformed to modern conditions in order to fulfill his educational purposes; (2) racial discrimination was against public policy and the institute was under a city-appointed board; and (3) racial discrimination by such a board violated the Constitution. After an extended trial, the Orphans' Court denied the application. In the course of Judge Bolger's opinion, the purpose of Professor Chein's expert testimony in the *Girard College* case is explained as follows:

The arguments of the petitioners collectively raise the question of the inherent harmfulness of the College, a private charitable school and orphanage, because of its racially restrictive admission policies, which they claim render it illegal and unconstitutional. Although the petitioners fail to present any citation or reference to legislation in support of théir position, they rely upon the following: their major premise is that we are now living in a mixed world and that the function of education, public and private, is to prepare children to take their places in it. Their minor premise is contained in the testimony of outstanding qualified experts in sociology, psychology and education. These witnesses, some of whom also testified in the *Desegregation* cases, stated that the modern educational concept is that it is indispensable, according to one witness [Professor Chein], and, according to others, the ideal or best policy, that mixed racial experience exist in school and that no amount of instruction can adequately compensate for the lack of it.

In short, Professor Chein's testimony was to the effect that the white orphan boys could not receive a proper education under the conditions of the contemporary world unless the Negro orphan boys were admitted to the institute. Professor Chein further testified that no amount of outside association or mingling could serve this purpose.

It is well to begin by admitting that Professor Chein's proposition (unlike Professor Clark's in the *School Segregation* cases) is not a matter of common knowledge. Professor Clark was attempting to prove that *Negro* pupils in general incur psychological harm from the inferior status incident to segregation. Professor Chein's proposition was that the *white* pupils in this institute incur psychological harm from the exclusion of non-whites and that the harm is so great under present social conditions as to deprive them of a good education. Professor Chein's principal statement in chief was:

Q. What would you say are the effects upon the majority group in a school which is so racially isolated that it is limited to members of that majority group?
A. Well, there are a number of effects. The prime effect in my opinion is that it deprives them of the experience of intergroup association in the course of which individuals develop the skills and the attitudes which enable them to function effectively in connection with members of other groups. The conditions of our society are such at the presest time that it is virtually impossible for a person to get along in our society without having to rub shoulders with members of other racial groups. They have to do business together. They meet in parent-teachers associations. They increasingly find themselves living in the same housing developments and so on and so forth. If they don't have the opportunity for direct personal experience with one another they are likely to develop false images and stereotypes and irrational

expectations and fears which prevent them from functioning most effectively together. This is something which is becoming increasingly true in our society. There was a time when a white person could go through life without having to rub shoulders with Negroes on an equal-status basis, to take one example. The effects of not being able to perceive one another realistically, therefore, were not so serious as today, and certainly if we can predict anything from the general trends in our large metropolitan centers it is not as serious at this very moment as it is likely to be four years, five years, or ten years from now, or as far as we can predict. The amount of inter-racial mixture and inter-racial mingling on an equal-status basis is necessarily increasing and the inability of individuals to perceive one another realistically and evaluate each other on the basis of their individual human characteristics becomes increasingly serious.

There are other effects. This one I regard as the prime effect, the prime consequence of segregated education on the members of the majority group.[5]

Opinions Based on Opinions Based on etc. Professor Chein testified further, "with regard to the statements that I made in my direct testimony I believe that there wouldn't be any substantial amount of controversy." In his direct testimony, he had been satisfied to make the more reserved statement that "it is the definite opinion of the majority of psychologists, of sociologists, and of anthropologists who are competent to judge with regard to these matters that segregation is indeed harmful not merely to the members of the minority groups which are segregated, but the members of the majority groups as well."

Here we come to a questionable use of terms. Professor Chein stated that the source of his knowledge about the opinions of psychologists, sociologists, and anthropologists was the opinion survey which he had helped to collect and which had been cited by the Supreme Court.[6] Let us assume for a moment that an opinion survey has some important scientific cogency. On that assumption, we have to take notice of a difference in terminology. In testifying, Professor Chein used the phrase "members of the majority groups," a phrase suitable to include the white orphan boys at Girard College. But this was not the terminology of the opinion poll. It had asked whether segregation has "a detrimental psychological effect on the group which enforces segregation, even if that group provides equal facilities for the members of the racial and religious groups which are segregated." It is purely conjectural whether the persons answering the question, so framed, meant to include children in the position of the white orphan boys at Girard College as a "group which enforces the segregation" and "provides equal facilities" for the segregated groups. The application would seem farfetched.

Professor Chein is too intelligent to overlook the nature of his "demonstration." In the very article which the Supreme Court cited, he wrote:

> Let there be no mistake. I have myself had occasion to argue in another connection that facts are not established scientifically by holding a poll among scientists concerning their preferences. Nor can issues of fact be settled by surveys of scientists' opinions.[7]

At the risk of underlining the obvious, it may be noted that in answering Professor Chein's poll, only 29.2 per cent of all respondents checked "own research" among the bases for their opinions, although the questionnaire permitted them to check multiple bases. As for the respondents who were psychologists, only 19.1 per cent checked "own research." Moreover, the questionnaire did not distinguish between Question I (relating to harm inflicted on the segregated group) and Question II (relating to harm inflicted on the group which enforces the segregation) for the purpose of answering Question III (the basis of the respondent's opinions). Thus, it is easy to see that some of the answers to Question III asserting "own research" may have related to research with the segregated groups only. These are, however, mere details; the real reply is the one I have just quoted from Professor Chein's article.

If Facts May Prove Inconvenient, Shun Them. Testifying in the *Girard College* case, Professor Chein made clear that not a single one of the following procedures was needed for his conclusions: (1) to make a psychological study of alumni of the institute; (2) to visit the institute at all; (3) to read through Stephen Girard's will or even the portion pertaining to the teaching of social relations; (4) to read the curriculum of the institute; (5) to know or become acquainted with the long-time president of the institute; (6) to discuss the question of contacts between the two races with any graduate of the institute or with any members of its faculty or any of its present students; (7) to attend in court while the long-time president of the institute was giving his testimony as to contacts and associations between the students and Negroes; (8) to become acquainted with the racial structure of the several neighborhoods to which the students go home on weekends; (9) to consider the list of chapel speakers and participants in entertainment programs at the institute; (10) to examine the records and achievements of alumni in business, community, church affairs, and professions; (11) to consider the proportion of alumni who have ever been committed for crimes; (12) to regard the judgment of educators as on a par with that of psychologists concerning the issues;

(13) to qualify or restrict the universality of his pronouncements, although admitting that the psychological reactions of individuals are different in different geographical sections; or (14) to allow for the possibility that other factors (such as making the institute coeducational) might deserve equal attention in the students' interest.

Professor Chein concluded his testimony by explaining why he saw no occasion for such inquiries:

> I don't believe that an extensive study of this kind would have very much bearing on the issue and there would be a problem. If one were to do a study which had any kind of bearing there would be a problem of the proper design of such a study. As I indicated, I think the further back one goes the less relevant the experience of the alumni is to the major factors that I was discussing here. Far back it was possible for an individual not to perceive — it was much easier for an individual not to perceive that the exclusion of one race was in fact a contradiction of the principle of the brotherhood of man or the equality of man under our laws. I think it is infinitely more difficult in the world today for an individual to fail to perceive that. I think, as indicated, thirty years ago, let's say, the alumni were much more likely to go through life without having to make a quick adjustment to the existence of members of another race on an equal-status basis. They would have had a series of very gradual experiences which would have built them into whatever degree of effectiveness to function they have, but the child who gets out of school today is much more quickly thrust into such a situation. If one were to do a relevant study I wouldn't do a study of the alumni, but of the very recent alumni possibly and the current school body to learn how they perceive the situation and so on, and this is not a very easy thing to do. One has to approach such matters with a certain degree of subtlety and finesse, otherwise one gets back the reasons the children think you want, which is one of the reasons why the head of a school is not in a position always to know what the children in his school are actually thinking and perceiving. But I don't think it is at all likely that any facts brought out in such a study would materially alter or would be in conflict with the things I have asserted. The children of Girard College are, after all, children; they are, after all, human beings, and what we know about human beings has relevance in predicting how they perceive things and how they feel and so on, but I think the major points wtih regard to which I testified are hardly controversial points today.

So saying, he seems to reason as follows: "We have no adequate method of study; we need for the purpose of *this* suit to state as a scientific proposition that all children are precisely the same in perceptions and feelings, though the proposition is denied by almost everything in modern psychological literature; the old alumni would be too unrepresentative anyhow; if we did have a method, we ought to apply it to the recent alumni and current school body, but this we have not even attempted; ergo, without inspecting anything on the scene or talking with anyone concerned in the situation, we conclude categorically that the proposition advanced in universal terms is scientifically true." It is not easy to comment on this kind of reasoning. At best, a quotation might be taken from Cohen and Nagel's *An Introduction to Logic and Scientific Method* to the effect that "no one considers that the valuable character of knowledge or the urgent need of it proves that we have it any more than the urgent need for other things proves that we have them." One thing is clear and certain: You cannot challenge a psychologist's investigations if he does not make any.

RESPONSIBILITIES OF THE LEGAL PROFESSION

The Lawyers. Most of us would agree that, if there is any single quality distinguishing the policy judgments of lawyers from those of the general community, it ought to be the quality of responsibility. Our daily experience prepares us and our millennial tradition admonishes us to maintain a posture of deliberation amid the currents and blasts of public enthusiasm. Society looks to us for the jural development of its values, trusting we will not revolve with every passing ideological fad.

If the testimony of social scientists seems vulnerable on inspection, then it is our professional duty to point out the shortcomings and advocate the use of better methods and standards. We ought no longer debate the general admissibility of testimony from authentic social-science sources; on the contrary, we ought to welcome and encourage evidence of this kind. Our studies and criticisms should be addressed rather to considerations of weight and materiality. While we ought to keep our minds receptive and open, open minds need not be drafty. Being servants of justice and officers of the court, we have an obligation to consider the quality and propriety of expert evidence before we offer it. In many instances, lawyers participate in projecting, planning, and assembling polls and studies and other items of social-science evidence. By doing so, we do not become sureties for the logical or scientific validity of the evidence; nevertheless at some point, if there is danger of misleading the court, we should either abstain from offering the evidence or, by our own questions, bring out the limitations on its objective demonstrability.

More important, however, it is a lawyer's duty to conduct thorough and searching cross-examinations of adversary experts. In this way, he serves more than the interest of his own client. Vigorous cross-examination serves the larger social interest (a) by exposing fallacies in the expert evidence and (b) by deterring experts from making assertions that will not hold water. If the prospect of skilled cross-examination can deter some laymen from committing perjury, it may also deter some experts from passing off wishes as facts.

In order to prepare for cross-examination, a lawyer should make himself thoroughly familiar with the methods and literature of the subject. He should endeavor to obtain advance information about adversary experts and the general purport of the testimony they are expected to give. When this information is not made available in advance, he should request an adjournment before conducting the cross-examination. If there is any advantage to which a scientist, of all men, is not entitled, it is the advantage of taking the other side by surprise.

The Judges. In the type of case we have had under consideration, the judge is ultimately responsible for the use he makes of the scientific testimony. Wherever possible, he should receive it in evidence, but if it is offered in order to invalidate an official act or policy, he should satisfy his own mind that the statement will stand probing and testing. Moreover, the judge should remember how seriously even his casual references may be taken. He ought to deliberate before saying, quoting, or citing anything that may imply, or be interpreted to imply, that he has ventured to adjudicate a contested issue of science. As Galileo insisted in his century and Holmes in ours, this is scarcely a judicial function.

The Law Schools. The implications for law schools are many and require consideration by many minds. One can hope that the schools will seek to approach this complex subject in a sophisticated manner. Memories seem to be strangely short. For example, the writings of William McDougall are not likely to be mentioned by Professor Chein, and law educators appear to forget all about them. Only a generation ago, McDougall was a leader in his profession; as recently as 1943 Roscoe Pound saw fit to assign reasons for not adopting McDougall's concepts of social psychology. Yet, anyone who has a sufficiently strong stomach to read McDougall's *Is America Safe for Democracy?* — a book published while he was professor of psychology at Harvard — will find it filled with racist slander, crude propaganda, and arrant nonsense. The book provided a cloak of pseudo-scientific respectability for agitation resulting in the Immigration Act of 1921 and the national origins quota system.

Social psychology is certainly not to be charged for all time with McDougall's sins against science. On the contrary, it is the law educators who will be blameworthy if they undertake the use of psychological theories and studies in a naive and credulous spirit. We cannot afford to settle for less than the truth. For if a license to purvey loose opinions as scientific facts is given to those who will testify on the egalitarian side, why is not a similar license available to the William McDougalls?

In general, the social psychologist will advise us more objectively when he sits in conference than when he testifies on the witness stand. But McDougall's example shows that the phrase "witness stand" must not be taken in a restrictively literal sense; an expert may also bear false witness within the pages of a book. Our search for truth requires an unremitting awareness of covert interests — interests ranging from the very finest to the basest — that may result in biased judgment. By leading our students to analyze statistical methods and probe beneath the surface of psychological writings, law teachers can help raise the whole level of performance in the social sciences. But there is no substitute for the vigilant exercise of critical intelligence. Where public justice is concerned, an educator has no more right to play the dupe than the deceiver.

From the 1955 Annual Survey of American Law.

The Lawyer as Scientist and Scoundrel

Now that we have reached the four hundredth anniversary of the birth of Francis Bacon, many will celebrate the occasion with uncritical enthusiasm and a few will pause to ponder it as it deserves. It deserves bold and honest consideration. Bacon's explicit legal philosophy, which Huntington Cairns has summarized for us with characteristic excellence,[1] presents a number of questions that, while highly perceptive and intelligent, seem comparatively manageable and comfortable. Far more urgent, I believe, are the deeper, more disquieting questions that history attaches to the character and jagged career of the man himself, whom Alexander Pope called — not without reason — "the wisest, brightest, meanest of mankind."

THE PHILOSOPHER'S PRACTICE VS. HIS PREACHING

Bacon was born on January 22, 1561, son of Sir Nicholas Bacon, an exemplary lord keeper of the seal, and nephew of Sir William Cecil, later Lord Burghley. After an education at Cambridge and the Inns of

Court, he practiced as a barrister while working his way, with the continual assistance of Elizabeth's favorite, the Earl of Essex, toward a post in the royal entourage. When Essex fell from favor and was tried and executed for treason, Bacon (at the age of forty) not only assisted the prosecution but also drafted, at the Queen's request, a public document justifying the proceedings. After Elizabeth's death, Bacon's family connections, brilliant personal endowments, and servile flatteries won him the favor of James and the royal favorite, Buckingham; they also won him the implacable opposition of Edward Coke. In 1617 Bacon was made lord keeper, in 1618 lord chancellor and Baron Verulam, and in January 1621 Viscount St. Albans. From these vertiginous heights he fell almost immediately. Accused of accepting numerous bribes and participating in gross acts of corruption, he sent an abject confession of guilt to the House of Lords. The sentence of the Lords was nominally severe but the King, responding to Bacon's groveling appeals, gradually remitted almost every penalty it contained; in net effect, Bacon suffered only imprisonment for four days and the loss of his membership in Parliament. He spent the remaining five years of his life revising and adding to his great philosophical writings. He died on April 9, 1626, full of glory and of shame.

Macaulay, whose appraisal of Bacon remains as interesting and luminous as ever,[2] finds it hard to explain just why the generations of posterity have been so very kind to Bacon's memory, why they extol his writings more and more as they extenuate or suppress the foulness of his corruptions. (Macaulay himself may have felt some of the same influences; like a true Victorian he does not mention what John Aubrey reported[3] about Bacon's profligate pederasty.) Let me try to answer Macaulay's puzzle by suggesting three more or less conscious motives that seem to account for the muting of the scandal. The first of these is obviously respectable: the professors of literature are moved to say little about Bacon's crimes because they rightly oppose condemning or censoring a book on the basis of the author's character. The second motive is rather harder to accept: the professors of philosophy draw away from the subject because it may prompt someone to ask whether, in view of Bacon's example, the systematic study of philosophy has any perceptible effect on human behavior. And the conjecturable motives of the third group, the lawyers, seem scarcely more attractive: lawyers, we surmise, generally prefer to forget Bacon's crooked dealings because they find them all too reminiscent of corruption and bribery in their own time and neighborhood. Thus Francis Bacon may be immortal in more than one sense.

Let us not lose sight of the man's wisdom and brilliance, or his penetrating insights into the workings of human nature and the methods of the law. No one ever preached a more practicable pursuit of worldly success. No one ever described more clearly the moral flaws and pitfalls that a good subject, statesman, or judge must avoid. It is a marvel to read him.

On the other hand, no one ever besmirched a higher judicial office than that of lord chancellor, or disgraced a higher philosophic reputation than Bacon's. Always preaching the life of science and intellect, he always followed the life of sensuality and dishonor. Lauding gratitude and fidelity, he helped to send Essex to his death. Donning the robes of lord chancellor, he inducted a new judge and lectured him in exalted terms on the need for integrity, self-discipline, and purity in judicial office — on the same day that he signed one of numerous decrees for which he had been paid in coins of gold.

Like so many others in every country and era, when Bacon saw no chance of brazening matters out, he turned to the contemptible old pretext that what he had done was usual and customary; he whined that he had simply yielded to the bad influences of his society. The lords, who presumably knew the practices of the times, spurned the plea. And how could they have done otherwise? For one thing, there were many notable examples before them of impartial judges, including Sir Thomas More and Bacon's own honorable father.[4] For another, there were several explicit passages in Bacon's writings which admonished, in meticulous detail, against the very sins that the author and his servants had committed. Pious pronouncements in the essay *Of Judicature,* the *New Atlantis,* and other works testified so loud that they drowned out the excuses.

What bearing has the enormity of Bacon's guilt on the worth of his philosophy? It is fascinating to watch philosophy teachers and lawyers squirm away from the discomforts of the question. Almost unanimously, they reply that we must judge philosophic propositions not by the life of the author but by the words of the text. How much more convenient this way! Forget the time, the place, the man and the vilenesses, they ask; attend only to the disembodied words. Would we say that a logician may not display irrationality in his private affairs or an academic skeptic may not flounder in credulity? To fret about contradictions between a man's philosophy and his behavior would be simply perverse.

Yet some few philosophers and lawyers do not consent to be silenced. Perhaps the basic trouble, or one of the basic troubles, with contemporary philosophy is that its academic purveyors do not take it seriously enough as a guide to life. Does not a genuine sage legislate with the deeds of his life as well as with the words of his pen? Is the study of philosophy a mere heaping-up of information, names of authors and schools, labels, formulas, and decorative culture? Some (Cardozo, for example) have maintained that philosophy is not worth disputing about unless it has much higher and more responsible pretensions. Albert Camus, in *The Myth of Sisyphus*, carried these pretensions to their logical limit, contending, like Nietzsche before him, that a philosopher who declared life not worth living could keep our respect only if he committed suicide. Thus a philosopher might have to die in order to prove that the business of his life had been serious. Camus winced at the familiar picture of Schopenhauer praising suicide while consuming a lavish dinner. When one considers the source, Bacon's lofty tributes to honor and integrity seem even more distasteful.

Surely the right path lies at neither of the extremes but somewhere between them. A man's philosophy must be something more than the sum of his discrete concepts and propositions, or why do we pay special heed when a saying is attributed to Socrates, Aristotle, or Spinoza? On the other hand, a philosophy scarcely loses *all* of its worth and wisdom when it is contradicted by the author's biography. The question is one of degree and function. If a philosopher's behavior makes a complete mockery of everything in his preachings, it seems more sensible to turn elsewhere for guidance. Not that the behavior would demonstrate that the doctrine was logically false, not at all; but rather that we could assess the doctrine more justly if we consulted some other source where our vision would be less impaired by the fogs of hypocrisy. Consequently, if one wishes to interest a law student in the rise of experimental philosophy, one may gladly direct him to Bacon; but if Bacon's name should become pertinent in a discussion of professional ethics, the main emphasis — it seems to me — should be placed on his downfall and hideous disgrace.

This I suggest is the first principal outcome of our reflections. We have an old English morality play before us. It is as though history had determined to present the most sweeping of lessons for the guidance of future generations. (Bacon himself wrote that his disgrace would serve as an example "these four hundred years," i.e., until 2021.) "Here," Clio declares, "is the superlative instance with which you shall warn yourselves. Here are intellect, wealth, family, prestige, literary genius, insight, worldly prudence, prophetic science, the favor of favorites capped with the favor of princes. Here are supreme success, noble rank, landed estates, great powers, and the highest judicial office in the kingdom. Here are the prompt esteem of scholars, the unstinted admiration of readers, and the sure prospect of an enduring philosophic monument. Yet for the lack of such rudimentary honesty as a peasant might grasp and practice, the man who possessed all these goods still deserves contempt after four long centuries. What price now your own intellectuality and sophistical keenness, your clever maneuvers and sly stratagems, your skill and specious wit? Do you fancy yourself sharper and more adroit than Francis Bacon, the renowned and execrated? If not, then avoid the fatal flaw that ruined his career. Without conscience no one can stand. The poorest is not defenseless if he possesses honesty; the richest is not secure if he lacks it."

SCIENTIFIC PHILOSOPHY INTOXICATED AND SOBER

When they come to assess Bacon's personal contribution to the advance of science and scientific method, recent historians are disposed to express considerable reserve and skepticism. Some say that his program went as far as could be expected with the limited mathematical apparatus of his time; others, holding that his inductive and experimental methods were worthless, set him down as a mere publicist of science, a sort of chanticleer whose crowing had nothing to do with the rise of science's sun. Of course, when one has an advantage of four hundred years in hindsight, it is easy to criticize and disparage. At any rate, whether or not Bacon devised anything of lasting value in methodology, everyone grants that he contributed enormously toward creating a favorable climate of opinion for controlled and purposeful experimentation. Though his own researches may have done little to bring on the new age of discovery and invention, he detected and announced its approach, hailed its material gifts, and like a good herald prepared the way for its reception. In many aspects, the modern world is an elaboration and fulfillment of Bacon's vision.

The vision he offered was rich, bold, and heady. In it, science would cease to concern itself with the fatuous debates of schoolmen; it would serve thenceforth as an instrument for the augmentation of human power and a technique for the subjugation and exploitation of nature. Truth would become an exact weapon in the armament of man's mastery. Experimentation would yield unlimited new knowledge, bringing in turn endless new power to the human species. Once men resolved to disregard scholastic authorities, ancient superstitions, and conventional inhibitions, they could begin on a new road leading them to conquest and empire: a conquest of comfort, abundance, health, and speed; an empire over all the dormant and arcane forces of nature. The propsect was intoxicating to behold. In the intervening eras, as multitudes of inventions and discoveries fulfilled and even surpassed Bacon's most ambitious prophecies, it was no wonder that a substantial segment of mankind — long accustomed to ignoring the metaphysicians, consulting the theologians, and heeding the witchdoctors — gradually came to pay supreme deference to the findings and pronouncements of the scientists.

Nor is it strange that some scientists have found mankind's new outlook and their own public prestige rather intoxicating. If hard and devoted work in a laboratory at last produces a good medical remedy, can the discoverer alienate us or forfeit our thanks by insisting ridiculously that his discovery is a panacea? Clearly not. Perhaps, if there were no such drunken boasts as his, no wild afflatus for him to look forward to, the prolonged labors and attendant disappointments of scientific inquiry would become unbearable. In any case, since excessive claims and grandiloquent prospectuses are a small price to pay for authentic genius, I do not think we need reproach Bacon for having unintentionally encouraged the "intoxicated" tradition in scientific philosophy. Nothing short of extreme enthusiasm could begin to overcome the inertias and resistances of his epoch. In him brashness was indispensable.

But what shall we say about some of the extravagances in our own century, particularly those that have emerged in fields like social psychology, psychoanalysis, opinion research and personality testing? They range from groundless conceit and harmless folly all the way to callous homicide. As murder has often been committed in religion's name, it was likewise committed in the prestigious name of science when Stalin construed Marxist economics to require the "liquidation" (a scientific term, no doubt) of millions of kulaks.

Uncritical scientism is one of the least satisfying cults ever devised to dupe mankind. Its chief appeal is to the ignorant and the credulous. Thoughtful scientists are generally too honest with themselves to succumb. They realize how difficult it is to control the complexities and volatilities of human transactions or to prescind them for experimentation. Surely scientists must rub their eyes and gasp at some of those naive passages scattered through the works of John Dewey, urging us to submit all our ethical problems to the methods of science and insisting "that there is nothing whatever that methodologically (*qua* judgment) marks off 'value-judgments' from conclusions reached in astronomical, chemical, or biological inquiries." On encountering passages of the sort, what can scientists do but smile mischievously and ask, "Over and above his *general* encomiums of scientific method, where does Dewey describe a single *specific* procedure for the experimental solution of an ethical problem?"

It is time to turn to what we call the "sober" tradition, the one to which Bacon really belonged. Whenever he came to discuss laws and lawmaking, he recalled his professional responsibility and wrote with soberness and restraint. Modernity tempered by prudence is the keynote of these pieces. Bacon finds that the philosophers who write about law are far too impractical and the lawyers who do so are far too preoccupied with the positive rules of one or two systems, that obviously the men best equipped to handle the subject are the statesmen, "who best understand the condition of civil society, welfare of the people, natural equity, customs of nations, and different forms of government," and that his own jurisprudential object must be "to go to the fountains of justice and public expediency." (Does this not remind one of Holmes?) Bacon's passages on law are replete with bright perceptions, subtle observations, and sound suggestions for reform; they draw their insights not from experiment but from experience. In point of fact, for all his fame as the great innovator and apostle of experiment, he admonishes explicitly:

> It is good also not to try experiments in states, except the necessity be urgent, or the utility evident; and well to beware that it be the reformation that draweth on the change, and not the desire of change that pretendeth the reformation.[5]

Today, I believe, the "sober" tradition is firmer and more influential than ever, particularly among the best-reputed psychologists, psychiatrists, and philosophers of science. Since the only way to repose an unlimited confidence in science is to know nothing about it, informed leaders in the respective disciplines generally exhibit an impressive modesty in their value-judgments. On occasion the modesty seems to approach agnosticism. Some of the ablest statements on the role of science and scientific philosophy have come from Professors Ernest Nagel and Hans Reichenbach.

Nagel declares it is not the primary responsibility of philosophy to direct men's actions. Philosophy's task, he says, is to provide "an astringent critique of the foundations of men's beliefs" and refine the intellectual tools which are used in evaluating proposed solutions for moral problems. Reichenbach, following Kant's sharp cleavage between cognition and volition, puts moral goals and imperatives entirely outside the realms of logic and science. (Hans Kelsen has long since made this theme familiar to lawyers.) Professor Reichenbach reserves, however, an important function for logic and science in the process of social valuation. He says that though irrelevant to the choosing of moral goals, they are quite useful in testing the implications and corollaries of moral imperatives, particularly when alternative imperatives compete for acceptance in a concrete situation.

Like many another philosophy teacher in our time, Professor Reichenbach has grown weary of students who stubbornly persist in expecting some sort of practical guidance. With arresting candor, he writes, "Whoever wants to study ethics, therefore, should not go to the philosopher; he should go where moral issues are fought out." (Here one wonders respectfully whether a motion to amend would be considered. If so, I suggest as a revised version, "Whoever wants to study ethics should not remain in the philosopher's pages or classroom; he should go where moral issues are fought out and take the philosopher with him.")

For a personal exemplar of the "sober" tradition, I find myself proposing one who is, to me at least, a most improbable choice: Sigmund Freud. Freud's utterances on many occasions were by no means entirely sober. Yet unless I misread the three volumes of Ernest Jones's great biography, there seems to have been something about the mere pendency of a concrete case in a court of law that prompted Freud to insist on the highest scientific integrity and responsibility. In 1924, at the time of the Loeb-Leopold murder case, though the *Chicago Tribune* offered him $25,000 or more to come and give his findings, Freud declined. He said with emulable dignity, "I cannot be supposed to be prepared to provide an expert opinion about persons and a deed when I have only newspaper reports to go on and have no opportunity to make a personal examination."

If I am not mistaken, Jones relates only two instances where Freud did give opinions for direct forensic use. The incidents are impressive. Both involved — as one might expect — a son's attack on a father; this was the kind of tragedy that would naturally call Freud's teachings to mind. But while the facts of the cases meet our expectations and preconceptions, can one say the same about Freud's expert opinions? To me they seem such models of level-headedness, good sense, and sobriety that I dare not hope for credence without quoting Jones's accounts in full:

[1922] in November the son of an old servant of Freud's shot his father, though not fatally, while the latter was in the act of raping the youth's half-sister. Freud did not know the youth personally, but his humanitarian nature was always moved by sympathy with juvenile delinquents. So, paying all the legal expenses himself, he engaged Dr. Valentin Teirich, the leading authority in that sphere and founder of an institution for the reform of judicial procedures in such cases, to defend the youth. He also wrote a memorandum saying that *any attempt to seek for deeper motives would only obscure the plain facts.* Professor Sträussler wrote a similar one, maintaining that the excitement of the moment caused a "short circuit" in the boy's mind which was tantamount to temporary insanity. This plea was accepted and the youth discharged.

[1931] Dr. Josef Hupka, the Professor of Jurisprudence in the University of Vienna, asked Freud to write a memorandum for him on the conclusions of the Innsbruck Medical Faculty about the case of Philipp Halsmann, who had been accused of killing his father. Hupka was engaged in defending the youth. Freud's comments concerned *the risk of taking too literally the concept of the Oedipus complex in adult life without unmistakable evidence of its operation.*

LIMITS FOR EXPERIMENTATION

I wish to suggest that, in the areas of scientific interest which impinge on government and law, there are limits to the permissibility of experimentation, that the limits are imposed by institutional factors on the one hand and moral factors on the other, and that they require much more attention and respect than lawyers, ethicists, or experimental scientists have been giving them.

In referring to *institutional* limits on experimentation, I mean merely that the characteristic purposes and methods of an institution can preclude the scientist from installing certain kinds of control and making certain kinds of trial. For example, even Bacon did not claim that when he took bribes he was only experimenting to ascertain precisely how much money would overcome a judge's sense of fairness.

One of the essential traits of legal institutions is that they can dispense neither with abstract general rules as implements nor with concrete individual transactions as subject matter. We of the law persistently invoke an authoritative generality couched in universal terms and just as persistently try to harness it to the uniqueness of *this* transaction, *this* statute, *this* controversy, *this* client. Apparently, nature, as the physicist and biologist know it, operates in an entirely different way. It seems to be heedless of the individual and to care only for the welfare of the species. Scientific philosophy, following the path of nature, has scorned or disregarded concrete individual phenomena ever since Socrates insisted that genuine knowledge pertained only to universals. Bacon put it that *philosophia individua dimittit* (philosophy discards individuals); John Dewey wrote on occasion that the word "individual" should be used only as an adjective; and the current spokesmen of analytic philosophy and symbolic logic assume the same conceptualistic stance.

These attitudes may seem curious to a sophisticated statesman or lawyer who knows that "General propositions do not decide concrete cases," that universals are futile in human affairs unless someone has sense and judgment to apply them productively, and that nothing is altogether "pure" in this world except perhaps a pure fool. Everything in the life of the law confirms William James's statement: "An infinite heterogeneity among things exists alongside of whatever likeness of kind we discover. . . ." And despite his later scientism, Dewey too, in his wisest book, *Reconstruction in Philosophy*, put an admirable emphasis on the concrete, specific situation as the proper focus for moral and social philosophy. Insights like these bring useful light to government and the administration of justice. An experienced lawyer does not hesitate to say, "Every case is like every other case and no two cases are alike."

It seems plausible that over a period of time experimental scientists will devise techniques to remove a few of the institutional impediments. For example, they may find a way to observe how jurymen act in jury rooms or how Supreme Court justices act in court conferences without impairing the freedom and spontaneity of the deliberations. But even if they achieved these difficult feats, we should still be left with the many prime individualities of the law. Law is the organ that tells a man in the present what he must do in the future because of what it decides to believe he did on some unique and unreproducible occasion in the past. What it tells him will depend in turn on a grand complex of imprecise and fluid beliefs — about past practices and decisions of its own, about present needs of the society, and about possible future consequences, projected, estimated, or simply fabricated. At its best — which can be superbly good — the whole legal process is pragmatic and empirical. Seldom is it experimentation in the scientific sense. Its objectivity is always imperfect. Indeed, for those in charge of it to follow Bacon's line and entirely "discard individuals" would be accounted no virtue on their part but a serious vice. These, then, are some of the most recalcitrant institutional limits.

The *moral* limits of experimentation have drawn less attention than they deserve. One can excuse John Dewey for being silent on the subject; he was a very old man when the world learned about Hitler Germany's satanic surgical and genocidal experiments, and he died before "brainwashing" acquired its current scientific precision and efficacy. When Dewey recommended experimentation and mentioned no limits, he simply failed to anticipate the kind of world we live in.

It is difficult to find a similar excuse for eugenicists, psychologists and others who after witnessing the spectacle of Nazi horror discern no moral problems in unlimited clinical experimentation. Of course, in the civilized societies of our day one does not resort to Nazi violence; one requests the subject of the proposed experiment to give his free consent. But can we rightly assume that when the consent is given, it is always morally acceptable?

One of the major malpractices of our era consists in the "engineering of consent." Sometimes this is effected simply by exploiting the condition of necessitous men, as in certain Indian states where thousands of consents to sexual sterilization have been purchased by offering a trivial bounty to the members of a destitute caste. Then again, consent may be "engineered" by the kind of psychologist who takes it for granted that his assistants and students will submit to experiments and implies a threat to advancement if they raise objections. Or the total community may "engineer" a consent, as when the President, the generals, and the newspapers call with loud fanfare for a heroic crew of astronautical volunteers to attempt some ultrahazardous exploit.

It is worth considering that the destitute Indians who accept payment for sterilization can at least know what they are consenting to; the psychological and astronautical subjects cannot. Moreover, though the astronauts are fairly certain of winning some species of glory, the lady who submits to hypnosis in the interest of science is certain of scarcely anything. Fortunately, there is evidence that responsible psychologists are becoming aware of the problem and are seeking to cope with it. Even a free consent must have moral limits in a society that honors human dignity and, honoring it, puts a ceiling price on truth.

Here again our reflections have strayed very little from events in Francis Bacon's fascinating career. Bacon prized experimentation with a passionate zeal that acknowledged no restraints or bounds. One cold day in the spring of 1626, while trying the experiment of preserving a chicken by stuffing it with snow, he contracted a severe chill, which a week later brought his life to an end. Thus through the manner of his death he bore witness to an unlimited faith in scientific philosophy.

Yet, we cannot help commenting, the philosophy was Bacon's own to attest, the venture his own to risk, the life his and no one else's to lose. Those who esteem the mode of his dying need not forget that as Attorney General he was one of the last English prosecutors to employ the rack. No money had been paid him to do it. In the mere hope of currying royal favor, Francis Bacon, herald of the new age of scientific experiment, artfully contrived a false charge against an old and harmless clergyman, tampered with the judges who were expected to preside at the trial, and personally interrogated the accused — the words we close with bear Bacon's signature — "before torture, in torture, between tortures and after torture."[6]

From the 1960 Annual Survey of American Law.

Drug Experiments and the Public Conscience

NOWADAYS there are many signs and traces of an increasing concern with the moral aspects of experimentation with drugs on human beings. I propose to approach the subject in the consumer perspective not only because my information and competence are limited to that capacity but also because I believe the moral position of the consumer needs special attention. In some respects, the consumer's moral responsibilities have been treated too lightly.

Though I bring no other qualifications to the discussion save perhaps a fixed disposition to take moral questions very seriously, I think I am well qualified as a consumer. Just ten years ago, when I was stricken with tuberculosis and my physician candidly informed me at the start that the outcome could not be prognosticated, I began a course of treatment with the relatively new drugs (isoniazid and P.A.S.) that had been developed for that disease. During the early months of the treatment, my best friend, the great jurist and humanitarian Jerome Frank, on one of his regular visits to my sickbed, told me the dismal news that he had become afflicted with leukemia. He added stoically, "Twenty years from now I suppose the biochemist will find a cure but it will be too late for me."

In past centuries two friends in such a position would probably have assumed that the Deity decided at the beginning of every year who should live and who should die during the twelve months to come. In our time, where else would one look but at the progress and posture of drug therapy? Whereas Judge Frank, carrying on bravely to the very end, died in January 1957, the drugs that I was given prepared my condition successfully for an operation that restored me to health. Thus I feel myself a qualified consumer on three distinct counts: (1) as one who would probably not be here at all without drug therapy, (2) as one who lost an irreplaceable friend because no known drug could cure his illness, and (3) as a citizen participating in collective social responsibility for the methods by which drug therapy develops and advances.

Looking at our subject in the consumer perspective, we have to admit that we find it vague, murky, and confused. Before proceeding further, it would be profitable to identify and remove, or at least reduce, some of the sources of the confusion. They are mainly *semantic* on the one hand and *emotional* on the other.

Let us recognize at the outset that most of the *semantic* confusion can be attributed to a rather complete change in our understanding of the term "experimentation." We are no longer in the age of Claude Bernard, nor, for that matter, in the later period when American judges in malpractice cases would castigate doctors with the phrase "experimenting on a patient." In point of fact, most of us have become sufficiently familiar with the requirements of scientific demonstration that we might insist on using some other phrase, like "trial treatment," to refer to mere empirical improvisations and innovations in the course of therapy or surgery. If we restrict the word "experiment" to the kind of systematic procedure with parallel controls that meets or approximates the requirements of scientific proof, we can avoid confusing it with various types of doctor-patient transactions that are more or less adequately covered by existing rules of professional ethics. By like token, we can avoid confusing it with the kind of trial that William James engaged in when he deliberately subjected himself to nitrous oxide gas intoxication. (Shortly after, he fluttered the academic dovecotes by announcing that the effects were strangely similar to those one got from reading Hegel.) What James did was undoubtedly interesting, but it was not a true experiment in our present-day sense.

Just as there are borderline situations in which what we may call "trial treatments" come very close to what we may call "experiments," so there are other situations in which experiments become so extensive that they approach a purposive alteration of the subject individual, or group, or population. For example, fluoridation of the water supply can be regarded as either experimentation or systematic alteration. The kind of manipulation of human beings by means of drugs that Aldous Huxley described in *Brave New World* would be a clear instance of purposive alteration. If we cannot completely separate the two concepts, we can usually distinguish one from the other.

I suggest that distinctions like these are indispensable to keeping emotionally sober in moral analysis. Our cultural history seems to indicate that proposals for changing familiar patterns of human behavior — or, as some would say, proposals for changing "human nature" — do not succeed or fail according to their rational merits but rather according to the manic or depressive condition of the general morale at the given moment. This explains the rise and fall of popular attitudes toward the genetic program outlined in Plato's *Republic* and the respective educational theories advanced by John Locke in his century and by Dewey and Watson in ours. Human plasticity looked like a glorious promise in the 1920's, became a threat by the time that Huxley published *Brave New World,* and invoked imminent horrors when Orwell wrote *1984*. The ethical factors were the same; it was the emotional morale that had changed.

There are other nonrational impediments to a sound moral analysis of our subject. On the one hand, there are elating factors such as the unmistakably great achievements of modern drug therapy, achievements so impressive and beneficent that they cannot be obscured even by the avarice of certain distributors or the shoddiness of advertising methods and promotion campaigns. There are plenty of good reasons for pride, if only it is kept sober.

But there are also deep-seated fears to reckon with, for the public has not forgotten the inhumane experiments conducted by supposedly respectable doctors in Nazi Germany. Moreover, ignorant people are likely to associate mysterious new drugs with weird magical secrets and the dangerous potions of alchemists and wizards. There is something frightening to them in the sheer power of the new therapeutic agents.

Thus, in the interest of reason, one of our first obligations is to guard against oscillations between an almost panic anxiety and an almost indifferent laxity. The thalidomide scandal initiated just such a cycle in this country, and those who claim that another such tragedy is inconceivable are as misled as those who look for it at every drug counter. A sound moral analysis ought to disregard special interests, whether governmental or industrial. To the extent that we see what is right we must declare it openly and without hesitation. As Lichtenberg said, "It is almost impossible to carry the torch of truth through a crowd without singeing someone's beard."

Although, considering the modernity of our problem, we could not expect to find much by way of guidance in an ancient source like the Bible, I think there is a certain episode in the life of King David that has distinct relevance to the morals of experimentation. We are told that King David, while waging war against the Philistines, had only a few of his best soldiers along with him, that a Philistine garrison was encamped in Bethlehem where a well of water could be found, and that David suffered from thirst and yearned audibly for a drink from the captive well. So three of his men broke through the enemy's army, drew water out of the well, and brought it back to their king. David, however, all of a sudden found himself loath to drink; he felt he could not even take a sip. Piously he poured the water upon the ground for an oblation to the Lord, saying, "Shall I drink the blood of men that went in jeopardy of their lives?"

As we see, David too had the problems of a consumer. Being not only a thirsty *man* but also a thirsty *king*, he faced a moral issue in both his individual and representative capacities, which made his predicament not dissimilar to ours. The episode seems to suggest that conscience imposes a ceiling on the human cost of social gains, even when they are most valuable and even when those who pay the cost are ready to bear it quite voluntarily.

II

The thalidomide tragedy of 1962 showed that it was not only the manufacturers and dispensers of drugs who needed to reassess their moral responsibilities. It also revealed a certain disease of hypocrisy affecting large portions of the American people. The hypocrisy manifests itself in two different but related syndromes, which for purposes of convenience we can call the "Pharaoh syndrome" and the "Pompey syndrome."

When ancient Pharaoh built a pyramid, it is possible that his more methodical overseers might have reported that the cost of construction had included some thousands or hundreds of thousands of human lives. Proper accounting would have computed these lives as part of the overall expense to the Egyptian throne; someone may even have kept comparative figures of mortalities from construction job to construction job. Be that as it may, Egyptian records do not say that anyone hesitated to expend a few, a few thousand, or a few hundred thousand workers.

Nowadays many Americans are satisfied to refer to the thalidomide episode and its consequences with some mildly regretful remarks about "the social cost of progress." To some of us, such remarks do not seem quite adequate. We suspect that it requires an authentic "Pharaoh syndrome" to convert misshapen babies with flippers for arms into mere items of "social cost." We grant, of course, that there is something conveniently impersonal about the phrase "social cost."

Of course, the Pharaoh syndrome is not restricted to developments in drug therapy; its traces can be found all through our society, perhaps most prominently in the profession of law. For example, some highly regarded American lawyers keep telling us that the United States Supreme Court ought not to interfere when legislation approved by the majority of the people persecutes the holders of unpopular political or religious views, because only by having their way and learning from their mistakes can the majority acquire the virtues of tolerance and self-restraint. What will happen to the persecuted individuals and the persecuted minorities while the majority educate themselves no one ventures to explain.

Along the same lines, Archdeacon William Paley used to insist on keeping capital punishment in force in England and extending it to a long series of offenses including petty thefts. Paley was honest enough to concede that the law might occasionally make a mistake and hang the wrong man. But he observed by way of consolation, "He who falls by a mistaken sentence may be considered as falling for his country, whilst he suffers under the operation of those rules by the general effect and tendency of which the welfare of the community is maintained and upheld." I wonder, was it Paley's theory that anyone who could swallow *that* for solace would have mighty little to lose by hanging?

The second or "Pompey syndrome" may be even more popular in this country. I have taken the name from young Sextus Pompey, who appears in Shakespeare's *Antony and Cleopatra* in an incident drawn directly from Plutarch. Pompey, whose navy has won control of the seas around Italy, comes to negotiate peace with the Roman triumvirs Mark Antony, Octavius Caesar, and Lepidus, and they meet in a roistering party on Pompey's ship. As they carouse, one of Pompey's lieutenants draws him aside and whispers that he can become lord of all the world if he will only grant the lieutenant leave to cut first the mooring cable and then the throats of the triumvirs. Pompey pauses, then replies in these words:

> *Ah, this thou shouldst have done,*
> *And not have spoke on't! In me 'tis villainy;*
> *In thee't had been good service. Thou must know*
> *'Tis not my profit that does lead mine honour;*
> *Mine honour, it. Repent that e'er thy tongue*
> *Hath so betrayed thine act; being done unknown*
> *I should have found it afterwards well done,*
> *But must condemn it now. Desist, and drink.*

Here we have the most pervasive of moral syndromes, the one most characteristic of so-called respectable men in a civilized society. To possess the end and yet not be responsible for the means, to grasp the fruit while disavowing the tree, to escape being told the cost until someone else has paid it irrevocably: this is the Pompey syndrome and the chief hypocrisy of our time. In the days of the outcry against thalidomide, how much of popular indignation might be attributed to this same syndrome; how many were furious because their own lack of scruple had been exposed! So many did not really care, did not even want to know what the new drugs might cost in terms of human injuries and fatalities. The dispensers of thalidomide had outraged the public by breaking an unwritten law — the law against interrupting the public's enjoyment of fruits with disagreeable revelations about the tree and the soil where the fruits have grown.

It is worth remembering that our descendants (assuming there are any) will study us as we study our predecessors under the headings of history and anthropology. Posterity will not fail to recognize the Pharaoh and Pompey syndromes in the behavior of our contemporary public. As we in our day can smile condescendingly at the primitives and ancients who practiced human sacrifice for what they considered to be the general good of the tribe or nation, future generations may ask how we could make human sacrifice more acceptable in our day by calling it "social cost." At least the ancients were honest; they called a spade a spade even when it was used to bury a human statistic of "social cost."

I suggest that on every side we need a more truthful and realistic set of attitudes if the development of new drugs is not to impose a general and intolerable burden of guilt. Though laws and regulations governing the distribution of experimental drugs are indispensable, their efficacy will largely depend on the fundamental attitudes of those who administer them, those who are subject to them, and those for whose protection they are enacted. Humaneness and safety require legislation but cannot be legislated. The attitudes to be cultivated must be rational, self-critical, and soberly responsible. I shall mention only a few specific applications; the bulk of the subject has been analyzed by others, particularly by Irving Ladimer in several fine articles.

When an experimenter with new drugs evinces a rational and responsible attitude, he has no need to resort to heroics or histrionics. For example, if he and his advisory panel find it necessary to employ a so-called double-blind procedure, which everyone concedes will increase the hazards of experimentation, he may be able to restrict the risk by rigorously assuming the very worst during the course of the experiment, that is, by assuming that each and every subject actually received the new drug and that there is imminent danger of toxicity and harmful side-effects in every instance.

As we approve of assumptions like these because they illustrate the attitude of responsibility, we may disapprove of the self-administration of untested drugs because it illustrates the resort to histrionics. If the director of an experiment has so little reputation for integrity that he can prove his good faith only by ingesting the drug himself, he is scarcely qualified for the post. Moreover, if the consent of the subjects can be obtained only through watching him as he tries the drug on himself, it is clearly not a willing and understanding consent.

There are many reasons to believe that, in general, experiments on human beings have been conducted in this country with a very high measure of prudence and caution. In point of fact, the average American consumer would have no misgivings about attitudes in the drug field if the drug companies, including the most respectable among them, had not so zealously resisted Senator Kefauver's bill that became the Drug Amendments of 1962. From the outset the resistance inspired a certain distrust. It seemed to be prompted by profit motives more than by concern for scientific advance. Then the thalidomide scandal broke, and the general clamor precipitated enactment of the Kefauver proposals, since which time, despite all the previous moanings of the companies' experts, the public has not noticed that scientific progress has halted or, for that matter, that drug companies are operating at a financial loss. Attitudes do vary from laboratory to laboratory and from company to company, and it would be unfair for us to generalize.

Nevertheless, on merely reading the Food and Drug Commissioner's regulations adopted pursuant to the 1962 Amendments, one is bound to notice that they throw little light on the moral problems of experimentation. In the first place, the regulations are expressly designed to protect the drug-consuming public, not the subjects of trials and experiments. In the second place, they allow the investigator in a specific situation to decide, according to his own professional judgment, that it is not feasible or that it is contrary to the best interests of subjects to obtain their or their representatives' consent to an experiment. I submit that it would be morally inexcusable for an investigator to act as judge in his own case and make such a decision alone. He can scarcely be a proper arbiter of the subjects' interest when they come into conflict with the progress of his enterprise, his career, and his professional zeal. In the third place, the commissioner's regulations say little or nothing about the conditions and limits of consent, that is, the conditions under which consent can be regarded as acceptable and the limits beyond which consent is morally nugatory.

One thing is clear: the conditions and limits of consent to human experimentation cannot be left entirely to statutes, regulations, and court decisions. In England there is no legislation specifically governing such questions, and in the United States the provisions are mainly peripheral. Yet the validity of consent has decisive moment in a consumer perspective. In all probability, there is no aspect of scientific research that the public can comprehend with equal clarity, which means that there is no aspect in which the public bears a clearer share of moral responsibility.

III

First there are the *conditions* of an acceptable consent. All writers agree that the consent must be "intelligent," which means, I suppose, that it must follow some sort of understanding of the procedure that is contemplated and the risks that are incurred. Though the writers do not discuss how intelligent a consenting subject must be, we may assume that if he does not realize that all experiments on human beings involve a wide margin of variability and unpredictability, he is not fit to give a valid consent. Nor is he sufficiently intelligent if he does not understand that, among the hazards of experimentation with a new drug, he must take account of his being deprived of some so-called tried and true remedy, the performance of which the investigator hopes to surpass. In accepting consents, a medical investigator ought to feel his moral duty with peculiar sensibility because, no matter how categorically the law or the professional code may assure him that he bears no doctor-patient relation to the consenting subject, the subject's attitude simply disregards all such distinctions. The law and the code to the contrary notwithstanding, he will rely on the doctor as *his* doctor.

This consideration does not make consents impossible to obtain and accept. It does serve to bar them when the parties stand in a previous confidential relationship to each other. Consequently, students should not be accepted as subjects except in institutions unrelated to their present or prospective studies, nor should employees be accepted unless their employer has no proximate interest in the investigation. Reasonable compensations for serving as subjects are entirely warranted provided they do not operate to purchase or coerce an unwilling consent, particularly from those who are poor or in hospital wards or derelict. It is clearly wrong to purchase the consents of prisoners by offering them a release or parole or any equivalent inducement that exercises a coercive effect. There is not much to say for a society that sends a burglar to prison for ten years and gives him to understand that he can be free in five if he subjects himself to medical experiments.

The investigator who desires a tranquil conscience must ultimately satisfy himself that the purported consents on which he acts are understanding and real. His scientific zeal should not blind him to the fact that certain individuals seek to become subjects for neurotic or masochistic motives. When motives like these come to his attention, he need not reject the consent; he need only make certain that it is based on a reasonably stable understanding rather than a violent and momentary impulse. If we were bound to reject every act and transaction in our society that might have a neurotic incentive, not much would remain for use.

This brings us to the consideration of certain situations in which even an understanding and intelligent consent will be morally unacceptable. Sometimes a consent will be unacceptable because of extrinsic circumstances that convert it into an exploitation of sickness or need, for example, the consents to irreversible sterilization that certain states in India have been purchasing from untouchables for small sums of money. At other times, a consent is unacceptable because of intrinsic circumstances, that is, circumstances having to do with the prospective consequences of the experiment and their relation to human dignity. One can conceive conditions under which a consent might be acceptable even where the experiment might involve a serious risk of death. Where however the experiment involves a serious risk of permanent physical or psychic mutilation, the consent should not be accepted. For example, a consent would be unacceptable if the experiment involved a serious risk of converting a subject who was mentally normal into a psychotic. On the other hand, as every physician knows, there are psychiatric conditions grievous or critical enough to warrant even the risk of psychic mutilation, but in such conditions the justification for taking the risk must be found in the possible benefit to the ailing subject, not alone in his consent or in possible increment of scientific knowledge.

The limits of acceptable consent will vary according to the society's evaluation of human life and dignity. Not long ago, Pope Pius XII stated that no person has the right to "involve his physical or psychic integrity in medical experiments or research when they entail serious destruction, mutilation, wounds or perils." In the same statement, reliance was placed on the theological distinction between a person's possessing a right of "use" and his lacking a right of "ownership" in his body, the inference being that what a person does not own, he cannot yield to another. I suppose that John Locke would have put the notion in different, natural-law terms and declared that a man does own his own body but he owns it inalienably. For my part, these analogies to the legal concepts of property titles seem, at best, merely redundant, like declaring that such and such a drug induces sleep because of its dormitive quality.

At worst the introduction of property-law analogies can be quite misleading. Though it is true that we have a right to use our bodies, the "use" has to be restricted; we certainly cannot use them entirely as we please or without moral limits. As for the legal concept of "owner-ship," it varies so much from legal system to legal system and from time to time that natural law can scarcely draw on it to deduce fixed moral principles, particularly when human dignity is at stake.

With all due respect, these analogies seem to approach the problem at the wrong end. As I see it, it is not primarily a question of what a subject can consent to, for under sufficiently extreme circumstances he may insist that he can consent to almost anything, and who has the right to contradict him without having had personal experience of just such circumstances? The moral impossibility is on the other side, *our* side. It is we who *cannot accept* certain consents that are ostensibly free and voluntary; it is we who are unable to accept a profit from human sacrifice. The ceiling price that we impose on scientific progress is the product of our own moral self-image, our enduring convictions and our social conscience.

Since the moral problems attached to experiment on human beings arise in highly specific and variable circumstances, the investigator will rarely find an easy formulary answer. Experience has shown the wisdom of consulting a group or panel of colleagues, who may not only assist in structuring the experiment but also influence its developing course. None of us can claim impartiality in his own enterprises; we all do well to seek detached, objective, and disinterested judgment. Merely as a matter of self-protection, the investigator ought regularly to seek outside counsel.

The practice of acting under group or panel supervision seems to have become quite general among scientists. The safeguards it affords, though highly desirable, are scarcely infallible; a researcher may find that his colleagues lack interest in the experiment, or they may lack moral sensibility, or they may unintentionally engage in a sort of logrolling maneuver, giving acquiescence in the expectation of receiving it from him for their own procedures. The advice of the appropriate committee of the American Medical Association is another available safeguard in doubtful cases, and presumably a trustworthy one as to scientific methods and definable risks.

It is however quite obvious that whatever else the American Medical Association may claim, it does not and cannot claim expertness in the resolution of moral problems. If, as we have indicated, the urgent need is to consider the problems of drug therapy in the consumer perspective, such an undertaking necessarily transcends the competence of the scientific professions. Saying this does not disparage the moral sensibilities of any group; the point is rather that since the consuming public takes the risk of becoming morally implicated in experiments on human beings, scientists alone cannot give the final answers or bear the entire responsibility. For these reasons, I recommend using a mixed panel to evaluate doubtful cases. Whether the adding of laymen would result in wiser moral decisions one cannot predict. What one can predict is that if, in morally debatable cases, the supervisory panel were to include one or two laymen, scientists would be protected against the severest peril that a decent human being is likely to encounter, that is, the peril of defending what is destructive and wrong because it is familiar, because one has become accustomed to it. The good things a man does can be made complete only by the things he refuses to do.

*An address delivered at Johns Hopkins University, November 1963,
and published in* Drugs in Our Society,
Johns Hopkins University Press, *1964.*

9

THE MEANING OF JUSTICE

*W*HEN *Edmond Cahn died on August 9, 1964, he left the unfinished manuscript of what was to have been his fourth book —*
The Meaning of Justice. *He had completed two chapters and part of a
third, which may have been the most important because it bore the
same title as the book itself. This chapter began with an example of a
gross injustice — the prosecution of an innocent woman for a crime
which never existed. When he had completed this section he wrote, in
his own hand, the heading of the next section of this chapter in which
he was attempting to define justice. The heading was "The Sense of
Injustice," which was, of course, the title of his first book.*

*In this beginning to a study of justice, Edmond Cahn was continu-
ing to apply the same consumer perspective which he had used in his
earlier books to explore the workings of the law. In his notes which he
left with the manuscript he wrote, "Justice is not a collection of
principles or criteria. . . . Justice is the active process of the preventing or repairing of injustice." His notes indicate that he was
developing other examples of public and private wrongs in order to
show how, in the process of correcting these wrongs, justice could be
done. The remaining chapter headings included "Justice in Legal
Analysis," "Justice in Negotiations" and "Justice Between Nations" —
all reflecting a concern with justice as an active process.*

*The unfinished manuscript, which appears in this chapter, evokes a
sense of sadness and wonder as we contemplate the unwritten pages.
But Edmond Cahn's own words — "contemplation bakes no loaves" —
quickly break the reverie. All of his writings, including this unfinished book, command us to return to the world of the present, for
justice will be done when ". . . the sense of injustice stirs once more
and calls men again to gird themselves."*

N. R.

Justice in Disfavor

FOR about two hundred years, philosophers and jurists have been depreciating the concept of justice. To some of them it seems redundant, to others flatulent and hypocritical. Still others declare that it is a word without shape or meaning and a mere emission of noise.

There are various ingenious ways to disparage a term if one has a mind to, and even to banish it from systematic discourse. To disparage justice, one need only yoke it to some other value that runs through one's philosophy — as David Hume does when he insists that "public utility is the *sole* origin of justice." Though this sort of treatment does not quite deprive the word of meaning, it leaves it close to superfluous, for if justice has no merit or significance save in utility to the public or, as others argue, in equality before the law, will not discriminating thinkers avoid using it and employ a term that is more precise and candid?

For candor too is at stake here, along with precision. If the criterion you really intend to put forward is public utility, or legal equality, or perhaps judicial objectivity, you can be charged with confusing the issue when you wave a cloak-word like "justice" — a cloak-word men use all too freely in order to divert attention from their own selfish purposes and hidden interests. Repeated often enough, the abuse may eventually compromise the use. Some socialists like Marx and Engels go so far as to contend that all talk of "justice" is mere abuse, that the very notion behind the word originated in men's assuming that an exchange should be "just" or "equal" when they bartered one commodity for another during primitive eras, and that, under modern conditions of industrial production, people who prate of justice are only seeking to provide a mask for capitalist exploitation. Hence it is that justice is an unfamiliar and uncharacteristic term in the legal literature of the Soviet Union. Soviet jurists commend a quite different standard, that is, "socialist legality," which is perhaps as high as a totalitarian society can ever aspire.

Nevertheless, the very making of a charge of hypocrisy would be vain if justice did not possess some remnant of practical meaning. Appearance cannot be used to disguise reality unless it has some substance, however sleazy, of its own. This much Marx and Engels impliedly concede to the concept of justice, and so too does the great utilitarian reformer Jeremy Bentham when he deems it, as he usually does, a mere facade for sinister interests.

Yet, on occasion, resistance to his reforms must make Bentham feel especially provoked, because we see him throw off his customary restraint. In such a mood, he declares that the name of "justice" has no substantive meaning at all, it is only a way "of intimating that a man is firmly persuaded of the truth of this or that moral proposition, though he either thinks he *need not,* or finds he *can't,* tell *why.*" This amounts to absolute rejection, which in our own day Alf Ross, an eminent Danish jurist, matches by saying: "To invoke justice is the same thing as banging on the table."

The selfsame period that saw justice decline so sharply among philosophers saw it rise dramatically in the discourse and affairs of almost everyone else. Bloody and cruel though the two centuries were, no previous era could rival their outpouring of declarations, manifestos and angry demands for justice, solemn guarantees, administrative provisions and institutional implementations for justice, election campaigns, mass uprisings and wars of independence for justice, international organizations and tribunals for preventive and punitive justice — a worldwide and irrepressible outcry for individual, social and transnational justice. Justice loudly demanded and sometimes won for the rights of women and children, religious minorities and labor unions, slaves and peons and serfs, injured and underpaid and unemployed workers, aliens and disenfranchised citizens, farmers and tenant-farmers, aged persons, unwed mothers and so-called "illegitimate" offspring, indigent persons in the courts, the blind and needy and sick, ethnic and racial minorities, Ireland and India and Israel and the colonial peoples on every continent, the congenitally handicapped and mentally disordered, political dissenters and conscientious objectors, the illiterate and ill-housed, and the survival-rights of future generations — all in all, justice has been a rather consequential word in the mouth of the common man.

In every free country, the ablest lawyers consciously inject considerations of justice when arguing their cases, the soundest judges seek to demonstrate that their decisions are not only correct but essentially just, and the most competent executives strive continually to maintain a public image of fair-dealing and justice. Peoples and nations stoutly declare that they regard justice as their highest interest; they insist on having it accorded to them; and they consent to being condemned and charged with reparations whenever they acknowledge that they have offended it. True, they may use the term loosely or hypocritically, as men often do when they talk about "life," "good," "love," "truth" or — for that matter — "utility"; nevertheless, all feel quite certain that justice possesses a meaning which no one can afford to dispense with.

This book* deals with the one meaning of justice that touches human beings most directly. Of course, there are many meanings to the word. Like other terms of ramified reference, justice has no single "true" definition; common usage speaks quite properly of a "justice" on the bench and of the "justice" of a tidy phrase or a good man's character. All the same, among the multitude of available meanings there is one that functionally surpasses the others; whether in discourse, action, or pedagogic influence, it is best of all because it serves human interests best. Our next two chapters define justice in this most functional of its meanings, and subsequent chapters portray it at work in the processes of law, the transactions of morals, and the destinies of nations.

The Shift to a Consumer Perspective

TRADITIONAL ACCEPTATIONS

W HY is it that able minds of some two centuries have turned against the concept of justice and denigrated it? How account for the wide gap between justice according to the philosophers (a superfluous if not entirely irrelevant term) and justice according to the people (a vital necessity of their lives)? Surely the authors we have mentioned have not been callous to ideal values, nor have they been preaching the kind of academic cynicism that certain professors affect in every generation in order to impress unsophisticated students. If men of the caliber of Hume, Bentham and Marx shock us by disparaging justice, it is not because they are engaged in striking classroom poses. It is rather because the conceptions of justice which they find about them are genuinely inadequate.

Yet inadequacy is not total worthlessness, nor is the inadequate

* This refers to Edmond Cahn's unfinished book *The Meaning of Justice.*

beneath esteem. In drawing on our legacy from the past, there is nothing easier to dismiss with ridicule than what is still partly true and suggestive. Consider, for example, the old folklore story about the blind men of India who go to discover what an elephant is like. Yes, it is simple and familiar but let us look before we smile it away. According to one version, the blind men are four in number and they feel the elephant's leg, tail, ear, and body respectively and announce that an elephant is like a log, a rope, a fan, and a thing without beginning or end (or, as some say, like a wall). In other versions, a fifth blind Indian, who encounters the tusk, says that an elephant is like a spear, and a sixth, who feels the trunk, insists that an elephant is like a snake.

Surely here is a neat parable full of hints for philosophy. In all its undertakings, philosophy seems to consist in nothing else than showing wherein each of the blind men of India is wrong and then showing wherein each of them is right. Each of the accounts is demonstrably false in so far as it takes a mere part for the whole beast and nevertheless each is demonstrably true in so far as it reports the part accurately. To a man unlucky enough to be impaled on an elephant's tusk the beast is indeed very like a spear and he feels little interest in the rest of its attributes. Concededly, it is proper fun to refute a partial, inadequate conception like his but the fun will be wasteful unless one searches the conception for its elements of truth.

In our study of justice, the old Indian parable provides a second hint. It invites us to notice that the elephant must have been lying still or the blind men would not have been able to examine him. Their reports show clearly that he was immobile the whole time and they were safe. This circumstance can make a profound difference to the meaning of any subject. As we shall soon see, old conceptions will no longer suffice and new conceptions will be required if the subject should somehow stir, rise and move.

Keeping these hints in mind, we can go on to inspect the main conceptions of justice and see why they have failed to satisfy many modern thinkers. This we can do without tracing the chronological details of the subject.[1] Here we need only consider the acceptations that have proved most influential:

That Justice Is the Division of Labor in a Political State According to Fitness. In this view the function of justice is to maintain social equilibrium and rational coordination, which it does by assigning each class of citizens an appropriate task and by forbidding them to trespass on the tasks of other classes. Plato's *Republic* presented such an acceptation, which still deserves consideration. While Plato would have used the principle of division of labor hierarchically to exclude all except the guardian class from the affairs of government, there is no reason why we cannot use it democratically to exclude the officers of government from the people's private affairs. If, as he thought, it is an effective shield against busybodies, can we not hold it as a shield against official busybodies? Surely if fitness is to be the measure of authority, we can rightly insist that no official is fit to censor beliefs or books.

In the *Republic* Plato wrote of justice with consummate thoughtfulness and eloquence. The eloquence set a dangerous example for lesser minds. Endeavoring to imitate it, a typical modern orator will inhale deeply and eulogize justice in a stream of reckless superlatives, declaiming with a wide sweep of the arm that it and it alone is "the sole end" of government and law. Listeners clap dutifully at the right places though most of them realize that government and law, which every society requires to serve a multitude of purposes, simply cannot have a single end. They may remember that, only a short time before, the selfsame speaker was declaring — likewise to applause — that "the sole end" of government and law was to maintain order in the community or encourage economic enterprise or provide social welfare or foster individual fulfillment or perhaps preserve civil liberties. If one takes pronouncements like these literally, one can feel as provoked as Bentham, but if one takes them the way a sensible woman takes her lover's compliments and impossible promises — for the ritualistic ululations that they really are — one can understand the audience's indulgence and avoid confusing "justice" entwined in bunting with "justice" in the responsible discourse of law and morals. Certainly Plato did not confuse the two.

In Plato's view of justice, one can see the traits that have characterized the concept ever since: it is equilibrial, abstract, rather static — and, above all, politically safe. If Plato is correct and justice implies that nonruling classes must attend strictly to their duties and let the ruling class attend to the duties of government, what philosophy could be more convenient for despots and their officers? No wonder that the *Republic* seems in every age to rationalize the more intelligent despotisms and the more audacious plans to manipulate human beings. At bottom, there can never be anyone fit for such absolute power over his fellows as a philosopher may wield in the hours of abstract reverie.

That Justice Is a Condition of the Psyche — Either Volitional or Emotional. Here again it was Plato who made the initial contribution by asserting that justice was "writ small" in the individual psyche whenever reason maintained an equilibrium there such as the guardians maintain in an ideal political state. Whatever its shortcomings, this acceptation has the advantage of recognizing that justice must somehow involve both reason and emotion — an insight in which Plato is wiser than modern authors who purport to reduce it to one or the other exclusively.

Improving on Plato's notion, which appeared to stress a merely internal order of harmony, Aristotle suggested that, while justice might be an internal condition, it looked directly toward the outside world and objective behavior. According to him, justice is an (internal) "state of mind" or "state of character" that disposes one to perform (external) just actions and behave in a just manner and desire what is just. This psychic acceptation has a progeny that continues with minor variations through such prestigious figures as Cicero, Ulpian, and Thomas Aquinas down to the present day. Ulpian's version, long the standard among lawyers, reads: "Justice is the steady and unceasing *disposition* to render to every man his due." (*Justitia est constans et perpetua* voluntas *jus suum cuique tribuendi*.) All of these are volitional acceptations of justice.

To them we may add the strictly emotional acceptations. The emotional acceptations offered by Bentham and Ross, which as we have already seen are entirely negative, need not detain us; if justice had no more intellectually respectable usage than they assume, we should probably agree with them in dismissing it. For a really ingenious instance of an emotional acceptation, we turn rather to John Stuart Mill in his capacity of thoroughgoing utilitarian. Mill subsumes justice to utility, making "the just" only a special genus or class of "the useful." Justice, he says, is merely a name for certain social utilities that are the most vital and imperative to human well-being. "It has always been evident that all cases of justice are also cases of expediency: the difference is in the peculiar sentiment which attaches to the former, as contradistinguished from the latter."

In this fashion, Mill, who provides several keen insights concerning our subject, tries to enclose the whole of it in a corner of the utilitarian domain. His fences can hardly stand the strain. He finds himself compelled to hold that whenever two men advance opposite and irreconcilable claims concerning what is just, "Social utility alone can decide the preference."

As an example, Mill says that if A contends that our courts act unjustly in punishing an offender not for his own sake but for the sake of the example to others, and if B claims the opposite, then since we cannot conclusively refute either of them, we must turn to social utility for a final criterion. But what sort of reasoning is this? Is it not the very essence of A's contention that in such cases the courts' action is unjust precisely *because* it follows the line of social utility (the example to others)? How can justice, which Mill asks us to identify with utility in its most vital and indispensable manifestations, be adjudged according to some other — and necessarily lesser — type of utility? Suppose John, a slave, contends that involuntary servitude is unjust while William, his owner, contends that it is just; is it credible that Mill would merely remit them and us to some criterion of social utility? We must try to think better of him.

This much, at least, we can infer about all of the psychic acceptations of justice: that in so far as they direct attention to volitional and emotional phenomena they are clearly correct and in so far as they halt at the threshold of external behavior they are clearly inadequate. A good state of mind or will or character that does not stir out of doors is too bland an acceptation. Tyrants and crooked officials would sleep well at night if they could persuade the world that "justice" involved no more than that.

That Justice Is Conformity with Law. In this view, which incidentally numbers among its exponents as esteemed and rigorous an ethicist as Immanuel Kant, whatever meets the precepts of law is just and whatever violates them is unjust. Fixing the standard of justice as it generally does according to the text of a constitution, a treaty, a statute, a judicial norm, or an administrative regulation, it may be called a "textual" acceptation. Obey the authoritative command and you do justice.

When we come to assess this acceptation, we find our task suddenly reversed. With other traditional notions of justice, it has been necessary to indicate the precise reasons for their unsuitability or inadequacy; here — because most people recoil too quickly from a textual acceptation and dismiss it out of hand — we are obliged to show how it makes sense at all. Long centuries of arbitrary, oligarchic, and unjust laws have created the general impression that justice and law are vastly disparate and that the main task of justice is to expose wrongful precepts in the law, resist their enforcement, and bring about their repeal. If laws and regulations can be cruel and unjust as some of them palpably are, how can anyone dare to equate what is just with what is legal? Such a doctrine would be fit for the citizens of a totalitarian state or for sheep.

Nevertheless, it has certain merits which we can by no means afford to overlook. For one thing, in a modern democratic society, the overwhelming majority of moral wrongs and injustices that officials may inflict on individuals or groups are legal wrongs as well and violations of express legal texts. The fact that texts do not automatically enforce themselves does not make them worthless. Surely there is nothing to blame in a text when it guarantees the poor man a fair and equal trial in court, guarantees the Negro child an equal opportunity for education, guarantees the vagrant that policemen will not beat him, and guarantees the Jewish worker that personnel managers will not discriminate against him; do not many of the severest social wrongs of our society consist precisely in dishonoring textual guarantees like these? When citizens protest against some official oppression or government scandal, it is much more often because the provisions of a legal text have not been obeyed than because they have. There are, of course, statutory texts that are unjust and cause grievous wrongs but they are quite few in comparison with the wrongs caused by failing to enforce just texts or by enforcing them unjustly. Take, for example, a case where the police and the prosecutor knowingly send an innocent man to prison for committing a robbery or a murder. Surely such a man does not complain against the laws forbidding robbery or murder, which he would concede to be entirely just, but rather against their being applied unjustly to him.

Without making a fetish of written texts, we have to own that they constitute our main technique for holding judges responsible for rational decisions. A judge untethered by a text is a dangerous instrument. The wisest and most honorable men on the bench, knowing this, can be seen searching continually for textual guides which will direct them and prevent their judgments from appearing like arbitrary acts of will. As for mediocre judges, they need textual discipline a hundredfold, which is why modern statutes seem so very complex and technical. The tedious clauses and minute details are necessary reflections on the general quality of judges. But if distrust of the judiciary is carried too far and causes too much particularizing, literalism may infect the bench and reduce the judges to automatons.

For this dilemma Aristotle offered a solution which he called "equity." Since a legislator framing laws can only lay down general prescriptions without regard to unusual or peculiar situations, equity empowers the judge to rectify the law when an unforeseen or deviant case arises. In such a case equity restores the troubled balance of justice. It does not presume to ignore or nullify the law; on the contrary, it too belongs to law, supplying a legal corrective for an excess of legal generalization. Once one recognizes the emollient influence of equity as immanent and potential *within* the law, it does not seem quite so odd to say that justice consists in conforming to law.

Yet, after all concessions have been made, our first unfavorable impression persists. We simply cannot acquiesce. Reason, experience, and history bring forward too many instances where a precept of law, far from serving as a fit model for justice, implements religious bigotry, oppresses the poor, or exploits the weak, where the consistent obscurantism of legal censorship belies every libertarian promise, and where custom is too rigid, phraseology too meticulous, and the bench too wooden to allow the slightest room for equity. There are too many human concerns where the more one gets of law, the more one suffers of injustice. The law is not thoroughly civilized anywhere. Justice would be tame indeed if it took all its goods and moved meekly into the house of legality.

That Justice Is Conformity with Natural Law. This is an ancient and widespread doctrine and it is unfortunate that, except for asserting that natural law exists and is discoverable by human reason, its adherents agree with one another on nothing else about it. Even within a single group they conflict extensively; for example, though Thomas Aquinas astutely points out all the contingent, local, customary, and ethnic factors that make natural law precepts highly variable in concrete cases, many writers who claim to follow his teachings ignore these reservations and declare that the precepts they happen to favor are universal, accessible to every man's reason, and forever immutable. There are almost as many notions of natural law as authors on the subject, and their differences are often diametrical. Since the precepts they offer consist mainly of moral rules and maxims (including many quite sound ones), it seems strange that they should have to call the entire fabric of the cosmos, especially the stars, to vouch for them. Calling moral principles "natural laws" does not seem very helpful, particularly when the immoral acts they forbid — like murder, robbery, incest, and sodomy — are so evidently natural.

While some of the ablest natural law writers regard "natural" precepts as mere ideal criteria by which to appraise a system of positive law, others say that natural law, being on a higher plane, nullifies unjust positive law completely, and still others (Thomas Aquinas among them) take a middle position, holding that the people must remain orderly and submit to an unjust law unless it violates divine law as interpreted by the church.

Historically, natural law has been invoked to support every conceivable doctrine from anarchic freedom to feudal oligarchy, and from social utopianism to the ethics of the jungle. John Locke employed it to rationalize the English Revolution of 1688, and Americans followed his lead in the Declaration of Independence. Whatever its defects, it will not become entirely obsolete as long as positive law fails to fill serious gaps. Its vocabulary may likely be heard whenever a regime begins to topple and a revolution requires a slogan. It is also convenient as a medium of international communication about basic human rights.

Yet when due honor has been paid, natural law remains today what it always has been in its most prominent versions – not a conception of justice but an assertion of political claims and pretensions. For if natural law is conceded the power to nullify positive law, the institution or man who has authority to lay down the natural law can thereby determine the law of the land. Precepts of natural law, once accepted from such a source, become immutable positive laws which all citizens must obey. No political authority could conceivably be more absolute or less democratic.

There is a vast difference between invoking natural law as one risks one's life during a revolution and invoking it to control particular acts of legislation in times of order and stability. The "natural" laws of revolution are like bayonets – as Napoleon said, not to be sat on. When the American Revolution was over and the people set up free governments, they swiftly composed bills of rights, federal and state, to convert so-called "natural" rights (and some other rights like trial by jury) into explicit and enforceable positive guarantees. They put their trust not in natural law but in positive constitutions, positive guarantees, and a government that would stand responsible to the people.

How right they were in these arrangements our own century has demonstrated. Under Hitler and Mussolini the German and Italian judges – extensively educated and indoctrinated though they were in natural law – did not once attempt to use it as a shield to defend the victims of racism and genocide. Servile and complaisant, they nullified nothing except the hope of justice. Currently, in the Republic of South Africa the judges are confronted with racist statutes of outrageous cruelty, and although some have bravely done what they could by way of palliation, none has ventured to nullify an enactment in the name of natural law. They too have shown that natural law is futile in an ongoing legal order, that it is weakest when men need it most.

The exclusive reliance on reason is one of the debilitating features of natural law, for reason, pure and unalloyed as we are told it must be, can do nothing but ask questions, engender doubts, and sketch static diagrams. The conformity of positive law to some pattern or other of "natural" precepts is an inert relation – fit to draw in a cool study and contemplate at ease. Natural law abstractions may be apt at rationalizing a revolution that is already under way or long since finished, but they cannot heat men's heads to start one. They do not move or impel. Nor do they furnish a judge with the materials he needs to defend his personal honor and official integrity when he is required to enforce a cruel statute. Thus, despite all its ramified history, the doctrine of natural law can scarcely disturb a modern despot if he feels secure in other respects.

THE OLD PERSPECTIVE AND THE NEW

It is startling to consider that for about two thousand years — from Aristotle's death to the seventeenth and eighteenth centuries — the classic philosophers of justice developed their theories while living under stern republican oligarchies, tyrannies, kingdoms, and empires. Aristotle himself, whose comprehensive treatment of the subject still remains the wisest and best of all, saw the close of an age and the twilight of Athenian democracy. During the next two millennia, while the liberty of philosophers to express their ideas might vary greatly from time to time and place to place, no one enjoyed the liberty of forming his basic ideas in a democratic milieu. In describing justice, some might use terms that seem tediously static and safe to us because they wished to please the prince, others because they hoped to instruct him, and still others because all the polities they saw about them or could imagine as likely to emerge in the world were strictly imperial, tyrannical or oligarchic.

This circumstance, of course, left distinct marks on their thinking. Almost inevitably it gave them a fixed and characteristic way of looking at justice, which was the imperial or official perspective. In shaping their notions of justice, they tacitly assumed a point of view that would be appropriate to a monarch or his ministers. It was only with the democratic revolutions of the seventeenth and eighteenth centuries that old acceptations, subjected to new tests and strains, came to appear more and more unsatisfactory. Consequently, when Hume and Bentham took the lead and disparaged the familiar appeals to "justice," they were actually recording the earth-tremors of a new epoch. The elephant, as it were, had risen and started to move.

Since the old imperial or official perspective is still evident almost everywhere, we need to understand the nature of its influence. For one thing, it is not necessarily cruel or oppressive in purpose. On the contrary, a ruler who employs it may act with entirely benevolent motives. . . .

Civilized men have retained the imperial perspective so long that they still find nothing incongruous in idealizing a ruler, whether divine or human, as a "good shepherd" of his flock, the people. They do not pause to consider in whose interest and for what eventual fate a shepherd — even the best of shepherds — tends and leads a flock.

The perspective men take goes a long way toward determining what values they will prize and preserve and what values they will merely tolerate and, if necessary, annul in their judgments. Rulers and jurists who adopt the imperial or official perspective evince a special predilection for keeping order and getting things done. Obedience, security, efficiency, and tangible results are their criteria. Should they consider justice at all, they would be prone to think of it in its equilibrial role; they would picture it as the repose the law produced in the scales when it returned a missing or stolen piece of property to its previous owner. But it would be only the preexisting equilibrium that their notion of justice would prompt them to restore, and how that particular equilibrium might have come about in the first instance would be no concern of theirs. Hence in former days they would restore the equilibrium with the same firmness and efficiency whether the missing item happened to be a stolen cow or a fugitive slave, and in our time they would find a certain aesthetic fitness in inflicting capital punishment for homicide because it seems to balance the account.

Most characteristic of those who use the imperial or official perspective has always been their quantitative way of valuing human rights. They measure efficiency by statistics and success by averages. Suppose, for example, statistics show that it would be easier to convict persons of crimes if police officers could enter private homes at will or arrest passersby who looked "suspicious"; they would loudly demand such a course, seeing only its wholesale results and caring little about its retail oppressions. Willingly such men would purchase order and safety, at least in the more elegant parts of the city, at the price of occasional awkward incidents of judges taking bribes, prosecutors using the third degree, or policemen beating their prisoners. Once in a while, if an innocent man is sent to prison or the electric chair, adherents of the old imperial or official perspective may be heard assuring him (or his widow) that the established system has a commendable average of performance and miscarries very seldom. This does not seem quite adequate.

Nevertheless, the old perspective still prevails almost everywhere among philosophers and jurists. After all, since mere statistics of miscarriages in the courts express no cruelty in themselves, one begins to discover cruelty in them only when one looks behind the aggregates and notices the individual cases as single instances. Yet how can modern philosophers be expected to do anything so unscientific as take single instances into account? A single instance is to a strictly scientific philosophy what a speck of dust is to a brand-new shoe; one brushes it off.

As for jurists, there is nothing that most of them scorn so thoroughly as a "naive" anxiety about the outcome of particular instances or cases. A system of government and law, they insist, would be no system at all if it were not impersonal, objective and indifferent. If it meets its social purposes over the long run, it works well enough for them. Accordingly, H. L. A. Hart, professor of jurisprudence at Oxford, says: "Justice constitutes one segment of morality primarily concerned not with individual conduct but with the ways in which *classes* of individuals are treated." In a related vein, Roscoe Pound, long the dean of Harvard Law School and American jurisprudence, writes that there are four "standpoints" from which to look at the law in the sense of a body of authoritative precepts, i.e., the standpoints of the lawmaker, the judge, the counselor, and the individual subject to the precepts. Then Pound declares his choice among the standpoints: "Can the different ideas reached from these four standpoints be unified? I submit that they can. They can be unified in terms of the idea from the standpoint of the judge." Here, one infers, is the reason why he entitles his fine book *Justice According to Law*. It would require a distinctly different standpoint and perspective to expound "Law According to Justice."

The new perspective, product of the democratic revolution that is still gaining momentum in our day, began to emerge during the seventeenth and eighteenth centuries. As the old point of view belonged to the *processors,* the new belongs to the *consumers* of law, government and justice. Modern democracy calls on its official processors to perform their functions according to the perspective of the consumers.

The results of this drastic shift can be infuriating. In the seventeenth century, John Lilburne told outraged English judges that, no matter how much it might expedite the business of finding him guilty, they must not require him to testify against himself. Then William Penn declared that the public interest in maintaining order and decorum in the streets did not warrant them in depriving him of freedom of speech and religion. In the eighteenth century, James Otis expostulated against taxing the colonists, and the Continental Congress against a long series of official trespasses on civil rights. No sooner was the disagreeable American war over than Charles James Fox pushed his Libel Bill to stop the time-honored judicial practice of condemning Britons to long terms in prison for telling plain truths about ministers of the Crown. Anyone with half an eye could see what would happen to Great Britain if agitators like Fox had their way and to America if the people should heed Jefferson and Madison and adopt a national bill of rights. Every guaranteed civil liberty and civil right took the country that much further from the easy old days of the Star Chamber, when there was no nonsense about obtaining search warrants, furnishing assistance of counsel, rejecting confessions taken at the rack, conducting jury trials, recognizing the right against self-incrimination, or presuming that a man was innocent until proved guilty.

How does a person become a consumer of justice and law? In any reasonably stable society, one consumes justice by being safeguarded and regulated from day to day as one fills his place in society; in this sense, one consumes public justice whenever one talks or writes, works or sleeps, buys or sells. One may also consume it in a more dramatic way, as by engaging in a lawsuit or being charged with a crime.

In a democracy, a citizen consumes justice still more extensively when he influences the shape of policy and legislation, casts his vote, and asserts the interests of a special group or of the whole community.

Finally, there is a third way to consume justice. It consists in the people's examining and assuming responsibility for what officials do in their name and by their authority — the unjust and evil acts as well as the beneficent and good.

A judge too has customarily been considered as consuming justice in the very process of dispensing it to others, for no one wholly puts off the man when he puts on the robe. The same status that makes a judge peculiarly vulnerable if law is used as an instrument of wrong simultaneously affords him means of protection. He is not required to give any legal effect to a transaction that the society regards as immoral or vicious, nor must he receive evidence that a prosecutor obtained through illegal means, or preside helplessly while a man is convicted of a crime that the police trapped him into committing.

One more example will be enough to show the shift from the old perspective to the new. In 1896 the United States Supreme Court, using the old perspective, held: that states and their officers could constitutionally impose a system of racial segregation; that their action in separating Negroes from white citizens did not imply that they were holding Negroes to be inferior; and that if Negroes suffered from such an imputation, they — the immediate consumers of the system — had no basis for making the inference. The Court said: "We consider the underlying fallacy of the plaintiff's argument to consist in the assumption that the enforced separation of the two races stamps the colored race with a badge of inferiority. If this be so, it is not by reason of anything found in the act, but solely because the colored race chooses to put that construction upon it."

In 1954, the justices looked at the selfsame facts in a consumer perspective. They held that, regardless of what a state or its officials might intend or protest, the very act of segregating Negroes stamped them as inferior, inflicted grievous harm on their sensibility and self-respect, and violated the Constitution's guarantee of equal protection of the laws. Nothing essential was different save the perspective. The perspective had changed from official processors to citizen consumers, and the meaning of constitutional equality had changed along with it.

In sum, adopting a consumer perspective involves investigating a transaction, a principle, or a concept through observation of the specific human targets it touches and the times and occasions when it affects them. One asks concretely whom does it concern and when, who needs it and why, who uses it and how, who gains from it and wherein? We propose now to look at the meaning of justice in this perspective of consumers.

The Marie Besnard Case*

S INCE our business now is with what justice means to consumers in their concrete experiences, we turn to the recent case that involved Mrs. Marie Besnard and her compatriots, the people of France. Marie and Léon Besnard, an affectionate but childless couple who lived in comfortable circumstances, suffered a number of family bereavements over a period of years. Finally, Léon, whose health had been failing for some time, passed away despite Marie's assiduous care, and shortly thereafter Marie lost her mother, whom she had also nursed devotedly. About a year and a half after Léon's death, the police exhumed his body, the state's expert claimed to have found lethal proportions of arsenic in it, the examining magistrate directed the exhumation of all of Marie's and Léon's relatives and friends who had been interred in the same cemetery over a period of years, and the police took Marie to prison — charged with murdering by poison eleven persons, including not only Léon, his parents and his sister but her own father and mother as well. The entire prosecution was baseless in fact and a deliberate frame-up.

What are the motives that bring about frame-ups? There are those that apply to the prosecutor and the police — such as professional ambition, newspaper clamor, the imperious demands of merchants' and veterans' associations, the desire to make a record for efficiency, the need to exculpate oneself or a political ally, callousness, stupidity or laziness, mere sadism, and — most dangerous of all — the lust to obtain a conviction at whatever cost once one has considered the evidence with an open mind and concluded mistakenly that the guilty

* In the unfinished manuscript this chapter was entitled "The Meaning of Justice."

person has been found. Motives like these may be quite impersonal in relation to the accused; he is only someone who chances to be at hand when a victim is needed. But there are other possible motives for frame-ups that are more personal in nature and apply directly to the accused — such as malice, envy and hatred, lust for his money if he has any, racial bigotry, religious bigotry, distrust of ethnic minorities, fear of political radicals, abhorrence of partisan opponents, and — quite frequently — the subconscious assumption that poverty means not only vulnerability but probable guilt as well. Motives like these can be fanned into fury if the accused happens to be charged with distributing illegal narcotics, disclosing security information, or administering poison — crimes that can easily stultify a policeman's judgment because they are so secret in the doing and so frightful in the consequences.

In Marie Besnard's case a dozen destructive motives converged against her. True, she was not poor, nor was she a member of a racial, religious or political minority; shall we say that in these respects her bad luck could have been much worse? Perhaps yes, perhaps no. If she had really been poor, the friends who proved false might not have been moved by envy and the relatives who seconded the prosecution might not have coveted her estate; and if she had really belonged to some minority group, the minority's organizations might have come to her aid and some of the newspapers might have investigated more carefully before pillorying her. All we know is that her ordeal lasted twelve years, five of them in prison.

It began when her supposed friend, Mrs. P——, who had lived under Marie's roof long enough to collect a number of family confidences, proceeded to soak them in the vinegar of envy, steep them in a thick concoction of malice, simmer them over the low fire of her own frustrations, season them with a clove of sex and a fistful of imaginary homicide, and serve them around the entire neighborhood. Soon a local ne'er-do-well submitted this witches' brew to the police, who proceeded to obtain the order of exhumation.

While Marie was in prison, the local police officer in charge tried relentlessly to extract a confession, and the examining magistrate did little to protect her rights under the law. The officer used a variety of devices to break her will. He interrogated her brutally; he deprived her of exercise, of any means of occupying herself, even of needle and thread with which to mend her clothes; he allotted other women to her cell — stool-pigeons — who took turns in keeping her awake through the nights, badgering her to confess, beating her, deceiving her with lying stories, endlessly chanting that her cause was hopeless and her destiny was execution. Meanwhile her attorneys were not permitted to see her; their letters were intercepted. For a time her mind swayed on the brink of complete breakdown. Her sanity was saved one happy day when a new superintendent assumed charge, halted these abuses, and treated the inmates like human beings. From then on, Marie could exult in being assigned to wash all the prison linen on Mondays and Tuesdays.

What then of the determination of her guilt or innocence? It was two and a half years after she was taken to prison before her court trial even began. After another two and a half years, she was allowed to leave the prison on furnishing a heavy bail, but her property, officially sequestered, was withheld from her because the case was still undecided. Twelve dreary years elapsed from the day she was led to prison before the trial resulted in a verdict. That is, for twelve years she had to remain under an undetermined public accusation of having deliberately murdered almost everyone in her family and her husband's. Meanwhile the greedy among her relatives and the unthinking as well as the envious among her neighbors felt sure that these horrible accusations could not possibly have held for so many years if they were not true.

Why all the delay? It was mainly the fault of the toxicologists. The performance of distinguished toxicologists in Marie's case was incompetent, irresponsible, and — in certain instances — downright dishonest. The men of science had it in their power to foil both the private injustices and the public ones, to explode the vicious gossip of the neighbors and frustrate the machinations of the police officer, to clear the whole muddled slate and inscribe the findings of truth on it. Instead, several of them, testifying at the respective hearings where Marie's life was at stake, acted like mere peacocks, fools, and frauds.

Through skillful and thorough preparation of the case's scientific aspects, Marie's lawyers were able to refute the experts time and again. At the first set of hearings, they showed that the prosecution's toxicologist — the "famous" Dr. B—— who "is never wrong!"— had made a botch of his chemical analysis. B—— claimed to have tested the eye of a corpse that had been interred for five years! He reported on several jars of remains over and above the number shipped to him for testing. He swore that by the naked eye he could distinguish arsenic rings from antimony rings and, when put to the test in open court, selected three tubes out of six as containing "arsenic" though all six contained nothing but antimony.

The court and lawyers agreed that a completely fresh examination must be made and the defense attorneys were permitted to name the experts. The men they chose held some of the highest scientific and academic posts in the country; their reports, which they submitted after a few months, were to prove as confused, contradictory, and unreliable as Dr. B——'s.

At the very first set of hearings, the defense had offered a perfectly plausible explanation of the whole mystery, which should have been tested and accepted at once. If the exhumed bodies (a dozen of them, all taken from the very same cemetery) were found to contain unusual amounts of arsenic, it was only because they had absorbed the arsenic from the cemetery soil. Simple enough, one would think. Yet the second set of experts did nothing but befog the explanation. When challenged in court, they admitted to having used contaminated instruments, to having confused their calculations, and to having tested for arsenic by using water that itself contained arsenic. The defense then produced some experts of its own, who showed with ease that the bodies had received the arsenic from the soil in which they lay. Nevertheless again there was no acquittal but an adjournment, again no exoneration for Marie but a new panel of scientific experts.

The new panel took six tedious years to file its report. Since all of France knew by than that the prosecution had blundered badly and its toxicologists ridiculously, the third trial featured a series of efforts to salvage their reputations. At first, the presiding judge tried to get Marie to blame all her alleged crimes on Léon, her husband whom she was supposed to have poisoned. This proving vain, he resorted to scolding the defense witnesses. But now it was shown that one of the prosecution experts had not only bungled his laboratory work but actually falsified his figures. Too much, too much. At last the tragic farce was over, the orations done, the lawyers silenced; after twelve years a jury was allowed to speak. The verdict, quickly reached, was "not guilty" on every count. The prosecution had been baseless from the beginning. No crime had ever been committed — no crime, that is, except the grave ones that were committed against Marie Besnard.

10

THE DEMOCRATIC
RESOLUTION

The Democratic Resolution

IN ancient times, the prophets of religion described a vision of such brilliance, beauty, and intensity that it has dazzled men's imaginations ever since. They pictured a sort of Golden Age — not, as the pagans said, hidden in the mists of the remote past but somewhere predictably ahead in the prospects of the future — when men would cease waging war against one another, would live in peace and quiet each under his own vine and fig tree, and would need no external regulation because their own hearts and inward parts would direct them rightly. When that day came, there would be no further occasion for governments, officials, punishments, or laws; men would be free to follow their own benevolent impulses.

The vision arose, of course, because of what the prophets and sages saw when they looked at governments and laws in their time: the apparently irresistible power of despots in Assyria, Babylonia, and Egypt, and subsequently in Macedon and Rome; the brutal systems of compulsion calling themselves governments; the codified injustices passing for laws; the scoundrels and hypocrites sitting as judges; and the desperate condition of the oppressed economic classes. If one could never expect that government would learn the ways of justice, one was driven to hope that justice would abolish government. Laws becoming more inflexible and judges more callous day by day, it seemed that God and man must turn from them and order the world in a radically different way, for even if, incredibly enough, some government or other should begin to act fairly and justly, it would nevertheless employ the old, repulsive methods of power and show the same ugly blotches of force and bloodshed. When the millennial age arrived to replace violence and oppression with harmony and freedom, all laws and governments would simply disappear.

The vision has flourished in almost every era since it was first announced, offering solace to a variety of religious mystics and quietists, encouragement to cooperative experiments such as Brook Farm, and occasional inflammation to the enterprises of anarchists. It attained a sensational though fugitive prominence in Marxist doctrine when Engels, in the name of dialectical materialism, said that the political state was only a transitional institution, and predicted that after the Communist revolution it would "wither away," Lenin followed with certain ambiguous statements that seemed to support the notion, and lesser Soviet theoreticians committed the indiscretion — for which they paid heavily in the purges of the 1930's — of treating the "withering away" as something that might come about soon and in Russia. Whether in a religious or a secular formulation, the vision still remains able to fascinate some highly diverse minds; to a world weary of oppression and conflict it apparently offers an ideal image of freedom and peace.

Nevertheless, like other utopian conceptions, it has also done some practical harm. People who trust that an approaching millennium will eradicate all social evils may be less concerned to resist them in the meanwhile, and people who believe that their institutions are so irredeemable that they must ultimately disappear or "wither away" may be slow to reform them. The millennial vision, while it offers men a noble social ideal, likewise provides them with a plausible excuse for accepting the status quo and leading a selfish, apolitical existence. Who would take the risks involved in struggling for justice and reform if all law were by nature brutal and all government by necessity oppressive? Until the millennium arrived and brought a society of perfect cooperation, one might do worse than attend to his own interest, pursue his own advantage, and try at whatever cost to survive. Law and government, one could argue, were merely necessary evils ordained to men by reason of their congenital sinfulness. Anyone bent on leading a virtuous life had better keep as far from them as possible.

Thus the ancient prophetic vision, for all its loftiness, exhibited deeply ambivalent implications. It extolled freedom and simultaneously put it beyond practical reach, compassionated the oppressed and impliedly deferred their liberation, criticized the evils of law and seemed to immunize them from correction. By picturing the time when the wolf would dwell beside the lamb, it let men infer that they need not improve the breed of their sheepdogs. These contradictions presented a profound dilemma.

The democratic resolution of the dilemma is, I believe, mankind's greatest single achievement in the ordering of political relations — an accomplishment of such wisdom, judgment, and insight that we are warranted in calling it corporate genius. To state it summarily first before mentioning its implications, the resolution consists, as it were, in *discounting the millennium* by realizing its promise of complete freedom here and now and by compressing it into the realms of conscience, thought, belief, and opinion. This resolution requires endless perseverance for a community to maintain, for no experiments are so difficult as those that grasp a slice of utopia and convert it into present reality. It is here and now, according to the democratic resolution, that a man possesses his full freedom of thought, the vine of his belief, and the fig tree of his conscience; in enjoying them he is completely secure, and government exists to serve as his safeguard. No creed, dogma, or orthodoxy can be imposed to constrict the free play of his intelligence.

For obvious reasons, the democratic formula does not provide a similar immunity to anyone's overt, social behavior; actions that may affect the welfare and safety of others must, of course, be subject to reasonable public regulation. Nevertheless, the resolution exerts a pervasive influence not only on the subjective but also on the objective, external side of the line. The democratic man's complete freedom of thought and his almost complete freedom of discussion serve to liberate not only his inner life but also his social transactions. It is never enough to say that he can merely think what he likes.

For how does the resolution proceed to develop the social regulations that he is expected to obey? By summoning the very mechanisms of thought, conscience, and communication to which it has secured the widest measure of freedom and using them to establish a continual flow of opinion mutually between citizen and citizen and reciprocally between citizenry and officialdom, culminating at intervals in the formal mandates of the ballot box. In this way, when the democratic process operates in accordance with its own specifications, it is able to accomplish much more than even Thomas Jefferson claimed for it. When true to itself, it not only derives the just *powers* of government from the consent of the governed, as he wrote in the Declaration of Independence; it also draws on the governed and their consent to warrant the just *applications and exercises* of the powers. On these terms, law, government, and official compulsion are provided with an unexceptionable moral basis. Freedom of inquiry and discussion on one side and justice of administration on the other are the twin pillars that together support the moral authority of a representative government.

The condition of democratic man is something new and young on the face of the earth, and his work of political creation is only beginning. In all the sad stages of human history, his is the first that, by grace of intelligence, can actually will the elements of a just society into practical existence. Now that he has commenced to discover his capacities and flex his desires, the work is visibly accumulating power and momentum. I see a world where no nation is accounted strong except in justice, rich except in compassion, or secure except in freedom and peace.

From The Predicament of Democratic Man,
Macmillan Company, 1961.

Notes

I N order to keep this volume within reasonable size, it was necessary
to delete or abbreviate some of the footnotes originally published
with the articles. In addition, a few deletions have been made in the
text in order to avoid duplication of material. It is with regret and
apologies to the reader that this has been done. However, the full notes
and text can be found by consulting the legal periodicals where these
articles originally appeared.

1: THE CONSUMER PERSPECTIVE

LAW IN THE CONSUMER PERSPECTIVE

1. The practice of grading beliefs according to conceived human costs is an indispensable step toward this sophistication. Cahn, *The Predicament of Democratic Man* (1961), pp. 154–158.
2. The perspective is described in *ibid.*, pp. 17–42. In "Fact-Skepticism: An Unexpected Chapter" [see pp. 315–323 — ED.] I endeavor to show its relation to fact-finding.
3. For a neat instance of the perspective, see the following remarks of Mr. Justice Harlan in Wood v. Georgia, 370 U.S. 375, 400 (1962). The Supreme Court held that Wood, a Georgia sheriff who, in a series of out-of-court statements, had harshly attacked a grand jury investigation into block-voting by Negroes, could not be punished for contempt since the record failed to disclose a clear and present danger to the administration of justice. Dissenting, Justice Harlan objected:
   "Indeed, the test suggested by the Court is even more stringent than that which it applies in determining whether a conviction should be set aside because of prejudicial 'outside' statements reaching a trial jury. In such cases, although the question is whether the rights of the accused have been infringed rather than whether there has been a clear and present danger of their infringement, it is necessary only to show a substantial likelihood that the verdict was affected, and it is no answer that each juror expresses his belief that he remains able to be fair and impartial. . . . The test for punishing attempts to influence a grand or petit jury should be less rather than more stringent."
4. See Cahn, *The Predicament of Democratic Man* (1961), pp. 30–42.
5. Reported *sub nom.* Brown v. Allen, 344 U.S. 443 (1953).
6. See People v. Mooney, 178 Cal. 525, 174 Pac. 325, *cert. denied*, 248 U.S. 579 (1918), and Mooney v. Holohan, 294 U.S. 103, 110 (1935).
7. On occasion, the bringing and conducting of a lawsuit may belong in this more creative category. As Mr. Justice Brennan has recently reminded us, litigation may be one of the most effective ways — sometimes the only effective way — to achieve redress of group grievances. NAACP v. Button, 371 U.S. 415, 430 (1963).
8. People v. Savvides, 1 N.Y.2d 554 (1956).
9. Brady v. State, 226 Md. 422, 174 A.2d 167 (1961); Brady v. Maryland, 373 U.S. 83 (1963).
10. Griffin v. United States, 183 F.2d 990, 993 (D.C. Cir. 1950).
11. Obviously, if as in the *Savvides* case the prosecutor knew of the perjury and did not disclose it, the Court will not listen to an argument that, since the proof of defendant's guilt was overwhelming, the episode was immaterial. As Judge Fuld put it, "The administration of justice must not only be above reproach,

410 [NOTES TO PAGES 24 TO 60]

it must also be beyond the suspicion of reproach." 1 N.Y.2d at 556, 136 N.E.2d at 854, 154 N.Y.S.2d at 887.

12. That innocent persons accused of crime are more likely to suffer from mistaken eyewitnesses than from deliberate perjurers would appear from the instances collected in Borchard, *Convicting the Innocent* (1932) and Frank and Frank, *Not Guilty* (1957).

13. See Cahn, *The Moral Decision* (1955), pp. 300–312.

14. Cahn, *The Sense of Injustice* (1949), pp. 1–27.

15. Greenman v. Yuba Power Prods., Inc., 377 P.2d 897, 27 Cal. Rptr. 697 (Sup. Ct. 1962).

16. Ballard v United States, 329 U.S. 187 (1946).

17. See Judge Frank's important warning against appellate judges' becoming so preoccupied with possible future cases that they overlook the interests of the actual parties before them and "never quite catch up with themselves." Aero Spark Plug Co. v. B. G. Corp., 130 F.2d 290, 295 (1942) (concurring opinion).

18. See Casey v. United States, 276 U.S. 413 (1928); Sorrells v. United States, 287 U.S. 435 (1932); Sherman v. United States, 356 U.S. 369 (1958); Masciale v. United States, 356 U.S. 386 (1958); cases collected in *1962 Annual Survey of American Law*, pp. 75–76; cf. Lopez v. United States, 373 U.S. 427, 434 (1963).

19. Though in the *Sherman* case the majority held that there had been entrapment, it reached the conclusion as a matter of law:
"We conclude from the evidence that entrapment was established as a matter of law. In so holding, we are not choosing between conflicting witnesses, nor judging credibility. . . . We reach our conclusion from the undisputed testimony of the prosecution's witnesses."
The ruling does not meet the trial judge's needs in the more usual case when a finding on entrapment involves a choice between conflicting witnesses.

2: THE BILL OF RIGHTS AND THE JUDGES

MADISON AND THE PURSUIT OF HAPPINESS

1. Parrington's position is sprinkled lightly with the salt of skepticism in Julian P. Boyd, *The Declaration of Independence* (1945), pp. 3–5, where "the pursuit of happiness" is linked with a variety of quotations to the effect that the happiness of society is the end of government. An admirably exhaustive collection of "happiness" references is to be found in a study by Herbert Lawrence Ganter entitled "Jefferson's 'Pursuit of Happiness' and Some Forgotten Men," *William and Mary Quarterly*, vol. 16 (2d series) (1936), p. 558. Mr. Ganter was on the track of what I consider the right source (*ibid.*, p. 564), but elected to leave it in favor of a theory of multitudinous sources — some rather farfetched in respect of both content and possible impact on Jefferson. Hence his references were not given adequate weight by Boyd, or by Dumbauld, *The Declaration of Independence and What It Means Today* (1950), pp. 60–61. See also Ford, "The Natural Law and the 'Pursuit of Happiness,' " *Notre Dame Lawyer*, vol. 26 (1951), p. 429. This interesting article presents the subject as shaped by theological views quite different from Locke's, Jefferson's, and Madison's. Of course, all modern expositions of "happiness" should be considered mediately or immediately in debt to Aristotle.

2. Jefferson's library inventories show that the editions he read were subsequent to and based on Locke's final revision of his *Essay* in the fourth edition, published in 1700. Early eighteenth-century printings (e.g., that of John Churchill, London, 1714) sometimes retained references to the second edition in the text, which went unobserved despite an "Epistle to the Reader" clearly showing that it was the fourth edition that lay in his hands.

3. See Irving Brant, *James Madison*, vol. 1: *The Virginia Revolutionist* (1941), p. 121. No catalog of Madison's books has been found, but Mr. Brant, in a

recent private letter, comments, "I should say that, considering the importance of Locke in Madison's thinking and in his day, it would be incredible if he did not have every work of Locke that was extant." Madison's remarkable summary in the 37th *Federalist* of the difficulties we encounter when we endeavor to communicate meanings accurately by means of words bears an intriguing relation to Locke's treatment of the same topic.

4. The following is based on the 10th *Federalist*, with some minor supplementation from the sequence beginning with the 37th. See Brant, *James Madison*, vol. 3: *Father of the Constitution, 1787–1800* (1950), chapter XIV.

THE FIRSTNESS OF THE FIRST AMENDMENT

1. Letter from Thomas Jefferson to James Madison, December 20, 1787. For a splendid account of developments leading to adoption of the Bill of Rights, see the third volume of Irving Brant's definitive biography, *James Madison: Father of the Constitution, 1787–1800* (1950), particularly chapter XXI.

2. This is an interesting qualification, for in his letter of December 20, 1787, he had expressed a preference for associating the judges in the President's veto power or investing them "separately with a similar power."

3. According to Mr. Brant, "All of Jefferson's private letters came by diplomatic pouch, and a dispatch of March 15 to Foreign Secretary Jay was received on June 2." Letter from Irving Brant to Edmond Cahn, October 18, 1955. I follow Mr. Brant in attributing this part of Madison's presentation to Jefferson's letter to him of March 15, 1789. See *ibid.*, p. 267.

4. A week later, on June 17, 1789, in the extended debate on the President's power to remove appointive officers without legislative concurrence, Madison said:

"It is therefore a fair question, whether this great point may not as well be decided, at least by the whole Legislature as by a part, by us as well as by the Executive or Judiciary? As I think it will be equally constitutional, I cannot imagine it will be less safe, that the exposition should issue from the legislative authority than any other; and the more so, because it involves in the decision the opinions of both these departments, whose powers are supposed to be affected by it. Besides, I do not see in what way this question could come before the judges, to obtain a fair and solemn decision; but even if it were the case that it could, I should suppose, at least while the Government is not led by passion, disturbed by faction, or deceived by any discolored medium of sight, but while there is a desire to all to see and be guided by the benignant ray of truth, that the decision may be made with the most advantage by the Legislature itself."

This presents an unintended but nonetheless excellent summary of the reasons for referring justiciable constitutional issues to the judges at all times after June 1789.

5. As late as May 27, 1789, there was still a note of uncertainty on this score. Madison wrote Jefferson on that day, "A Bill of rights, incorporated, perhaps, into the Constitution, will be proposed. . . ."

6. In Mr. Brant's view, Madison's original resistance to a bill of rights was due to his apprehension "that limitations of language and public opinion might render the basic freedom, that of religion, too narrow for security. If it were infringed, prejudice and intolerance would tear down everything else." Mr. Brant concludes, "Charged with the task of drawing a bill of rights, the very apprehensions which made him hesitate spurred him to superlative performance." *Ibid.*, p. 275.

7. Commencement Address by Justice Black at Swarthmore College, June 6, 1955.

8. Feldman v. United States, 322 U.S. 487, 501–502 (1944) (dissenting opinion).

9. Of course, Jefferson was profoundly interested in popular education. Opening the Great Dialogue with Madison, he freely asserted he was "not a friend to a very energetic government" because it generally led to despotism; then by way of emphasis through contrast, he pointed to the sound judgment that could

be expected from an informed people (at least so long as it retained an agricultural base). Letter from Thomas Jefferson to James Madison, December 20, 1787. But as will be seen, it remained for Justice Black to confer jural status on the community's First Amendment right to receive intelligence, to learn and to advance.

10. Marsh v. Alabama, 326 U.S. 501 (1946); Tucker v. Texas, 326 U.S. 517 (1946). The rationale of the *Marsh* opinion had been adumbrated in Martin v. Struthers, 319 U.S. 141, 143 (1943). See also the dissenting opinions in Beauharnais v. Illinois, 343 U.S. 250, 268–270, 274–275 (1952); Breard v. Alexandria, 341 U.S. 622, 650 (1951); Dennis v. United States, 341 U.S. 494, 580 (1951).

11. Feldman v. United States, 322 U.S. 487, 501 (1944) (dissenting opinion).

12. United Nations reports illustrate the extraordinary value of this approach when applied to international communication of intelligence. See the Universal Declaration of Human Rights Article 19, adopted by the General Assembly of the United Nations on December 10, 1948.

13. *The Odes of Horace,* book III, ode iii (Dunsany tr., 1947), p. 82.
    To the justices of the Supreme Court, the south wind may feel unusually stormy these days. But informed Americans understand that worthier things than wind come from the South; and as for the uninformed, they can profit by noting that Alabama produced Hugo L. Black.

3: FREEDOM OF THE PRESS

CORRESPONDENCE WITH DAVID BEN-GURION: A DEBATE

1. EDITOR'S NOTE: These lectures have been included in this volume. See "The Libertarian Standard" (p. 134) and "Responsibility for Defamation" (p. 147).

4: CHURCH AND STATE

THE "ESTABLISHMENT OF RELIGION" PUZZLE

1. Brant, *James Madison,* vol. 6: *Commander in Chief, 1812–1836* (1961).

2. Everson v. Board of Educ., 330 U.S. 1 (1947); Illinois ex rel. McCollum v. Board of Educ., 333 U.S. 203 (1948); Zorach v. Clauson, 343 U.S. 306 (1952); McGowan v. Maryland, 366 U.S. 420 (1961), together with Two Guys from Harrison-Allentown v. McGinley, 366 U.S. 582 (1961), Braunfeld v. Brown, 366 U.S. 559 (1961), and Gallagher v. Crown Kosher Super Mkt., Inc., 366 U.S. 617 (1961).
    I have not listed Doremus v. Board of Educ., 342 U.S. 429 (1952), because in it the majority of the Court, on grounds of mootness and lack of standing to sue, refused to decide the merits (state statute provided for reading five verses of Old Testment at opening of each school day).
    Nor have I included Torcaso v. Watkins, 367 U.S. 488 (1961), where, without a single dissent, the Court struck down a Maryland test-oath requiring "a declaration of belief in the existence of God" in order to qualify for public office (in this instance, the exalted office of notary public). With a friendly pat on McCollum's head, Justice Black, writing for the Court, described the seventeenth- and eighteenth-century abuses of religious test-oaths and the peculiar odium attached to them by our early settlers. It is an eloquent and moving opinion. Yet the same historical apparatus that embellishes and enriches it likewise operates to narrow the scope of its holding. Following very closely after McGowan, which it cites without reservation, Torcaso indicates no intervening change of attitude. It does reiterate reassuringly the Everson and McCollum statements that government cannot "aid all religions."

3. Brant, *James Madison,* vol. 1: *The Virginia Revolutionist* (1941), pp. 244–247; Brant, "Madison: On the Separation of Church and State," *William and Mary Quarterly,* vol. 8 (3d series, no. 1) (1951), pp. 3–7.

4. EDITOR'S NOTE: Reprinted in full as Appendix A to the original publication of this article in *1961 Annual Survey of American Law*, p. 571; and in *New York University Law Review*, vol. 36 (1961), p. 1274.

5. The passage is most conveniently available in *The Political Writings of Thomas Jefferson* (Dumbauld ed., 1955), pp. 36–38. Among other things, it shows that in 1782 as in 1789 Jefferson consistently advocated a bill of rights as a *legal* safeguard, not as a mere basis for appeal to the spirit of the people. Here is his 1782 answer, *ibid.*, p. 38, to what Judge Learned Hand taught on the subject:

"[I]s the spirit of the people an infallible, a permanent reliance? Is it government? Is this the kind of protection we receive in return for the rights we give up? Besides, the spirit of the times may alter, will alter. Our rulers will become corrupt, our people careless. A single zealot may commence persecution, and better men be his victims. It can never be too often repeated that the time for fixing every essential right on a legal basis is while our rulers are honest and ourselves united."

6. EDITOR'S NOTE: Reprinted in full as Appendix B to the original publication of this article in *1961 Annual Survey of American Law*, p. 590, and in *New York University Law Review*, vol. 36 (1961), p. 1293.

7. Of course, the provisions and reservations that eventually became the Ninth and Tenth Amendments were designed to take care of this very difficulty. Yet even as he submitted them to the Congress, Madison again acknowledged his semantic misgivings. *Annals of Congress*, vol. 1 (1789), p. 456.

8. For instances of Madison's acts, see Brant, "Madison: On the Separation of Church and State," *William and Mary Quarterly*, vol. 8 (3d series, no. 1) (1951), and references *passim* in Brant, *James Madison*, vol. 6: *Commander-in-Chief, 1812–1836* (1961). It is obvious that Madison would have agreed with Judges Dye and Fuld who dissented in Engel v. Vitale, 10 N.Y.2d 174, 176 N.E.2d 579, 218 N.Y.S.2d 659 (1961), *petition for cert. filed*, 30 U.S.L. Week 3116 (U.S. Oct. 3, 1961) (no. 468) (upholding so-called "non-denominational" prayer in public school classrooms, objecting pupils presumably being excused).

9. The date was January 1, 1802. For the full text in which the phrase occurs, see *The Writings of Thomas Jefferson*, vol. 16, p. 282 (A. E. Bergh ed., 1907).

10. Brant, "Madison: On the Separation of Church and State," *William and Mary Quarterly*, vol. 8 (3d series, no. 1) (1951), p. 14. It is not claimed here that Madison was aware of the extent to which he had gone beyond Jefferson's position.

11. Though he baffled Justice Harlan by doing so (see Lathrop v. Donohue, 367 U.S. 820, 852 [1961]), Justice Black was on solid historical ground when, dissenting in International Assn. of Machinists v. Street, 367 U.S. 740 (1961), he quoted Madison's Memorial and Jefferson's Bill *Id.* at 790. To the libertarians of the seventeenth and eighteenth centuries, "establishment" denoted any variety of official compulsion that might violate "the equal rights of conscience."

12. The dichotomy was employed explicitly in a leading "free exercise" case:

"Mr. Jefferson afterwards, in reply to an address to him by a committee of the Danbury Baptist Association (8 id. 113), took occasion to say: 'Believing with you that religion is a matter which lies solely between man and his God; that he owes account to none other for his faith or his worship; that the legislative powers of the government reach actions only, and not opinions, —I contemplate with sovereign reverence that act of the whole American people which declared that their legislature should "make no law respecting an establishment of religion or prohibiting the free exercise thereof," thus building a wall of separation between church and State. Adhering to this expression of the supreme will of the nation in behalf of the rights of conscience, I shall see with sincere satisfaction the progress of those sentiments which tend to restore man to all his natural rights, convinced he has no natural right in opposition to his social duties.' Coming as this does from an acknowledged leader of the advocates of the measure, it may be accepted almost as an authoritative declaration of the scope and effect of the amendment thus secured. Congress was deprived of all legislative power over mere opinion, but was left free to reach actions which were in violation of social duties or subversive of good order." — Reynolds v. United States, 98 U.S. 145, 164 (1878). It may be significant that when Justice Black quoted Jefferson's "wall of separation" metaphor in Everson, he took it from the Reynolds opinion. 330 U.S. at 16.

13. I dealt with the subject in more detail in *The Predicament of Democratic Man* (1961), p. 99.

14. But Madison did not adopt the theory of psychological determinism expressed in the opening phrases of Jefferson's Bill. These phrases were deleted by the Virginia legislature before the Bill was enacted.

15. In 1764, Voltaire (addressing the Christian world tactfully as *"Insensés. . . . Malheureux. . . . Monstres. . . . !"*) summarized the matter succinctly, *"On vous l'a déjà dit, et on n'a autre chose à vous dire: si vous avez deux religions chez vous, elles se couperont la gorge; si vous en avez trente, elles vivront en paix."* Voltaire, *Dictionnaire Philosophique* (J. Benda ed., Paris), verb. *Tolérance* II, p. 269.

16. In 1790, Madison amended a census bill so as to avoid enumerating clergymen, lest the government be put in the position of "ascertaining who [are] and who are not ministers of the gospel." Brant, "Madison: On the Separation of Church and State," *William and Mary Quarterly*, vol. 8 (3d series, no. 1) (1951), pp. 17–18.

17. In all likelihood, it was the zealous Baptist evangelists, jailed continually for their preachings and preaching continually from their jails, who exemplified the need for an express guarantee of freedom of *speech* in the federal Bill of Rights.

18. *The Federalist*, no. 51 (Cooke ed., 1961), p. 352. For years, I have restrained my desire to quote this fervent affirmation of Madison's in the 51st *Federalist* because partisans of Hamilton claimed it for him. Now, however, I feel free to use it. In 1961, the attribution of the 51st *Federalist* to Madison became not only authoritative but general as well. Brant, *James Madison*, vol. 6: *Commander-in-Chief, 1812–1836* (1961), p. 428.

ON GOVERNMENT AND PRAYER

1. 370 U.S. 421, 431–432 (1962). Life might be a lot more harmonious in this country if everyone would use a certain maxim that we owe to Baltasar Gracián, the astute seventeenth-century Spanish Jesuit. Gracián advised, *"Hanse de procurar los medios humanos como sino huviesse Divinos, y los Divinos como sino huviesse humanos."* In English this amounts to: "Use human means as if there were no divine ones, and divine as if there were no human ones." Gracián, *The Art of Worldly Wisdom* (Jacobs [1892] tr., Ungar ed., 1960), maxim ccli.

2. Madison's "Detached Memoranda." See note 4 below. *"Obsta principiis"* means "Resist the beginnings."

3. See discussion of the dichotomy in "The 'Establishment of Religion' Puzzle." As far as I have been able to find, Jefferson's very first statement of this all-important principle appears in his "Outline of Argument," set down in the summer or fall of 1776, in preparation for the debate on disestablishment. See *The Papers of Thomas Jefferson*, vol 1 (Boyd ed., 1950), p. 537. The exact notes are:

> True line betw. Opn. or tendcy. of opn. — & *Overt* act.
> humn. 1 nothg. t. d. wth. Opn. or tendcy. — only Overt acts.

4. See Madison's "Detached Memoranda," *William and Mary Quarterly*, vol. 3 (3d series, no. 4) (1946), pp. 560–561. EDITOR'S NOTE: The entire portion of the "Detached Memoranda" that relates to church and state is reproduced as Appendix C to the original publication of this article in *1962 Annual Survey of*

American Law, p. 693; and in *New York University Law Review*, vol. 37 (1962), p. 981.

5. This seems a fitting place to note that Madison was as solicitous of the rights of Jews and Roman Catholics as of those of Protestants and deists. In asserting the equal freedom of all "sects," he applied the word to non-Christian as well as Christian religious groups. For an instance of his benevolent attitude toward Jews, see his letter of May 15, 1818, to Mordecai M. Noah, *Writings of James Madison*, vol. 8, p. 412 (G. Hunt ed., 1908). For an instance of his benevolent attitude toward Roman Catholics, see his remarks on the floor of Congress, January 1, 1795, *Annals of Congress*, vol. 4 (1795), p. 1035.

6. Justice Douglas, concurring in Engel v. Vitale, notes the element of "captive audience." 370 U.S. at 442. A captive audience, as I understand it, is one that assembles and remains for one purpose but finds itself used for another. This is precisely what happens when parents send their children to school for secular education and the school exploits their presence by conducting prayers.

7. It will be remembered that the Orthodox Eastern Church parted finally with the Papacy over an insertion of only two words (*filioque*) in the creed.

8. Consistency goes out the window. The people who have always said that parents have a "natural right" to control their children's education and have cited Pierce v. Society of Sisters, 268 U.S. 510 (1925), to prove it are the very ones who now affront the parents by insisting on collective prayers in the public schools.

9. Foolish men, once in the saddle, beguile themselves with the dream that they will always remain there; it is this illusion that makes persecutors. Prudent men know better. Roger Williams said: "And oh! since the commonweal cannot without a spiritual rape force the consciences of all to one worship, oh, that it may never commit that rape in forcing the consciences of all men to one worship which a stronger arm and sword may soon (as formerly) arise to alter." Madison gave the warning in his Memorial and again in the "Detached Memoranda." Justice Black sounded it clearly in Engel v. Vitale when he said, "The First Amendment was added to the Constitution to stand as a guarantee . . . that the people's religions must not be subject to the pressures of government for change each time a new political administration is elected to office." 370 U.S. at 429–430.

10. In Madison's time, as today, the senators and congressmen who insisted on having chaplains open their proceedings by praying that God might send them wisdom, enlightenment, and concord, would habitually arrive late, chat in the halls and committee rooms, and pay no attention to the prayers. There is little in the history of the United States Congress to indicate that, on reaching their destination, the chaplains' prayers have received more serious interest than at their place of origin.

11. Matthew 6:7. The following verse is also worth pondering.

12. *New York Times*, September 3, 1962, p. 8, col. 5.

6: ON THE LEGAL PROFESSION

ETHICAL PROBLEMS OF TAX PRACTITIONERS

1. 8 N.J. 433 (1952).

2. 88 U.S. 441 (1874).

3. Here we have a good illustration of the risks one incurs in using a quotation in the course of extemporaneous remarks. I quoted Holmes accurately but out of context: he was referring only to strict compliance with formal statutory conditions attached to the government's consent to be sued. Rock Island R.R. v. United States, 254 U.S. 141, 143 (1920). I feel confident, however, that Holmes would approve my wider application of his aphorism.

7: FACT-SKEPTICISM

SKEPTICISM IN AMERICAN JURISPRUDENCE

1. For Leslie Stephen dangling over a precipice and evaluating his beliefs, see Annan, *Leslie Stephen: His Thought and Character in Relation to His Time* (1952), pp. 83–84. This book will surely interest any student of Holmes or of the period.
2. Cossio, "Jurisprudence and the Sociology of Law," *Columbia Law Review*, vol. 52 (1952), pp. 356, 479.
3. See Cahn, "Authority and Responsibility," *Columbia Law Review*, vol. 51 (1951), p. 838.
4. *The Spirit of Liberty: Papers and Addresses of Learned Hand* (Dilliard ed., 1952). This book reflects a magnanimous and superlatively gifted personality.
5. Hand, "The Future of Wisdom in America," *Saturday Review*, November 22, 1952, p. 10.
6. In Montesquieu, *Histoire Veritable* (Caillois ed., 1948), p. 62 (an intriguing work made public only two generations ago), the author tells of an Egyptian king who was at the point of launching a military expedition and consulted the oracles to ascertain whether it would be successful. The various oracles contradicted one another so flatly that the monarch was thrown into a state of perplexity and indecision. Finally he had recourse to a philosopher. The philosopher commented, "Majesty, men were not made to know the particular desires of the gods, but only to know their general desires. . . . Irresolution has all the effects of timidity and even worse. The gods have given you armies, and you undoubtedly have prudence and courage. These are the oracles which you must consult."
7. This radiant phrase occurs in Shakespeare's *Henry IV*, Part II, Act iv, Scene I, l. 94.

"COURTS ON TRIAL": AN ANALYSIS

1. The best literary instance of Gestalt emergence is Robert Browning's magnificent *The Ring and the Book*.

FACT-SKEPTICISM AND FUNDAMENTAL LAW

1. The report, on behalf of a commission on the penal system of Austrian Lombardy (1792), appears as an appendix in Cesare Cantù, *Beccaria e il Diritto Penale* (Florence: G. Barbera, 1862), p. 369. I have suggested that Beccaria obtained this new insight from none other than Maximilien Robespierre. "Preface for Americans" in Arthur Koestler, *Reflections on Hanging* (1957).
2. In his concurring opinion in Griffin v. Illinois, 351 U.S. 12, 21 (1956), Justice Frankfurter observed that "capital offenses are *sui generis*"; dissenting in the same case at p. 28, Justice Burton said, "There is something pretty final about a death sentence." Thus they anticipated their respective positions in Reid v. Covert, 354 U.S. 1 (1957) and demonstrated the multivalence of the "insight of irreversibility."
3. Excerpt from letter of Hugo L. Black to Edmond Cahn, dated January 18, 1957, quoted with the writer's permission.
4. As one of his final gifts of wisdom to us, Zechariah Chafee said, "There is an admonition by Justice Holmes which is often repeated by judges as a reason for regretfully respecting the numerous recent sedition laws and possible bills of attainder which have been adopted by tremendous majorities in legislatures. For example, Justice Frankfurter quoted it after the rider in the Lovett case had passed the House of Representatives by a vote of 5 to 1: '[It] must be remembered that legislatures are ultimate guardians of the liberties and welfare of the people in quite as great a degree as the courts.' Remembered by whom?

So far as I can see, this is a maxim which judges constantly remember and legislatures always forget. I wish it were the other way round." Chafee, *Three Human Rights in the Constitution* (1956), pp. 160–161.

5. AFL v. American Sash Co., 335 U.S. 538, 550 (1949) concurring opinion; Kovacs v. Cooper, 336 U.S. 77, 95–96 (1949) concurring opinion.

6. 341 U.S. 494, 526 (1951) concurring opinion.

7. United States v. Carolene Products Co., 304 U.S. 144, 152 n.4 (1938). The intellectual elements of the preferred position doctrine are at least as old as the republic. Cahn, "The Firstness of the First Amendment" (1956) [see pp. 86–104 — ED.]

8. Ullmann v. United States, 350 U.S. 422, 428 (1956).

9. Moreover, Justice Frankfurter follows the same method (i.e., he grades the respective constitutional guarantees) when the issue is of a somewhat different nature, to wit, whether "the Constitution follows the flag." Here he calls it the "fundamental right" test. Reid v. Covert, 354 U.S. 1, 53 (1957) concurring opinion.

REFLECTIONS ON HANGING: PREFACE FOR AMERICANS

1. Ambard v. Attorney-General [1936] A.C. 322, 335.

2. Bridges v. California, 314 U.S. 252, 270 (1941).

3. Fisher v. United States, 328 U.S. 463 (1946).

4. Durham v. United States, 214 F.2d, 862 (D.C. Cir. 1954).

5. For information on lesser palliatives, see *Report of Royal Commission on Capital Punishment* (1953), p. 182. The American experience with the death penalty is the subject of an excellent symposium, edited by Professor Thorsten Sellin, in *Annals of The American Academy of Political and Social Science*, vol. 284 (November 1952).

6. Louisiana v. Resweber, 329 U.S. 459 (1947).

7. "What Medicine Can Do for Law" in Cardozo, *Selected Writings* (M. E. Hall ed., 1947), p. 381.

8. This new idea of Beccaria's emerged in his report for a commission on the penal system of Austrian Lombardy (1792). The report appears as an appendix in Cesare Cantù, *Beccaria e il Diritto Penale* (Florence: G. Barbera, 1862), p. 369. The most probable source of Beccaria's new insight was — of all men — Maximilien Robespierre!

   The relation between Robespierre and capital punishment constitutes one of history's most edifying moral dramas. No man ever opposed the penalty more earnestly. A few years before the Revolution, he resigned his office as criminal judge rather than pronounce the sentence of death. As late as 1791, when the short-lived Legislative Assembly of the Revolution debated the question of abolishing capital punishment, Robespierre uttered this brilliant appeal, which apparently came to Beccaria's notice:

   "Hear the voice of justice and of reason! It cries that human judgments are never certain enough that society can inflict death on a man condemned by other men, themselves subject to error. Even if you could imagine the most perfect judicial system, if you could find the most honorable and enlightened judges, you would still leave room for error or bias. Why deny yourselves the means of repairing them? Why condemn yourselves to being unable to extend a rescuing hand to oppressed innocence? Of what use are sterile regrets, illusory reparations that you may accord to vain shadows and insensible ashes?" — Charles Lucas, *Receuil des débats* (Paris: Béchet, 1831), p. 85.

   Then came the crisis and the turn. In December 1792 Robespierre ruthlessly demanded the execution of Louis XVI, whether guilty or innocent, as a political measure to preserve the peace and safety of the nation. The demand prevailed. Robespierre had destroyed part of himself. The ensuing events were called "The Terror."

9. 28 U.S.C. § 1495, § 2513.

10. State v. Sheppard, 165 Ohio St. 293 (1956).
11. Testifying before the Royal Commission on Capital Punishment in 1950, Justice
    Felix Frankfurter of the United States Supreme Court said:
    "I am strongly against capital punishment for reasons that are not related to
    concern for the murderer or the risk of convicting the innocent, and for reasons
    and considerations that might not be applicable to your country at all. When
    life is at hazard in a trial, it sensationalises the whole thing almost unwittingly;
    the effect on juries, the Bar, the public, the judiciary, I regard as very bad. I
    think scientifically the claim of deterrence is not worth much. Whatever proof
    there may be in my judgment does not outweigh the social loss due to the
    inherent sensationalism of a trial for life. I am speaking about my country, not
    yours. Any opinion I may give is subject to one's bias on the question of capital
    punishment; so, naturally, I view every system that mitigates the imposition of
    capital punishment with favour. . . . I myself would abolish it." — Frankfurter,
    Of Law and Men (1956), p. 81. Though this is, in some respects, a very strange
    statement, it points correctly to the evil effects of sensationalism.
12. "He who desires to inflict rational punishment does not retaliate for a past
    wrong which cannot be undone; he has regard to the future, and is desirous
    that the man who is punished, and he who sees him punished, may be deterred
    from doing wrong again. He punishes for the sake of prevention." Plato,
    Protagoras (Jowett tr.), p. 324.
13. Smith v. Baldi, 344 U.S. 561 (1953).
14. I quote this seemingly scandalous characterization from Chief Judge Biggs's
    splendid dissent in the Court of Appeals. 192 F.2d 540, 549. For lack of space,
    my summary omits several very disturbing circumstances recounted by Chief
    Judge Biggs.
15. Douglas, "A Challenge to the Bar," Notre Dame Lawyer, vol. 28 (1953), p. 503.
16. Statement furnished to me by Judge Frank expressly for this preface.

FACT-SKEPTICISM: AN UNEXPECTED CHAPTER

1. EDITOR'S NOTE: James Fitzjames Stephen, "On the Uncertainty of Judicial Fact-
   Finding," excerpted from his introduction to The Indian Evidence Act — Cal-
   cutta (1872), printed as an appendix to the original publication of this article in
   1963 Annual Survey of American Law, p. 613; and in New York University Law
   Review, vol. 38 (1963), p. 1025.
2. Our sources include Leslie Stephen, The Life of Sir James Fitzjames Stephen
   (1895); Leslie Stephen's sketch of Sir James Fitzjames Stephen in Dictionary of
   National Biography, vol. 54 (Lee ed., 1898), pp. 164–168; and Dr. Leon Radzino-
   wicz's excellent Selden Society Lecture on "Sir James Fitzjames Stephen and
   His Contribution to the Development of Criminal Law" (1957).
3. No one who has read Courts on Trial and noticed its phenomenal collection
   of fact-skepticism references will be astonished to learn that such a collection
   could not be quite complete; the wonder is that the author found as many
   kindred thinkers as he did. In a passage with which Frank was long acquainted,
   Henry S. Maine had furnished a direct lead to Stephen's discussion. Maine,
   Village-Communities (4th ed., 1881), p. 310. But copies of Stephen's Indian
   Evidence Act being relatively scarce, Frank read Stephen only at the end of
   1949.
4. Frank, " 'Short of Sickness and Death': A Study of Moral Responsibility in
   Legal Criticism," New York University Law Review, vol. 26 (1951), pp. 559–562.
5. 237 U.S. 309 (1915) (refusing a hearing on habeas corpus despite allegations of
   mob disorder and uproar in the trial court). Readers who are not familiar with
   the case of Leo Frank (no relative of Jerome Frank's) should be informed: (a)
   that the evidence pointed overwhelmingly to Frank's innocence, (b) that the trial
   judge explicitly stated his doubt as to Frank's guilt in the bill of exceptions but
   because he overlooked writing the same expression in his order denying a
   motion for a new trial, the Supreme Court of Georgia declined to take note

of his doubt and refused Frank a new trial, (c) that after the ignominious decision of the United States Supreme Court, the Governor of Georgia, having received further proof, which he did not disclose, that Frank was innocent, commuted the death sentence to life imprisonment, and (d) that, shortly thereafter, a Georgia mob took Frank from the State Prison and hanged him. By a majority vote of the lynch mob, it was decided not to burn the corpse but to let the undertaker return it to Brooklyn where Frank's parents lived. *American State Trials*, vol. 10, chapters vi–xii, pp. 182–414 (Lawson ed., 1918); sources collected in *Universal Jewish Encyclopedia*, vol. 4 (1941), p. 395.

6. Hand, *The Spirit of Liberty* (3d ed., 1960), pp. 62–63. Whether this statement contains anything beyond Voltaire's conclusion in *Candide* (*"il faut cultiver notre jardin"*) the reader may judge for himself.

7. 219 U.S. 219, 245 (1911), striking down an Alabama criminal statute that compelled peonage (by making the failure to perform labor contracted for without repaying moneys loaned by the employer prima facie evidence of fraud). Hughes wrote for the Court. Holmes wrote a dissenting opinion in which Lurton joined.

8. 217 U.S. 349, 382 (1910), striking down an elaborate and sadistic mode of punishment inherited in the Philippine Islands from the former Spanish dominion and holding that the Eighth Amendment prohibits not only those punishments that were deemed "cruel and unusual" in 1689 or 1789 but also modes of punishment that violate modern standards of humane justice. Here Holmes joined in White's dissenting opinion.

9. Some seem too callous to let even this circumstance move them. One wonders what could conceivably have sufficed to interest the justices who were responsible for the decision in Frank v. Mangum, 237 U.S. 309 (1915), or, for that matter, the two who dissented in Moore v. Dempsey, 261 U.S. 86, 92 (1923).

10. 237 U.S. at 345, Hughes joining in the dissenting opinion. Leo Frank did not die entirely in vain. See Moore v. Dempsey, 261 U.S. 86, 90 (1923). The great current example is Fay v. Noia, 372 U.S. 391 (1963), where Justice Brennan's admirable opinion for the Court gives habeas corpus its full historical efficacy while the dissenting opinion attempts to exhume Frank v. Mangum, 237 U.S. 309 (1915). Of course, all any state needs to do in order to obviate federal intervention in cases of this sort is to afford a genuinely adequate remedy for its own mistake or misconduct.

8: SOCIAL PSYCHOLOGY, EXPERIMENTATION AND THE LAW

A DANGEROUS MYTH IN THE SCHOOL SEGREGATION CASES

1. 163 U.S. 537 (1896). There have been signs of a campaign to transform Mr. Plessy into a heroic asserter of Negro rights. This will take some doing, at least if people read Plessy's petition. He alleged that he was "seven eighths Caucasian and one eighth African blood; that the mixture of colored blood was not discernible in him, and that he was entitled to every recognition, right, privilege and immunity secured to the citizens of the United States of the white race," etc. *Id.* at 538.

2. Davis v. County School Board, 103 F. Supp. 337 (E.D. Va. 1952), no. 4 in the Supreme Court.

3. Clearly, counsel followed the right strategy in offering the expert testimony for whatever the several courts or judges might find it worth. The younger Pliny, an extraordinarily successful advocate, insisted at some length that since different minds may be persuaded by different arguments, the advocate ought to develop and present them all, neglecting none. Pliny, *Letters*, book I, xx (Loeb ed., 1931), vol. 1, pp. 70–72. (It is barely possible that a phrase in this passage suggested Holmes's metaphor of "the jugular.")

4. Clark, "Desegregation: An Appraisal of the Evidence," *Journal of Social Issues,*

vol. 9, no. 4 (1953), p. 3. It would relieve me to learn that I have read Professor Clark too literally, but general opinion indicates that I have not.

5. "The Effects of Segregation and the Consequences of Desegregation: A Social Science Statement," *Minnesota Law Review*, vol. 37 (1953), p. 427.

6. For Professor Clark's testimony that this is the test "generally accepted as indications of the child's sensitivity to race as a problem," see no. 2, Briggs v. Elliott (the South Carolina case), Transcript of Record, p. 86. Professor Clark suffered from inflicting the test on the Negro children. No. 4, Davis v. County School Board (the Virginia case), Transcript of Record, p. 251.

7. No. 2, Briggs v. Elliott (the South Carolina case), Transcript of Record, pp. 87–90.

8. A bit later, the number was stated as "400 times." *Id.* at 96.

9. Thus in original; probably should be "pressures."

10. Professor Clark testified that a graduate student at Columbia had used the test on white children with his permission, but he had not obtained the results. *Id.* at 96. Yet it would seem that trying the test on white children would be the very first and most obvious way to begin ascertaining whether it had any probative value when given to Negro children.

11. In the attractive account cited above in note 4, Professor Clark described the close collaboration between the NAACP lawyers and the scientists, and went on to remark: "In fact, there were times when the lawyers could speak as social psychologists and the social psychologists began to sound like lawyers. In spite of this mutual accommodation, however, a clear distinction of roles and responsibilities had to be maintained for effective collaboration." Clark, "Desegregation: An Appraisal of the Evidence," *Journal of Social Issues*, vol. 9, no. 4 (1953), p. 6. It seems possible that the distinction of roles would be maintained more satisfactorily if the social psychologist's primary motive in maintaining it were strict fidelity to objective truth rather than "effective collaboration."

For an example of the kind of methodological criticism we need from the social scientists, see Hoebel, *The Law of Primitive Man* (1954), pp. 272–274. The instance discussed by Professor Hoebel likewise involved a very flabby attempt to "demonstrate" an assertion that on its face would seem entirely plausible to the lay mind.

Under the circumstances, some readers may feel inclined to credit Chief Justice Warren with Mephistophelean wit in that famous "footnote 11" (the accolade to the social psychologists which we have already mentioned). In the footnote, the Chief Justice lists various works published between the years 1944 and 1952. The *latest* of these discloses: "*Unfortunately for scientific accuracy and adequacy, thoroughly satisfactory methods of determining the effects of prejudice and discrimination on health of personality have not yet been devised, nor has a sufficient number of studies dealing with the various minority groups been made.*" (Emphasis supplied.) Witmer and Kotinsky, *Personality in the Making* (1952), pp. 139–140.

12. In *1953 Annual Survey of American Law*, p. 811, n. 30; and *New York University Law Review*, vol. 29 (1954), p. 485, n. 30, I proposed a canon for interpreting a certain limited class of writing. If valid, the canon would elucidate a writing in which, after a long controversy, one of the parties concedes that the opponent's position has been the right one. Without quoting or repeating last year's exposition, to which I hope some of my present readers will refer, I may summarize the "canon of concession" in three aspects: (1) viewed as rhetoric, the conceding disputant's statement will tend to emphasize any newly advanced reasons for coming to the conclusion he had previously rejected, because the new reasons are the face-savers; (2) viewed as definition, his statement will seem to imply that his adhesion to the conclusion is restricted by the new, face-saving reasons; and (3) viewed as prediction of his future behavior, the face-saving reasons and implied restrictions tend gradually to disappear — unless some later occurrence should happen to renew their pertinence and force.

If I may venture now to apply this canon to the Brown opinion, treating it as a concession in the long debate with Mr. Justice Harlan's Plessy dissent, then it seems to suggest an adequate explanation of Chief Justice Warren's references to psychological writings. In this analysis, the data of social psychology would constitute, at most, convenient face-savers. Applied to them, the canon of concession helps us to understand their rhetorical usefulness. If they did have a definitional function (which I contest), it would also clarify that.

Is anyone temerarious enough to predict whether the Supreme Court will make further face-saving references to the data of social psychology in cases of this kind? Not I. However, it is fair to comment that, according to the canon of concession, the significance of any such references would sooner or later shrink to the disappearing point in "equal protection" doctrine — unless some independent factor should emerge to vivify them. Face-saving reasons generally do not outlast the occasion that calls them forth. So much may be said safely. Saying more would be wrapping the future in a formula, a thing foolish to attempt and impossible to accomplish.

THE LAWYER, THE SOCIAL PSYCHOLOGIST AND THE TRUTH

1. EDITOR'S NOTE: See "A Dangerous Myth in the School Segregation Cases," pp. 329–325.
2. "The Lawyer's Role in Modern Society: A Round Table," *Journal of Public Law*, vol. 4 (1952), p. 8.
3. Comments attributed herein to Professor Chein are excerpted from his letter addressed to Will Maslow, counsel of the American Jewish Congress, December 21, 1954, and are published with consent of Professor Chein and Mr. Maslow. A copy of this letter is on file in the *New York University Law Review* offices.
4. Girard Trust, 5 Fiduciary Reporter 449 (1955). For reasons that are not pertinent to Professor Chein's testimony, I think the result in the case was erroneous.
5. EDITOR'S NOTE: This and the following quotations from testimony are taken from the Transcript of Record, Girard Trust, 5 Fiduciary Reporter 449 (Orphans' Ct., Phila. Co., Pa., 1955).
6. Deutscher and Chein, "The Psychological Effects of Enforced Segregation: A Survey of Social Science Opinion," *Journal of Psychology*, vol. 26 (1948), p. 259.
7. Chein, "What Are the Psychological Effects of Segregation Under Conditions of Equal Facilities?" *International Journal of Opinion and Attitude Research*, vol. 3 (1949), p. 230.

THE LAWYER AS SCIENTIST AND SCOUNDREL

1. Cairns, *Legal Philosophy from Plato to Hegel* (1949), chapter 6.
2. See Macaulay, *Essay on Bacon*. Lord Campbell's sketch in Campbell, *Lives of the Lord Chancellors of England*, vol. 3 (1857), chapter 51, is factually reliable to the extent it follows Macaulay. Though inaccurate, Campbell at least expressed a moral revulsion equal to Macaulay's; unlike some of our contemporaries, he did not shrug off bribe-taking as a "common practice in those days."
3. Aubrey's *Brief Lives* (Dick ed., 1950), p. 8. Though ordinarily I place little reliance on Aubrey's gossip-mongering, I credit him on this matter: (a) because his friendship with Thomas Hobbes and Hobbes's with Bacon establish a direct chain of testimony, and (b) because pederasty fits the known facts of Bacon's behavior.
4. Across the Channel during the same century Saint-Simon recorded a comparable instance of extensive judicial corruption. *Saint-Simon at Versailles* (Norton ed., 1958), p. 97. But no matter how prevalent corruption may be at a given time, it is never to be deemed incorporated into the mores as long as men continue to call it "corruption."
5. While it is possible to regard these conservative statements as mere insurance

against political disfavor, I think that anyone who reads Bacon's jurisprudential pieces will probably conclude that he meant them quite sincerely.
6. See *The Letters and the Life of Francis Bacon*, vol. 5 (Spedding ed., 1869), p.
94. Torture and experimental science were intimately linked in Bacon's thinking. See Collingwood, *The Idea of History* (1946), p. 269.

9:   THE MEANING OF JUSTICE

THE SHIFT TO A CONSUMER PERSPECTIVE

1. EDITOR'S NOTE: The original manuscript indicated that an appendix was to
have contained a conceptual history of justice.

Bibliography of the Writings
of Edmond Cahn

BOOKS

The Sense of Injustice — An Anthropocentric View of Law, New York University Press (1949). Reprinted in paperback, with a personal epilogue by the author, A Midland Book, Indiana University Press (1964).

The Moral Decision — Right and Wrong in the Light of American Law, Indiana University Press (1955). Reprinted in paperback, A Midland Book, Indiana University Press (1958).

The Predicament of Democratic Man, Macmillan Company (1961). Reprinted in paperback, A Delta Book, Dell Publishing Co. (1962). Reprinted under the title *Common Sense About Democracy,* Victor Gollancz, Ltd., London (1962).

Social Meaning of Legal Concepts, Nos. 1–4 (editor), New York University Press (1948–1952).

Supreme Court and Supreme Law (editor), Indiana University Press (1954).

The Great Rights (editor), Macmillan Company (1963).

ARTICLES AND REVIEWS

1927–1944

The Contractual and Proprietary Status of Married Women in Civil Law, with Particular Reference to the Law of Louisiana. Unpublished Doctor of Jurisprudence Thesis (1927).

Something Old Under the Sun, *Loyola Law Journal,* vol. 10 (1929), p. 41.

The Fiduciary of the Future, *St. Johns Law Review,* vol. 5 (1930), p. 32.

Undue Influence and Captation, *Tulane Law Review,* vol. 8 (1934), p. 507.

Restraints on Disinheritance, *University of Pennsylvania Law Review,* vol. 85 (1936), p. 139.

Testamentary Construction — The Psychological Approach, *Georgetown Law Journal,* vol. 26 (1937), p. 17.

Estate Corporations, *University of Pennsylvania Law Review,* vol. 86 (1937), p. 196.

State Gift Tax Jurisdiction, *University of Pennsylvania Law Review,* vol. 87 (1939), p. 390.

Book Review (Attorneys General of the States, *Constitutional Immunity of State and Municipal Securities*), *National Lawyers Guild Quarterly,* vol. 2 (1940), p. 281.

Book review (Strayer, *Taxation of Small Incomes*), *Columbia Law Review*, vol. 40 (1940), p. 361.

Book review (Tax Policy League, *How Shall Small Business Be Taxed*), *National Lawyers Guild Quarterly*, vol. 3 (1940), p. 54.

Federal Regulation of Inheritance, *University of Pennsylvania Law Review*, vol. 88 (1940), p. 297; and *New Jersey Law Journal*, vol. 63 (1940), p. 281.

The Trustee as Insurer, *Trusts and Estates*, vol. 70 (1940), p. 605.

Time, Space and Estate Tax, *Georgetown Law Journal*, vol. 29 (1941), p. 677.

Some Reflections on the Quest of Substance, *Georgetown Law Journal*, vol. 30 (1942), p. 587.

Local Law in Federal Taxation, *Yale Law Journal*, vol. 52 (1943), p. 799.

Book review (Curran, *Excess Profits Taxation*), *Lawyers Guild Review*, vol. 4 (1944), p. 51.

Federal Taxation and Private Law, *Columbia Law Review*, vol. 44 (1944), p. 669; and *Taxes — The Tax Magazine*, vol. 23 (1945), p. 168.

1945

Jurisprudence, *1944 Annual Survey of American Law*, p. 1153.

Contract or Gift? Analysis of Recent Gift Tax Cases — New Canons of Interpretation, *Trusts and Estates*, vol. 80 (1945), p. 489.

Book review (Everett ed.: Bentham, *The Limits of Jurisprudence Defined*), *Lawyers Guild Review*, vol. 5 (1945), p. 275.

Book review (Gaa, *Taxation of Corporate Income*), *Lawyers Guild Review*, vol. 5 (1945), p. 344.

1946

Jurisprudence, *1945 Annual Survey of American Law*, p. 1231.

Justice, Power and Law, *Yale Law Journal*, vol. 55 (1946), p. 336.

Book review (Buckland, *Some Reflections on Jurisprudence*), *Lawyers Guild Review*, vol. 6 (1946), p. 563.

Book review (Paul, *Federal Estate and Gift Taxation; 1946 Supplement*), *Tax Law Review*, vol. 2 (1946–1947), p. 289.

1947

Jurisprudence, *1946 Annual Survey of American Law*, p. 1193.

Book review (Paton, *A Text-Book of Jurisprudence*), *Columbia Law Review*, vol. 47 (1947), p. 521.

Book review (Sayre ed.: *Interpretations of Modern Legal Philosophies — Essays in Honor of Roscoe Pound*), *Lawyers Guild Review*, vol. 7 (1947), p. 230.

1948

Jurisprudence, *1947 Annual Survey of American Law*, p. 1099.

Freedom, Order and Law, *New York University Law Quarterly Review*, vol. 23 (1948), p. 20.

An Outline of Three Great Systems. In Cahn ed.: *Social Meaning of Legal Concepts*, No. 1, *Inheritance of Property and the Power of Testamentary Disposition*, New York University Press (1948), p. 1.

Book review (Lewin, *Studies in African Native Law*), *Texas Law Review*, vol. 26 (1948), p. 695.

Book review (Jessup, *A Modern Law of Nations*), *Standard*, October 1948, pp. 30–31.

Book review (Schoch ed.: *The Jurisprudence of Interests, Latin American Legal Philosophy*), *Columbia Law Review*, vol. 48 (1948), p. 973.

1949

Jurisprudence, *1948 Annual Survey of American Law*, p. 915.

Goethe's View of Law — With a Gloss Out of Plato, *Columbia Law Review*, vol. 49 (1949), p. 904.

Book review (Husson, *Les Transformations de la Responsibilité: Étude sur la Pensée Juridique*), *New York University Law Quarterly Review*, vol. 24 (1949), p. 245.

Book review (Cairns, *Legal Philosophy from Plato to Hegel*), *Columbia Law Review*, vol. 49 (1949), p. 286.

1950

Jurisprudence, *1949 Annual Survey of American Law*, p. 1020.

Book review (Cohen, *Reason and Law — Studies in Juristic Philosophy*), *Cornell Law Quarterly*, vol 35 (1950), p. 941.

Book review (Frank, *Courts on Trial — Myths and Reality in American Justice*), *Yale Law Journal*, vol. 59 (1950), p. 809.

Book review (Goodhart, *Five Jewish Lawyers of the Common Law*), *New York Times Book Review*, April 30, 1950.

Book review (King, *Melville Weston Fuller — Chief Justice of the United States 1888–1910*), *New York Times Book Review*, June 11, 1950.

Book review (Lauterpacht, *International Law and Human Rights*), *New York Times Book Review*, October 1, 1950.

Book review (Reppy ed.: *David Dudley Field — Centenary Essays*), *Columbia Law Review*, vol. 50 (1950), p. 402.

1951

Jurisprudence, *1950 Annual Survey of American Law*, p. 847.

Authority and Responsibility, *Columbia Law Review*, vol. 51 (1951), p. 838.

Ego and Equality, *Yale Law Journal*, vol. 60 (1951), p. 57.

What Makes a Successful Tax Lawyer? A Tax Law Review Symposium (editor), *Tax Law Review*, vol. 7 (1951), p. 1.

Book review (Hamburger, *Morals and Law — The Growth of Aristotle's Legal Theory*), *Harvard Law Review*, vol. 65 (1951), p. 363

Book review (Hendel, *Charles Evans Hughes and the Supreme Court*), *New York Times Book Review*, February 11, 1951.

Book review (Pound, *Justice According to Law*), *New York Times Book Review*, November 25, 1951.

Book review (Biddle, *The Fear of Freedom*), *New York Times Book Review*, December 2, 1951.

1952

Jurisprudence, *1951 Annual Survey of American Law*, p. 861.

Madison and the Pursuit of Happiness, *New York University Law Review*, vol. 27 (1952), p. 265.

The Inherent Radicalism of the Legal Profession, *New York University Law Review*, vol. 27 (1952), p. 408.

The Unreasonables: 1952–1962, *New Republic*, June 23, 1952, p. 13.

Ethical Problems of Tax Practitioners, *Tax Law Review*, vol. 8 (1952), p. 1.

Book review (Sayre, *An Introduction to a Philosophy of Law*), *New York University Law Review*, vol. 27 (1952), p. 182.

Book review (Kruse, *The Community of the Future*), *Journal of Legal Education*, vol. 5 (1952), p. 224.

Book review (Vanderbilt, *Cases and Other Materials on Modern Procedure and Judicial Administration*), *New York University Law Review*, vol. 27 (1952), p. 879.

Book review (Botein, *Trial Judge — The Candid, Behind-the-Bench Story of Justice Bernard Botein*), *New York Times Book Review*, April 27, 1952.

Book review (Cohen, *Murder, Madness, and the Law*), *New York Times Book Review*, November 30, 1952.

1953

Skepticism in American Jurisprudence, *New York University Law Review*, vol. 28 (1953), p. 852. In *1952 Annual Survey of American Law*, p. 765.

The Editor's Secret, *New York University Law Review*, vol. 28 (1953), p. 922; and *Tax Law Review*, vol. 8 (1953), p. 495.

Book review (Howe ed.: *Holmes-Laski Letters — The Correspondence of Mr. Justice Holmes and Harold J. Laski 1916–1935*), *New York University Law Review*, vol. 28 (1953), p. 764; and *Virginia Quarterly Review*, vol. 29 (1953), p. 272.

Book review (Hale, *Freedom Through Law — Public Control of Private Governing Power*), *New York Times Book Review*, January 18, 1953.

Book review (Horowitz, *The Spirit of the Jewish Law*), *New York Times Book Review*, September 13, 1953.

1954

Atavism in American Jurisprudence, *New York University Law Review*, vol. 29 (1954), p. 473. In *1953 Annual Survey of American Law*, p. 799.

Book review (Douglas, *An Almanac of Liberty*), *New York Times Book Review*, November 14, 1954.

1955

A Dangerous Myth in the School Segregation Cases, *New York University Law Review*, vol. 30 (1955), p. 150. In *1954 Annual Survey of American Law*, p. 809.

John Marshall — Our "Greatest Dissenter", *New York Times Magazine*, August 21, 1955.

Book review (Griswold, *The Fifth Amendment Today*), *New York Times Book Review*, January 30, 1955.

Book review (Jackson, *The Supreme Court in the American System of Government*), *New York Times Book Review*, July 10, 1955.

Book review (Rodell, *Nine Men — A Political History of the Supreme Court from 1790 to 1955*), *New York Times Book Review*, August 28, 1955.

1956

Foreword to Calamandrei, *Procedure and Democracy*, New York University Press (1956).

The Lawyer, the Social Psychologist and the Truth, *New York University Law Review*, vol. 31 (1956), p. 182. In *1955 Annual Survey of American Law*, p. 655.

The Firstness of the First Amendment, *Yale Law Journal*, vol. 65 (1956), p. 464.

Can the Supreme Court Defend Civil Liberties? Hillman Reprint Series no. 9 (1956), p. 18.

Louis Dembitz Brandeis, 1856–1941. In Pollack ed.: *The Brandeis Reader*, Oceana Publications, Inc. (1956), p. 21.

Brief for the Supreme Court, *New York Times Magazine*, October 7, 1956.

Book review (Douglas, *We the Judges — Studies in American and Indian Constitutional Law from Marshall to Mukherjii*), *New York Times Book Review*, January 22, 1956.

Book review (Elman, ed.: *Of Law and Men — Papers and Addresses of Felix Frankfurter, 1939–1956*), *New York Times Book Review*, May 27, 1956.

1957

Preface to Koestler, *Reflections on Hanging*, Macmillan Company (1957).

Jurisprudence, *New York University Law Review*, vol. 32 (1957), p. 133. In *1956 Annual Survey of American Law*, p. 582.

Jerome Frank's Fact-Skepticism and Our Future, *Yale Law Journal*, vol. 66 (1957), p. 824.

Eavesdropping on Justice, *Nation*, January 5, 1957, p. 14.

Book review (Howe, *Justice Oliver Wendell Holmes — The Shaping Years, 1841–1870*), *New York Herald Tribune Book Week*, March 10, 1957.

Book review (Wittenberg ed.: *The Lamont Case — History of a Congressional Investigation*), *New York Times Book Review*, October 13, 1957.

1958

Fact-Skepticism and Fundamental Law, *New York University Law Review*, vol. 33 (1958), p. 1. In *1957 Annual Survey of American Law*, p. 575.

A Lawyer Looks at Religion, *Theology Today*, vol. 15 (1958), p. 100.

Some Reflections on the Aims of Legal Education, *Journal of Legal Education* (1958), p. 1. In Hawley ed.: *Comparative Legal Education — The Papers of the Ankara Conference on Comparative Legal Education* (1959), p. 11.

The Doubter and the Bill of Rights, *New York University Law Review*, vol. 33 (1958), p. 903. In *1958 Annual Survey of American Law*, p. 687.

Book review (Kelsen, *What Is Justice? — Justice, Law, and Politics in the Mirror of Science*), *New York University Law Review*, vol. 33 (1958), p. 1056.

Book review (Douglas *The Right of the People*), *New York Times Book Review*, January 19, 1958.

Book review (John P. Frank, *Marble Palace — The Supreme Court in American Life*), *New York Herald Tribune Book Week*, October 19, 1958.

1959

Consumers of Injustice, *Social Research*, vol. 26 (1959), p. 175; and *New York University Law Review*, vol. 34 (1959), p. 1166.

In *1959 Annual Survey of American Law*, p. 655; and London ed.: *World of Law*, vol. 2, Simon and Schuster, Inc. (1960), p. 574.

Private Interviews and Community Views, *Journal of Legal Education*, vol. 11 (1959) p. 513.

Book review (Mason, *The Supreme Court from Taft to Warren*), *New York Times Book Review*, January 18, 1959.

Book review (Christman ed.: *The Public Papers of Chief Justice Earl Warren*), *New York Times Book Review*, July 12, 1959.

Book review (Countryman ed.: *Douglas of the Supreme Court — A Selection of His Opinions*), *New York Times Book Review*, August 9, 1959.

1960

The Juristic Approach to Moral Problems: A Case Study, *Yearbook of the Central Conference of American Rabbis*, vol. 70 (1960), p. 184.

Book review (Black, *The People and the Court — Judicial Review in a Democracy*), *New York Times Book Review*, March 6, 1960.

Book review (Gellhorn, *American Rights — The Constitution in Action*), *New York Herald Tribune Book Week*, March 6, 1960.

Book review (Douglas, *America Challenged*), *New York Herald Tribune Book Week*, June 12, 1960.

Book review (Montgomery, *Sacco-Vanzetti — The Murder and the Myth*), *New York Times Book Review*, September 18, 1960.

Book review (Levy, *Legacy of Suppression — Freedom of Speech and Press in Early American History*), *New York Herald Tribune Book Week*, October 16, 1960.

Book review (Hazard, *Settling Disputes in Soviet Society — The Formative Years of Legal Institutions*), *New York Times Book Review*, November 6, 1960.

1961

The Lawyer as Scientist and Scoundrel; Reflections on Francis Bacon's Quadricentennial, *New York University Law Review*, vol. 36 (1961), p. 1. In *1960 Annual Survey of American Law*, p. 587.

The "Establishment of Religion" Puzzle, *New York University Law Review*, vol. 36 (1961), p. 1274. In *1961 Annual Survey of American Law*, p. 571.

The Jewish Contribution to Law, *Jewish Frontiers*, May 1961, p. 12; and *Jerusalem Post*, March 31, 1961.

How to Destroy the Churches, *Harper's*, November 1961, p. 33.

Book review (Douglas, *A Living Bill of Rights*), *New York Herald Tribune Book Week*, February 12, 1961.

Book review (Peltason, *Fifty-eight Lonely Men — Southern Federal Judges and School Desegregation*), *New York Times Book Review*, September 17, 1961.

Book review (Cohen, *The United Nations — Constitutional Developments, Growth and Possibilities*), *New York Herald Tribune Book Week*, November 12, 1961.

1962

Justice Black and First Amendment "Absolutes": A Public Interview, *New York University Law Review*, vol. 37 (1962), p. 569.

Defects in Israel's Legal System, *Congress Bi-Weekly*, May 28, 1962, p. 10; reprinted as Surgeons with Carpenter's Tools, *Jerusalem Post*, April 24, 1962.

On Government and Prayer, *New York University Law Review*, vol. 37 (1962), p. 981. In *1962 Annual Survey of American Law*, p. 693.

The Parchment Barriers, *American Scholar*, vol. 32 (1962–1963), p. 21.

Book review (Kirchhermer, *Political Justice — The Use of Legal Procedure for Political Ends*), *New York Times Book Review*, January 14, 1962.

1963

Introduction to Frank, *Courts on Trial — Myth and Reality in American Justice*, Atheneum Publishers (1963).

Introduction to Marke and Lexa ed.: *International Seminar on Constitutional Review* (1963).

Law in the Consumer Perspective, *University of Pennsylvania Law Review*, vol. 112 (1963), p. 1.

Fact-Skepticism: An Unexpected Chapter, *New York University Law Review*, vol. 38 (1963), p. 1025. In *1963 Annual Survey of American Law*, p. 613.

Thomas More Among the Lawyers (Collins ed.), *New York University Law Review*, vol. 38 (1963), p. 813.

1964

Drug Experiments and the Public Conscience. In Talalay ed.: *Drugs in Our Society*, Johns Hopkins University Press (1964), p. 255. Reprinted as Limits for Experimentation; in Ladiner and Newman, *Clinical Investigation in Medicine — Legal, Ethical and Moral Aspects* (1964), p. 111.

Defamation Control vs. Press Freedom: A Current Chapter in Israel, *Journal of Public Law*, vol. 13 (1964), p. 3.

Posthumously

Book review (Todd, *Justice on Trial — The Case of Louis D. Brandeis;* Mendelson ed.: *Felix Frankfurter — A Tribute*), *New York Herald Tribune Book Week*, September 6, 1964.

How Democracy Unites Us, *Congress Bi-Weekly*, Third Dialogue in Israel, November 9, 1964, p. 34.

Introduction to *A Man's Reach — The Selected Writings of Judge Jerome Frank*, Macmillan Company (1965).

Public Schools, Flag Salute. In *New Catholic Encyclopedia* (scheduled for publication in 1966).

Justice. In *New Encyclopedia of Social Science* (scheduled for publication in 1968).